Robert Gream Hall

Hall's essay on the rights of the Crown

The privileges of the subject in the sea shores of the realm

Robert Gream Hall

Hall's essay on the rights of the Crown
The privileges of the subject in the sea shores of the realm

ISBN/EAN: 9783337271367

Printed in Europe, USA, Canada, Australia, Japan

Cover: Foto ©Suzi / pixelio.de

More available books at **www.hansebooks.com**

HALL'S ESSAY
ON THE RIGHTS OF THE CROWN

AND THE

PRIVILEGES OF THE SUBJECT

In the Sea Shores of the Realm.

SECOND EDITION, REVISED AND CORRECTED,
TOGETHER WITH EXTENSIVE ANNOTATIONS,

AND REFERENCES TO THE LATER AUTHORITIES IN ENGLAND, IRELAND, SCOTLAND, AND THE UNITED STATES.

By Richard Loveland Loveland,
OF THE INNER TEMPLE, BARRISTER-AT-LAW.

WITH AN APPENDIX, CONTAINING

I.—LORD CHIEF JUSTICE HALE'S "DE JURE MARIS."
II.—THE CASE OF DICKENS v. SHAW.
III.—MR. SERJEANT MEREWETHER'S SPEECH.
IV.—FORMS IN USE BY THE BOARD OF TRADE.

LONDON:
STEVENS & HAYNES,
Law Publishers,
BELL YARD, TEMPLE BAR.

CHISWICK PRESS:—PRINTED BY WHITTINGHAM AND WILKINS,
TOOKS COURT, CHANCERY LANE.

PREFACE TO SECOND EDITION.

HIS edition of an "Essay on the Rights of the Crown in the Sea Shore," by ROBERT GREAM HALL, of Lincoln's Inn, Barrister-at-Law, (which was first published in 1830,) contains the whole of the original text, with annotations and references to the later cases which have been decided in the English, Scotch, Irish, and American courts. These notes are distinguished from those of the first edition by being placed within brackets.

With a view of materially increasing the usefulness of the work, and facilitating references, numerous errors occurring in the original have been corrected, and an Appendix has been added, containing Lord Chief Justice Hale's well known "De Jure Maris," the case of Dickens v. Shaw, and (by kind permission of H. A. Merewether, Esq., Q.C.,) Mr. Serjeant Merewether's speech in the Court of Chancery, Dec. 8, 1849, upon the claim of the Commissioners of the Woods and Forests to the sea shore and the soil and bed of tidal harbours and navigable rivers; also certain Forms in common use by the Board of Trade in dealing with the interests of the Crown in such property.

Should this edition of a work (which for a long period has been out of print and with difficulty procured), prove an assistance to those engaged in cases relating to the foreshores of the country, the editor will be fully compensated for the time and trouble expended upon it.

Temple, *February*, 1875.

INTRODUCTION.

HE following Essay is published with no other pretensions than as collecting, from the text writers and decided cases, the principal points of law upon the subject; with a commentary upon such of them as would seem to have been rather loosely laid down by the authorities. It is a subject which, as matter of dispute or discussion, does not, from the nature of things, often come before the Courts of Westminster for judicial decision; (although it has, of late, been more frequently canvassed than usual;) it is, however, a topic by no means unimportant or uninteresting, as affecting both public and private rights. It is remarkable, that the principal authority, generally quoted and relied upon, is the "Treatise de Jure Maris," published, some time ago, by Mr. Hargrave, in a collection of Law Tracts, from a MS. ascribed by him, upon apparently sufficient grounds, to Lord Hale. Even this authority is com-

cipal design of which regarded the Ports and Customs. How far the work was considered, by Lord Hale himself, as sufficiently revised for publication, does not appear. It is, no doubt, a valuable present to the profession, and in deference to its generally admitted authority, the Treatise in question has been made the basis of the following Essay.

Lincoln's Inn, 8, New Square,
January 16, 1830.

SUMMARY OF CONTENTS.

I.

HALL'S ESSAY.

HE principal points of law discussed therein are these:—

Page

1. That the dominion and ownership of the British Seas, and of the creeks, bays, arms, ports, and tide-rivers thereof, are vested, by our law, in the Crown . . 1-7
2. That this ownership includes *aquam et solum;* both the water, its products and uses, and the land or soil under the water . . . . ibid.
3. That such ownership includes the shore, as far as the reach of the high-water mark of the [medium high tide between the springs and the neaps] 9
4. That the land subject to spring tides, and high spring tides, is no part of the sea, or sea-shore; but belongs to the title and ownership of the *terra firma*. 10-13
5. That by grant from the Crown, a subject may have a lawful ownership of a certain portion of the sea, its creeks, bays, arms, ports, or tide-rivers, and of the shores thereof, *tam aquæ quam soli* 6, 14
6. But that such grants must have a date anterior to the statutes restraining the alienation of Crown lands . . . 106, 107
7. That no distinction exists at law, between the title or proofs of title to such land covered with water, and the title to *terra firma*. 14
8. That where the ownership claimed by a subject in any such *districtus maris*, or tide-river, or shore, cannot be proved by the production of the grant, such ownership can *no otherwise* be established than by adverse possession, under the Statutes of Limitation 22-26

	Page

9. That such ownership cannot be supported by "prescription," properly so called, against the King, and never could, at any period, be so supported under the feudal law . 16, 21-31

10. That the proofs of title, where the grant itself is not forthcoming, to such *districtus maris aut littoris* must be *paris materiæ* with those required to prove title to inland estates 32, 33

11. That proof, by prescriptive evidence, of a right to a franchise, liberty, or easement in or out of the soil, is no sufficient evidence of title to the freehold and inheritance of the land itself, whether such land be *terra firma* or *pars maris* 39

12. And consequently, that the ownership of a several fishery, or of the franchises of wreck, of flotsan, jetsan, and ligan, or of royal fish, or of ports, or the liberty of digging for sand, or shells, &c., will not be sufficient to establish an absolute ownership over the soil itself, where such rights are enjoyed against the Crown . . . 20, 55-65, 71-77, 78-103

13. And, therefore, neither the express *grant* of a franchise, or liberty, nor "prescription" for such (which supposes a grant) can be construed to include the soil, or freehold, against the Crown, by implication, or presumption 20, 65, 103

14. That "alluvion," properly so called, belongs to the ownership of the freehold of the adjacent *terra firma*, subject to such interests in others as such ownership is liable to . 108-128

15. That "derelict" land, properly so called, belongs to the Crown, as land suddenly and by manifest marks left by the sea 128-135

16. That islands produced out of the British Seas, and the creeks, bays, arms, ports, and tide-rivers thereof, belong, like derelict land, to the Crown 140

17. Unless the soil under the water out of which such islands are produced, previously belonged to a subject . . . ibid.

18. That the title of a subject to the soil of a *districtus maris*, viz. to the soil of any creek, bay, arm, port, or tide-river, or to the shore, in no substantial respect differs from a title to *terra firma* 32, 34

19. That it is more for the public advantage that the ownership of subjects should be limited to the *terra firma*; and consequently, that by the rule of law, as well as of public policy, claims set up to tracts of sea, or of ports, or tide-rivers, or of the shore, ought not to be *favoured* against the Crown 104, 220

Summary of Contents.

Page

21. As to the public right to dig for sand, shells, &c., on the shore 186-217
22. Remarks on the case of Dickens *v.* Shaw . . . 217-220

II.

HALE'S (C. J.) DE JURE MARIS . . . . App. i-xliii

III.

THE CASE OF DICKENS *v.* SHAW . . . . App. xlv-lxviii

IV.

MR. SERJEANT MEREWETHER'S SPEECH IN THE COURT OF CHANCERY, Dec. 8, 1849, upon the Claim of the Commissioners of Woods and Forests to the Sea Shore, and the Soil and Bed of Tidal Harbours and Navigable Rivers; the nature and extent of the Claim, and its effects upon such Property . . . . App. lxix-cvii

V.

FORMS USED BY THE BOARD OF TRADE RELATING TO THE RIGHTS OF THE CROWN IN THE SEA SHORE . . . . App. cix-cxxv

INDEX cxxvii

TABLE OF CASES.

₊ *The references in Roman numerals are to pages in the Appendix.*

		Page
ABBOT of Benedict Hulme, Case of	.	57, xvii, lxxxiii
„ Ramsay, Case of .	.	118, xxvi, lxxxvii
„ Peterborough, Case of		119, xxvi, lxxxvi
„ St. Austin, Case of	. .	. xi, lxxxvi
„ Tichfend, Case of	. .	. xviii, lxxxi
Adams *v.* Frothingham	. . .	. 112
Alcock *v.* Cooke	. . .	. 81
Allen *v.* Donelly		. 47
Alston's Estate, *In re*		15, 46
Anglesea, Marquis of, *v.* Hatherton, Lord	. . .	. 89
Anonymous		. 41
Arnold *v.* Munday		. 186
Ashworth *v.* Brown . . . ᠂ . .		. 50
Attorney-General *v.* Chamberlaine	. . .	. 99
„ „ *v.* Chambers . .	. 3, 9, 13, 15, 109, 110, 111	
„ „ *v.* Cleaver		. 45
„ „ *v.* Farmen		. 7, 104
„ „ *v.* Hanmer		. 18
„ „ *v.* Johnson		. 43
„ „ *v.* Jones		. 18
„ „ *v.* London (Mayor, &c., of)	. .	. 5, lxxv
„ „ *v.* Lonsdale		. 43, 44, 45, 99
„ „ *v.* Matthias		. 197, 202
„ „ *v.* Parmeter		. 45, xcv
„ „ *v.* Rees		. 99
„ „ *v.* Richards		. 45, 168
„ „ *v.* Roll (Sir Samuel), and others		. . xxiv
„ „ (of Cornwall) *v.* St. Aubyns	.	. xcviii, cvi

Table of Cases.

	Page
Attorney-General v. Terry	44
,, ,, v. Turner	104
Aubrey v. Fisher	159
BADGER v. South Yorkshire Railway Company	48
Bagott v. Orr	13, 41, 46, 96, 105, 167, 175, 181, 186, 207
Bailey v. Appleyard	36
Ball v. Herbert	48, 161, 163, 176, 215
Banks v. Ogden	112
Banne River, Case of	20, 41, 65, v, xciv
Barnes v. Mawson	103
Baron of Barclay's Case	84, 152, xiii, xxxii
Barry v. Arnaud	81
Barwick v. Matthews	201
Beaufort (Duke of) v. Swansea (Mayor)	15, 78, 82, 100, civ
Belfast Dock Act, *In re*	15, 18, 162
Benedict Hall v. Mason	86
Benedict Hulme, Abbot of, Case of	57, xvii, lxxxiii
Benest v. Pipon	16, 26, 92, ciii
Benett v. Costar	46
Bickett v. Morris	44, 99
Blakemore v. Glamorgan Canal Company	45
Bland v. Lipscombe	196, 202
Blewitt v. Tregonning	37, 197
Blundell v. Caterall	3, 13, 105, 156, 176, lx, ci
Bodenham v. Hill	lxx
Bridger v. Richardson	192
Bridges v. Highton	45, 88
Bridgwater (Duke of), Trustees v. Bootle-cum-Linacre	15
Brooke v. Spering	ci
,, v. Chadbourne	48
Brown v. Mallett	45
,, v. Perkins	43
Bullstrode v. Hall	xcvii
Burnell v. Bishop of Bath and Wells	130
Buszard v. Capel	34
CALMADY v. Rowe	15, 18, 78, 82, 89, 96, 100
Carlisle (Mayor of) v. Graham	51
Carter v. Murcot	3, 41, 46, 53, 77
Chad v. Tilsed	50, ci

	Page
Child v. Winwood	103
Christ Church, Canterbury, Prior of, Case of	138, xxxii
Clowes v. Beck	198
Colchester (Mayor of) v. Brooke	3, 43, 44, 51, 140
Commonwealth v. Bilderback	44
„ v. Charlestown	13, 48
„ v. Chapin	72
Coningshed, Prior of, Case of	xvi
Constable, Sir Henry, Case of	15, 29, 77, 82, xxiv, xli, xciii
„ Sir John, Case of	xciii
„ v. Nicholson	197, 198
Cornfield v. Coryell	186
Cortelyou v. Van Brunt	61
Cowper (Earl) v. Baker	198
Crichton v. Collery	51
DAY v. Day	48
Delaware and Maryland Railway Company v. Stump	48
Den v. East New Jersey	4
Devonshire (Duke of) v. Hodnett	51, 72
„ „ v. Smith	72
Dewell v. Sanders	72
Dickens v. Shaw	19, 20, 21, 40, 78, 81, 91, 92, 94, 108, 170, 175, 178, 179, 181, 182, 184, 186, 208, 209, xlv
Diggs v. Hamond	lxxxvii
Doe v. Thomas	88
Donegall (Marquis of) v. Lord Templemore	15
Duberly v. Page	195
Dunstan v. Tresider	201
Dunwich v. Sterry	41, 81
Dyce v. Hay (Lady J.)	198
EAST Haven v. Hemingway	45
Edgar v. Special Commissioners for English Fisheries	50
Edleston v. Crossley	45
Eduljee Byramjee, Ex parte	106
Emans v. Turnbull	93, 109
Embleton v. Brown	16, 47
Evans v. Rees	88
Exeter (Mayor of) v. Warren	135
FEATHER v. Reg.	21
Fife (Earl of) v. Woods and Forests Commissioners	22
Fitzpatrick v. Robinson	37

	Page
Fitzwalter's (Lord) Case	41, 42, 49, 53, 56, 85
Fleet v. Hegeman	186
Ford v. Lacey	128
Foreman v. Free Fishers of Whitstable	18
Fowler v. Sanders	72
Free Fishers of Whitstable v. Gann	7
Freery v. Cook	68
GAMMELL v. Commissioners of Woods and Forests	193
Gann v. Free Fishers of Whitstable	3, 43, 70
Gateward's Case	199, 212
Georgetown v. Alexandria Canal Company	45
Gifford v. Lord Yarborough	128
Gould v. Carter	44
Gray v. Bond	176, cii
Grimstead v. Marlow	202
HACCHESHAM Case	xii, lxxxii
Haight v. Keokuk	21
Hall v. Whillis	186
Hamilton v. Donegall (Marquis of)	49, 50, 72
Hammond v. Digges	78, xxiv
Hamond v. Pearson	45
Hancock v. York Railway Company	43
Hanmer v. Chance	24
Hart v. Hill	93
Harvey v. Lyme Regis (Mayor of)	10
Hayes v. Bridges	35, 49, 50, 76
Healy v. Thorne	15, 18, 19, 92
Heron, Sir Edward, Case of	12, ix, xxiii
Holford v. Bailey	50, 51, 69
,, v. George	70
Hollis v. Goldfinch	48, 75, 101
Hopkins' Academy, Trustees of, v. Dickenson	141
Horne v. Mackenzie	13
Howard v. Ingersole	163
Howe v. Stowell	93
Hoyle v. McCunn	176
Hudson v. McRae	202
Hull and Selby Railway Company, In re	109, 112, 119, 120, 129
IPSWICH Dock Company v. St. Peter's, Ipswich (Overseers of)	6, 16, 89
Ipswich (Inhabitants of) v. Brown	61, 174

Table of Cases. xvii

	Page
JACKSON v. Halstead	66
Jenkins v. Harvey	37, 135
Jersey Case	xxxvii
Johnson v. Barrett	xcvi
„ v. Wyard	197
Jones v. Soulard	141
KINLOCK v. Neville	48
Kinnersley v. Orpe	88
LA PLAISANCE Bay Harbour Company v. City of Monroe	21
Leaconfield v. Lonsdale	70, 72
Ledyard v. Ten Eyck	48
Legge v. Boyd	81
Le Strange v. Rowe	15, 18, 100, 198
Little v. Wingfield	47, 50
Lloyd v. Jones	196, 202
Lockwood v. Wood	202
Lord v. Sydney Commissioners	21
Lord Advocate v. Graham	22
„ v. Hamilton	3
Lowe v. Govett	10, 13, 92
MACALISTER v. Campbell	18
McCannon v. Sinclair	16, 89
Mace v. Philcox	156, 186
Macfarlin v. Essex County	203
Macmanus v. Carmichael	4, 21
Macnamara v. Higgins	197, 199, 207
Malcolmson v. O'Dea	3, 4, 42, 48, 50, 68, 72, 87, 88
Maldon v. Woolvet (Mayor of)	192
Mannall v. Fisher	50
Marshall v. Ulleswater Steam Navigation Company	4, 42, 55, 59, 62, 66
Martin v. Waddell	186, civ
Melvin v. Whiting	61, 68, 203
Memphis (Corporation of) v. Overton	49
Menzies v. Breadalbane	99, 168
Middleton v. Pritchard	4, 49, 141
Miles v. Rose	4
Moore v. Griffin	93
Moulton v. Wilby	70
Monmouth Canal Company v. Hill	48
Municipality No. 2 v. Orleans Cotton Press	110
Murgatroyd v. Robinson	23

Table of Cases.

	Page
Murphy v. Ryan	4, 37, 42
Murray v. Sermon	112
NEVILLE, Case of Sir Henry	79, 83, xxv, lxxxv
New Orleans v. United States	112
Nicholson v. Williams	135, 198
Norbury v. Kitchen	43, 45
Northumberland (Duke of) v. Houghton	51
O'NEILL v. Allen	47, 50
Orford (Mayor of) v. Richardson	41, 49, 52
Outram v. Morewood	39
Oxenden v. Palmer	198
PADWICK v. Knight	197
Palmer v. Rouse	81
Parker v. Cutler	186
Parnaby v. Lancashire Canal Company	45
Parrett Navigation Company v. Robins	45
Partheriche v. Mason	62
Pauline, The	81
Peake v. Tucker	67
Peck v. Lockwood	186
People v. Canal Appraisers	4, 21, 141
Perley v. Langley	197, 203
Perrott v. Bryant	16, 89
Peterborough, Abbot of, Case of	119, xxvi, lxxxvi
Peyroux v. Howard	13
Phillips v. Rhodes	93
Philpot's Case	x, xcv, cvii
Pierse v. Lord Fauconberg	48
Pitts v. Kingsbridge Highway Board	197, 198, 206
Plymouth and Sutton Poole, Case of	138, 146, xxxii, xcviii
Pollard's Lessee v. Hagan	4
Port of Toppesham, Case of	57, 137, 145, xviii, xxxii, lxxx
Post v. Munn	43
„ v. Pearsall	197, 202
Prior de Coningshed, Case of	xvi
„ of Christ Church, Canterbury	138, xxxii
„ of Stoke	xvi
„ of Tinmouth	x, lxxxi
RACE v. Ward	197

Table of Cases. xix

	Page
Rawstorne v. Backhouse	70
Rebeckah, The	21
R. v. Bedfordshire (Inhabitants of)	39
„ v. Betts	45
„ v. Commissioners of Sewers in Pagham	99, 167
„ v. Ellis	76, 82, 89, 90
„ v. Forty-nine Casks of Brandy.	21, 81, 103
„ v. Gee	16
„ v. Landulph (Inhabitants of)	16
„ v. London (Mayor of)	21
„ v. Montague	4, 75
„ v. Musson.	16
„ v. O'Connell and others	lxx
„ v. Oldsworth	131
„ v. Pagham Commissioners	99, 167
„ v. Randall	45
„ v. Russell.	44, 45
„ v. Smith	13, xxxii, c
„ v. Stimpson	3, 47
„ v. Tindall.	140
„ v. Trafford	99, 169
„ v. Two Casks of Tallow	81
„ v. Ward	43, 45, 99, 169, ciii
„ v. Watts	45
„ v. Yarborough, Lord.	13, 109, 120—128, 130
„ v. York, Archbishop of	106
River Banne, Case of	20, 41, 65, v, xciv
„ Severn, Case of	84, xiii, xxxii
„ Thames, Case of	x, lxxxiv, xcv, cvii
Rogers v. Allen	49, 90
„ v. Brenton.	197, 262
„ v. Jones	48
Rolle v. Whyte	70
Rose v. Graves	45
Rowe v. Brenton	xcix
„ v. Granite Bridge Corporation	4, 13
Rumney (Corporation of) Case of	129
St. Austin, Abbot of, Case of	xi, lxxxvi
Sale v. Pratt.	93, 197, 203
Saulet v. Sheperd.	112
Scratton v. Brown.	13, 15, 18, 19, 32, 81, 87, 89, 149, cii
Seebkristo v. East India Company	111

Table of Cases.

	Page
Severn River, Case of	84, xiii, xxxii
Seymour *v.* Lord Courtney	68
Shakespear *v.* Peppin	195
Shinberge's Case	xiii, xxxii, lxxvi
Shuttleworth *v.* Le Fleming	23, 49, 50, 67, 68
Simpson *v.* Dendy	101
Smart *v.* Dundee (Council of)	99, 111
Smith *v.* Kemp	41, 67
„ *v.* Stair (Earl of)	10, 13, 99
Somerset (Duke of), *v.* Fogwell	20, 62, 76
„ „ *v.* France	89
Stanley *v.* White	103
Stevens *v.* Paterson and Newark Railway Company	4
Stewart *v.* Greenock Harbour Trustees	111
Stoke, Prior of, Case of	xvi
Stone *v.* Augusta	163
Storer *v.* Freeman	48
Stuart *v.* Clark's Lessee	141
Sutherland (Duchess of) *v.* Watson	3
Sutton Marsh, Case of	131, xi, xxiv, xxviii
Sutton *v.* Buck	80
Swans, Case of	civ
TALBOT *v.* Lewis	81
Taylor *v.* Perry	101
Thames River, Case of	x
Tichfend, Abbot of, Case of	xviii, lxxxi
Tinmouth, Prior of, Case of	x, lxxxi
Tisdall *v.* Parnell	88
Todd *v.* Dunlop	99, 111
Toppesham Case	57, 137, 145, xviii, xxxii, lxxx
Treat *v.* Lord	48
Trematon Case	138, 146, xxxii, xcviii
Tyrwhitt *v.* Wynne	91, 101
UPTON *v.* Dawkins	67
VANHAESDANKE'S Case	12, ix, xxiii
Vaughan *v.* De Winton	101
WALTON-CUM-TRIMLEY Manor, *In re*	15, 88
Wandsford, Lady, Case of	12, ix
Ward *v.* Cresswell	41, 174
Warren *v.* Matthews	41, 46, 54

Table of Cases.

	Page
Waterloo Bridge Proprietors v. Cull	16
Waters v. Lilley	202, 203
Webb v. Bird	23
Wedderburn v. Paterson	141
Weekly v. Wildman	202
Weld v. Hornby	72
Wenman v. Mackenzie	88
White v. Crisp	43, 45
„ v. Phillips	43
Whitstable Fishers v. Foreman	43
Wild v. Holt	101
Wilkinson v. Proud	23
Williams v. Blackwall	43, 70
„ v. Wilcox	3, 43, 69, 70, 140
Willingale v. Maitland	198
Winch v. Thames Conservators	48
YARBOROUGH, Lord, Case of	13, 109, 120—128, 130
ZETLAND (Earl of) v. Glover Incorporation of Perth	141

AN ESSAY ON THE RIGHTS OF THE CROWN

IN THE SEA-SHORES OF THE REALM, Etc.

Of the King's Title to the British Seas.

HE British Seas, sometimes called the Four Seas, are those which encompass the coasts of England, Scotland, and Ireland. To the west they not only include the sea between Great Britain and Ireland, but extend over the Atlantic Ocean, which washes the western coasts of Ireland : this western part of our sea is subdivided ; for, so much as runs between England and Ireland is called St. George's Channel, or the Irish Sea; and the sea on the west coast of Scotland is sometimes named the Caledonian, Deucaledonian, or Scottish Sea, and sometimes the North Sea. To the east we have the German Ocean, which is bounded principally by the opposite coasts of Germany, and the United Provinces (now Belgium) ; lastly, to the south there is the British Channel, or Sea, which runs along the

The British seas, and the king's title therein.

French coast, and, comprehending the Bay of Biscay, ends with the northern coast of Spain. (*a*)

Over the British seas, the King of England claims an absolute dominion and ownership, as Lord Paramount, against all the world. Whatever opinions foreign nations may entertain in regard to the validity of such claim, yet the subjects of the King of England do, by the common law of the realm, acknowledge and declare it to be his ancient and indisputable right. (*b*)

This dominion and ownership over the British seas, vested by our law in the King, is not confined to the mere usufruct of the water, and the maritime jurisdiction, but it includes the very *fundum* or soil at the bottom of the sea. "The sea is the King's proper inheritance," (*c*) and he is "Lord of the Great Waste," both land and water; "*tam aquæ quam soli.*" Selden, (*d*) in his celebrated treatise on the Dominion of the Seas, would seem to contemplate this ownership of the King, as combining both jurisdiction and ownership; the one, indeed, would seem to involve the other, if Selden's doctrine to its full extent be admitted.

There are eminent writers upon natural and upon national law, who have controverted Selden's doctrines, and have denied the King of England's exclusive dominion, and consequently his ownership over the British seas; but however this may be, and probably will ever continue, *vexata quæstio* between such writers, we know that the writers on the common and municipal law of England, as well as the

<small>The king's title to the British seas, includes both the sea and the land covered by it.</small>

(*a*) Hargrave's notes to Co. Litt. 107, b. being a summary of the 1 Ch. 2d Book of Mr. Selden's Mare Clausum. [Woolrych, pp. 4, 5. Jerwood's dissertation on Rights of Sea-Shore, p. 13.]

(*b*) 1 Roll. ab. 528, l. 15. 2 Roll. ab. 168 and 170, lines 42 and 43. 3 Leo. 73. Co. Litt. 107 and 260 b. Callis 39. 2 Molloy, 207, 9th ed. Black. Com. 264. Hale, De Jure Maris, Appendix, post, vii. and xv., and see the cases cited post on the Fisheries, which admit this to be settled law. [Woolrych, p. 433.]

Of the King's Title to the British Seas. 3

decisions of our judicial courts, all speak the same language, and appropriate the dominion of the British seas *tam aquæ quam soli*, to the King. (*c*)

This dominion not only extends over the open seas, but also over all *creeks, arms of the sea, havens, ports*, and *tide-rivers*, as far as the reach of the tide, around the coasts of the kingdom. All waters, in short, which communicate with the sea, and are within the *flux* and *reflux* of its tides, are part and parcel of the sea itself, and subject, in all respects, to the like ownership. This is abundantly proved by the cases hereinafter referred to, where the public *right of fishing* in the creeks, arms of the sea, havens, ports, tide-rivers, &c., of the kingdom has been, in many instances, established upon the principle that they are *part of the sea*, and of the King's dominion, and as such, liable to the common law right of the subject to fish therein ; of which right we shall, in a future page, take notice. (*f*)

It includes all creeks and arms of the sea, and tide-rivers, as far as in the reach of the tides.

(*e*) [Angell on Tide Waters, p. 3.]
(*f*) [The soil of the sea, estuaries, and navigable rivers, within the British dominions, was originally in the Crown, and remains so still, except in those cases where it can be proved to have legally passed into the hands of private persons. Phear on Rights of Water, p. 41. See Malcolmson *v.* O'Dea 10 H. of L. cases 593 ; R. *v.* Stimpson 32 L. J. M. C. 208 ; Att.-Gen. *v.* Chambers per Alderson, B., 4 De G. M. and G. 206 ; S. C. 23 L. J. Chan. 665 ; Blundell *v.* Caterall per Bayley, J., 5 B. and Ald. 304 ; Carter *v.* Murcot 4 Burr 2164 ; but subject to the right of passage over them, see Gann *v.* Free Fishers of Whitstable Co. 11 H. of L. cases 192 ; S. C. 20 C. B. N. S. 1 and 35 L. J. C. P. 29; Colchester, Mayor of, *v.* Brooke 7 Q. B. 339; S. C. 9 Jur. 1090. In England it is held to be the property reserved to the sovereign; but in Scotland it is presumed to be granted as part and pertinent of the adjacent lands, under the burthen of the Crown's right as trustee for the public uses. Bell on Law of Scotland, 5th edit. 251. See Duchess of Sutherland *v.* Watson 6 Macph. 199, Jan. 1868. The doubt which seems to have existed, as to the ownership of the soil of navigable rivers (see Williams *v.* Wilcox 8 Ad. and E. 333), is now set at rest by Lord St. Leonards, in the case of The Lord Advocate *v.* Hamilton

Of the King's Title to the British Seas.

Lord Hale, in the treatise ascribed to him,(g) aptly compares the King's property in the sea and tide-rivers, creeks, &c., to the ownership of lords of manors in the common or waste lands of the manor. The soil and freehold of the

of the Crown to the alveus or bed of a river, it really admits of no dispute; beyond all doubt the soil and bed of a river (we are now speaking of navigable rivers only) belongs to the Crown." As to the soil of a lake, see Marshall *v.* Steam Navigation Co., 3 B. and S. 732; Bell's Principles on Law of Scotland, 651; Phear, p. 13. A river is *primâ facie* navigable in which the tide ebbs and flows: Murphy *v.* Ryan, 2 Ir. R. C. L. 143; see also Malcolmson *v.* O'Dea 10 H. of L. cases 618, per Willes, J.; Rex *v.* Montague 4 B. & C. 598; Miles *v.* Rose 5 Taunton, 705; Woolrych on Waters, pp. 40, 411; Schulte's Aquatic Rights, p. 128. This question has occupied the attention of the Courts in America more than in this country, owing to the large rivers there, which are non-tidal, though for many miles navigable; and while some of their Courts have held that tides are necessary to make a river navigable in law, others have held navigability in fact to be navigability in law. See McManus *v.* Carmichael 3 Iowa 1-52; Middleton *v.* Pritchard 3 Scam. (Ill.) 510; Rowe *v.* Granite Bridge Corporation, 38 Mass. (21 Pick.) 344, 347; People *v.* Canal Appraisers, 33 New York (6 Tiffany) 461, 500: Pollard's Lessee *v.* Hagan, 4 Miss. (3 How.) 212; Child *v.* Starr, 4 Hill (N.Y.) 369; Den *v.* East New Jersey, 15 Howard, U. S. Sup. Ct. Rep. 426; and remarks in Stevens *v.* Paterson and Newark Railway Company, 34 New Jersey Law (5 Vroom) R. 532; Angell on Tide Waters, pp. 38 & 76; Angell on Watercourses, 6 edit. p. 730; Houck on Navigable Rivers, p. 26, *et seq*. The management of the rights and interests, belonging to the Crown, in the shores and bed of the sea, and the rivers of the United Kingdom, as far as the tide flows, was by 29 and 30 Vict. c. 62, s. 7, transferred from the Commissioners of the Woods and Forests to the Board of Trade in the following terms:—" From and immediately after
" the thirty-first day of December, one thousand eight hundred and
" sixty-six, all such parts and rights and interests as then belong to
" her Majesty in the right of the Crown of and in the shore and bed
" of the sea, and of every channel, creek, bay, estuary, and of every
" navigable river of the United Kingdom, as far up the same as the tide
" flows (and which are hereinafter for brevity called the foreshore)
" except as in this Act provided, shall, subject to the provisions of this
" Act, and subject also to such public and other rights as by law exist
" in, over, or affecting the foreshore, or any part thereof, be and the
" same are hereby transferred from the management of the Commis-
" sioners of the Woods and Forests to, and thenceforth the same shall

Of the King's Title to the British Seas. 5

waste belong to the lord, but subject to certain rights of the manorial tenants; such as common of pasture, piscary, turbary, ways, &c., claimed and enjoyed by them, by the custom of the manor, in and out of such waste lands. So

of the Board with respect to the foreshore and bed of the sea are, *inter alia*, to protect the Crown's rights, to ascertain in what parts of the coast the Crown has parted with its rights, in what parts the rights of the Crown are undoubted, and in what parts the title is doubtful; to prevent encroachments on the foreshore, to protect navigation and other public interests, and to sell, lease, or license the use of and otherwise deal with the soil, where expedient so to do, under the powers contained in 10 Geo. 4, c. 50; 2 and 3 Will. 4, c. 1 and 112; 3 and 4 Will. 4, c. 69; 5 Vict. c. 1; 8 and 9 Vict. c. 99; 14 and 15 Vict. c. 42; 15 and 16 Vict. c. 62; 16 and 17 Vict. c. 56; and 29 and 30 Vict. c. 62 (see Forms, post, Appendix cix.) The 10 Geo. 4, c. 50, s. 60, enables the Treasury to grant their consent for a class of cases, instead of in each individual case, and by the 62nd section of the same Act, the necessity of a survey is dispensed with in cases where the land is obviously not worth a survey; the 16 and 17 Vict. c. 56, s. 5 gives power, with the consent of certain authorities, to compromise and settle disputed claims; and the 29 and 30 Vict. c. 62, s. 11 dispenses with the necessity of any consent to compromises. See also Board of Trade Arbitrations, &c., Act 37 and 38 Vict. c. 40.]

(*g*) De Jure Maris, Appendix, post, vii.
[Mr. Serjeant Merewether in a case of the Att.-Gen. *v.* London Mayor and Corporation (see Appendix, p. lxxv.), speaking of the authorship of this work, says, "I have now to advert to a treatise, " which I am well assured has led to much misconception respecting " this supposed principle of law (Rights of the Crown to the Sea- " Shore, &c.) It is a treatise familiarly called Lord Hale's, but I have " every reason for thinking, as far as regards the book published by " Mr. Hargrave, that it is not Lord Hale's; at least, I would venture " so far as to say that there is no sound reason for assuming that it is " so;" but see remarks of Mr. Jerwood in his Dissertation, pp. 32 and 45, which was published shortly after the Serjeant's speech, and was written with special reference thereto; also Phear, p. 47, note *m*; Black's report on the Manor of Tranmere, p. xxx. An American writer goes so far as to say that, " deprived of Lord Hale's name, the Law " as laid down in the treatise referred to, in relation to rivers, would " hardly ever have been recognized in this country; it was the name " of that great jurist that dazzled our judges, and caused some of them " to disregard the plainest principles of common reason." Houck on

the king is lord of the great waste of the sea, subject to certain beneficial rights and privileges of fishing, navigation, &c., immemorially enjoyed by his subjects therein, by the custom of the realm, which is the common law. (*h*)

The title of the King of England to the land or soil *aquâ maris cooperta*, is similar to his ancient title to all the *terra firma* in his dominions, as the first and original proprietor and lord paramount. It is a fundamental principle of our laws of property in land, that all the lands in the realm belonged originally to the King; and, according to the feudal principles of our ancient laws of tenure, the landowners of England are, to this day, *tenants* to the King, holding their lands of him, as their lord paramount.

That part of the land which the King and his ancestors have never granted out to the subject, remains to the King, as his *demesnes*, in absolute ownership.(*i*) The *terra firma* of England has become, almost entirely, the property (by grant and tenure) of the subject; but the *terra aquâ maris cooperta* still remains to the King in wide and barren ownership. (*k*)

Some rare and antique instances may indeed be found of actual grants, by Kings of England, of certain portions of land *under the sea, i.e.* of both sea and land, to a certain extent. These grants have been made in such places where some creek or bay has afforded the means of exclusive possession. Thus, the tract ascribed to Lord Hale, and before quoted, recites a grant of King Canute "de terrâ insulæ Thanet, tam in terrâ quam *in mari* et *littore* ;"(*l*) and another of William the First, " Abbati Sancti Augustini de

---

(*h*) [See the case of the Ipswich Dock Co. *v.* Overseers of St. Peter's, Ipswich, 7 B. and S. 344, and remarks of Blackburn, J., therein. Angell on Tide Waters, p. 24. De Jure Maris, Appendix, post, viii.]

(*i*) Madd. Formulare Anglicarum, 202.

totâ terrâ Estanore, *et totum littus usque medietatem aquæ;*" and the author of the tract adds, " If the King will grant lands adjacent to the sea, together with a thousand acres of land covered by the sea adjoining, such grant will pass the soil itself; and if there should be a recess of the sea, leaving such a quantity of land dry, it will belong to the grantee." (*m*)

Callis, (*n*) in his book on Sewers, says, "I take it, it is very "*disputable* whether grounds, before they be relinquished " by the sea, may be gained by *charter* and *grant* from the " Crown ; *I suppose they may.*" But if such grounds could not be gained by *charter* or *grant*, it would seem to follow that they could not be claimed by *prescription;* for nothing can be prescribed for, which could not have had a lawful beginning by grant: Callis, however, in the very same place, says, "A subject cannot have the grounds to the *low* " water-mark, *but by* custom or *prescription ;*" and he adds, that "the subject *may* have the grounds of the sea, to the " *low* water-mark, and that no *custom* can extend the " ownership of a subject *further.*" (*o*) But he adduces no authority, and there seems no sufficient reason why prescription or custom should not give title, as well to a specific portion of sea, or of a creek or arm of the sea, as of the shore. The true question is, whether *prescription* or *custom* will give title to either. But of this more hereafter.

Having stated the law to be that the king is absolute owner of the ground or soil under the surface of those seas which are within, or parcel of, the British dominions;—let

(*m*) [De Jure Maris, Appendix, post, xv.]
(*n*) Callis on Sewers, p. 53 ; [but see Free Fishers of Whitstable *v.* Gann 11 C. B. n. s. 387, and remarks of Erle, C. J., and Lord Chelmsford in the same case 11 H. L. 218 ; see also Schulte's Aquatic Rights, 110 ; Angell on Tide Waters, 286 ; and the case of Att.-Gen. *v.* Farmen, 2 Levinz, 171.]

us proceed to distinguish the lines drawn by the law, between the *terra firma*, the *sea-bottom*, and the *sea-shore*.

<small>Distinctions between terra firma, sea-bottom, and sea-shore. Tides and inundations.</small>

The waters of the sea, being liable to fluctuation, sometimes rise above and overflow the land, and at other times retire from and leave the land dry. These fluctuations of the waters are of two different characters; they are either periodical and according to the regular course of natural causes and effects: or, 2ndly, *extraordinary* fluctuations, such as happen irregularly and rarely. The periodical and regular fluctuations are called the *tides;* and are thus distinguished from extraordinary *inundations*, and *floods*, as well as from sudden and unusual recessions or derelictions of the sea. The manner, extent, and permanency of these changes will be found to govern and determine the ownership of the soil affected; and our inquiry, therefore, will be directed to ascertain how far these changes in the natural character of the *locus in quo* will, in the consideration and judgment of law, alter or affect the pre-existing title.

<small>Sea-bottom.</small>

In legal, as well as common parlance and intendment, the *sea-bottom* is that soil which is "*semper aquâ maris co-operta*," and *never* known to become dry by changes of the surface of the sea. But with regard to the "*terra firma*," or dry land, although, in common speech, it imports land wholly exempt from the action of any of the tides, yet it would seem that the legal *terra firma* ranges down to the ordinary high-water mark. In the Roman law, the shore extended "quatenus hybernus fluctus maximus excurrit," a boundary line equivalent, as it would seem, to the limits of our high spring tides. But with us it has been long settled, that *that* portion only of the land adjacent to the sea, which is alternately covered and left dry by the *ordinary* flux and reflux of the tides is, in legal intendment, the *sea-shore;* although

<small>Terra firma.</small>

<small>Sea-shore.</small>

Limits of the Sea-shore. 9

more extensive meaning,(*p*) taking in all that extensive belt of waste ground or strand of sand, shingles, and rock, which encircles the British Isles, liable to the action of *every kind* of tide, and of which a part, next the land, is seldom covered by the water, even at the *highest spring tides*. But, in fact, no more of this unreclaimed tract is, at law, *sea-shore*, than that portion which lies between the *high-water* and *low-water mark*, at *ordinary* tides. (*q*)

(*p*) Callis, pp. 54 and 55, in his book on Sewers, makes a distinction between *coast* and *shore*: "coast," says he, "certainly contains both sea and banks;" but he tells us, that "shore at every full sea is covered by the waters." He also quotes the Gospel of St. Matthew, c. 13, v. 2, where our Saviour "went into a boat, and sat, and all the multitude stood on the *shore;*" and Callis thence learnedly infers, "that the *shore* "was the dry-land *quia* they '*stood* thereon,' and it was a great quan- "tity of ground, for thereon stood a multitude; and it was near the "brink of the water, because they heard Jesus speak unto them out of the ship,"—a mode of proving a legal argument, not so much followed now, as in the quaint times in which the learned reader on Sewers lived and argued. We may observe, however, that as it was a *lake*, without tides, on which Jesus embarked, it could not, properly, be said to have a "shore," according to our legal understanding of that term; it had "*ripam*," but not "*littus*." [See also Angell on Tide Waters, p. 67.]

(*q*) [This point has been finally decided, by the case of the Att.-Gen. *v.* Chambers, 4 De G. M. & G. 206; in which Ld. Ch. Cranworth was assisted by Maule, J., and Alderson, B. "The principle," says his lordship, "which gives the shore to the Crown is, that it is "land not capable of ordinary cultivation or occupation, and so is in the "nature of unappropriated soil. Lord Hale gives as his reason for "thinking, that lands only covered by the high spring tides do not belong "to the Crown, that such lands are for the most part dry and manoriable; "and taking this passage as the only authority at all capable of guiding

Marginalia: Tides, three kinds of. High spring tides. Spring tides. Neap tides. As to the soil subject to spring tides.

The law takes notice of three kinds of tides: (r)—

1st. The high spring tides, which are the fluxes of the sea at those tides which happen at the two equinoctials.

2nd. The spring tides, which happen twice every month at the full and change of the moon.

3rd. The neap, or ordinary tides, which happen between the full and change of the moon, twice in the twenty-four hours.

In one book (s) it is said that the lands overflowed by spring tides are called *sea-greens*, and they have been *supposed* to be *inter regalia*, in England; but in Scotland they are private property.

In the marshy districts and fens along the coasts of the sea, creeks, and tide-rivers, the lands which are subject to the action of the *spring* tides, are of considerable extent and value, and by no means so barren and unprofitable as the ordinary sea-shore or strand. These marshes, indeed, are in many places "manoriable," as Lord Hale expresses it,— and the right to embank and enclose them against the effects of the high spring and spring tides, and reduce them to a completely cultivable state, is of no small importance to the lords of adjacent manors, and the owners of the adjacent *terra firma*. In Dyer 326, and 2 Roll. Abr. p. 170, pl. 13, the following quotation is given, "22 lib. Ass. Ca. 93, *de* "*alluvione, accrescentiâ et inundatione maris seu fluminis subito*

" in thinking that the medium line must be treated as bounding the " right of the Crown." In Lowe *v.* Govett, 3 B. and Ad. 863, it was held that where land was covered by the high water of the ordinary spring tides, but not by the medium tides, in the absence of proof as to acts of ownership, the soil must be presumed to have belonged to the owner of the adjoining estate, and not to the Crown. As to when goods are said to be "landed," see Harvey *v.* Lyme Regis, Mayor of, 4 L. R. Ex. 260.]

(r) [De Jure Maris, Appendix, post, xxiii. See also Smith *v.* Earl of

Spring Tides.

" *et extraordinarie per vehementes tempestates, et quando per*
" *naturales et ordinarios fluxus maximos* (*viz.* spring tides)
" *qui fiunt bis quolibet mense, differentia magna est.*"(*t*) Here, it seems the *spring* tides (fluxus maximos) are termed " naturales et ordinarios," being the same terms as also used for the *neap tides*. They are " natural," and periodical, but certainly not " ordinary," compared with neap tides.

Callis, also, would seem, though incorrectly, to consider *spring* tides as *ordinary* tides. "It is certain," says he, " that, at spring tides, the sea useth to overflow the marshes " in Lincolnshire and Norfolk, and returneth within a short " space again; these being *usual* and *annual*, be not accounted " grounds left or gained from the sea; so, because the " marshes and sands in Lincolnshire be overflown every " twelve hours, and then dry again, they are not accounted " grounds left or gained from the sea, because the sea hath " daily her recourse thereon."(*u*)

But, if the *spring* tides are deemed *ordinary* tides, and the marshes subject to the spring tides are not accounted grounds gained from the sea, then such marshes might seem to be "*partes maris, et marisci*," and to belong to the king. Callis, however, does not expressly so state the law; and the inference afforded by the case in Dyer,(*v*) as will appear by reference, is *contra*, and more in favour of the subject, and against the King's title; for the "*magna differentia*" there allued to, is this; viz. that all sudden and unusual inundations, which totally deface all the land-marks, will convert such inundated land into sea-bottom and sea-shore, and, as *such*, it will belong to the King; but that the more regular and periodical inundations of the spring tides, do not, by overflowing the lands, change their legal land-marks and

---

(*t*) Dyer 326, Roll. Abr. 2, p. 170, l. 43.
(*u*) Callis on Sewers, p. 50.

High Spring Tides.

<small>Spring tides not "ordinary" tides.</small>

ownership, nor, consequently, convert them, for the King's benefit, into sea-bottom or sea-shore; and if they are not sea, or sea-shore, they must be part of the *terra firma* adjoining. Relatively speaking, it would seem that the spring tides, though *periodical*, can scarcely be denominated "*ordinary*," when there are other tides which take place daily, and more regularly, viz. the *neap* tides. Besides, the land subject to spring tides, is, for the greater part of the year, dry land.

<small>As to soil subject to high spring and spring tides.</small>

Wherefore, as the authorities almost uniformly describe the "shore," as that which lies within the "*ordinary* flux and reflux of the tides," it would seem to be most correct to consider the soil which is subject to the "high spring tides," and the "spring tides" as part of the adjoining *terra firma*, and belonging to the same title; and that, when such tides have ceased to act, the soil returns to the owner of the adjoining land. "That this is law," says Lord Hale, (*x*) " in " regard to *high spring tides*, is admitted on all hands, but " with regard to the *spring tides*, some hold that common " right speaks for the subject; unless the King hath a pre- " scription, or usage, to entitle the Crown; for this is not " properly *littus maris*. And, therefore, it hath been held, " that where the King makes his title to land, as *littus maris*, " or *parcella littoris marini*, it is not sufficient for him to " make it appear to be overflowed by spring tides of this " kind; p. 8, Car. 1, *in Camerâ Scacarii*, in the case of " Vanhacsdanke for lands in Norfolk; and so I have heard " it was held p. —, 15 Car. B. R. Sir Edward Heron's case, " and Trin. 17 Car. 2, in the case of the Lady Wansford for " a town called the Cowes, in the Isle of Wight." In Appendix, post, ix. he says more decidedly, "the King's title is only to lands that are usually overflowed at ordinary tides." Upon the whole, it may be regarded as good law at

Shore. 13

this day, that the *terra firma*, and right of the subject, in respect of title and ownership, extends beyond the lines of the *high spring* tides and *spring tides*, and down to the edge of the high-water mark of the *ordinary* or *neap* tides; and that the Scotch and English Law are, in this respect, the same.(*y*) {*Terra firma* includes land subject to high spring and spring tides.}

Below this ordinary high-water mark, down to the low-water mark, *i.e.* between the ordinary high and low-water marks, lies the *shore* or *littus maris*. This shore, throughout the coasts of England, as well of the sea, as of crecks and tide-rivers, doth, *de jure communi*, belong to the King. (*z*) In this respect, as matter of title, it would seem to be part of the *fundum*, or sea-bottom, which, as before said, belongs also to the king. " Our Common law of England," says Callis, (*a*) " doth much surpass in reason either the Imperial {The shore, or littus. Is the King's.}

(*y*) [See Att.-Gen. *v.* Chambers, 4 De G. M. and G. 206; Lowe *v.* Govett, 3 B. and Ad. 863; Smith *v.* Earl of Stair, 6 Bell, App. Cases, 487. Observations attributed to Lord Brougham, and note *q* ante, p. 9.]

(*z*) See pp. 2 and 41 for authorities; most of the cases relating to the king's ownership of the sea, and to the rights of fishing, either expressly or impliedly admit the king's ownership in the *shore*. See particularly the cases of Bagott *v.* Orr. 2 Bos. and Pul. 472; Blundell *v.* Catterall, 5 Barn and Ald. 268, Dav. Rep. 55; and the King *v.* Smith and others, 2 Dougl. 441, as to the shore of tide-rivers. [It was urged in this case, that the river Thames above London Bridge was not " navigable," although it was flowing and reflowing, inasmuch as the tide beyond that limit was occasioned by the pressure and accumulation backward of fresh water; but the distinction attempted was, by Lord Mansfield, pronounced new and inadmissible; it was taken for granted, however, that the water was salt, the case stating that the Thames was navigable. In Horne *v.* Mackenzie, 6 Cl. and Fin. 628, the question was, what was to be considered " river" and what " sea," and the direction was " that the thing to be looked for was the fact of " the absence or prevalence of the fresh water, though strongly impreg- " nated with salt;" this was, however, held to be bad. See as to ownership of shore in America, Commonwealth *v.* Charlestown, 18 Mass. (1 Pick.) R. 180; Chapman *v.* Kimball, 9 Conn. R. 40; Peyroux *v.* Howard, 7 Peters (U. S. Sup. Ct.) R. 324; Rowe *v.* Granite Bridge Corp., 38 Mass (21 Pick.) 344, 347.] See also the cases of the King *v.* Lord Yarborough, 3 B. and C. 91, and Scratton *v.* Brown, 4 B. and C. 485.

"or the Civil law, for (by our law) it is said *Rex in ea habet* "*proprietatem, sed populus habet usum ibidem necessarium.*"

Of the title which a subject or corporate body of subjects may have in a portion of sea-shore or sea.

As all the land of England, whether *terra firma*, sea-shore, or sea-bottom, belonged originally (according to our laws of tenure) to the King; and as the ownership of a subject, in or over any part of it, could only be derived by *grant* from or through the King, it might seem to follow that every claim of the subject, or of a Corporate body of subjects, to any part of the sea-shore, or of the shores of tide-rivers, must be supported by precisely the *same* evidence of *title* as a claim to any inland estate, as against the King's *primâ facie* title. Nor does it appear how the King's right and claim to the sea-shore, or shore of tide-rivers, or any part thereof, can be rebutted by any other kind of evidence than that which would be called for by our courts of law in a case of *inland title.* It is presumed that the *sea-shore* is legally and technically speaking "*land*," as is the adjacent *terra firma*, in all cases of disputed title between the King and a subject, and between subject and subject.

Title to any part of the shore must be proved and supported as inland titles are.

Grants of the sea-shore by the King.

The Kings of England have frequently, and from the most ancient times, exercised their right of ownership in the sea-shore, by making *grants* thereof to the subject, accompanying grants of the *terra firma* adjoining, and by similar forms of grant. Thus the King might grant a manor (*b*) "cum littore maris adjacente," and the shore itself will pass, though *in gross*, and *not parcel of the manor*. He might also grant a manor, or land contiguous to the sea, *cum maritimis incrementis*, and that will pass the "jus alluvionis," *i.e.* land left by the retirement of the sea." Thus, King John granted to the Abbot de Bello Loco, "alveum "super quem Abbatia fundata est, à vado de Hartford cum "fluctu maris in ascendendo et descendendo inter utramque

and Grants of Shore.

" ripam."(*c*) So William I. granted, "Abbati sancti Augus-
" tini de totâ terrâ Estanore et *totum littus* usque medie-
" tatem aquæ."(*d*) Such also was the grant of Canute,
quoted before ; (*e*) and the muniments of title to many
manors on the sea-coasts, will probably furnish similar
express grants of the *littus*, or sea-shore, together with the
manors themselves. In Sir Henry Constable's Case (*f*) it
is said, " that it was resolved by the whole Court that the
" soil on which the sea flows and ebbs, (*g*) *i. c.* between the
" high-water mark and low-water mark, *may* be *parcel* of the
" manor of a subject."(*h*) Indeed, there is no doubt but that
a subject may be owner of a portion or tract of shore, by
ancient *charter* or *grant* from the Crown.

<small>The shore may be made the subject of express grant.</small>

(*c*) Ib. xv.   (*d*) Ib. xv.
(*e*) P. 6 ante, and see also 4 Inst. for two other instances. Even Grotius admits that there *may* be private ownership in some creek, or small part of the sea, or tide-river, although he founds such ownership on "primary occupation." Grotius, Mare Lib. ch. 5 and 7.
(*f*) 5 Co. 107.
(*g*) 2 Roll. Abr. 170 ; Dyer, 326 ; Scratton *v.* Brown, 4 B. and C. 485.
(*h*) [Continuous acts of ownership exercised by the grantee upon the sea-shore between high and low-water mark may be called in aid to prove the shore to be parcel of a manor : Calmady *v.* Rowe, 6 C. B. 861 ; and see Att.-Gen. *v.* Jones, 33 L. J. Exch. 249 ; Walton cum Trimley manor *in re* 28 L. T. N. S. 12 ; S. C. 21 W. R. 475 ; Healy *v.* Thorne, 4 Ir. Com. Law R. 495 ; *in re* Belfast Dock Act, 1 Ir. Eq. R. 128 ; Le Strange *v.* Rowe, 4 F. and F. 1048 ; Donegall, Marquis of, *v.* Lord Templemore, 9 Ir. Com. Law Rep. 374. And modern usage is admissible in evidence to show that such sea-shore was part of the manor ; Beaufort, Duke of, *v.* Swansea, Mayor of, 3 Exch. 413 ; Dickens *v.* Shaw, Appendix, post, xlv. ; also Jerwood, p. 74. Juries may presume an ancient lost grant from the Crown, from long-continued acts of ownership exercised by the adjoining proprietor on the sea-shore : see *in re* Belfast Dock Act, 1 Ir. Eq. R. 128 ; Att.-Gen. *v.* Chambers, 4 De G. and Jo. 55 ; *Re* Alston's Estate 5 W. R. 189 S. C. 28 L. T. 337 ; and cases cited in Taylor on Evidence, 6th edit. vol. i. p. 144, *et seq*. As the shore, says Hale, C. J., Appendix xxiv., may be parcel of a manor, so it may be parcel of a vill or parish : see Calmady *v.* Rowe, 6 C. B. 880 ; but, *primâ facie*, it is extra parochial : see Duke

Of Title to the Shore by Prescription.

But it is also laid down, in the tract ascribed to Lord Hale, (*i*) as well as by Callis,—that a title to the *soil,* as well at the *bottom* of the sea, as upon the *sea-shore,* may be acquired and possessed by the subject by " *Prescription.*" The doctrine of the Treatise is, that there are *two* ways by which a subject may acquire a right to such soil or shore ; 1st. By the King's Charter or Grant. 2nd. By *custom* or *prescription.* (*k*) Callis, (*l*) indeed, goes so far as to say that " a subject *cannot* have the ground to the low-water mark, " *but* by custom and prescription." But in this he is clearly wrong.

As the ownership claimed by a subject to any portion of the sea-shore is in opposition to and in derogation of the King's *primâ facie* title, it will be proper in this place to consider, with attention, the grounds upon which the King's subjects are supposed to found their titles to any part of the sea-shore when claimed by them against the King's ancient right and dominion. Neither good policy, nor public utility will, it is conceived, incline towards the claim of the individual subject ; and it may be presumed that, the exclusive ownership of the sea-shore, or of any of the creeks, or arms of the sea, or of the ports or tide-rivers, or any part of them, ought, whenever set up by a subject, to

B. 4; Ipswich Dock Company *v.* Overseers of St. Peter's, Ipswich, 7 B. and S. 310; R. *v.* Gee, 1 E. and E. 1068 ; Reg. *v.* Musson, 8 E. and B. 900 ; but see 31 and 32 Vict. c. 122, s. 27; and further, as to public and private rivers, McCannon *v.* Sinclair, 2 E. and E. 53, S. C. 5 Jur. N. S. 1302 ; see also Proprietors of Waterloo Bridge *v.* Cull, 5 Jur. 1288 ; Perrott *v.* Bryant, 2 Y. and C. 61 ; Rex *v.* Landulph inhab. of, 1 Mood and R. 393. Still the shores of the sea and beds of navigable rivers are part of the adjoining counties, and justices have power to convict persons charged with fishing in such waters, where there is a private right of fishery, Embleton *v.* Brown, 6 Jur. N. S. 1298.]

(*i*) [See Jerwood, p. 45, and Serj. Merewether's Speech, Appendix, post, lxxiv.]

(*k*) [See Appendix, post, xv. See Benest *v.* Pipon, 1 Knapp, 60.]

be regarded and construed *stricto jure*,—in favour of the Crown, *pro bono publico*.

It has already been premised, that the *terra firma* of England has become, almost entirely, transferred to and vested in the King's subjects, by grants from him. Without adverting to obsolete modes of tenure, and division of property, it will suffice to explain further that, as against the King, the subject holds his landed estate under two general denominations of title, according to the two most prevailing divisions of landed property, viz. into manors, which are tracts of freehold land, accompanied by peculiar rights and privileges; and naked freeholds, or freehold lands, unaccompanied by any such manorial rights and privileges. *Copyholders* are mere *tenants* of the lord of a manor.

As, however, claims set up to portions of the sea-shore, and to the shores of tide-rivers, are almost invariably made by *lords of manors*, in right of their manors, it will simplify our subject, and answer every useful purpose, if we discuss the question of right and title to the "shore," chiefly with reference to the ownership claimed therein by lords of adjacent manors.

We have already shown that any of the King's subjects, whether lords of manors, or not, may have a right and property in portions of the sea-shore, by ancient *express grant* from the King. (*m*) With regard to claims founded on grants of manors, it need only be remarked, that the title to the "shore" will depend wholly upon the construction of the metes and bounds of the grant. Thus, if the boundary be expressed to be "down to the *sea*" or "bounded on one side by the *sea*," or any similar phrase, it is presumed the ordinary *high-water mark* must be deemed the intended line, and not the low-water mark, for the whole

(*m*) P. 15, ante.

shore is "quasi pars maris;" or, as Bracton expresses it, "quasi maris accessoria."(*n*) But, if the boundary line be expressed to be "down to the low-water mark," or extend to any ascertainable line beyond low-water mark, this will be tantamount to a grant of the *sea-shore*. So, if the grant extend to any known and distinct limits within the sea, or tide-river—as " usque filum aquæ," or " medietatem aquæ," &c. In fact, the land granted, whether situate upon the coast or inland, is co-extensive with the words of grant, and no more. (*o*)

A manor on the sea-coast does not necessarily include the shore.

If a manor on the coast be granted by the same form of words as is used to grant an inland manor, nothing but *terra firma* would pass by such grant; no part of the " sea-shore" would be included in such grant. In a former page (*p*) we are told, that the King might grant a *manor*, " cum littore maris adjacente," and the shore will pass, though in *gross*, and *not parcel of the manor*. So that it is evident a

(*n*) Lib. 1, cap. 2, and lib. 2, cap. 12.

(*o*) [A patent of James the First granted the priory of Holmpatrick and also the four Islands to the priory belonging, to wit the island called Shennick, &c., and the patent used the large general words, granting wreck of the sea, flotsam, jetsam, &c. and all the appurtenances to the priory belonging. It was held that these words, coupled with the proof of enjoyment for 70 years of the foreshore, by letting to tenants to take seaweed, &c., were sufficient evidence to support a finding that the shore passed under the grant, Healy *v.* Thorne, 4 Ir. C. L. R. 495, and the soil of the shore between high and low-water mark may pass under the term "waste" in a grant, Att.-Gen. *v.* Hanmer, 27 L. J. Ch. 837, S. C. 4 Jur. N. S. 751 ; see Scratton *v.* Brown, 4 B. and C. 485, per Bayley, J., and Att.-Gen. *v.* Jones, 33 L. J. Ex. 249; or "ripa," *in re* Belfast Dock Act, 1 Ir. R. Eq. 128, 139, or " anchorage, &c.," see Foreman *v.* Free Fishers of Whitstable, 4 L. R. E. and I. App. 266, 2 L. R. C. P. 688 ; Le Strange *v.* Rowe, 4 F. and F. 1048, Calmady *v.* Rowe, 6 C. B. 861; also under other terms, Macalister *v.* Campbell, 15 D. B. and M. Session-Court, 490. As between the Crown and the Duchy of Cornwall, all mines between high and low-water mark, in the county of Cornwall are by 21 and 22 Vict. c. 109, vested in the Prince of Wales, as part of the soil and territorial possession of the Duchy, see Phear, p. 49.]

(*p*) P. 14, ante.

Franchises of Wreck.

sea-coast manor does not *necessarily*, by reason of its locality, include the *shore* within the *precincts*.(*q*) Some grants of manors on the coast may include, *expressly*, not only the "*shore*," but also *wreck*, and *royal fish, flotsam*, &c., and a *separate fishery ;* others may comprise the shore, but none of these liberties, profits, or franchises; and others may contain all these, or one of these privileges only, and no grant of the shore at all. (*r*)

It is agreed on all hands that *wreck*, or *royal fish*, are (under the technical denomination of *franchises*) *separate and peculiar species of property*, in the hands of subjects, and distinct from the property of the soil. If, therefore, one species of property be expressly granted, and another kind clearly omitted, it would seem to be contrary to the ordinary and acknowledged rules of construction to *presume*, or infer, a grant of that *one* which is omitted, *unless* it be *so* essential to the enjoyment of the *other*, as to render the implication or inference, in common sense, *necessary*. It is equally agreed, on all hands, that one man may have the soil of the shore; another man the franchise of wreck; another the liberty, or profit *à prendre*, of a private fishery, &c., and all this may be upon the same line of coast, and on the same spot of shore. "The property in such land" [the shore] "is *primâ facie* in the Crown. It *may*, how-" ever, be in a subject; and *different* rights, in that descrip-" tion of property, may be vested in a subject, *according to* " *the terms of grant.* The King may have granted to a " subject the soil itself, or the privilege of fishing, &c." *Per* Bayley, J. in Scratton *v.* Brown, 4 B. and C. 485.

In like manner as it does not necessarily include the regalia of wreck, royal fish, &c.

(*q*) Non a nudâ terrarum quæ oceano pulsantur *occupatione*, sed ab ipso maris *usu* ejusmodi privato ; Seld. lib. 2, cap. 2 ; *i.e.* the absolute private use of it *for all* purposes, and not one, or two only,—and *that* excluding all other persons. See post, p. 84.

(*r*) [See Dickens *v.* Shaw, Appendix, post, pp. xlvii., lxiv. Healy *v.* Thorne, 4 Ir. R. C. L. 495. See post, 82.]

These rights and titles, therefore, it would seem, are not, in respect of their subject matter, dependent upon each other, or necessarily linked together. The grant of the *sea-shore* down to low-water mark, is one thing; and the grant of *wreck* is *another* thing; nor does it appear ever to have been established that the possession of the franchises of Wreck, or of Royal Fish, by an express grant, *totidem verbis*, conferred also a title to the shore itself. The rule, "*expressum facit cessare tacitum*," applies as strongly to such form of grant, as to any other form.

Neither is it necessary to the full enjoyment of all, or any of these grants of *wreck, separalis piscariæ*, &c., that the soil of the shore should accompany them; it is clear that the King, or a subject under him, may retain the soil, subject and without prejudice to such usufructuary rights, vested in some other individual. It would seem, therefore, too much to contend that an express grant of any one, or more of these "franchises," will *per se* carry the soil of the "sea-shore;"(*s*) and it should be remembered, that the King's grants to a subject are, by the rule of law, to be construed strictly, and in the King's favour, and more by the letter thereof, than a grant from one subject to another; in which case the grant is construed most in favour of the grantee.(*t*)

(*s*) ["The privileges of 'wreck' and 'royal fish' have been separated "from the other incidents, which would attach to ownership of the shore, "and vested in the Crown as distinct incorporeal rights. This fact is of "no importance, while both the property of the shore, and the owner-"ship of these rights, remain in the hands of the Crown; but when a "subject has established a claim by grant to either of them, it often "requires to be remembered that there is no mere implication or pre-"sumption to carry the other with it." Phear, p. 52. See also Dickens *v.* Shaw, Appendix, post, p. xlv.]

(*t*) In Dav. Rep. 55, it is distinctly laid down, that "the grant of the king passes nothing by implication."—The great case of the fishery of the river Banne, Ireland. In the Duke of Somerset *v.* Fogwell, this doctrine is distinctly recognized by Mr. Justice Bayley, who says, "in

Our next enquiry is, whether a Lord of a Manor or any other subject, or a Corporation Sole or Aggregate, may also acquire an ownership in the sea-shore, by *prescription*. The learned writer already quoted (Lord Hale), clearly alludes to that kind of prescription, or usage, which supports such franchises and usufructuary rights, liberties, and profits, as were just now mentioned, viz. wreck, royal fish, separate fishery, &c., the immemorial use and enjoyment whereof will, *per se*, support a title to them. (*u*)

It may be concluded from some of our best authori-

Enquiry whether a title to any part of the sea-shore c be acquired by "prescription."

" grants from the Crown, nothing passes unless the intention is *mani-*
" *fest* that it should pass ;" 5 B. and C. 875 ; Jerwood, 60.

[In Feather *v.* R., 6 B. and S. 283, S. C. 35, L. J. Q. B. 204, and 12 L. T. N. S. 114, Cockburn, C. J. says, " It is established on the best
" authority, that in construing grants from the Crown a different rule
" of construction prevails from that by which grants from one subject
" to another are to be construed. In a grant from one subject to
" another, every intendment is to be made against the grantor, and in
" favour of the grantee, in order to give full effect to the grant ; but in
" grants from the Crown, an opposite rule of construction prevails.
" Nothing passes except that which is expressed, or which is matter
" of necessary and unavoidable intendment, in order to give effect to
" the plain and undoubted intention of the grant ; and in no species
" of grant does this rule of construction more especially obtain than in
" grants which emanate from, and operate in derogation of, the prero-
" gative of the Crown ;" and he then cites the language of Lord Stowell in the case of the Rebeckah. 1 Ch. Rob. 227, 230.

The rule in England, that a grant from the Crown is strongly construed against the grantee (Feather *v.* Reg. 6 B. and S. 283 ; Lord *v.* Commissioners of Sydney, 12 Moore, P. C. 496 ; R. *v.* London, mayor of, 1·Cr. M. and R. 12 ; R. *v.* 49 casks of brandy, 3 Hag. Adm. R. 271 ; and Forsyth's Constitutional Law, 175), applies to grants from the United States. " All public grants," says Chan. Manning, " are to " be strictly construed, and nothing passes under them by impli-
" cation ;" La Plaisance Bay Harbour Co. *v.* City of Monroe, Walker's Chan. R. 155 ; McManus *v.* Carmichael, 3 Iowa, 1-53 ; Haight *v.* Keokuk, city of, 4 Iowa, 200 ; People *v.* Canal Appraisers, 33 N. Y. (6 Tiffany), 461. In Iowa the Supreme Court expressed similar views. An additional reason for the rule mentioned is, that the United States Government holds all the public lands as a mere trustee ; see McManus

ties, (*x*) that a title to "*land*" or freeholds corporeal cannot be supported by *prescription*. The words of Blackstone are, " no prescription can give a title to lands, and other corpo-" real substances, of which more certain evidence (of title) " can be had ;"(*y*) and he states this more certain evidence to be "corporeal seizin and inheritance." Now, there are two grounds of title to land :—1st. By *Grant*. 2nd. By what is called *adverse possession*, founded on the *Statutes of Limitation*. A title by "adverse possession," under the *Statutes of Limitation*, is, indeed, sometimes spoken of as held by "prescription;" but at common law, as at present understood, "prescription alone, it is conceived, confers no *title* to freehold land. In the Scotch law,(*z*) *positive* prescription is said to be "the acquisition of property, by the pos-" sessor's continuing his possession for the time which the " law has declared sufficient for that purpose." *Negative* " is the loss or omission of a right, by neglecting to follow " it forth, or use it during the whole time limited by the " law."(*a*) Erskine's Principles, p. 372. In the French Code it is laid down, " la prescription est un moyen d'acquérir ou " de se libérer par un certain laps de temps, et sous les " conditions detérminées par la loi." And this "moyen d'acquérir" is applied to *lands*, as well as to *incorporeal* rights. But when, in our law, the word is used in its technical sense, it does not correctly apply to a title to freehold lands or corporeal hereditaments.

(*x*) 2 Roll, Abr. 264, l. 3. Co. Litt. 48 a, 113 b, 114 b, 195 b. Vin. Abr. title, Prescription.

(*y*) 2 Blac. Com. 264, and see Doct. and Stu. Dial. i. cap. 8, Finch 132, and see note to Com. Dig. title Franchise, where it is said, "land cannot be claimed by prescription." Hammond's Ed.—The *text* there, from Co. Litt. 114 b, has only relation to a "tenant in common," and see p. 52 post, and accord. Litt. Sect. 310.

(*z*) See Ld. Advocate *v.* Graham, 7 D. B. M. 183.

Prescription as giving Title to the Shore. 23

Adverse possession of land without the aid of statute law, is no *title*; but prescription, as a title to incorporeal rights, is everything without statute law.(*b*) In prescription for a customary privilege, immemorial usage is allowed to raise the presumption of an ancient grant.(*c*) But as to land,

(*b*) [See 2 and 3 Will. 4, cap. 71. The right to a given substratum of coal lying under a certain close is a right to land, and cannot be claimed by prescription; but a right to take coal in another's land may be; Wilkinson *v*. Proud, 11 M. and W. 33; see Phear, p. 68, n. It has been held that negative easements are not within the Prescription Act, which only deals with easements which are used in and upon the servient tenement, and are capable of interruption by the owner of the servient tenement. Neither can prescription apply to a right which has been expressly prohibited by statute, unless the grant be presumed to have been made before such statute was passed; nor can such right be claimed against the public, if it directly operate as a nuisance to a public right or franchise. Webb *v*. Bird, 10 C. B. N. S. 268; 31 L. J. C. P. 335; Murgatroyd *v*. Robinson, 7 E. and B. 391, 26 L. J. Q. B. 233.]

(*c*) "The several modes of establishing an old title by pleading a "lost grant, &c., often proved insufficient to meet cases of real "hardship," says Mr. Phear. "For instance, enjoyment might have "been sufficiently long and adverse to render a disturbance of it "most unjust, and yet it might be possible for the opposing party to "defeat the pleas, by showing that its actual commencement was in- "consistent with them; or, even if the enjoyment necessary for sup- "porting the plea were proved, circumstances adverse to the legal "inception of the right might be shown, notwithstanding that the pre- "sent enjoyment ought, in all justice, to be entirely unaffected by "them. The statute 2 and 3 Will. 4, c. 71, known as the Prescrip- "tion Act, offers a remedy for some of these cases." Phear, p. 83.

[In Shuttleworth *v*. Le Fleming, 19 C. B. N. S. 687; S. C. 34, L. J. C. P. 309. To a declaration in trespass for breaking and entering the plaintiff's close and landing fishing nets there, the defendant, amongst other things, pleaded, that the land was part of the shore of an inland lake, and that he, and all his ancestors, for sixty years before the suit, enjoyed as of right and without interruption a free fishery in the said water, with the right of landing their nets on the shore, &c., and to these pleas the plaintiff demurred. In delivering judgment, Montague Smith, J., said :—"The demurrer raises the question whether the rights "so pleaded to belong to the plaintiff in gross, are within the Prescrip- "tion Act, 2 and 3 Will. 4, c. 71. The construction of the statute whether there was or was not an ancient grant, is immaterial to the *effect* of the statute; for the statute may be a bar to the "best title in the world," and confirm the worst against all presumption.

The common law was peculiarly strict in all questions of title to the freehold, and realty. But upon questions of minor right,—as upon the enjoyment of some petty convenience, or benefit derived from the land,—it was not so

" has arisen in the courts, it has not been decided. We are now called
" upon to determine it; and upon consideration of all the provisions
" of the Act, we are led to the conclusion that rights claimed in gross
" are not within it. The fifth section gives the key to the true con-
" struction of the Act. It professes to enact forms of pleading appli-
" cable to all rights within the Act theretofore claimed to have existed
" from time immemorial, which forms it declares shall, in such cases,
" be sufficient. Those forms have clearly relation to rights which are
" appurtenant to the land, and to such rights only. The whole prin-
" ciple of the pleading assumes a dominant tenement, and an enjoy-
" ment as of rights by the occupier of it. The proof must, of course,
" follow and support the pleading. It is obvious that rights claimed
" in gross cannot be so pleaded or proved." See also Gale on Easements, 151.

By sect. 1 of the Act, claims to right of common and other profits *à prendre* are not to be defeated after thirty years' enjoyment, by showing only that such right was first taken or enjoyed at any time prior to such period; and when such right shall have been so taken for sixty years it shall be deemed absolute and indefeasible, unless it had been taken by consent or agreement.

And by sect. 2, in cases of claims of right of way or other easements, the periods are twenty and forty years. " It may be remarked," says Mr. Phear, " that in making use of this Act whenever the mere alle-
" gation of right, and not immemorial usage, was originally sufficient,
" the general issue will render everything under this Act available to
" rebut it; but when the allegation of immemorial usage was neces-
" sary, the user given by the Act must be alleged, and the general
" issue will only traverse that; other defences must be pleaded spe-
" cially. It may be added that claims under this Act may be made
" in respect of enjoyment by the occupiers of land without alleging the
" right of the owner of the fee;" but although by sect. 6 no presumption in favour of the claims is to be derived from a user short of thirty years, the statute does not take from such shorter user its weight as

strict; such claims, therefore, as a right of way, a right to fish, or a right to dig turf, or a right to pasture cattle, were allowed, upon the proof of a continued acquiescence on the part of the owners of the soil, for a time beyond memory of man. " Not that the Court believes" (as Mr. Butler(*d*) well observes) "that any actual grant of such right once existed;" but upon the general political principle of quieting possessions. (*e*)

But immemorial usage *alone*, without the aid of statute law, will not, it is conceived, raise a title to land at this time of day; and especially not against the Crown. Whatever may have been the "old law," as explained by Bracton,(*f*) and Coke,(*g*) previously to the statute of Merton (20 Hen. 3), yet, from the time of that statute, title to land by length of time of possession, or, as Bracton borrows it from the civil law, " *usucaptio*," has depended upon statute law. Whether, under the feudal system, " usucaptio" was ever a valid ground of title to land, *as between subject and subject*, we need not stop long, in this place, to inquire; our inquiry being into the effect of such act against the Crown. It is said that, previously to the statute of Merton, "what " length of time was necessary to give such right [to land,] " was not defined by the law, but was left to the discretion " of the *Justices;*" (*h*) and it would seem to have been fixed by those Justices of whose discretion in this matter we have the earliest record, that no " seizin could be alleged " by the demandant in a real action, but from the time of " Hen. I." This discretion of the Justices has, it is considered, ceased since the stat. of Merton, as regards title to the freehold and inheritance of lands. (*i*)

(*d*) See his note Co. Litt. 261 a.
(*e*) Taylor on Evidence, 6 edit. p. 146.
(*f*) Lib. 2, fo. 51, 52.   (*g*) 1 Inst. 114 b.

It is to be noted, however, that neither the "discretion of the Justices," anterior to the statute law, nor the statute law itself, for a long period after the stat. of Merton, enabled a subject to make title to land, "by length of time of possession," *against the Crown*. The maxim "*nullum tempus occurrit Regi*" prevailed, until a period much later than the stat. of Merton.

Against the King, therefore, as it would seem, "prescription" or "usucaptio" did not, by our common or feudal law, give title to lands; and, consequently, it is contended, not to lands of the Crown covered by the sea, or upon the sea-shore. (*k*) It is by the statute law *alone*, without any reference to the "old law" of prescription between subject and subject (whatever that law might have been), that adverse possession will, by lapse of time, prevail against the King's original and paramount title. These statutes are comparatively recent, so far as they affect the Crown; and are not founded upon any principle or right of prescription against the Crown, known to have prevailed in our feudal system of laws prior to those statutes. (*l*)

Since the statute of Merton, therefore, as regards the law between subject and subject; and both *before* and since *that* and subsequent statutes, as regards the law between the Crown and a subject, there has existed and still exists a sufficiently marked distinction between "prescription" for certain usages or rights, and title to land under the statutes of limitation. Mr. Butler, in his annotations (*m*) on Co. Litt., has touched upon this part of our subject, but would seem to have adopted the doctrine of Lord Hale, in regard to titles to the "sea-shore," and to have considered such titles as capable of being made good by prescription. He first

Mr. Butler's doctrine considered.

Prescription as giving Title to the Shore. 27

explains the distinction between titles, founded in *common right*, which is an ownership conferred by mere act of law, and titles acquired by the act of the party, and which are in derogation of such common right. "In inquiries," says he, " of this kind, where it is said that a person is entitled
" to the right or property in question, by *common right*, but
" that it *may* belong to another, it is intended to say, that
" the right or property in question is, by common law,
" annexed to the particular capacity of the party, or to
" some property of which he is owner; yet, that it is not so
" inseparably or inalienably annexed to this capacity or
" ownership, but that the party may transfer it to another.
" So that in all these cases, the presumption is in favour of
" him to whom the right or property is said to belong by
" common right; yet this does not exclude the possibility
" of its belonging to another. To another, therefore, it *may*
" belong; but if he claim it, he must prove his title to it.
" On the other hand, the party to whom it belongs of *com-*
" *mon right* is under no obligation of showing his title to it;
" to him, in the intendment of the law, it belongs till there
" is proof of the contrary. To exemplify this doctrine, the
" lord of a manor is lord of the soil of the manor of common
" right; (*n*) that is, if it be admitted or proved that he is lord
" of the manor, his right to the soil necessarily follows so far
" that it is not incumbent on him to produce any proof
" of it. He may, therefore, of common right, dig for gravel,
" unless it is to the prejudice of his tenants. But this right
" is not inseparable or unalienable from the seignory. The
" lord may grant it (*i.e.* the right to dig gravel) to the
" tenants; to the tenants, therefore, it may belong. But if
" they claim it, it is incumbent on them to prove their title

" to it. There are two ways of doing this,—one by showing
" the grant from the lord, the other by *prescription;* that is,
" by proving an immemorial usage of it, which, in the eye
" of the law, always presupposes a grant. Now, prescrip-
" tion is shown by producing repeated and unequivocal
" instances of the immemorial usage or exercise of the
" right contended for; the tenants, therefore, in the case
" we have mentioned, if they cannot produce the original
" grant, must, to make out their title to dig for gravel,
" produce repeated and unequivocal instances of their hav-
" ing done it immemorially. If they do this, they esta-
" blish their title to the right in question. But, though the
" lord is not called upon in the first instance to prove his
" title; yet, when it is claimed by others, he may disprove
" their claim by showing he has done acts inconsistent with
" it. Thus, if, on the one hand, the tenants can prove, by
" repeated instances, that they have exercised the right in
" question of digging for gravel, the lord may, on the other
" hand, show that in all, or a considerable number of these
" instances, the parties have been presented at his court, or
" otherwise punished for the acts in question, and this may
" destroy the effect of the evidence in their favour, arising
" from the instances adduced by them. In the same man-
" ner, the lord may show that they have dug only in one
" particular spot of the waste, at particular times, or for a
" particular purpose; by this he may circumscribe their
" right as to the place, time, and manner of its enjoyment.
" It should also be observed, that though it is said that pre-
" scription presupposes a grant, and non-user presupposes a
" release, it is not that, strictly speaking, the courts always,
" in these cases, *really believe* that such a grant, or such a
" release, is actually executed; but because for the sake of

Prescription as giving Title to the Shore. 29

" therefore determine in the same manner as they would
" determine if the very instrument of grant or release were
" produced." The learned writer then goes on to say
(quoting from Lord Hale), " as to the *soil between high and
" low-water mark* at ordinary tides, this, of common right,
'' belongs to the King. It *may*, however, belong to a subject
" by grant or *prescription*. Sometimes it is parcel of the
" adjacent manor: sometimes of the adjacent vill, or parish:
" sometimes it belongs to a subject in gross;" "still, how-
" ever," says Mr. Butler, "it belongs of common right to
" the King; it is therefore incumbent on the subject to
" prove his right. This may be done by producing the
" grant. Hale, ib. ch. 4, 5, 6. (*o*) Sir Henry Constable's case,
" 5 Rep. 107. But as it is part of the possessions of the
" Crown, *jure coronæ*, it does not pass by general words, and
" therefore to establish a right to it under the grant, it must
" contain such words as either *expressly*, or by *necessary*
" *implication*, convey the soil. If the grant cannot be pro-
" duced, it can *no otherwise* be proved than by 'prescrip-
" tion,' that is, as we observed before, by repeated unequi-
" vocal and immemorial *usage*. As to *ports*, there is a
" very material and important distinction between the *fran-
" chise* of a port and the *property of its soil*. As to the
" franchise; by the common law, a port is the only place
" where a subject is permitted to unlade *customable* goods.
" This privilege constitutes what is called the franchise of a
" port. To create the franchise of a port is part of the royal
" prerogative. *But this does not in anywise affect the pro-
" perty of the soil.*" "It may be considered as a striking
" instance of the respect of the law of England for private
" property, that though it entrusts the King with the pre-
" rogative of originating ports, and though the use of the
" adjacent soil is essentially necessary to the existence of a

(*o*) [Appendix, post, pp. vii. xiv. xxiii.]

"port, the law does not permit the King to take any part of the soil from the owner; so that, if the soil is not the property of the King, it is necessary to secure the property of the shore beforehand, for the purposes of the port.(*p*) The franchise belongs to the King of common right, but by charter or *prescription*, it may be, and frequently is, the right of the subject. The soil generally belongs to the owner of the port; but it is going too far to say that it belongs to him of common right. The mere grant of a port would not, in a *modern* charter,(*q*) pass the soil; but *perhaps* it would be sufficient in an *ancient* charter to pass it, if no evidence to the contrary could be shown; and it certainly would be considered as sufficient to pass it in an ancient charter, if accompanied with the additional circumstance of immemorial usage." The learned annotator then adds:—"Having thus shown to whom the soil of the shore and of ports belong by common right, it remains to state succinctly the nature of the evidence by which the right to it may be proved to exist in another.(*r*) It may be done by showing that he, and those under whom he claims, have immemorially, frequently, and without restriction to any part of the soil, dug gravel,(*s*) fetched away seaweed or sand, or embanked against the sea. If it be claimed to be part of a manor, the right of commonage for the cattle of the lord and the tenants; the prose-

---

(*p*) This renders it the more necessary to preserve the King's right to the shore, and to be strict in the proofs of title against him.

(*q*) It is said in Comyn's Dig. title Navigation (from 1 Rol. ab. 528), that a grant of a *port* "is not good, for a subject cannot have it." As to the *soil*, indeed, no modern grant can be made of it by the king, by reason of the statutes against the alienation of crown lands.

(*r*) Hale, De Jure Maris, Appendix, post, xxiv. xxv.

(*s*) Yet copyholders do not acquire a right to the soil by proving an immemorial custom to dig gravel or sand. Why, therefore, should such act, by a lord of a manor, in the shore, raise a title in him,

Prescription as giving Title to the Shore. 31

"cution and punishment of purprestures in the court of a
"manor; its being included in the perambulations, *and
"every other act by which the right to the soil of inland pro-
"perty is established,* may be given in evidence in support of
"it. The right to wreck of the sea, or royal fish by pre-
"scription *infra manerium,* is a strong presumption for the
"shore's being a parcel of the manor. Lord Hale's expres-
"sion is very strong; perchance (says his lordship), the shore
"is parcel almost of all such manors as by prescription
"have royal fish or wrecks of the sea within their manors.
"But it should be observed, that though wreck is frequently
"parcel of a manor, it is a royal franchise, and belongs of
"common right to the Crown. But by *grant* or *prescription*
"it may, and, in fact, frequently does belong to a subject,
"sometimes *in gross,* but oftener as *parcel of his manor,*
"parish, or vill, adjacent to the sea."

Mr. Butler, in the foregoing note, adopts the doctrine of the treatise he quotes, that a title to the soil of the sea-shore may be founded on prescription. He tells us also, that the same evidence which is allowed to establish inland title, may be adduced in support of titles to portions of the sea-shore; but he does not say that such evidence, and *no other,* MUST be adduced. On the contrary, we find that *wreck, royal fish,* a *separate fishery, right of digging sand, &c.* are also adduced as good evidence of title to the *land* or soil itself. This, however, it will be admitted, is not evidence which would support a title to inland property. *Mr. Butler's opinion as to the proofs of title to the ownership of the sea-shore, considered.*

Rights and privileges which do not imply or confer a title to the soil of inland estate.

Common of pasture, of turbary, of piscary estovers, rights of digging brick earth, or marl, and rights of way, in manors, are rights analogous to those of wreck, separate fishery, and digging of sand, &c. on the shore, and yet none of these analogous rights are allowed to give title to the soil. Neither can the form or mode of pleading a title to these incorporeal rights or privileges, be used in pleading Analogous privileges in the sea-shore have no greater effect.

a title to land. Wreck, and a right of way, are both founded on the like grounds of title, viz. either *grant* or *prescription*, which prescription is, in substance, evidence or proof of usage, or custom, beyond memory of man, and which usage raises the presumption of an ancient grant of such privileges.(*t*)

<small>The shore is, technically, land.</small>

Now, we have it laid down, as before quoted, that a title to land, *i. e.* freehold estate, cannot be founded on "prescription." (*u*) Are we then to conclude that the land or soil on the sea-shore is not, in legal intendment, or consideration, "*land*"? It is apprehended that no distinction whatever exists in legal construction, between the land on the shore, and land in the interior. Accordingly, in Scratton *v.* Brown, (*v*) the "shore" is expressly regarded, by the Court, as "land," in all its technical attributes, as a corporeal hereditament held by tenure, and as a "moveable freehold." The Court said, "where the grantee has a freehold in that which the "Crown grants, his freehold shifts as the sea recedes or en- "croaches."

<small>Acts which are evidences of an inland title are evidences of title to sea-shore.</small>

There can be no difficulty in agreeing with Mr. Butler, that those acts which are evidence of title to inland estates, are equally available to prove a title to the land on the shore. Thus, for instance, if I inclose a piece of waste land in the interior, and cultivate it, this is an act *prima facie* denoting title; *so,* if I inclose by an embankment a piece of the sea-shore; for these are both actual taking seizin and possession of the land. If I can prove such seizin for a period of sixty years, in regard to such piece of land, whether on the coast or inland, the *statute law* confirms my title to such piece of land. Land on the coast, as well as land in the interior, may equally be acquired by adverse possession, and the statutes of limitation. When possession of land is taken adversely to the king's ownership, or to

---

(*t*) [See now 2 and 3 Will. 4, c. 71, and ante, p. 23, note *b.*]
(*u*) Ante, p. 22.   (*v*) 4 B. and C. 485.

the ownership of a subject, the law requires that there should be some manifest act or acts of the party demonstrating an intention to assume the *territorial* ownership of the *locus in quo*. The intrusion or disseizin must be such as the statute may recognize as the substantial territorial acquisition which it (the statute) was intended to act upon and confirm. The statute was not passed for the purpose of confirming a partial ownership in the land ; such as a right to dig marl, or to pasture cattle, but the *droit droit*, or absolute ownership. Such, therefore, ought to be the positive and unequivocal nature of the possession taken. There is no difficulty in admitting a title to a *districtus maris*, under an *express* grant from the Crown. But there seems some difficulty in determining what acts shall be considered sufficiently forcible and exclusive to oust the King's ownership in a certain *districtus maris*, still continuing open to the action of the tides. Every attempt of this kind is a *wrong;* and the less intitled to aid from the law, as being a wrong against the Crown. How far certain acts, more equivocal, but less difficult than are required in inland titles, will be held sufficient evidence of *ouster* and possession, in cases of *districti maris*, against the king, is not very clearly settled ; but that there *are* acts sufficient to constitute *seizin* at law of certain portions of land covered by the sea, as so much *land*, seems to be allowed by the books. If this be so, it will *a fortiori* be admitted that the *sea-shore* is *land*, and capable of grant and conveyance (for it has been granted, and conveyed) from one person to another, like other lands ; and it must therefore follow, that such shore is capable of *seizin* in law ; and it will also be admitted that portions of the sea-shore are *capable* of being taken such exclusive possession of, as, under the statutes of limitation, will ultimately make a good title. This forcible and exclusive possession of a portion of the sea-shore may be taken ad-

34   *The Shore cannot be appendant to a Manor*

versely to another individual, which is a *disseizen;* or against the King, which is an *intrusion;* and such disseizen or intrusion, may, after sixty years, by virtue of the statutes of limitation, work a good title to the disseizor, or intruder. The sea-shore, therefore, does not seem to be that species of property which, in its nature, requires from the indulgence of the law, a more relaxed, and less certain evidence of title than inland property.   There is no necessity for our law to admit other evidence of title to the shore, than it calls for in regard to inland estate.

<small>Prescription concerns things appendant or appurtenant.</small>

Lord Coke (*x*) tells us, that "*prescription* is regularly *the mother of things appendant or appurtenant;*"(*y*) and he then proceeds to distinguish between what may, and what may not be appendant or appurtenant; from which an inference is clearly deducible that "*land*" cannot be appendant or appurtenant to *land.* (*z*)   " A thing corporeal," says he, " can-

---

(*x*) Co. Litt. 121 b., 122 a.

(*y*) " Concerning things appendant or appurtenant, two things are im-
"plied ; first, that prescription (which regularly is the mother thereof)
"doth not make anything appendant or appurtenant, unless the thing
"appendant or appurtenant agree, in quality and nature, to the thing
"whereunto it is appendant or appurtenant ; as a thing corporeal, can-
"not properly be appendant to a thing corporeal, nor a thing incorpo-
"real to a thing incorporeal. But things incorporeal, which lie in grant,
"as advowsons, villeins, commons, and the like, may be appendant to
"things corporeal, as a manor, house, or lands, or things corporeal to
"things incorporeal, as lands to an office.   But yet, as hath been said,
"they must agree in nature and quality, for common of turbary, or es-
"tovers, cannot be appendant, or appurtenant to *land,* but to a house,
"to be spent there. Secondly, That nothing can be properly appendant or
"appurtenant to anything, unless the principal or superior thing be of
"perpetual subsistence, and continuance; for example, an advowson,
"that is said to be appendant to a manor, is *in rei veritate* appendant to
"the demesnes of the manor, which are of perpetual subsistence, and not
"to rents or services, which are subject to extinguishment and destruc-
"tion."   Co. Litt. 121 b, 122 a.

(*z*) It has been expressly decided, that " land cannot be appurtenant to land."   Buszard and others *v.* Capel and another, 8 B. and C. 141.

as Prescriptive Rights may be.

not be appendant to a thing corporeal."(a) But if the shore be land, then the shore cannot be appendant or appurtenant to adjacent land, or manors, or be prescribed for as such. The phrase "parcel of," signifies "*pars totius*," and denotes that the thing is an integral part, and homogeneous. But if *wreck* be *appendant*, and yet be allowed to carry the shore with it, then the *shore* is in effect appendant, but according to Lord Coke, this cannot be. It may be further observed (as marking the distinction between things which may, and things which may not be prescribed for) that *spiritual* persons may, and regularly do *prescribe for tithes*, because they are *incorporeal* hereditaments, when owned by spiritual persons; but *lay impropriators* cannot *prescribe* for tithes because impropriate tithes, in lay hands, are not incorporeal hereditaments, but *real estate*, and of *freehold* quality, and have "the nature and all the incidents of temporal inheritances, "and are sued for and recovered in the temporal courts in "like manner as lands and other hereditaments."(b) Hence a title to lay tithes, can no more be made "*by prescription*,"

Distinction between things whic may, and things whic may not be prescribed 1

"indenture, T. B. demised to W. R. J. and G. J. all that wharf next "the river Thames, described by abutments, together with all ways, "paths, passages, *easements*, profits, commodities, and *appurtenances* "whatsoever, to the said wharf belonging; and that by the indenture, "the exclusive *use* of the land of the river Thames, opposite to, and in "front of the wharf, *between high and low-water mark*, as well when "covered with water, as dry, for the accommodation of the tenants of "the wharf, was demised, as *appurtenant* to the wharf,—but that the "land itself between high and low-water mark was not demised." Lord Tenterden, C. J. said, "it is difficult to understand how the *exclusive* "*use* [of the land] could be demised, and the *land* not.—If the mean- "ing of this finding be that the land itself, [*i. e.* between high and low- "water mark, in other words, ' shore or *littus*',] was demised *as appur- "tenant* to the wharfs, that would be a finding that one piece of land "was appurtenant to another, which in point of law, cannot be." [An exclusive right of fishing for oysters, may be prescribed for as appendant to land : Hayes *v.* Bridges, 1 Ridg. L. and S. 390.]

(*a*) Co. Litt. 121 b.

than a title to lands. (c)   The very change from a spiritual to a lay inheritance, at once destroys all title by *prescription*. (d)

The essence of a prescriptive right is the *usage*. Proof of the usage, and proof of its having been in use *time out of mind*, are equally necessary. (e)   The thing claimed is the use, viz. a right to do, or enjoy in future, that which has been, and is proved to have been heretofore time out of mind, done or enjoyed.   It is not the claiming one thing, *because* another thing has been used or enjoyed.   Proof that a common of pasture, or a road, or the franchise of wreck has been immemorially enjoyed, is confirmatory of my title to enjoy such common, or road, or wreck, in future.   This right or privilege is not tangible, but exists only in the eye

(c) Toller 18.
(d) ["The mode of proof which is technically called prescription," says Mr. Phear, p. 68, "can only be employed to establish rights originating "in a grant, *i.e.* almost exclusively incorporeal rights, and referring to this "argument of Hall's, he says, and for this reason considering it inappli-"cable to prove a title to the ownership of the shore itself, he has devoted "much space in his excellent treatise to showing how seldom the ques-"tions raised between private claimants and the public have amounted "to questions of actual ownership and therefore how little there is to "support the common dictum, that such ownership can be established "by prescription."   "His observation," continues Mr. Phear, "is very "just if the word prescription be always understood in its narrowest "sense, as pointing only to the quantity of enjoyment requisite for esta-"blishing a right ; but it will be found on examining the cases therein "referred to, that 'prescription' was used in them to express merely "that the right in question could not be assailed after long enjoyment, "and was not there intended to specify further, that such enjoyment, "either really or constructively had the immemorial duration which "is characteristic of prescription in its technical sense, and which "gives a title, as opposed to the limited enjoyment which the statutes "of limitation rendered protective of possession.   This general em-"ployment of the word prescription is common enough in our text "writers."]

[A plea of prescription is supported if the party prove a right more extensive than that pleaded ; but the right must be of such a nature that it may comprehend the right pleaded.   Coleridge, J., in Bailey *v.* Appleyard, 8 Ad. and Ell. 167, S.C. 3 N. and P. 257.]

Seizin and Prescription distinguished. 37

and contemplation of law. Either the express grant, or the continued and immemorial usage, is the best possible evidence the law can procure of the franchise or privilege claimed, and therefore it rests content with such evidence.(*f*)

The law requires the very best evidence of the right which the nature of thing's will allow. Wherefore, if I claim a title to a thing which is tangible, and capable of seizin and manual possession, the law requires proof of such seizin or manual possession, either past or present, or both, as the best evidence that I have made it mine. The reason given (as before said) why land cannot be claimed by prescription is this, that it is a thing capable of more certain evidence of ownership(*g*) than those things which lie in prescription are capable of; viz. of a transfer of the actual possession,—*i.e.*, the land itself, from one to another,—from the last owner to the present. This actual transfer is called livery of seizin; and prescription never was, and is not now allowed to supply the place of seizin, in questions of titles to things of which seizin can be given.(*h*) Prescription is the allegation

(*f*) [In Blewitt *v.* Tregonning, 3 Ad. and Ell. 583, Littledale J. says :— " If evidence establishes a user as far back as memory goes, and there " does not appear to be any time at which it did not exist, that is proof "of prescription." In Jenkins *v.* Harvey, 1 Cr., M. and R. 894, Alderson, B. says :—" If an uninterrupted usage of upwards of seventy years, " unanswered by any evidence to the contrary, is not sufficient to " establish a right like the present (receipt of toll for coal imported into " the port), there are innumerable titles which could not be sustained." In Fitzpatrick *v.* Robinson, 1 Hud. and Br. 585, it was held that a user by the public of an open strand or waste, does not necessarily lead to the inference that the owner of the soil has abandoned his right to it and given it to the public ; and in Murphy *v.* Ryan, 2 Ir. C. L. R. 143, it was held that the public cannot acquire by immemorial usage any right of fishing in a river in which, though it be navigable, the tide does not ebb and flow ; for the word "navigable," used in a legal sense as applied to a river in which the soil *primâ facie* belongs to the Crown, and the fishing to the public, imports that the river is one in which the tide ebbs and flows.]

and proof of a *usage*, not *occupation*. The shore must be not merely *used*, but so *occupied* as of necessity to involve actual seizin or possession of it. If I prove such usage of it as is tantamount to seizin and exclusive possession, that is, in fact, showing title by *adverse possession*, and not by *prescription*, and it remains to be seen by the statute law whether my possession can be supported. Or, the land may be used as a mere convenience, as for a road, or as a fishing-place; and if I prove such use of a road, or such custom to fish there, to have existed time out of mind, I have proved certain specific rights which the common law allows and confirms to me, without statute law. In such case I have made good my title to a *distinct* species of property from the land itself: why should the law go further, and *that* even against the King, by tacking to it a right to the very soil itself?(*i*)

Prescriptive rights are no doubt all founded on *presumptive* evidence, and therefore it is that land cannot be prescribed for; *i.e.* presumed in point of title.(*k*) To say that the shore lies in prescription, is placing it on a par, in point of title, with mere easements, which is surely incorrect.

<small>to evidence boundaries titles.</small> As to the evidence to particular *limits* and *boundaries* of estates, it is to be remembered, that in every such enquiry

<small>that "*tenants in common* may be by title of prescription, as if the one " and his ancestors, or they whose estate he hath in one moietie, have " holden in common the same moietie with the other tenant which " hath the other moietie, and with his ancestors, or with those whose " estate he had *undivided* time out of mind." To this Lord Coke subjoins, " but joint tenants cannot be by prescription, because there is " survivor between them, but not between tenants in common." There seems also another exception, Co. Litt. 121, 122, as to lands annexed to an office, which is an incorporeal *hereditament*, to which lands may be appendant or appurtenant, and pass by *deed* of grant of the office only,—but it appears that there must be a "deed, and secondly, the " thing to which the land is appended must be *ejusdem generis, i.e.* an " *hereditament*, which franchises, commons, and liberties are not."</small>

Prescriptive Rights no proof of Title. 39

of metes and bounds, the titles to the *estates* of which some particular spot in question is claimed to be *parcel*, are not disputed, but are admitted to be good, according to the strict rule of evidence of title to lands; the question only refers to and concerns the metes and bounds of the respective estates. But, as against the Crown, *reputation* does not seem admissible in such question.(*l*) It has also been refused between two private disputants.(*m*) There is no doubt but that *written* documents, or sixty years' quiet possession, under the statutes of limitation, will prevail over all verbal testimony, or prescriptive—which is presumptive evidence, however strong. Where there is nothing but presumptive evidence on both sides, except that one has positive possession, the Courts of law do no more than refuse to disturb the possession.

Now, as between the King and a subject, in respect of the sea-shore, there can be *presumptive evidence but on one side only*, the King's right is not presumptive, but a legal title of the strictest kind; the common law itself is the King's evidence of title, and no better can exist; and presumptive evidence must necessarily be inferior to it.(*n*) In the absence of any grant or documentary title, the only other title to land is, it is conceived, by adverse possession, ratified and confirmed by the statutes of limitation. Can, then, adverse possession, or seizin of the soil of the sea-shore be *legally proved* by mere evidence of a right of wreck, a right of fishery, or the privilege of digging sand? Are these such uses of the land itself as necessarily carry with them the seizin and possession of such land? It is difficult to admit this doctrine. If the *freehold* of the shore were intimately

The king's title is positive, and by the common law.

Adverse possession of the shore may be confirmed by statute law but not by prescriptive rights to wreck, &c.

(*l*) 2 Roll. Abr. 186, pl. 5, tit. Prerogative.
(*m*) See Outram *v.* Morewood, 14 East 331, note. [R. *v.* Inhab. of Bedfordshire, 4 E. and B. 535, 541 ; 24 L. J. Q. B. 81. See also cases cited in Taylor on Evidence, and Hunt on Boundaries, 226, *et seq.* See

and *essentially* connected with the franchise of wreck, or those other franchises, liberties, or usufructory privileges which are enjoyed thereon, then indeed a title to the one could not be made good without involving with it the title to the other. But if we examine the nature and quality of these franchises, liberties, and privileges, which are noticed by our law, we shall find that they not only do not *necessarily* involve or carry with them the soil of the sea-shore, but that they may, and generally do, actually exist separate and distinct from the ownership of the shore,—as such examination is not foreign to our subject, we will consider these franchises and privileges in their order.(*o*)

The franchises, liberties, profits, and advantages derivable from the *sea*, may be considered as follows :—

1st. Fishing,(*p*) public and general, or private and several.

2nd. The use of the sea for the transportation of merchandise in traffic, and for ports, or for any other purpose of use or enjoyment to which it can be applied.

3rd. The perquisite of what in our law is called Wreck,(*q*) being the unclaimed ships and cargo wrecked on the shore.

(*o*) [See remarks on case of Dickens *v*. Shaw, post.]

(*p*) Whale, sturgeon, and porpoise, whenever and by whomsoever caught in the British seas, are the property of the Crown by royal prerogative. They each constitute what in our law is called a royal franchise. Such franchises, however, were formerly granted away by the Crown to a subject; limited within certain districts, as a manor, hundred, &c. In Scotland, salmon seems to have been inter regalia. See Erskine's Principles.

(*q*) Wreck is also a royal franchise, and with the perquisites called flotsam, jetsam, and lagan, was formerly often granted within certain territorial limits to the subject, as within a manor, hundred, &c. 1 Bl. Com. 290.

The above regalia, or royal franchises, are possessed by the Crown, not in respect of the land or soil of the shore, or the ownership of the sea, but by the royal prerogative, in distinct and peculiar ownership.

"[Whenever goods floating on the sea, or stranded below high-water

the Sea and from the Shore. 41

The uses and profits of the *shore* are,—1. Fishing ; (r) 2. Wreck, and its accompaniments flotsam, &c. ; 3. Egress and regress, and right of Way, for the purpose of navigation, fishing, bathing, and other uses of the sea ; 4. Ports ; 5. The digging and carrying away its soil and materials for building, ballast, manure, &c.

And of the shore.

Now, as we have already attributed the absolute ownership of the sea, and sea-shore, to the King, *ab origine,*—it might be thought that the above perquisites are absolutely his own, and grantable exclusively to any one of his subjects. But according to the acknowledged law of the land, although the King is owner of this great waste, *yet the common people of England have regularly a liberty of fishing in the sea, and creeks and arms thereof, and in navigable rivers within the tides, as a public common of piscary.*(s)

" their owner, they *ipso facto* vest in the Crown as wreck ; if they formed
" portion of a ship, or its cargo, out of which none of the crew nor any
" domestic animal escaped alive, they become immediately the absolute
" property of the Crown ; in other cases, the vesting in the Crown is
" for temporary protection only until the lapse of a year and a day,
" during which time the original owner may come in and revest them
" in himself : but at the expiration of that period, without any claim
" having been made by the owner, the title of the Crown becomes, as
" in the first instance, indefeasible." Phear, p. 99 (note). See authorities cited in Dunwich *v.* Sterry, 1 B. and Ad. 831. " At common law
" a distinction is made between wreck which is stranded, and that
" which is sunk in the sea or floats on its surface : the first is termed
" wreck proper, and the latter bears the name of flotsam, jetsam, or
" lagan, according to the circumstances," &c. Phear, p. 99, and see post p. 80, and statutes concerning wreck.]

(r) De Jure Maris, Appendix, post, viii.

(s) Lord Fitzwalter's case, 1 Mod. 105. Anonymous, 6 Mod. 73. Warren *v.* Matthews, 1 Salk. 357. Smith *v.* Kemp, 2 Salk. 637. 16 Vin. 354, pl. 1. Ward *v.* Cresswell, C.B. 14 and 15 of Geo. II. Sir J. Davy's Rep. 57. Willes, 265. The great salmon-fishery on the River Banne in Ireland. See also Bro. Abr. Prerog. pl. 35, and 6 Bac. Abr. 398. Carter *v.* Murcot, 4 Burr. 2163. Plowd. 315. Bro. Abr. Custom, pl. 46. Fitz. Abr. Barre, pl. 93. Bagott *v.* Orr, 2 Bos. and Pull. 472. Mayor of Orford *v.* Richardson, 4 T. R. 438, and see 7 Comyn. Dig. 70.

Public right of fishing in the sea.

This public or general right of fishing in the sea, claimed by the subject, is a beneficial privilege enjoyed by British subjects, time out of mind. (*t*) Whether, in fact, it was originally a public grant from the King, or whether it was a reservation by the people of such right, when they vested the rest of the property of the sea in him, or whether it be one of those natural and necessary rights which, like the air we breathe, has ever been free and unquestioned in enjoyment, is immaterial; for the conclusion is the same; viz. that such right of fishing has immemorially belonged to, and been enjoyed by the public, and that, in point of title, it is admitted to be held and enjoyed *by common right, i.e.* by the common law, and custom of the Realm. (*u*)

Navigation.

The use of the sea, *as a great high way*, for the transportation of merchandise, or any other purpose for which

---

Lib. 2, ch. 1. Here it is observable that Bracton makes no distinction between those parts of rivers which are, and those which are not, within the flux and reflux of the tides. The public right does not seem to extend above the tides. See accord, Lord Fitzwalter's case, Per Hale, C. J. 1 Mod. 105. Dav. 57 [and Hall's Profits à Prendre, 307. Murphy *v.* Ryan, 2 Ir. C. L. R. 143. Taylor's Evidence, part 1, cap. 5, p. 133, 6th edit.]

(*t*) [See Sea Fishery Act, 31 and 32 Vict. c. 45.]

(*u*) [" When the soil of the shore, as is generally the case, is in the " Crown, the rights of the public in the sea, and tidal waters, such as " fishing and navigation, &c., are 'natural rights,' accruing to them as " *cestui que trustent* in possession ; but that when a private individual " holds the shore, such of these rights as remain to the public have " become, strictly speaking, 'easements.' However, in the latter case, " the private owner cannot have a more advantageous position than his " grantor the Crown, and must therefore be subject to all public rights, " unless he can prove an immemorial title to exemption. Hence, in all " cases, the rights of the public in the sea and its shore are *primâ facie*, " and must be treated as 'natural rights'; while those of a private indi- " vidual, whether his claim extends to territorial possession or not, can " rest upon no other foundation than the strict construction of a grant." Phear, p. 52. See Malcolmson *v.* O'Dea, 10 House of Lords Cases, 593 ; Marshall *v.* Ulleswater Steam Navigation Co. 3 B. and S. 732 ;

Public Right of fishing in the Sea. 43

its waters can be usefully navigated, is also a liberty or privilege belonging of common right to the people of England, by the same title as the fishery.(*v*)

(*v*) [The right of navigation belongs by law to all the subjects of the realm, and is paramount to the right of fishing ; where a part of the sea coast or shore, being the property of the Crown, and giving *jus privatum* to the King, is granted to a subject for uses, or to be enjoyed so as to be detrimental to the *jus publicum* therein, such grant is void as to such parts as are open to such objection, if acted upon so as to effect nuisances by working injury to the public right, or it is a grant which does not divest the Crown, or invest the grantee ; Att.-Gen. *v.* Parmeter, 10 Price, 378-412 ; Att.-Gen. *v.* Johnson, 2 Wils. 87. The right to anchor is a necessary part of the right to navigate ; this right never could have been interfered with by grant from the Crown, but evidence of mere immemorial usage will not support a claim to dues for anchorage, and it cannot exist merely in respect of the use of the soil, it must be founded on proof that the soil of the claimant was originally within the precincts of a port or harbour, or that some service, or aid to navigation, was rendered by the owner of the soil, who claims the dues. Gann *v.* Free Fishers of Whitstable, 11 House of Lords Cases, 192 ; Whitstable Fishers *v.* Foreman, L. R. 2 C. P. 688 ; 4 E. and I. app. 266 ; see as to the public right of navigation Att.-Gen. *v.* Lonsdale, 7 L. R. Eq. 377 ; Colchester, mayor of, *v.* Brooke, 7 Q. B. 339 ; Williams *v.* Wilcox, 8 Ad. and E. 329 ; R. *v.* Ward, 4 A. and E. 384 ; also Williams v. Blackwall, 32 L. J. Ex. 174 ; Post *v.* Munn, 1 Souths (New Jersey) R. 61 ; Angell on Tide Waters, p. 80 ; Houck, 146 ; Phear, 53 ; Angell on Watercourses, 554.

[If property be placed in the channel of a public navigable river, so as to create a public nuisance, a person navigating is not justified in damaging such property by running his vessel against it, if he has room to pass without so doing, for an individual cannot abate a nuisance, if he is no otherwise injured by it than as one of the public (Colchester, mayor of, *v.* Brooke, 7 Q. B. 339 ; Brown *v.* Perkins, 12 Gray 89, 101-102) ; and therefore the fact that such property was a nuisance is no excuse for running upon it negligently : and there is no

44 Public Right of fishing in the Sea.

But wreck, and royal fish, are royal franchises, belonging exclusively to the King, by the prerogative of the Crown, or to individuals, deriving them, as an exclusive private

excess, if a vessel, which cannot reach her place of destination in a single tide, remains aground till the tide serves ; although, by custom or agreement, a fine may be payable to the lord of the soil for such grounding. Colchester, mayor of, *v.* Brooke, 7 Q. B. 339.

[A riparian proprietor has no greater right to use the alveus of a tidal than a non-tidal river, and therefore cannot construct a jetty so as to injure the property of others or interfere with navigation. Att.-Gen. *v.* Lonsdale, L. R. 7 Eq. 377. See also Bickett *v.* Morris, 1 L. R. Sc. App. 47, and Angell on Tide Waters, p. 95.

[In the Att.-Gen. *v.* Terry, L. R. 9, Chan. Appeals, 423, a wharf owner drove piles into the bed of a river extending the wharf so as to occupy 3 ft. out of a breadth of about 60 ft. available for navigation. It was held that this was such an obstruction as would be restrained at the suit of a municipal corporation empowered by Act of Parliament to remove obstructions.

[In the court below, the Master of the Rolls held that an owner of land at the side of a public navigable river has no right to erect on the bed of the river, for the benefit of his own trade, any structure, whether any actual obstruction to the navigation of the river will or will not be thereby occasioned; and any benefit to his own trade is too remote to be held for the advantage of the public generally, and so to justify the erection. See American cases, Gould *v.* Carter, 9 Humph. (Tenn.) 369; Commonwealth *v.* Bilderback, 2 Pars. (Penn.) 447.

[No amount of collateral benefit, resulting from any manner of obstruction to the local community, can divest it of its character of a nuisance, an abridgment of the right of navigation can only be justified when the erection is productive of a greater public benefit. R. *v.* Russell, 6 B. and C. 566. This case was a trial by indictment for a nuisance by erecting staiths in a river, and the jury were directed to acquit the defendant if they thought that the abridgment of the right of passage, occasioned by such erections, was for a public purpose, and produced a public benefit, and if the erections were in a

Public Right of fishing in the Sea. 45

possession from the Crown. For the present we will confine our view to the *fishery*.

indictment, and that the question to have been taken was, whether the navigation and passage of vessels on a navigable river were injured by the erections in question. See R. *v.* Ward, 4 A. and E. 384.

[But it is not necessary that any interruption of, or interference with, the public rights should amount to a nuisance, Reg. *v.* Betts, 16 Q. B. 1022; 19 L. J. Q. B. 501; R. *v.* Ward, 4 A. and E. 384; Gates *v.* Blencoe, 2 Dana (Ken.), 158; that is a question for the jury, Reg. *v.* Randall, Cas. and M. 496; R. *v.* Russell, 3 E. and B. 942. As to the abatement by injunction, &c., where an individual has sustained damage different from and independent of that which is sustained by the rest of the public, see Bridges *v.* Highton, 11 L. T. N. S. 653; Rose *v.* Groves, 6 Sc. N. R. 653; Edleston *v.* Crossley, 18 L. T. N. S. 15; Norbury *v.* Kitchen, 18 L. T. N. S. 501; Blakemore *v.* Glamorganshire Canal Co. 1 My. and K. 154; Att.-Gen. *v.* Richards, 2 Anst. 603; Att.-Gen. *v.* Cleaver, 18 Ves. 211; Att.-Gen. *v.* Lonsdale, 7 L. R. Eq. 377; and see remarks of Chancellor Kent in 2 John, ch. 382, and Georgetown *v.* Alexandria Canal Co. 12 Peters (U. S.) 91. By the customary law of Connecticut, a riparian has the right of soil between high and low water mark, so as to enable him to construct wharves; but before the soil had been so reclaimed, the right of fishing on the flats remains common. E. Haven *v.* Hemingway, 7 Connect. R. 186. See Angell on Watercourses, p. 743.

[In Brown *v.* Mallett, 5 C. B. 599, which was an action against an owner of a vessel sunk by accident, for injuries received by another vessel coming in contact therewith, Maule, J., laid down the following principles:—That it is the duty of a person using a navigable river with a vessel of which he is possessed, and has the control and management, to use reasonable skill and care to prevent mischief to others, and the liability is the same whether his vessel be in motion or stationary, floating or aground, under water or above it, and this liability may be transferred with the transfer of the possession and control to another person, and on the abandonment of such possession, control, and management, the liability also ceases. See also Hamond *v.* Pearson, 1 Campb. 515; but it is also clear from Rex *v.* Watts, 2 Esp. 675—"that from an unavoidable accident pro-
" ducing the wreck of a vessel, an indictment cannot be preferred
" against the owner for not removing the impediment to navigation
" which it creates. There is no reason for throwing on the owner any
" special share in the consequence of what may be considered as a
" misfortune, both to him and to the public." See White *v.* Crisp, 10 Ex. 312; Parrett Navigation Co. *v.* Robins, 10 M. and W.

46   *Public Right of fishing in the Sea.*

Public fishery.   The public right, (*x*) or common of piscary, (*y*) claimed and allowed by the common law to the people of England in the sea, extends, not only over the open sea, but over all bays, creeks, ports, havens, arms of the sea, and tide-rivers, up to the reach of the tide, (*z*) and also, as it would seem, *over and upon the sea-shore itself,* for such kinds of fish as are usually caught upon the rocks, and sands of the coast. (*a*) But in some cases, statute law has set bounds to the exercise of this right, in respect of seasons, particular kinds of fish, and manner of fishing. (*b*) There are also other excepted cases; viz. where private individuals, (*c*) or Corporate bodies, claim and enjoy a separate fishery, in some par-

---

Geo. 2, c. 22, s. 3; 54 Geo. 3, c. 159, s. 19; and 10 and 11 Vict. c. 27.

[The Board of Trade is enabled, by the various powers contained in The Railways Consolidation Act, 8 and 9 Vict. c. 20, s. 17; The Harbours, Docks, and Piers Clauses Act, 10 Vict. c. 27, s. 12; The Harbours Transfer Act, 25 and 26 Vict. c. 69, and the Railways Clause Act, 26 and 27 Vict. c. 92, ss. 13 to 19, to protect the foreshore from being injuriously affected by the construction of such works, as to which these statutes refer, and in the case of Bills for all such works, the Board of Trade take care to see that these Acts are incorporated.]

(*x*) In Anonymous, 6 Mod. 73, it is said, that the King's grant could not bar the public of their right to fish, and as it is a rule that nothing can be *prescribed for* which might not have a lawful commencement by *grant*, it would follow, that no such thing as a separate fishery in the sea, or tide-rivers, could exist if this were good authority. But, 6 Mod. 73 is clearly not law, so far as regards *ancient* grants, and was overruled in Carter *v.* Murcot, 4 Burr. 2163. The doctrine of 6 Mod. 73 is also held (as to the sea) in 2 Com. 431, and is supported in a note (see this note cited in p. 53 post) to Carter *v.* Murcot. At this day the King cannot, by grant, abridge the general public right, nor has any such right existed in the Crown since Magna Charta.

(*y*) [See Benett *v.* Costar, 8 Taunt. 183, 1 B. and B. 465, sc.]

(*z*) See the cases cited p. 41, ante.

(*a*) Bagott *v.* Orr, 2 Bos. and Pul. 472.

(*b*) [See Woolrych, p. 85, *et seq.*]

(*c*) Dav. Rep. 57 a. Carter *v.* Murcot, 4 Burr. 2163 ; Warren *v.* Mat-

Public Right of fishing in the Sea.

ticular places, in derogation and exclusion of the general right.(*d*)

This divides the right of fishery into "communis piscaria," or the public common of piscary mentioned above, and the *several*, or *private* fishery belonging to particular owners, and excluding all other persons. The *several* fishery is claimed and enjoyed by *prescription*, or *ancient usage*, presupposing a grant, or by express grant from the Crown, anterior to Magna Charta.(*e*)

Several or private fish

(*d*) [" This public right is an established principle, and whether the
" opinion of those writers, who class this right among the *jura regalia*,
" be preferred, or that, on the other hand, of those who hold the right to
" be *jus publicum vel commune*, it is nevertheless certain that, *primâ
"facie*, the liberty in question is general." Woolrych, pp. 76, 85 ;
Angell on Water Courses, p. 73. And where there is reasonable evidence
to show that the question of title raised by a defendant is *bonâ fide*,
the jurisdiction of magistrates is at end. R. *v.* Stimpson, 32 L. J. M. C.
208 ; but see Embleton *v.* Brown, 6 Jur. N. S. 1298. "As a public
" right, belonging to the people, it *primâ facie* vests in the Crown ;
" but such legal investment does not diminish the right, or counteract
" its exertion." Schulte, p. 15.]

(*e*) [In Allen *v.* Donelly, 5 Ir. C. L. Rep. 229, the petitioner claimed an exclusive right of fishing in an arm of the sea, and a public navigable river, and the petitioner prayed that he might be quieted in possession by an injunction. The respondent relied on the general common law right of fishery in the sea, but it was held that the Court had jurisdiction to entertain such a suit, and the petitioner need not be left exclusively to his common law remedy. In O'Neill *v.* Allen, 9 Ir. C. L. R. 132, the plaintiff in support of a claim to a several fishery in the open sea, proved an adventurer's certificate of the year 1666, acts of ownership by parties unconnected with the person found entitled to the fishery by the certificate, were proved from 1668 to 1701. No such act was proved from that date to 1798, but from 1798 to 1857 there was undisturbed user by the O'Neill family, from whom the plaintiff derived. It was held that a several fishery was rightly found, that the granting of a patent subsequently to 1668 might have been presumed ; but that 17 and 18 Car. 2, c. 2, rendered such presumption unnecessary. Whether a several fishery is such a franchise as can be lost by non-user was not decided, but if it were, the absence of evidence of user from 1701 to 1799, did not amount to proof of non-user. See also Little *v.* Wingfield, 8 Ir. C. L. Rep. 279 ; and 11 Ir.

48   Public Right of fishing in the Sea.

The public fishery includes a right of egress and regress, &c.   As the public right of fishery cannot be enjoyed without making use of the sea-shore for egress and regress, and for other essential conveniences which the fishery requires in order to be carried on with effect, the use of the *sea-shore*, (*f*)

C. L. Rep. 63; Malcolmson *v.* O'Dea, 10 House of Lords Cases, 593. And, in the United States, the right of fishery may be granted by the States in the navigable waters in their borders, to individuals, provided the free use of the waters for purposes of navigation and commercial intercourse be not interrupted; 1 Kent Com. 489; Rogers *v.* Jones, 1 Wend. 237. An exclusive right, however, must be shown, and if it can be shown, it may be exercised exclusively, though the presumption is against it, unless a prescriptive right, or express legislative grant, can be given in evidence; for such right shall not be presumed, but the contrary, *primâ facie*. Schulte, 70. See Commonwealth *v.* Charlestown, 18 Mass. (1 Pick.) Rep. 180; Storer *v.* Freeman, 6 Mass. R. 435; Delaware and Maryland Railway Co. *v.* Stump, 8 Gill and J. (Md.) 479; Day *v.* Day, 4 Ind. 262. See also Angell on Watercourses, p. 70, 6th edit.

(*f*) We do not speak here of the "*ripa*," or bank, which is adjacent *terra firma*, but of the *sea-shore* only. But for all reasonable purposes of safety and convenience in fishing, and navigation, the *ripa*, or immediate *terra firma*, is, by common right, subject to the free egress and regress of the public. Bro. Abr. Tit. Custom, pl. 46. But this does not extend to any *permanent* appropriation of such *ripam*. Nor will it authorise *towing-paths* to be made. Ball *v.* Herbert, 3 T. R. 253. Towing is not navigation, properly so called. But, it seems, towing-paths, and other modes of moving, raising, and securing vessels, and fishing-boats, &c. upon the adjacent *terra firma*, may well be acquired and enjoyed by usage, or prescription, as a local easement, S. C.

[In this case, Kenyon, C. J., said he remembered when the case of Pierse *v.* Lord Fauconberg, 1 Burr. 292, was sent to that Court from the Court of Chancery, and it was then the current opinion in Westminster Hall, that the right of towing depended on usage, without which it could not exist. See Winch *v.* Conservators of Thames, 7 L. R. C. P. 458; S. C. 41 L. J. C. P. 241; Badger *v.* S. Y. R. Co. 1 E. and E. 347; Monmouth Canal Co. *v.* Hill, 4 H. and N. 427; Kinlock *v.* Nevile, 6 M. and W. 795; Hollis *v.* Goldfinch, 1 B. and C. 205; Angell on Water Courses, 6th edit. 740, on Tide Waters, 176; Woolrych, 164; Brown *v.* Chadbourne, 31 Maine, 23, 26; Treat *v.* Lord, 42 Maine, 552, 563; Ledyard *v.* Ten Eyck, 36 Barb. 102. The supreme Court of Illinois, and that of Tennessee, have, however, decided agreeably to the civil law, that the right of

Several or Private Fishery. 49

for all purposes essential to the enjoyment of the right of fishery, necessarily accompanies such right. But it is quite clear that the public use of the shore, for the public exercise of the fishery, *does not impeach the King's ownership or property in the soil itself.* (*g*) Wherefore, the King remains owner of the shore, liable to such use of it by his subjects, as their ancient common of piscary therein, and in the waters around it, naturally calls for; and this would seem to include a public *right of way* to and fro over the sea-shore.

A *several* or *private* fishery(*h*) is claimed, not only against the King's original right, but against the general public right of the subject. It may be either in gross, (*i*) *i.e.* an absolute personal right, or privilege attaching to the individual, or Corporate body of individuals (as many Religious Houses formerly had); or it may be appendant or appurtenant to manors; and *this*(*j*) not only in navigable rivers, and arms of the sea, but in creeks, ports and havens; and in *certain known limits in the open sea, contiguous to the shore.* In 2 Com. 431, the contrary is held, as to the *sea;* but in 4 T. R. 437, Mayor of Orford *v.* Richardson, where both a *several*, and a *free* fishery were prescribed for, Lord Kenyon said, " there can be no doubt but that there may be a *pre-*

Several fishery.

In gross.

Or appendan or appurtenant.

---

river, but included the right to land, and to fasten to the shore, as the exigences of navigation may require; and that such was a burthen upon the owner of the land, which he must bear as a part of the public easement. Middleton *v.* Pritchard, 3 Scam. (Ill.) R. 520; Corp. of Memphis *v.* Overton, 3 Yerg. (Tenn.) R. 390.

(*g*) See Lord Fitzwalter's Case, 1 Mod. 106; Dickens *v.* Shaw, Appendix, xlvii.
(*h*) See post, further, on this kind of fishery, [and Phear, p. 64.]
(*i*) [Shuttleworth *v.* Le Fleming, 19 C. B. N. S. 687.]
(*j*) De Jure Maris, Appendix, post, xv. [see Hayes *v.* Bridges, 1 Ridg. L. and S. 390; Hamilton *v.* Donegall, Marquis of, 3 Ridg. 311; Rogers *v.* Allen, 1 Camp. 39.]

"*scriptive* right in a subject to a several fishery in an arm
" of the sea."(*k*)

Fishing, in practice, may be of two kinds, *viz.* 1. with nets, hooks, or other moveable apparatus; 2. or by means

(*k*) [A several fishery passes under the words "all the salmon fisheries, pyke, eyle, and other fishings of and in the river," Ashworth *v.* Brown, 7 Ir. Jur. O. S. 315, Q. B.; and a " free fishery" *primâ facie* means a " several fishery," per Willes, J. in Shuttleworth *v.* Le Fleming, 19 C. B. 697. The definition of a several fishery in 13 and 14 Vict. c. 88, s. 1, is " all fisheries lawfully possessed and enjoyed as such, under any title whatever, being a good and valid title at law, exclusively of the public, by any person or persons, whether in navigable waters, or in non-navigable, and whether the soil covered by such waters be vested in such persons or in any other persons." In Holford *v.* Bailey, 13 Q. B. 426, the words " sole and exclusive" were held to be equivalent, at all events after verdict, to a " several fishery." Undisturbed possession of the right for sixty years and upwards is some evidence to entitle the jury to presume a legal grant. Little *v.* Wingfield, 8 Ir. C. L. Rep. 279, also 11 Ir. C. L. R. 63. See also 2 and 3 Will. 4, c. 71, s. 1; evidence of a continuous practice for upwards of sixty years, wholly unresisted, for a corporation to grant licenses to fish in a navigable tidal river, and to obstruct and warn those who fish without a license is sufficient evidence for a jury to conclude that the corporation was owner of a free fishery : Mannall *v.* Fisher, 5 C. B. N. S. 856; see Malcolmson *v.* O'Dea, 10 H. L. cases 593; O'Neill *v.* Allen, 9 Irish C. L. Rep. 132; Chad *v.* Tilsed, 2 B. and B. 403. But although long exclusive enjoyment of a right to a several fishery in a public navigable river, is sufficient *primâ facie* evidence, upon which to presume that the Crown had granted a separate right before Magna Charta, yet the omission of all mention of the right in any probably true inventory, taken since that period, of all the possessions of the then alleged owner, of that right, or any reasonable ground for considering that the user had not been exclusive, but in common with other persons, may be sufficient to negative such presumption ; even if a fishery may pass as appurtenant to land—see Hayes *v.* Bridges, 1 Ridg. L. and S. 390 ; Hamilton *v.* Donegall, Marquis of, 3 Ridg. 311— it cannot be appendant to a several pasture ; Edgar *v.* Special Commissioners for English Fisheries, 23 L. T. N. S. 732, C. P. A corporation which had an immemorial right to an oyster fishery in a navigable river, became in 1740, by the ouster of several of its members, unable to continue, or to carry on the management of the fishery. In 1763, the corporation was re-incorporated by charter, under the old

Public Fishery distinguished.

of wears, (*l*) stakes, or fixed enclosures or fishing places. Now, it is obvious, that the public right of fishing cannot be carried on by the latter modes, since an enclosure by one person excludes others.

Fishing with nets, hooks, &c. may, according to the treatise De Jure Maris, be "either as a liberty, without the "soil; or arise by reason of (*m*) or in concomitance with "the soil itself, and the proprietorship of it." Now, as the public cannot claim the soil under the sea or of the shore

<small>As to fishing with nets, &c</small>

There having been no actual dissolution, the fishery never passed to the Crown; and though the corporation had granted a license to certain persons to dredge, &c., this did not operate as a demise of the fishery, so as to put the corporation out of possession; Colchester, mayor of, *v.* Brooke, 7 Q.B. 339. And where a several fishery is legally granted before Magna Charta, it does not merge by forfeiture to the Crown: Northumberland, Duke of, *v.* Houghton, 5 L. R. Ex. 127. Where the Crown grants by patent the soil and bottom and a several fishery in a navigable river, and enjoyment under that patent was shown, it was held to be evidence that the Crown was seized in fee at the time of making the grant, but the several fishery must have been created before Magna Charta, if so it can be granted afterwards: Devonshire, Duke of, *v.* Hodnett, 1 Hud. and Bro. 323; as to the law of several fisheries in America, see Houck, p. 137, *et seq.*

[Trespass lies for breaking and entering the "several" or "sole and exclusive" fishery of one person over the soil of another and disturbing the fish: Holford *v.* Bailey, 13 Q. B. 426; 18 L. J. Q. B. 109, Ex. Cham. If the *locus in quo* is an arm of the sea, and yet a several fishery be claimed, it is not sufficient in answer to such plea, simply to deny the public right, but the plaintiff is bound to set up his exclusive claim in a replication: Crichton *v.* Collery, 19 W. R. 107, Ir. Exch.

[Where a several fishery exists in a tidal river, the waters of which have permanently receded from one channel and flow in another, it cannot be followed from the old to the new channel: Carlisle, mayor of, *v.* Graham, 4 L. R. Ex. 361; 38 L. J. Ex. 226, S. C.]

(*l*) See De Jure Maris, Appendix, post, xviii. for numerous instances of these wears.

(*m*) Sed q. By reason of? for the mere ownership of the soil does not exclude the *public right* of fishing in the sea, even when the King is such owner; therefore, the mere ownership of the soil in a subject, is not, *per se*, a sufficient ground for an exclusive private fishery in the

52   *Whether a Several Fishery*

<!-- marginalia: The public fishery is a floating right, with nets, &c., only. -->

itself, the *public* fishing of the subject is a floating liberty of fishery, with nets, hooks, &c.; whereas the *several*, or private fishery, may be claimed, either as an individual personal right of fishing with nets, hooks, &c. *in loco*, the soil or shore whereof belongs to the King or to any private subject; or it may be claimed as appendant, or appurtenant to the ownership of the adjoining manor, or freehold.

<!-- marginalia: The public fishery and the private are incompatible with each other. -->

The public fishery and private fishery are incompatible (*n*) with each other. So also is a right to fish with nets, hooks, &c. (moveable machinery) incompatible with a fixed fishery. No fishery with nets, hooks, &c. can be enjoyed by the public, or even by one person, in a place where another enjoys a *private* right to make wears and enclosures; and yet both these kinds of fishing may be enjoyed in waters, the shore and soil of which belong to another; nor can such owner of the soil or shore prevent the other from exercising his paramount right to fish. Thus, all the subjects of the Realm have a right to fish in the sea or any creek thereof, or in a tide-river, the shore and soil of which place of fishing belong to the King, or to the lord of the manor. Or the lord of the manor alone, may have a separate fishery, not only exclusive of his manorial tenants, but also of all other persons; or some other individual may have a separate fishery, exclusive of the lord, and all other persons, or a *free* fishery in common with the lord.

<!-- marginalia: Private fishery considered, as giving colour of title to the sea-shore. -->

As the private or several fishery alone, gives colour of title to the sea-shore, or soil itself, it will be necessary for us to consider this private right more minutely.

That the ownership of the sea-shore, or the soil under

(*n*) In the case of Mayor of Orford *v.* Richardson, 4 T. R. 437, Buller, J. said, " one party is to prove that this is an arm of the sea, in which, " *primâ facie*, every subject hath a right to fish ; the other is to esta-
" blish a prescriptive right *which destroys the general right.*"

gives Title to the Shore. 53

the sea to any given distance, should include a right to fish, seems reasonable enough ; and, accordingly, the King's general right of ownership to the shore and sea-bottom, doubtless entitles him to fish, in common with his subjects. In like manner, if the King have conferred such ownership of any part of the shore on a subject (as on a lord of a manor), the general right of fishery does not exclude the lord. (*o*) But the mere ownership of the shore, whether possessed by the King, or by a lord of a manor, will not entitle the owner to establish a *separate* fishery, and exclude the public. In fact, the mere ownership of the soil will not, it would seem, confer or include a right to a separate fishery in the sea or tide-rivers, whether by nets and lines, or by wears and enclosures. (*p*) The right to exclude the public can only be supported by prescription, *i. e.* by evidence of immemorial usage. A several and exclusive fishery, immemorially enjoyed by an individual subject, or a corporate body, will exclude the public right. The common law gives stability to a right thus immemorially enjoyed ; and although the public may claim a preference, where the usage is doubtful, yet, where the usage is proved to have existed on the side of the individual, and to have been acquiesced in by the public, time out of mind, the public will be excluded, precisely as if such private fishery had been granted by the King himself, to the individual.(*q*)

The ownership of the soil of the shore does not entitle such owner to establish an exclusive fishery.

(*o*) If a man claim to have " communiam piscariam," or " liberam piscariam," the owner of the soil shall fish there. Co. Litt. 122 a.
(*p*) " In case of a *private river*, the lord's having the soil is good evi-
" dence to prove that he has the right of fishing, and it puts the proof
" on them that claim *liberam piscariam;*" " but in case of a river that
" flows and reflows, and is an arm of the sea, there, *primâ facie*, it is
" common to all, and if any will appropriate the privilege to himself,
" it lies on his side."—Per Hale, Ch. J. [in Lord Fitzwalter's case] 1 Mod. 105.
(*q*) In a note to Carter *v.* Murcot, 4 Burr. 2165, the following

54 Ownership of Shore does not include a

It seems certain that the *mere ownership* of the soil will not *exclude* the public, or authorise the owner to exclude the public fishery; for no subject can take more than the King had to grant, out of the shore or sea-bottom, and therefore the grantee must have taken his grant, subject to the public common right of piscary, to which the sea and *sea-shore* were liable, even in the King's hands. Therefore, although the ownership of the soil may afford some colour, or pretext to the claim of the individual to a private or several fishery, yet, unless such owner, and the former

"ing to some authorities, every navigable river, as far as the sea
" flows and reflows, is an arm of the sea, and it may perhaps not
" be unreasonable to admit such property may be by *prescrip-*
" *tion*, in some such navigable river; but in the sea or in such
" rivers as have free communication with the sea, where the catching
" of fish cannot diminish the stock, more than it could in the sea,
" the right which the subjects confessedly have, to fish there, ought
" not to be suffered to be restrained, either by *prescription,* or by the
" *King's grant;* for it is a principle incontestable, that all customs,
" prescriptions, and royal charters, that are either contrary to reason,
" or the good of the commonwealth, are void ; and it is apparent that
" all such restrictions are against both, and are injurious to the public
" in hindering a large supply of fish, as well as a means of livelihood
" to many particular persons, without any benefit to the public, or to
" any but monopolists, and inhancers of the price of fish ; but in rivers
" not having a free communication with the sea, the case is quite
" different ; for if the fishery there is made private property, the same
" would be preserved, and produce more, than if all persons were
" allowed to fish there, for by that means the breed would be in a
" manner destroyed, as is the case in many rivers not supplied by the
" sea." No modern grant can be made by the King of a separate, or free fishery in the sea, or on the sea-coast, or *in* navigable rivers. Since the time of Henry II. all grants from the crown of this kind of fishery have been contrary to statute* law, *viz.* Magna Charta, and the Charter of Henry III. and subsequent Acts of Parliament ; and therefore, if a grant *be produced*, it must be dated so far back ; the consequence is, that these kind of fisheries are always *prescribed for.* An ancient grant was put in, in the case of Warren *v.* Matthews, 1 Salk. 357, and probably others may be found, particularly to ancient Abbeys.

owners of such soil, have immemorially excluded the public, by means of a separate fishery, prescribed for, and *proved*, or founded in express ancient grant, the public right will prevail.

It is not, therefore, the ownership of the soil, but immemorial usage or prescription, and ancient grant, which support the several and exclusive fishery; and if so, then, it seems singular to hold (as Lord Hale seems to do), that a several fishery by means of wears, or fixed stakes, &c., " *is the very soil itself :*"(*r*) *i.e.* that such kind of fishery can, *per se*, be sufficient to confer a title to the soil itself. For, if the ownership of the soil will not confer an exclusive fishery (which in the eye of the law is a *minor* right, and rather an adjunct to the soil), why should the mere right to fish confer a *greater*, and in the eye of the law a more valued right, to land itself, thus making the greater an adjunct to the less? This is reversing the law rule, " *majus dignum continet et trahit ad se minus dignum.*" Why is it not enough to construe it a separate fishery, of the kind proved according to the prescription? Why should the mode of fishing, which is varied according to the kind of fish, their habits and haunts, be construed into an ownership of the soil? A right to catch fish by nets or wears, is still, in either case, no more than a mere right of fishery. Why should the owner of the land around be deprived of the soil where the private fishery *was* once enjoyed by *another*, but which has ceased, by the permanent drying up of the waters? (*s*)

Nor does an exclusive fishery give title to the soil.

The doctrine that the ownership of the soil affords a presumption in favour of a separate right of *fishery*, does not involve the same consequences of law, as saying, that a

(*r*) De Jure Maris, Appendix, post, xvi.
(*s*) Co. Litt. 4 b. [See Marshall *v.* Ulleswater Steam Navigation Co.

separate fishery gives a right to the soil, for *this* involves the question of title to *land*, and the form or mode of supporting that title. To say that if I prescribe for, and prove a separate fishery, I thereby gain the ownership of the soil, is as much as to hold that I may prescribe for an ownership in the soil; *i.e.* that a title to land, or fee simple estate, may be supported by prescription; a doctrine denied by some of our best authorities.(*t*) It is also remarkable that, when we get *beyond* reach of the tides, and the river is no longer *pars maris*, the doctrine is, that the ownership of the adjoining land, is good presumptive evidence that such owner has the exclusive right of fishing,—per Lord Hale, Ch. J. in Lord Fitzwalter's case, 1 Mod. 105;—but as soon as we get *within* the flux and reflux of the tides, the doctrine is reversed, and the ownership of a private fishery, is *said* to be good presumptive evidence of title to the soil itself. This, in itself, seems singular doctrine.

A freehold, or title to land, is one right and thing, and a fishery is another, and the rights and titles to these several things are not supported in like manner. A fishery, as well as any other franchise, liberty, profit or easement (as a right of road or way over another man's ground, or a right to pasture cattle on the manorial waste or common) may, as before explained, either be founded on express grant, or prescriptive usage; whereas, a title to land must be founded either on express grant, or on what is called "*adverse possession;*" which is not what our common law intends by "*prescription.*"

It is remarkable, that the cases of separate fisheries, cited in the treatise ascribed to Lord Hale, Appendix xviii. *et seq.*, by way of authority that a separate fishery carries the soil, do all use the term *piscaria*, which signifies merely a fishery; and not one assumes an ownership of the soil, in virtue of the "piscaria," even where it is claimed as "separalis." In some cases the "piscaria" and the sea-shore are mentioned separately; thus, "the Earls of Devon had, not " only the port of Toppesham, but the record tells us, that " the *Portus* et *Piscaria*, et *mariscus* (*u*) (marsh) de Toppes- " ham spectant Amiciæ Comitissæ Devon."(*x*) The only plausible instance adduced by the learned writer to prove that a separate fishery includes the ownership of the soil, does not seem, upon examination, to support such doctrine.

"Trin. 10, Ed. 2. B. R. Rot. 83, Norfolchiæ.—The abbot
" of Benedict Hulm,(*y*) impleads divers, for fishing in riparia
" quæ se extendit a ponte de Wroxam, usque quendam
" locum vocatum Blackdam. Pending the suit, the King's
" Attorney came in, and alledged for the King, quod
" prædicta riparia est brachium maris, quæ se extendit in
" salsum mare, et est riparia Domini Regis salsa fluens, ubi
" naves, et battelli, veniunt et applicant extra magnum
" mare carcati et discarcati quiete, absque tolneta, seu
" custuma aliqua dando, et est *communis piscaria* quibus-
" cumque; et dicit quod presentatum fuit, in ultimo itinere,
" coram Solomone de Roffa, et Sociis Justiciariis itineran-
" tibus in comitatu isto, quod prædecessor prædicti Abbatis
" fecit purpresturam super dominum regem in riparia præ-
" dicta, gurgites plantando in eadem, et appropriando sibi
" prædictam *piscariam tenendo tanquam separalem;* per
" quod consideratum fuit, quod gurgites illæ amoverentur,
" et quod prædicta aqua remaneret *communis piscaria.* Et
" petit quod nunc procedatur ad aliquam inquisitionem
" inde capiendam quousque præfati justiciarii super recordo

(*u*) De Jure Maris, Appendix, post, xviii. See also lxxx.
(*x*) "Mariscus" will pass the soil. Co. Litt. 4 b. But "Piscaria" will not.
(*y*) Case of the Abbot of Benedict Hulm, quoted from De Jure Maris,

" et processu prædictis certiorentur. Thereupon search is
" granted, and the record certified; and afterwards, a pro-
" cedendo was obtained; and issue being joined, it was
" found for the Abbot, and judgment and execution given
" against the defendants for the damages; viz. £200."

"Upon which record," says the learned writer, "these
" things are observable :—

" 1st. That, *de communi jure*, the right of such arms of
" the sea belongs to the King.

" 2nd. That yet, in such arms of the sea, the subjects in
" general have, *primâ facie*, a common of fishery, as in the
" main sea.

" 3rd. That yet, a subject may have a separate right of
" fishing, exclusive of the King, and of the common right
" of the subject.

" 4th. That in this case, the right of the Abbot to have
" a several fishing, was not a bare right, liberty, or profit
" *à prendre;* but the right of the very water, and *soil itself;*
" for *he made wears in it.*"

With deference, however, to such eminent authority, it
does not seem very observable, upon this record, that the
Abbot *had* the right of the "water, and *soil* itself," *because*
he made wears in it.(z) Nothing more, in fact, appears, than
that the Abbot by making wears, claimed to have *piscariam
tanquam separalem* (a private fishery), which, on trial, was
allowed against the King, who claimed the fishery in favour
of all his subjects as an open right. (a) That separate

(z) [Jerwood, p. 54.]
(a) P. 34, Ed. I. B. R. Rot. 14 Kancia Prior de Coningshed implacitat Abbatim de Ferneys pro prostratione Gurgitis in aquâ de Ulverstone. Defendant justified, because *each end of the wear* was fastened
upon the abbot's land. The abbot replies, quod Wilhelmus de Lancaster Dominus de Kendal dedit prædecessori domus suæ prædictæ

Several Fishery, nor the Fishery the Shore. 59

fisheries, by means of water sluices, wears, &c., may, and frequently do, belong to subjects in right of their manors, and as appendant to their manors, &c., there can be no doubt, for these may be prescribed for. That the soil where these separate fisheries are, *may* be "*parcel of*" (*b*) a manor (*i.e.* within the boundaries and *parcel*, as the other lands within the manor are parcel) is also admitted.—In the principal creeks and tide-rivers of England, and in the flat and marshy districts upon the coasts, these fisheries, some with, and some without the soil, are not unfrequent. But, it does not follow, that because they *may* be good in point of title by prescription, *as fisheries*, they confer also a title to the soil itself, without other evidences.

Lord Coke, in his Com. on Litt. 4 b, says, "if a man be " seized of a river, and by deed do grant, 'separalem " piscariam' in the same, and maketh livery of seizin, " ' secundum formam chartæ,' the soil doth *not* pass, for " the grantor may take water there, and *if the river become* " *dry he may take the benefit of the soil;* for there passed " to the grantee but a particular right. For the same " reason, if a man grant '*aquam suam*,' the soil shall *not* " pass, but the pischary within the water passeth. And " land covered with water shall be demanded by the name " of so many acres 'aquâ coopertas,' whereby it appeareth " that they are distinct things."(*c*)

There certainly exists a difference of opinion amongst the authorities, as to whether a "*separate* fishery" neces-

---

Rastall's Entries, trespass in pischary, pl. 4. Prescription for *several fishing*, in aquâ maritimâ fluente et refluente in seizonabili tempore cum 7 stallis separatis *separalis piscariæ fixis pro retibus*. Vide de Jure Maris, Appendix xvi.

(*b*) The phrase "*parcel of*" does not seem synonymous with "appendant" or "appurtenant."

(*c*) [See Marshall *v.* Ulleswater Steam Navigation Co. 3 B. and S.

Separate Fishery on the Shore does

Mr. Hargrave's opinion that a separate fishery does not give title to the soil.

sarily, and *per se*, includes the soil or not. This question is ably considered by Mr. Hargrave in a note to Co. Litt. 122 a, note 7,(*d*) and he concludes in the *negative*. After quoting a passage in 1 Inst. 122, relative to this subject, as follows: "A man may prescribe to have *separalem* piscariam "in such a water, and the owner of the soil shall not fish "there; but if he claim to have *communiam* piscariam, or "*liberam* piscariam, the owner of the soil shall fish there," Mr. Hargrave observes, "According to this passage, owner-"ship of the soil is *not* necessarily included in a several "fishery, and common of fishery and free fishery are the "same thing." He then refers to Judge Blackstone's doctrine, who lays it down, "that the ownership of soil is essen-"tial to a *several* fishery; and that a *free* fishery differs "both from *several* fishery and *common* of fishery: from the "former, by being confined to a public river, and not "necessarily comprehending the soil: from the latter by "being exclusive." 2 Black. Com. 8 Ed. 39. Mr. Hargrave replies to this: "We doubt whether this distinction may "not be, in a great degree, questionable. 1. In respect to a "several fishery,—where is the inconsistency in granting "the sole right of fishing, with a reservation of the soil, "and its other profits? Bracton expressly takes notice "of such a grant; for his words are, that one may 'servi-"'tutem imponere fundo suo quod quis possit piscari cum "'eo, et ita in communi, vel quod alius per se ex toto.' "Brac. fo. 208 b. There are also numerous other authori-"ties for it; the old books of entries agreeing that one may "prescribe for a *several* fishery against the *owner* of the "soil; to which should be added the three cases of Eliza-"beth, cited by Lord Coke. See Lib. Intrat. 162 b, 163 a, "Rast, Entr. 597 b, and the books cited under the letter d, "in fol. 4, B, and under m here, and the cases referred to

not necessarily include the Soil. 61

" under the * on the other side. Nor do we understand
" why a *several* piscary should not exist *without* the soil, as
" well as a several pasture,(*e*) as to which latter we have
" already shown the doctrine to be settled, *supra*, n. 6.
" The chief reasons which occur against Lord Coke seem
" to be these :—Several writs, never applicable except to
" the soil, lie for a piscary; such as a præcipe quod reddat,
" monstraverunt de rationabilibus divisis, and trespass,
" which latter writ is particularly insisted on by Lord Ch.
" J. Holt; Dav. 55 b; Hugh Comm. Orig. Wr. 11 W. Jo.
" 440; 1 Ventr. 122; 2 Salk. 367; Skinn. 677. Suum
" liberum tenementum is a good plea to trespass for fishing
" in a several piscary; 17 E. IV. 6; 18 E. IV. 4; 10 H.
" VII. 24, 26, 28. The soil will pass, as it is said, by the
" grant of a piscary; Plowd. 154. But all these objections
" may be repelled. The writs relied on will not always lie
" for a piscary. Thus, if a præcipe quod reddat is brought
" of a piscary in the water of another person, the writ is
" bad, and a quod permittat is the proper remedy; Fitz.
" Abr. Briefe, 861; F. N. B. 23 i; and note b of the 4to ed.
" Besides, in the cases of actions for trespass in a several
" piscary, or at least in some of them, the writ seems in
" effect to state a several piscary in the plaintiff's own soil,
" which therefore proves nothing as to the sense of several
" piscary without further explanation; Reg. B. R. Orig. 95 b;
" Carth. 285; Skinn. 677. The plea liberum tenementum
" may be replied to by prescribing for a several piscary.
" See the books before cited, as to such a prescription.
" Though the *grant* of a piscary generally may *perhaps* pass
" the soil, yet it will not, if there are any words to denote a
" different intention; as where one seized of a river grants
" a several fishery in it, which is the case put by Lord Coke

(*e*) [See Melvin *v.* Whiting, 24 Mass. (7 Pick.) 79; Cortelyou *v.* Van

"in another place; and much less will the soil pass when "there is an express reservation of it; ante 4 b, and n. 2, "there. Hence, as it should seem, the arguments are short "of the purpose; for, at the utmost, they only prove that a "*several* piscary is presumed to comprehend the soil, till "the contrary appears, which is perfectly consistent with "Lord Coke's position, that they *may* be in different per- "sons, and *indeed appears to us the true doctrine on the* "*subject*."(*f*)

Comments. But the doctrine thus noticed by Mr. Hargrave is not, as applied to the Crown, precisely the same as when applied between subject and subject; nor is it the same when applied to the soil *beyond or above* the flux and reflux of the tides, as when applied to the soil upon the *shores* of the sea and tide-rivers. Admitting that a *several* fishery, in waters *not* subject to the tides, and, therefore, no part of the sea, may, between one subject and another, be made ground of presumption (where there is no proof to the contrary), that the soil goes with it (although from what is before said, p. 53 *et seq.* a presumption of that kind does not seem *necessary*), it may be insisted, that between the *flux* and *reflux* of the tides, every such presumption is against the right of the Crown, and that implication is not to be made against the King. A very modern case would seem to justify this distinction; the case is that of the Duke of Somerset *v.* Fogwell,(*g*) in which letters patent of the 44th of Eliz. were given

(*f*) In Partheriche *v.* Mason, 2 Chitty's Cases, temp. Mansfield, 661, Lord Kenyon is made to say, "there is no reason why a person may "not have a several fishery in *alieno solo*." But the Report adds, "SED "PER CURIAM, where a man has a several fishery, the presumption is, "that he has the soil; *that* presumption is conclusive, *if not opposed*." But this was said of a fishery in a river *not within the tides* though navigable. *Within* the tides the presumption *is* always *opposed* by the King's title; see also Lofft. 364; [Marshall *v.* Ulleswater Steam Navigation Co. 5 B. and S. 732; Hall's Profit à Prendre, p. 310, *et seq*.]

in evidence, by which she granted to Edward Seymour, Esq., his heirs and assigns, "all those domain lands and " manors of Berry Pomeroy and Bridgetown Pomeroy, and " the castle of Berry Pomeroy, with all their rights, mem-" bers, liberties and appurtenances, in the county of Devon, " then lately parcels of the lands, and possessions, and here-" ditaments of T. Pomeroy, Kt.;" and after making use of general words to pass the lands, &c. and tithes of Berry, her majesty granted " *all waters, fisheries*, &c. to the afore-" said manors, castle, and premises, and to each and every " of them belonging, or appendant, known, accepted, held, " used, or reputed or deemed as part or parcel of the same " premises." There were also produced two fines, one levied in 2 Ed. VI., and the other in 2 and 3 William and Mary, of the manor, &c. "*ac de separali piscariâ de aquâ de Dert.*" It was also proved that the present Duke and his ancestors had, since 1765, regularly received a rent for the *fishery* in the river Dart, which was a navigable and *tide-river*. In the course of the argument, the doctrine of Judge Blackstone "that ownership of the soil is essential to a several fishery,"—and the contrary doctrine of Lord Coke, before quoted,(*h*) and the argument of Mr. Hargrave in the text, were mentioned and commented on. The question, whether the words of the letters patent, "all waters, fisheries, &c." and the words in the fines, "separalis piscaria," carried the *soil*, was not the principal question; but was mooted in reference to the effect of a lease of the "separalis piscaria" made without deed. If the "separalis piscaria" were a *territorial* hereditament, including the soil, then such lease was good; but if "separalis piscaria" were merely an *incorporeal* hereditament, then a grant by deed was necessary to vest such hereditament in the lessee. In the latter case, an action of trespass brought by the Duke, as plaintiff, was well brought; but if the parol demise was good, then the action should have been brought in the name of the lessee. The Court decided that the fishery in question was not a *territorial*, but an *incorporeal* hereditament, and required a grant, by deed, to divest it from the Duke. Mr. Justice Bayley, in delivering the judgment of the Court, said, "No " conveyance of the right of fishing, or of the soil, was pro-" duced at the trial, but it appeared not to be an *ordinary* fish-" ing, resulting to the owner of the adjoining land in respect " of the land, *but a fishery in a navigable river, where the* " *tide flows and reflows*, and, therefore, in the nature of a " royal franchise, which Sir William Blackstone calls a *free* " fishery.(*i*) Such a franchise could not be created after " Magna Charta, but there was evidence in this case from " which its existence from time beyond legal memory might " be presumed." Then, after alluding to the words, "sepa-" ralis piscaria" in the fines, and quoting the words of Lord Coke, as just now quoted,(*k*) the learned judge proceeds: "in " the case here put (that from Lord Coke),(*l*) the grant was " made by the owner of the soil, capable of granting it, and " yet a grant 'separalis piscariæ,' followed up by livery, " which properly applies to a thing corporeal, *did not convey* " *the soil*, livery being made secundum, &c. If then a " fishery only is granted, nothing passes but a right to take " the fish, and to use such means as are necessary for that " purpose; which is, in truth, nothing more than a liberty " to fish; the grantee has no property in the water, none " in the soil. And this is a case where the grant is made " between subject and subject, and, consequently, is to be " construed against the grantor, a principle inapplicable to " grants made by the Crown, whereby nothing passes,

(*i*) 2 Com. 39.   (*k*) P. 56, ante.
(*l*) But Lord Coke's case was not between the flux and reflux of the

not necessarily include the Soil.

" unless the intention that it should pass is manifest." After quoting the case of the river Banne, from Davis 55, in which there was a grant by letters patent from the Crown, of "omnia castra, messuagia, &c. *piscarias, piscariones, aquas, aquarium, cursus*, &c.," the learned judge proceeds: "It was held that the fishery of the Banne did not " pass by the grant of the land adjoining, and by general " grant of all piscaries, &c.; for that it was a *royal* fishery, " not appurtenant to the land, but a fishery in gross, and " was by itself part of the inheritance of the Crown; and " that general words by the King would not pass such a " special royalty, which belongs to the Crown by preroga-" tive; and it was further agreed, that *the grant of the King* " *passes nothing by implication*. It was contended in argu-" ment, that the owner of a several fishery must be pre-" sumed to be owner of the soil. That *may* be true, where " the terms of the grant under which he claims are un-" known [*i.e.* it is presumed, where he claims by prescrip-" tion]; but when they appear, and are such as convey an " incorporeal hereditament only, the presumption is de-" stroyed." This last remark of the learned Judge may, however, be considered as applied to a case between subject and subject,—not where a subject claims the soil against the *King* in right of a several fishery between the flux and reflux of the tides,—by prescription, or by "a grant, the terms of which are unknown;"—for to *presume* the owner of such fishery to be owner of the soil, is taking the soil from the Crown, by a presumption not necessary. First, a grant from the Crown is presumed :—but of what? Of a separate fishery. But such grant, if produced, would not carry the soil :—why then should the presumed grant do so? —is it because the terms of it "are unknown"? This would be singular reasoning; for we know that the doubtful terms of an actual grant by the Crown are construed strictly *in favour* of the Crown; and yet we are told that a grant, the terms of which are so much more doubtful, as to be "unknown," may be construed most *against* the Crown. It is presumed that the words of the learned Judge, as well as of Mr. Hargrave, had reference only to "several fisheries" in waters *not* within the flux and reflux of the tides; and even to that extent they both seem to speak with doubt, using the phrase "may be."(*m*)

With regard to a "free fishery," as distinguished from a "several fishery," Mr. Hargrave remarks, in continuation of the note before quoted, "Both parts of the description of a " 'free fishery' seem disputable, though, for the sake of dis-

(*m*) [In Marshall *v.* Ulleswater Steam Navigation Co., 3 B. and S. 732, 748; 6 B. and S. 570, Cockburn, Ch. J., says: "It is admitted " on all hands that a several fishery may exist independently of the " ownership of the soil in the bed of the water. Why then should such " a fishery be considered as carrying with it, in the absence of negative " proof, the property in the soil? On the contrary, it seems to me that " there is every reason for holding the opposite way. The use of water " for the purpose of fishing is, when the fishery is united with the " ownership of the soil, a right incidental and accessory to the latter. " On a grant of the land, the water and the incidental and necessary " right of fishing would pass with it. If, then, the intention be to " convey the soil, why not convey the land at once, leaving the acces- " sory to follow? Why grant the accessory that the principal may pass " incidentally? Surely such a proceeding would be at once illogical " and unlawyerlike,—the greater is justly said to comprehend the less, " but this is to make the converse of the proposition hold good. A " grant of land carries with it, as we all know, the mineral which may " be below the surface; but whoever heard of a grant of the mineral " carrying with it the general ownership of the soil? Why should a " different principle be applied to the grant of a fishery,—which may

Free Fishery. 67

" tinction it might be more convenient to appropriate *free*
"*fishery* to the franchise of fishing in *public* rivers, by deri-
" vation from the Crown; and though in other countries it
" may be so considered, yet, from the language of our
" books, it seems as if our law practice had extended this
" kind of fishery to all streams, whether private or public,
" neither the Register nor other books professing any dis-
" crimination. R. 95 b; Fitzh. N. B. 88 g; Fitzh. Abr.
" Ass. 422; 4 E. 4, 28, 17 E. 4, 6 b, 7 a; 7 H. 7, 13 b;
" Cro. Ch. 554; 1 Ventr. 122; 3 Mod. 97; Carth. 285;
" Skinn. 677. Again, it is true that, in one case, the Court
" held free fishery to import an exclusive right, equally with
" several piscary, chiefly relying on the writs in the Reg.
" 95 b, and the 43 E. 3, 24. But then this was only the
" opinion of two Judges against one, who strenuously in-
" sisted that the word 'libera,' *ex vi termini*, implied
" ' common,' and that many judgments and precedents were
" founded on Lord Coke's so construing it. Smith *v.*
" Kemp, 2 Salk. 637; Carth. 285. That the dissenting
" Judge was not only unwarranted in the latter part of his
" assertion, appears from two determinations a little before
" the case in question. See Upton and Dawkins, 3 Mod.
" 97, and Peake and Tucker, cited in Carth, 286, in marg.
" We may add to this, the three cases cited by Lord Coke
" as of his own time; and that there are passages in other
" books which favour his distinction. See Cro. Ch. 554;
" 17 E. 4, 6 b, 7 a; 7 H. VII. 13 b."

The phrase "*free fishery*,"(*n*) seems a technical phrase, answering to "*free warren.*" Now, one or *more* individuals may have "free warren" in another man's land, and "free fishery" in a river of the soil of which another individual is owner. In a "free fishery," the owner of the soil is not

[marginal note: stinction tween era, separalis, and communis, piscaria.]

excluded.(*o*) But in "separalis piscaria" he may be.—Thus "separalis" is opposed to "libera," *tanquam species generalis*, to show that "no one else"(*p*) can share in the fishery. Thus A may prescribe for "libera piscaria," in the *locus in quo*, in common with B;—and B prove that in such place, he, B, has "separalis piscaria,"—which excludes A; yet C may be owner of the soil. But "separalis piscaria" necessarily excludes C as well as A, whereas "libera piscaria" does not. Thus there is "libera piscaria," "separalis piscaria," and "communis piscaria," which latter is not a *franchise* like the former, but a common right, *sui generis*. But, "libera piscaria" being a "franchise," is, like "free warren," generally found where the soil is in another, and by no means involves, or carries with it the soil. It may be further observed that the word "*separalis*" seems to apply peculiarly to that kind of private fishery which is carried on by means of weares, and other artificial fixed apparatus, which being the labour of the individual, cannot be used by others, and like his nets, or the moveable apparatus, are his own property. This mode of fishing was (like the oppressive forest laws) ever obnoxious to our ancestors, but more especially as being obstructions to commerce and navigation.(*q*)

(*o*) Co. Litt. 122. [See Hall's Profit à Prendre, p. 312; Paterson, 46.]
(*p*) See accord. 5 Burr. 2814, per Lord Mansfield, in Seymour *v.* Lord Courtney. In that case, also, the Court declined giving any opinion "whether a person can have a several fishery *without* being owner of "the soil."
(*q*) [A "free fishery," *primâ facie*, means "a several fishery," per Willis, J., in Shuttleworth *v.* Le Fleming, 19 C. B. 697. See Melvin *v.* Whiting, 24 Mass. (7 Pick.) R. 79; Freary *v.* Cook, 14 Mass. R. 488. In Malcolmson *v.* O'Dea, 10 H. of L. cases 593, Willes, J., says, "Some "discussion took place during the argument as to the proper name of "such a fishery, whether it ought not to have been called in the plead- "ings, following Blackstone, a 'free' instead of a 'several' fishery. "This is more of the confusion which the ambiguous use of the word

From the earliest times, it was no uncommon act of the legislature to destroy these weares and fixed fishing-places, as nuisances to navigation. By Magna Charta it was declared, "omnes kidelli deponantur de cetero penitus per " Thamaesiam et Medwayam per totam Angliam, *nisi per* " *costeram maris.*" And this statute was seconded by others that were more effectual, viz. 25 Ed. III. c. 4, 1 H. IV. 12, and 12 Ed. IV. c. 7 ; and other subsequent statutes, whereby such weares and stake fisheries were abated from time to time; not only in rivers, but *along the sea coasts.* " And, by force of this last statute," says Lord Hale, " weares, which were prejudicial to the passage of vessels, " were to be pulled down ; and accordingly it was done, in " many places."(*r*) And he adds, " The exception of weares " upon the *sea-coasts* [in Magna Charta], and likewise fre-" quent examples, some whereof are before mentioned, " *make it appear* that there might be such private interest, " not only in point of *liberty*, but in point of *property*, on " the sea-coast, and below the low-water mark ; for such " were regularly all weares. But, as by the statutes of " 25 Ed. III. c. 4 ; 45 Ed. III. c. 2 ; 1 H. IV. c. 12 ; " 4 H. IV. c. 11 ; and other statutes, the erecting of new " weares, and 'inhancing '(*s*) of old, is provided against, in " navigable rivers ; and by other statutes, particular provi-

Exclusive fixed fishe discountenanced by law.

" fol. 13, down to the case of Holford *v.* Bailey, 13 Q. B. 444, where it
" was clearly shown that the only substantial distinction is between an
" exclusive right of fishery, usually called several ; sometimes free
" (used in 'free warren '), and a right in common with others, usually
" called ' common of fishery ;' sometimes 'free' (used as in 'free port').
" The fishery in this case is sufficiently described as a several fishery,
" which means an exclusive right to fish in a given place, either with
" or without the property in the soil."]

(*r*) [De Jure Maris, Appendix, xix.]
(*s*) [This is supposed to be a mistranslation of lever, for levying or setting up: per Lord Denman in Williams *v.* Wilcox, 8 A. and E. 335,

"sion is made against weares new or old, erected in parti-
"cular ports, as in the port of Newcastle, by the statute of
"21 H. I. c. 18; in the port of Southampton, by the
"statutes of 11 H. VII. c. 5; 14 H. VIII. c. 13; in the
"rivers Ouse and Humber, by the statute of 23 H. VIII.
"c. 18; in the river and port of Exeter, by the statute of
"31 H. VIII. c. 4; in the river of Thames, by the statutes
"of 4 H. VII. c. 15; 27 H. VIII. c. 18; 3 Jac. c. 20;
"and divers others; so, by the statute 3 Jac. c. 12, all new
"weares *erected upon the sea-shore*, or in any haven, harbour,
"or creek, or within five miles of the mouth of any haven
"or creek, are prohibited, under a penalty."(*t*)

(*t*) See De Jure Maris, Appendix xix. [All new fixed nets, not legally existing in 1862, are illegal, and any person may destroy them : Williams *v*. Blackwall, 32 L. J. Ex. 174, S. C. 2 H. and C. 33, 9 Jur. N. S. 579, 11 W. R. 621 ; and L. T. N. S. 252 ; Moulton *v*. Wilby, 32 L. J. M. C. 164. A weir appurtenant to a fishery, obstructing the whole or part of a navigable river, is legal, if granted by the Crown before the commencement of the reign of Edward I., and such grant may be inferred from evidence of its having existed before that time. If the weir, when so first granted, obstruct the navigation of only a part of the river, it does not become illegal by the stream changing its bed, so that the weir obstructs the only navigable passage remaining. But where the Crown had no right to obstruct the whole passage of a navigable river, it had no right to erect a weir obstructing a part, except subject to the rights of the public ; and, therefore, in such a case, the weir would become illegal upon the rest of the river being so choked that there could be no passage elsewhere. Williams *v*. Wilcox, 3 N. and P. 606 ; 8 A. and E. 314. See Gann *v*. Whitstable Free Fishers, 11 H. L. c. 192 ; 35 L. J. C. P. 29 ; Rawstorne *v*. Backhouse, 3 L. R. C. P. 67 ; Holford *v*. George, 3 L. R. Q. B. 640, London Law Magazine, vol. 28, p. 325. The statute 12 Ed. 4, c. 7, relates to navigable rivers only, and though weirs in navigable rivers are illegal unless they existed before the time of Edward I., such an easement might be acquired in private waters by grant from other riparian owners, or by enjoyment, or by any means by which such rights may be constituted. Rolle *v*. Whyte, 3 L. R. Q. B. 286. See Leconfield *v*. Lonsdale, 5 L. R. C. P. 657 ; Hall's Profit à Prendre, p. 308 ; Paterson's Fishery Laws, c. 4 ; and Jerwood, p. 83. As to salmon fisheries, see

It is further observed by the learned writer (Lord Hale), upon the above legislative acts, "that they did *no way dis-* " *affirm the propriety*, but only remove the annoyance ; and " though they prohibit the thing, yet they *do admit* that " there may be such an interest lodged in the subject, " though below the low-water mark, whereby a subject " may not only have a liberty, *but a right or propriety of* " *soil.*" (*u*)

In reply to this, it is to be observed, that it does not appear how these statutes admit *a weare or fishing sluice* to be sufficient evidence of a title to the soil, which is the inference intended by Lord Hale ; or that the weare is anything more than a mere fishery. They go no further than admitting the existence of such an interest, franchise, or liberty, as a "separalis piscaria," in a subject, to be exercised by means of weares, &c., so that in the exercise of such right, he be careful not to injure or interrupt other paramount general rights of the public. Not only is a separate or private fishery thus restrained ; but the ownership of the soil, even in the King himself, cannot be made a ground for obstructing the subjects in general, in the navigation of the seas or tide-rivers. Whether the obstruction or nuisance be a weare, or a mere wall, it is equally a nuisance, if in prejudice of the *jus publicum ;* for, as the learned author truly observes,(*x*) "the *jus privatum*, that is " acquired to the subject by *grant, patent*, or *prescription*, " must not prejudice the *jus publicum*, wherewith public " rivers and arms of the sea are affected for public use."

No inference from the St tutes against weares, &c. that such exclusive fisheries car the soil.(*v*)

The frequent nuisances occasioned by the formation of weares, and fishing sluices (attested by the numerous statutes in force against them), would warrant their being

72 Grant of Several Fishery does not carry

Weares and several fisheries, being opposed to the jus publicum, to be construed strictly.

construed *stricto jure,*(*y*) and to include nothing more than the fishery. Nor is it desirable (in a public view) to afford to lords of manors any additional, or easier means of establishing a title to the *soil on the sea-shore*, or the creeks, or arms of the sea, or in the public rivers, than is allowed to them in regard to *terra firma* titles; especially, as such ownership is so capable of being perverted to the public annoyance.

Distinction between several fisheries places not within the tides, and in the sea and tide-rivers.

There may be a difference, too, very fairly taken, betwixt the grant of a separate fishery, in rivers, streams, and lakes, which are not connected by the tides with the sea, and therefore not subject to the "jus publicum," and the grant of a separate fishery in parts of the sea, creeks, havens, or tide-rivers; which grants, being to the prejudice of public rights and benefits, are, and ought to be, more strictly construed than in cases where there are no public rights to be sacrificed.

In Weld *v.* Hornby,(*z*) the question was whether an ancient weare heretofore constructed of wicker work and brush-wood, might be converted into one of stone, and it was decided that it could not. Lord Ellenborough, C. J. said, "The erection of weares across rivers was reprobated in the "earliest periods of our law. They were considered as "public nuisances. The words of Magna Charta (ch. 23) "are, that all weares from henceforth shall be utterly pulled "down by Thames and Medway, and through all Eng-"land, &c. And this was followed up by subsequent acts "(vide 12 Ed. IV. c. 7), treating them as public nuisances, "forbidding the erection of new ones, or enhancing, strait-

(*y*) See Dewell *v.* Sanders, Cro. Jac. 491, and Fowler *v.* Sanders, Cro. Jac. 446.

(*z*) 7 East 195. [As to weirs, see Hamilton *v.* M. of Donegall, 3 Ridg. P. C. 267; Leconfield *v.* Lonsdale, 5 L. R. C. P. 694; D. of Devonshire *v.* Smith, Alc. and Nap. 442; Malcolmson *v.* O'Dea, 10 House of Lords C. 593; D. of Devonshire *v.* Hodnett, 1 H. and Br.

the Shore, and is to be construed strictly.

" ening, or enlarging of those which had aforetime existed.
" I remember that the stalls erected in the river Eden, by
" the late Lord Lonsdale, and the Corporation of Carlisle,
" whereby all the fish were stopped in their passage up the
" river, were pronounced in this Court, on a motion for a
" new trial, to be illegal, and a public nuisance. Now here
" it appears that, previous to the erection of this complete
" stone weare, there had always been an escape for the fish
" through and over the old brushwood weare, in which those
" of the stream above had a right; and it was not com-
" petent for the defendant to bar them of it by making an
" impervious wall of stone through which the fish could not
" insinuate themselves, as it is well known they will through
" a brushwood weare, and over which it is in evidence that
" the fish could not pass, except in extraordinary times of
" flood. And however twenty years' acquiescence may bind
" parties whose private rights only are affected, yet the
" public have an interest in the suppression of public
" nuisances, though of longer standing. No objection,
" however, of this sort can apply to the case, where the
" action was commenced within twenty years after the
" complete extension of the stone weare across the river,
" by which, it is proved, that the plaintiff has been injured.
" Then, however general the words of the ancient deeds
" may be, they are to be construed, as Lord Coke says,
" ' by evidence of the manner in which the thing has always
" ' been possessed and used.' " Nothing is said in this case
from which we can infer that the court considered the
weare as giving title to the soil. It is treated throughout
as a mere fishery.

It will hardly be contended, that an express grant of a "piscaria" without more words will pass the whole shore of a manor, which shore *may be of several miles in extent;*

A shore of a manor is often of several miles in extent,

74 *Grant of a Several Fishery does not carry*

whilst the weare may be of but a few yards.

implied, or presumed grant do so? It is also singular law to hold, that a weare or fishing-place, which may cover only a few yards of shore, should give title to the whole shore, throughout the whole extent of the manor, which may be several miles along the coast, creek, or tide-river.

Now, if we nowhere find a case in point, where the right to the soil on the shore, or under the sea, or an arm thereof, or a tide-river, is *solely* supported on the basis of a prescriptive right of fishery, either separate or common; and, if we find this separate fishery frequently put down by statutes, as nuisances and encroachments on the *jus publicum*;—and that these statutes nowhere notice the separate fishery, as conferring the soil itself, or otherwise than as a mere "piscaria" and nuisance;—and if we likewise know that fisheries are, in legal title and intendment, mere franchises, and usufructuary liberties or privileges, and are, technically, a distinct species of property and ownership from the soil, and as such, founded either in express ancient grant, or on immemorial usage or prescription; we may be allowed to doubt, whether either an ancient grant of, or a prescription for, any fishery, *eo nomine*, however private, will support a title to the soil itself.

An express grant of a separate fishery, and no more words, will not (it is considered) include the soil.

With respect to the express ancient grant, it does not appear how it could be construed to include the soil itself; for suppose the King to have granted, in some creek or arm of the sea, to W. S. the exclusive fishery thereof, by means of weares, stakes, &c., without any express words of grant of the soil itself, and the whole creek became suddenly dry land, by the permanent retreat of the waters, it would not be consistent with the received rules of construction, to construe such grant into a grant of the land. As well may it be said that the franchise of *free warren*, or even

the Shore, and is to be construed strictly. 75

land. (*a*) It may plausibly be urged that an inclosure by means of a weare, or by stakes, &c., is a virtual appropriation of the soil within it, because no one can make use of it without breaking such inclosure. But in answer to this it may be contended, that the weare or inclosure was made for no other purpose than to catch fish ; *as to the land*, the inclosure was not made *eo intuitu*. It is different from an *embankment* made expressly to secure land from the water. If the place where the weare stands should become dry land, the *fishery* is destroyed ; and that which was a lawful inclosure for catching fish, may be unlawful when used for asserting a title to grow corn there. The prescription is necessarily gone, when the subject matter of it, and the medium through which it was exercised, is destroyed ; when such a prescription, dependent upon the water, has ceased to exist, what is left to support a title to the dry land ? The grantor of the franchise or liberty would seem to recover his exclusive dominion again. (*b*) If a weare were placed on the sea-shore, still, on the recess of the tide, the soil within may be of much use for ballastage, or for manure, building materials, &c. (*c*) without injury to

Distinction between weares and an embankment.

(*a*) But Lord Coke tells us, " if a man grant to another to dig turves " in his land, and to carry them away at his will and pleasure, the land " shall *not* pass, because but part of the profit is given." Co. Litt. 4 b. Plowd. 154 is contra, and makes it carry the soil ;—but the better opinion is with Coke.
(*b*) See p. 59, ante, and see Co. Litt. 4 b ; and see accord. what is said per Bayley, J. in the case Rex *v*. Montague, 4 B. and C. 603, as to the ceasing of rights by natural causes.
(*c*) See p. 59, ante, where it is said, that the owner of the soil, though he grant a separate fishery, " may take the water," and also " make profit of the soil when dry." In the case Hollis *v*. Goldfinch, 1 B. and C. 213, the ownership of four *hatches* or *water sluices* made on the banks of a canal was adduced as evidence of title to the soil of the banks ; on this evidence Lord Tenterden observes, " It is said that " the demise of the *hatches* imports that they belong to the lessor, and

76 *Grant of a Several Fishery does not carry*

the fishery; and what should prevent him, who granted the fishery only, from claiming all the right and uses in the soil that are not inconsistent with his grant, and also the soil itself, when the fishery has ceased to exist by natural causes? Indeed, if the law acknowledge a separate fishery as a distinct species of property, and rank it amongst franchises differing essentially both in title and estate from an inheritance and title to land, it is impossible to admit that the grant in question (which is one only of the many usufructs of the sea or sea-shore) can include the land itself.(*d*) As to prescription, the rule is, that it presupposes a grant; but no other grant can be presupposed than such as is tantamount to the fishery prescribed for; and if so, a presupposed grant of a separate fishery cannot reasonably go further than the actual grant of such fishery.

As to other franchises of wreck, &c.

We will next proceed to consider, in their order, the several other rights, franchises, and uses which arise from or are claimable in respect of the sea and sea-shore; because the learned writer, in the treatise alluded to, in order to establish his doctrine,—that the sea-shore may belong to the subject by "prescription," as well as by charter or grant, —not only quotes the *private fishery*, but various other

" also belong to him; but that is a conclusion which by no means
" follows, because, if they were necessary for the purpose of main-
" taining the navigation of the river, the undertakers (of the canal) had
" a right to place those hatches there, *although they might not be*
" *owners of the soil.*"

(*d*) In a case in 1 M. and S. 666, the King *v.* Ellis, Bayley, J. observes, " I should doubt very much if the grant of a fishery would
" convey the soil, and everything underneath it, as all the minerals,
" though I can conceive that it might pass so much of the soil as is
" connected with the fishery." As this was a fishery with *staked nets*, q.
Whether the right to drive stakes for that purpose is more than an easement? [See Duke of Somerset *v.* Fogwell, 5 B. and C. 875, per Bayley, J., and Hayes *v.* Bridges, 1 Ridg. L. and S. 420. per Finu-

the Shore, and is to be construed strictly.

franchises, rights, and usufructs, the enjoyment of which, by a subject, will, as he concludes, support a title to the soil of portions of the sea and sea-shore. Lord Hale says,(*e*) " It may not only belong to a subject, *in gross*, which pos-" sibly may suppose a grant before time of memory, but it " *may* be *parcel* of a manor." "And this," says he, " it is " agreed, 5 Reports, 107, Sir H. Constable's case,(*f*) and the

And their giving title to the soil.

(*e*) [Appendix, post, xxiv.]

(*f*) The words of this case are these : " It was resolved by the whole " court that the soil on which the sea flows and ebbs, sc. between the " high and low water mark, *may* be *parcel of the* manor of a subject," and Dyer, 326, b, is cited as accord. 2 Roll. Abr. 170 has also the same words. But this doctrine of Lord Coke may be freely admitted without admitting that " it may be parcel of the manor" by *prescription ;* Lord Coke does not in the above resolution say *that;* the resolution in fact seems to be directed against the doctrine of the civil law writers, who hold that there can be no ownership in the " shore " at all.

The phrase " parcel of," signifies that when the subject has the shore, he has it as *pars totius,*—as he holds the rest of the lands of the manor —and does not in any wise release him from proving it to be " parcel," by the same kind of evidence as is required for the title to all the other parcels of land in the manor. In a note to Carter *v.* Murcot, 4 Burr. 2165 it is said, " in 1 Sid. 149, prescription was admitted to be a title to " the soil of a river, within the flux and reflux of the sea, which is a " consequence from its being allowed in 5 Co. 107. 2 Roll. Abr. 170 " pl. 12, that it may *by prescription* be part of a manor." But the word *prescription* is not to be found either in the resolution in 5 Co. 107, or in 2 Roll. Abr. 170 pl. 12. In Siderfin the words are, " and in this case " it was repeatedly affirmed, and denied by no one, that the soil of all " rivers (cy-haut), where there is fluxum et refluxum, is in the King, " and *by no means* (nemy—) in the lords of manors, sans prescription," and no authority whatever is quoted. Callis also quotes Constable's case as an authority, " that a subject's manor may extend to low-water " mark by *prescription.*" See p. 55. Coke, however, upon *his own* authority, and not as giving the resolution of the court,—adds (alluding to a 'case of replevin, Fitz. Replev. 41), " on which I observe three " things. 1. That wreck may be claimed by prescription," [which is admitted.] " 2. That forasmuch as a ship cannot be wreck, scil. cast " on the land, but between the high-water and low-water mark, " thence it follows that *that* was parcel of the manor," q.e.d., for according to this doctrine, prescription for a *lesser* thing, a mere franchise. viz. wreck.—gives title to a *greater* thing. viz. land.—and

"Book of 5 E. 3, 3, cited accordingly. And according to
"this was the resolution cited, Dy. 316, to be between
"Hammond and Digges, p. 17, Eliz.;—accordingly it was
"decreed in the Exchequer Chamber, p. 16, Car. inter.
"Attorney-General *v.* Sir Sam. Roll, Sir Rd. Buller, and
"Sir Thos. Arundell, per omnes Barones. *And the evidences
"to prove this fact are commonly these;* constant and usual
"fetching gravel, and seaweed, and sea sand between the
"high-water and low-water mark,(*g*) and licensing others
"so to do; *enclosing* and *embanking* against the sea, and
"enjoyment of what is so inned; enjoyment of *wrecks* hap-
"pening upon the sands; presentment and punishment of
"purprestures there, in the court of a manor; and such
"like;" and he adds, "it not only *may* be parcel of a
"manor,(*h*) but, *de facto*, it many times is so; and *perchance*
"it is parcel of almost all such manors as, by prescription,
"have *royal fish*, or *wrecks* within their manors. For, for
"the most part, wrecks and royal fish are not, and indeed
"cannot be well left above the high-water mark, unless it
"be at such extraordinary tides as overflow the land: but
"these are perquisites which happen between the high-water
"and low-water mark; for the sea withdrawing at the ebb,
"leaves the wrecks upon the shore,(*i*) and also those greater
"fish which come under the denomination of royal fish.
"He, therefore, that hath wrecks of the sea or royal fish, by
"prescription *infra manerium*, it is a great presumption that
"the shore is part of the manor, or otherwise he could not
"have them. And consonant to this is the pleading in Sir

Lord Hale's doctrine, that wreck and royal fish raise a presumption of ownership in the shore.

that against the King. Besides, the conclusion is a non sequitur, for wreck may be cast upon the shore, and yet belong to one who has *only* the franchise. [See Jerwood, p. 57.]

(*g*) [See Dickens *v.* Shaw, Appendix, post, lvi.]

(*h*) [Calmady *v.* Rowe, 6 C. B. 861; Beaufort, Duke of, *v.* Swansea, 3 Exch. 413.]

do not carry the Shore. 79

"Henry Neville's case, 5 E. 3, 3, and Rastall's Entries, 684, "transcribed out of the record, M. 14. E. 1. Rot. 432, where "an Abbot, prescribing for wreck belonging to his manor, "doth it in this form :—Ipseque et omnes prædecessores "sui Abbates Monasterii prædicti, et dominii ejusdem "manerii, per totum tempus prædictum, habuerunt et "habere consueverunt, *ratione manerii* prædicti, omnimodo "bona *wreccata* super mare, et ut wreccum super terram "projecta, per *costeram maris*, in quodam loco, ubi mare, "secundum cursum suum pro tempore fluxit et refluxit, à "quodam loco vocato M. in parochiâ de L. &c." And in the following plea an Abbot prescribes to have "Wreccum "maris *infra*(*k*) præcinctum manerii, sive dominii sui pro"jectum, et Flotsan maris infra præcinctum manerii de"veniens; quodque prædictum dolium vini fuit wreccum "maris, per mare projectum, super littus maris apud S. "infra precinctum manerii sive dominii illius."(*l*)

Pleading in Sir Henry Neville's case.

We may collect from the foregoing quotations(*m*) that the learned writer considers not only a separate fishery, by wears, stakes, &c., but also a right to royal fish, to wrecks, to flotsan, jetsan, and ligan, and lastly, a usage to dig and carry away sand, seaweed, &c., or to make embankments

Comments on such doctrine.

(*k*) Mr. Hargrave, in a note to Co. Litt. 107 A. n. 115, observes upon this word, that on many occasions it may be of importance thoroughly to understand the phrase *infra*, or, as according to classical style it ought to be, *intra*; and he construes infra quatuor maria to mean intra quatuor maria. In like manner, in the abbot's plea, *infra* was used for *intra*, although infra præcinctum manerii means, according to ordinary construction, *below*, and not *within* the precincts of the manor. Lord Coke uses the word intra, and not infra. "Intra quatuor maria," within the four seas; "extra quatuor maria," *beyond* the four seas: 260 b, Co. Litt. But in his third Inst. 113, he uses the phrase, "infra corpus comitatus" for "intra corpus comitatus;" and in Constable's case he uses "infra præcinct. manerii" for "intra."

and inclosures of portions of the shore, may all be adduced (by prescription) in support of a title to the land or soil of the shore itself.(*n*) He does not say that *all* these are necessary together: we may infer, indeed, from his language, that *all* of them are *not* necessary to raise an absolute title to the ownership of the sea-shore itself; but he does not inform us whether any one, or more, of them will suffice, or which of them is *essential.*

Royal fish. Now, with regard to the franchise of royal fish (which are whale, sturgeon, and porpoise), this is reckoned by Blackstone(*o*) *inter regalia,* and one of the King's ordinary branches of revenue, and one of the flowers of the Crown. Those fish are claimed on account of "their superior excel-"lence," according to Blackstone, who vouches for the royal taste, not in right of the sea-shore, but by royal prerogative, and from the most remote antiquity. Whether thrown on shore, or caught in the sea, or on the coast, they are the property of the King, not of the catcher, even in a private fishery.(*p*)

Wreck. In like manner wreck (when no owner can be found) is part of the King's ordinary revenue, in right of his royal

Flotsan, &c. prerogative, and is a flower of the Crown. So also flotsan, jetsan, and ligan, are perquisites of the Crown. These royal rights and franchises are *not* claimed by the Crown as part of or appurtenant to the *ownership* of the sea-shore, nor enjoyed in virtue of such ownership. They belong to the Crown in virtue of the *royal prerogative.*(*q*) They are regarded as "*nullius bona,*" and allotted to the King by the law, for

(*n*) De Jure Maris, Appendix, post, xxiv.
(*o*) Blackstone's Com. vol. i. p. 289, 13th ed.
(*p*) Black. vol. i. p. 290. [See Paterson's Fishery Laws, 24 and 165; Stewart on Fishery Rights, Scot. p. 46.]
(*q*) Bracton, 2 Vent. 188, and 5 Co. 108, Constable's case; Sutton *v.*

Franchises which do not carry the Shore. 81

want of other ownership. The King might grant them, or any one of them, to a subject, *without any grant of the shore*. (*r*) So, he might grant the wreck to one person, and royal fish to another, and the shore itself to a third person. (*s*) There are not wanting instances where lords of manors on the coast are possessed of, and can prescribe for, *both* these royal franchises, or but *one* of them, and yet have never had or claimed the ownership of the shore itself. (*t*)   All or any of these rights may be and often are held without any right to the shore.

Wreck and royal fish are no part of the realty; they may indeed be prescribed for by the lord of the adjacent manor, and may be and commonly are attached as franchises to the *manors* on the sea coast; but still they are prescribed for on the ground of immemorial usage, or are proved by   These rights are no part of the realty.

(*r*) And see Scratton *v*. Brown, 4 B. and C. 485.
(*s*) Anon. 6 Mod. R. 149.
(*t*) [The grantee of "wreck" has a special property in all goods stranded within his liberty, and may maintain trespass against a wrongdoer for taking them away, though such goods were part of a cargo of a ship from which some persons escaped alive to land, and though the owners within the prescribed time claimed and identified them, and before any seizure on behalf of grantee (Dunwich bailiffs *v*. Sterry, 1 B. and Ad. 831); but to constitute wreck the goods must have touched the ground (Pauline, 2 Rob. Adm. R. 358), though they need not have been left dry: Rex *v*. Forty-nine Casks of Brandy, 3 Hag. 257; see also R. *v*. Two Casks of Tallow, ibid. 294. But if timber is found without an apparent owner, having broken away from its fastenings and drifted out to sea, it is not "wreck" within 17 and 18 Vict. c. 104, s. 458, so as to entitle the finders to salvage in respect of their services: Palmer *v*. Rouse, 27 L. J. Exch. 137; 3 H. and N. 505, S. C. "Wreck" will not pass under general words: Alcock *v*. Cooke, 2 M. and P. 625. See further, ante, p. 40, and Dickens *v*. Shaw, Appendix xlv.; Talbot *v*. Lewis, 6 C. and P. 603; the Pauline, 2 Rob. Adm. p. 358; Phear, p. 52, and note in p. 99; Angell, on Tide Waters, 289, &c. Goods thrown on the shore by the violence of the waves are "wreck" within the provisions of 3 and 4 Will. 4, c. 52, s. 50; Legge *v*. Boyd, 1 C.B. 92; S. C. 14 L. J. C. P. 183; see also Barry *v*. Arnaud, 10 A. and E. 646. Disputed title to "wreck" by 17 and 18 Vict. c. 104, s. 472, may be decided by two justices in the same manner in which disputes as to salvage are therein directed to be determined, and by the same Act the Board of Trade has

express grant, and are not claimed in right of (*ratione*) the ownership of the sea-shore. It is nowhere said, nor could it be intended, that a mere grant of so many acres of seashore, or sea bottom from the King, would pass, *inclusive*, the royal franchises of wreck and royal fish; and yet these might seem to be more reasonably attached to the shore than the shore attached to them; and if the rule "*accessorium non ducit sed sequitur suum principale*" be applicable at all, it were much more reasonable to hold that the ownership of the soil is evidence of the franchises before mentioned (which, however, it is not), than that these rights, or any of them, are proof of title to the shore. It is difficult to conceive how all or any one of these rights, together or separate, can confer a different title to a different thing, viz. the soil. I may obtain the royal fish from the King, and wreck from another man to whom the King once granted it; I may *prescribe* for my title to one, and produce an express *grant* of the other, and yet the soil of the shore remain where it was. (*u*) I may prescribe for all these rights, but that is not prescribing for or proving another right; each right must be supported on its own title; nor does it appear why the prescribing for wreck should confer a title to the soil, more than prescribing for wreck should confer a title to a separate fishery, or to royal fish, which clearly it will not do.

As to the observation that "a right to wreck or to royal
" fish cannot be well had above high-water mark, for the
" sea withdrawing at the ebb, leaves the wreck or royal
" fish upon the shore, and consequently that he who hath
" wreck of the sea, or royal fish, by prescription, infra
" manerium, it is a *great presumption* that the shore is part
" of the manor, as otherwise he could not have them," (*x*)

Franchises which do not carry the Shore. 83

—it may be replied, that this does not seem to be a *necessary* consequence; for wreck, or royal fish, may clearly be granted, *per se, without* the shore; so far as the shore is essential to the enjoyment of the franchise, it will be subject to egress and regress for that purpose; (*y*) nor does it appear what should prevent the grantee from claiming the wreck, or royal fish, although the shore may remain with the King; it is not *necessary*, in order to make the grant of wreck perfect, that more should be conceded than egress and regress. (*z*)

Now, if it be not *necessary*, that in order to enjoy the wreck, the grantee should be owner of the soil of the shore, no *presumption* necessarily follows that he is such owner. If I have common of pasture upon the waste lands of a manor, I must go upon the waste for the purpose of pasturing my cattle, and yet no presumption of ownership of the soil is raised on that account. The pleadings in Neville's case, (*a*) quoted by the learned writer, do not set up any title to the shore. Sir H. Neville merely claims wreck, ratione manerii, *i.e.* wreck in right of, or as appurtenant to the *manor*, and passing with the manor into the hands of all owners for the time being of the manor, but nothing is said as asserting a claim to the shore, *ratione wrecci*. (*b*)

The other authority, of the abbot's plea, (*c*) assumes the wreck and flotsan to be *infra*, or (according to Mr. Hargrave) *intra* præcinctum manerii, and it asserts the "dolium vini" to have been cast "super littus maris, *apud S*. infra præcinctum manerii sive dominii illius."(*d*) It may be agreed

The abbot's plea considered.

xxv. R. *v.* Ellis, 1 M. and S. 662. See Calmady *v.* Rowe, 6 C. B. 861, and Beaufort, Duke of, *v.* Swansea, Mayor of, 3 Exch. 418.]
(*y*) 6 Mod. R. 149. (*z*) [See Appendix, post, p. lxvi.]
(*a*) 5 E. 3, 3, p. 79, ante.
(*b*) [Jerwood, pp. 54, 55. Serj. Merewether's speech, Appendix, post,

that the abbot considered the shore as within the precincts; although the next antecedent is the locus in quo, viz. S.—which *locus* the plea states to be *within* the manor. But admitting the plea to intend that the shore, as well as the place S., was within the precincts, yet he was not prescribing for or claiming a title to anything else but wreck and flotsan; *and he certainly did not claim or prescribe for the shore in virtue of his title to the wreck.* The shore might or might not be his, and within the boundary of his manor; (*e*) but nothing appears to show *that it was his because the wreck was his;* or that his prescription for the wreck was *allowed* evidence of a title to the shore; the shore was not in dispute at all. The form of plea, in both these cases, does not show a title to the shore in right of the wreck. Nor is it *necessary* to show a title to the shore, in order to prove a title to wreck.

Case of Barons of Barclay for the soil of the River Severn.

It is proper here to notice a case, which is cited at considerable length in the treatise ascribed to Lord Hale,(*f*) and which appears to be the only case cited by him from which the doctrine now under consideration seems to derive any material support. The learned writer quotes it as a case with the decision of which he was personally familiar. " In Scaccario, Car. ——— upon the prosecution of Sir
" Sackville Crow, there was an information against Mr.
" John Smith, farmer of the Lord Barclay, setting forth
" that the river of the Severn was an arm of the sea, flow-
" ing and reflowing with salt water, and was part of the
" ports of Gloucester and Bristol, and that the river had
" left about 300 acres of ground, near Shinbridge, and
" therefore they belonged to the King, by his prerogative.
" Upon not guilty pleaded, the trial was at the Exchequer
" bar, and by a very substantial jury of gentry and others
" of great value."

Case of the River Severn.

"Upon the evidence," proceeds his Lordship, "it did
"appear, from unquestionable proof, that Severn, in the
"place in question, was an arm of the sea, flowed and re-
"flowed with salt water; was within and part of the ports
"of Bristol and Gloucester; and that within time of
"memory these were lands newly gained and inned from
"the Severn; and that *the very channel of the river did,*
"*within the time of memory, run in that very place where the*
"*land in question lies;* and that the Severn had *deserted it,*
"and the channel did then run above a mile towards the
"west." (*g*)

On the other side, the defendant, claiming under the
title of the Lord Barclay, alleged thesè matters, whereupon
to ground his defence, viz. :—

"1st. That the barons of Barclay were, from the time
"of Henry the 2d, owners of the great manor of Barclay." Q. e. d.

"2d. That the river of the Severn, usque filum aquæ,
"was, time out of memory, *parcel* of that manor."

"3d. That, by the *constant custom of the country,* the
"filum aquæ of the river of Severn was the common *boun-*
"*dary* of the manors on either side of the river."

"When the state of the evidence was opened, it was
"insisted upon that the river in question was an arm of
"the sea, a royal river, (*h*) and a member of the King's port,
"and therefore lay *not in prescription to be part of a manor.*
"But the Court overruled that exception, and admitted
"that even such a river, though it be the King's in point
"of interest, *prima facie,* yet it may be by *prescription* and
"usage time out of mind parcel of a manor.".

(*g*) In Lord Fitzwalter's case, 1 Mod. 106, Hale, Ch. J. says, "In the
'Severn there are particular restraints, as *gurgites,* &c., but the soil
"belongs to the lord on either side, and a *special* sort of fishery
"belongs to him likewise, but the common sort of fishery is common
"to all."—And in some other place the Severn is said to be "an un-

Case of the River Severn.

" Thereupon the defendant went to the proofs, and insisted
" upon many *badges* of property or ownership, as (viz.)"

"That the lords of the manors adjacent to this river, and
"particularly those of that manor, had all *royal fish,* taken
"within the river opposite to their manors usque filum
"aquæ."

"That they had the sole right of salmon fishing."

"That they had all wrecks cast between high-water and
"low-water mark."

"That the lords of the manors adjacent had ancient *rocks*
"or fishing-places, and *wears,* or such as were of that nature,
"within the very channel."

"That they had from time to time granted these fishing-
"places, some by lease, some by copy of court roll, at their
"several manors, by the names of '*rocks,*' *wears, statches,*
"*boraches, putts,* (*i*) *and that they were constantly enjoyed, and*
"*rent paid by those copyholders and leaseholders.*"

(*i*) These four last are all *artificial* apparatus for taking the fish, as their names import. Gurges, which is sometimes translated " weare," is a *natural* formation in the river, and, by Lord Coke, is said to be "a deep pit of water, a gors, or gulfe, and consisteth of *water and* " LAND, and by that name the soil shall pass." Co. Litt. 5 b. He takes no notice of " weares," as a fishery, nor of the *other* words in the text. Callis, 255, tells us, that the " kidelli," mentioned in Magna Charta, are " weares," and yet, by stat. 25 Ed. 3, c. 4, " all mills, *weares,* " stanks, stakes, *and kiddels* which were *set* in the time of King Edward " (grandfather of Edw. 3.), and after, whereby ships and boats were "disturbed, should be *pulled down.*" In stat. 12 Henry 4th, weares and fishgarths are mentioned together as nuisances, and in a case Benedict Hall *v.* Mason, quoted by Callis, 262, a weare and fish-guard are put together, and mentioned as " having been letten by the late Queen (Eliz.) at yearly rents, with the profits of fishing." This weare, which was stated to have been built of *timber and stone,* was demolished as a nuisance. According to Plowd. 154, " by the grant of "a *pool,* the soil *and wear* shall pass, because it is included in the " word ; for by one book a formedon lies de *gurgite.*" Here the "*soil*" and " *wear*" are distinguished.* Ld. Coke, however, translates " stag-

Case of the River Severn.

"That by common tradition and *reputation* the manors "on either side Severn were *bounded* one against another by "the filum aquæ, and divers *ancient depositions* produced, "wherein it was accordingly *sworn by very many ancient* "*witnesses.*"

"That the increases happening by the reliction of the "river were constantly enjoyed by the lords adjacent."

"These," says the learned writer, "and many other *badges,* "were opened, and were most effectually made good by "most authentical evidences and witnesses. But before the "defendant had gone through one half of his evidence, the "Court, and the King's Attorney-General, Sir John Banks, "and the rest of the King's Counsel, were so well satisfied "with the defendant's title, that they moved the defendant "to consent to withdraw a juror, which, though he were "very unwilling, yet, at the earnest desire of the Court and "the King's Counsel, he did agree thereunto. *So* that "matter rested in peace, and the lands, being of the yearly "value of £200 and better, are enjoyed by the Lord Bar-"clay and his farmers, quietly, and without the least pre-"tence of question, to this day."

By this report of the case it is made to appear, that the Court declared that the soil of such a river (*i. e.* the Severn, a tide-river and arm of the sea) may, by *prescription* and usage time out of mind, be parcel of a manor. No grant whatever of the soil of the river to the Barons *appears* to have been produced on the trial. The great manor of Barclay, as it would seem, was *admitted* to belong to the Barons; the title to the *manor*, therefore, was not disputed:

Comments on the case of the Barons of Ba clay.

num, a pool," and "gurges, a deep pit of water," but says nothing of the weare, which, in fact, may be constructed in a marsh or lake, stagnum (pool), gurges (pit of water), or in the river course, or on the seashore. So, the word "sea-grounds" will, it seems, pass a portion of sea-shore.—Scratton *v.* Brown, 4 B. and C. 485, [and see Malcolmson

the true question was, whether such manor comprised or included within its limits the soil of the river or not. Now this was a mere question of *boundaries* of a manor, the ownership of which was not disputed. This manor was *asserted* to extend usque *filum aquæ;* and whether it did or did not extend so far, was the question. (*k*) Two distinct kinds of evidence were adduced to prove a title to the soil; the first kind was that which has been just now controverted; viz. that the Barons, owners of the manor, had immemorially enjoyed the franchises and liberties of wreck, royal fish, and separate fisheries, by wears, borachiæ, &c. The other kind of evidence was such as has, in later times, been admitted to support titles to inland estates; viz. *copyhold grants,* (*l*) *leases,* and taking rents, &c., surveys, records, terriers, and evidence of old witnesses, and ancient depositions to the *boundaries* of the manor.(*m*) These, in the absence of the grant, are admitted as evidence of boundaries to inland estate. But mere reputation, or common tradition, will not alone, it is conceived, be sufficient to support a title to the freehold. (*n*) So, perhaps, the evidence to the

(*k*) [Jerwood, p. 48.]

(*l*) See 2 T. R. 53; 4 T. R. 514, 669; 10 East, 206; 14 East, 331; 2 Roll Ab. 186, pl. 5. [Ancient leases are good evidence, showing the ancient state of possession; entries on court rolls of fines and presentments, Walton cum Trimley Manor, 21 W. R. 475 S. C.; 28 L. T. N. S. 12; bills and answers in Chancery between parties litigating the title, Malcolmson *v.* O'Dea, 10 House of Lords cases, 593; see also Tisdall *v.* Parnell, 14 Ir. C. L. Rep. 23; verdicts in former actions, and an award, where the party or his predecessors were privy to it, Wenman *v.* Mackenzie, 5 E. and B. 447; Evans *v.* Rees, 10 A. and E. 151; Kinnersley *v.* Orpe, 2 Douglas, 517; but an unauthenticated M.S. report of a trial 140 years back, of an action of trespass, and of the charge of the Ld. Ch. Baron (which was received in the Court below) is a document which ought not to be admitted in evidence: Bridges *v.* Highton, 11 L. T. 653.]

(*m*) 1 Maule and Sel. 81, and 687, 689. Doe *v.* Thomas, 14 East, 323.

(*n*) See p. 39, ante, nor does the question, as to what kind of evidence custom of the country, as to *boundaries*, "affecting a whole district of manors," may have been good evidence in this case. (*o*) The custom, however, of one *manor* is not evidence of the custom of *another*. (*p*)

It is admitted, that a man may be owner of a definite tract of sea, or river, if it be capable of demarcation ; but yet the required evidence of the boundary line, (*q*) whether of old *terra firma*, or of land covered with water, is legally and technically stricter than when an easement is claimed by prescription, founded on usage. If it be admitted (as it was in the principal case) that a man is owner of the Great Manor of B. such manor must have its boundaries and limits, both on the land side and on the water ; and it is competent for me to prove, by evidence, those limits, and witnesses are in such case admissible evidence. Lord Hale tells us, (cap. 6.) " That the shore may not only be parcel " of a manor, but also of a vill or parish ; and the evidence " for that will be, usual *perambulations, common reputation*, " known *metes and divisions*, and *the like*. (*r*) Now all this is " evidence to *boundaries ;* but 'wreck' or 'a fishery' is no "evidence to boundaries."

The evidence ought to establish such acts, on the part of the claimant and his ancestors, as far back as the statutes of limitation require, as are in their nature the most effectual

particular close is part of an estate, appear yet to be fully settled. See also Phillipp's Evidence, [10th edit. vol. 1. p. 170.]

(*o*) R. *v*. Ellis, 1 Maul and Sel. 662, per Ld. Ellenborough.

(*p*) D. of Somerset *v*. France, 1 Strah. 658, and cases cited in Phillipp's Ev. 10th edit. vol. i. p. 497. [Jerwood, p. 48. Anglesea, marquis of, *v*. Hatherton, Lord, 10 M. and W. 218 S. C. 12, L. J. Exch. 57.]

(*q*) It is the practice to "beacon out" the limits of appropriated portions of shore, or sea-grounds ; and these " beacons " are evidences of boundaries. See Scratton *v*. Brown, 4 B. and C. 485, [Calmady *v*. Rowe, 6 C. B. 881.]

(*r*) But see p. 39, ante, [and McCannon *v*. Sinclair, 5 Jur. N. S. 1022 ; Ipswich Dock Commissioners *v*. Overseers of St. Peter's, Ipswich, 7 B.

for acquiring and retaining the *possession* of the land. These acts must be *eo intuitu*, having for their express and manifest object the seizin and possession of it. These acts must also have been *continued* for the time required by the statutes of limitation. At the time the foregoing case was tried, the ancient time of Richard I. was the period of limitation, and it is expressly stated, that the Barons of Barclay had held the manor from the time of Richard I., *nor was this controverted*. The evidence went to prove that, during all the time they were lords of the manor, the Barons had made a series of copyhold grants of various portions of the disputed soil, and leases also, which were overt acts (*s*) of ownership; and the evidence as to boundaries went as far back as living testimony could go.

We are not informed what part of the evidence adduced in this case prevailed most with the Court; we know which would do so in a case of inland title at the present day; and our object is, to separate from this mass of evidence that which was valid from that which was not.

This case, indeed, presents a precedent for those to follow, who, without a grant, have to make good a similar claim; for every kind of evidence (except the "taking sand") which could give colour of title to the soil was amassed upon the trial; but it does not inform us whether *all* this evidence was *necessary*, or if not all, what part of it was essential in establishing the title to the bed of the river. (*t*) In other cases, therefore, where but one, two, or three of these proofs are adduced, we are left to the principles of the common law to determine whether such proof be legal evidence or

(*s*) See accord. Rogers, and others, *v.* Allen, 1 Camp. 309; and see 5 T. R. 412.
(*t*) But see Lord Ellenborough's comments on this case in the King

Case of the River Severn. 91

not; as, for instance, whether wreck, or royal fish (and on the sea-coasts these are the most common attributes of manors), will alone, without more substantial evidence, support a title to the sea-shore, or to soil under the sea. (*u*)

With regard to *terra firma*, there is no difficulty as to the nature of the *acts* required to testify seizin and possession. These are such as occupation, and taking possession or seizin, inclosing, letting, (*x*) and taking rent, cultivating and making profit of the soil, land-marks, perambulations, and other acts which savour of *ownership, i.e.* which common sense acknowledges as acts of appropriation and occupation, and which naturally flow from continued and exclusive possession; and these acts must have continued for the period required by the statutes of limitation. Nature of the acts required to give title to terra firma.

It may be a question what other acts, besides those just noticed, shall be said to attest an appropriation and personal possession of the soil under the water, in a tract of sea or sea-shore, whilst it continues sea or sea-shore. There must be something in the acts themselves evidencing the "animus habendi, possidendi, et appropriandi,"—not the usufruct of the water merely,—*but of the soil itself under it.* (*y*) The acts of ownership must not be more appropriate to the *water* than to the *land*. They ought to savour of the land itself, and be the natural result of the personal and exclusive occupation of the soil itself. The animus piscandi, or wreccum capiendi, is not animus solum appropriandi. Acts of fishing, continually used, do at last establish a *right* to fish in future; and this is embodied by our law into a "fishery," a technical and distinct species of property and ownership. Why should those acts go further? That

(*u*) [See remarks on case of Dickens *v.* Shaw, post.]
(*x*) But see Tyrwhitt *v.* Wynn, 2 Barn. and Ald. 554.

which those acts savoured most of they were allowed to give a title to, viz. a fishery; and by the same reasoning, that only which savoured most of the soil, ought to give a title to that soil; that which savours most of one kind of property and ownership, can hardly be said to savour most of another kind of property and ownership. The usufruct of the water vanishes with the water, (z) and where both usufruct and water are gone, it seems singular to construe such usufructuary right, now no more, into proof of a new species of ownership in the land, and *that* in derogation and to the ousting of the King's original property in such land.

Digging for sand, &c.

With regard to the "constant and usual fetching of sea-sand, seaweed, and gravel, between the high-water and low-water mark, and licensing others so to do;" (a) and embanking against the sea, and enjoyment of what is so "inned;" these, it must be admitted, are all acts likely to be done by the owners of the soil; and they afford colour, that he who does these acts is such owner: but these acts *may* be usurpations or intrusions on the King's ownership, and *prima facie* are so. (b)

(z) See 4 Rep. 88. and Co. Litt. 4 b.
(a) [See case of Dickens *v.* Shaw, Appendix, post, p. li.]
(b) [The lord of the manor cannot acquire an exclusive right to cut seaweed below water-mark, unless by grant from the King, or such long and undisturbed enjoyment, as to give him a title by prescription. The sea is the property of the King and so is the land beneath, except such part as is capable of being occupied without prejudice to navigation, and of which a subject has either a grant from the King, or has exclusively used for so long a time as to confer on him a title by prescription: Benest *v.* Pipon, 1 Knapp Rep. 68. Nor is there at common law a general right in the public of entering on the sea-shore to take seaweed even between high-water and low-water mark: see Howe *v.* Stowell, 1 Alcock and Nap. 348; Healy *v.* Thorne, 4 Ir. C. L. R. 495; for Scotch cases see Paterson's Compendium of English and Scotch Law, p. 6. But seaweed thrown up by extraordinary tides belongs to the

being Evidence of the Title to the Shore. 93

As to the right of digging for sand, the authorities show that this may, and often does exist, without conferring any title whatever to the land ; for similar rights are exercised by the tenants in the wastes of a lord's manor, and yet the tenants have no title to the soil; but such rights are mere profits *à prendre*.

A custom to dig sand or seaweed is analogous to the customary right of digging turf, or brick earth, or sand, or coal, or minerals, in the waste lands of a manor, by the customary tenants. Such custom is good, but it does not raise any title to the land ; it is a mere usufructuary liberty, or right of commonage in the lord's waste, supported by express grant, or by usage and prescription. It further appears, that a single individual may possess similar rights, exclusive of all others, *in alieno solo*. (c) But if this be so, then there is only one instance in which seaweed is mentioned, where he says "the shore may be part and parcel of a manor, and the evidences " to prove this fact are constant and usual fetching of seaweed, &c."
" This passage," says Angell, "would seem to indicate that the learned
" author considered the public to be, *prima facie*, entitled to seaweed.
" For if he had not so considered it, then the circumstance of its being
" exclusively taken by the lord of the manor, could not be received as a
" proof of his adverse right of property in the shore."

[In Howe *v.* Stowell, 1 Alcock and Nap. 348, which was an action of trespass for breaking and entering the plaintiff's close, a plea of justification that the close was the sea-shore, and that all the subjects of the King had the right to enter and carry away the seaweed left by the tide, and that the defendant being such subject entered, was held to be bad.

[For law in America see Emans *v.* Turnbull, 2 John's (N.Y.) R. p. 314, Kent, C.J. ; Chapman *v.* Kimball, 9 Connect. R. 38 ; 3 Kent, Com. 522 ; Philips *v.* Rhodes, 48 Mass. (7 Met.) R. 322 ; Moore *v.* Griffin, 9 Shep. (Me.) R. 350 ; Sale *v.* Pratt, 36 Mass. (19 Pick.) R. 191.]

(c) " If a man *grant* to another to dig turves in his land, and to carry
" them at his will and pleasure, the land shall not pass, because but
" part of the profit is given." Co. Litt. 4 b. So " If a man *prescribe*
" or allege a custom to have and enjoy *solam vesturam terræ*, from such
" a day to such a day, hereby the *owner of the soil* shall be excluded to
" pasture or feed there : so he may *prescribe* to have *separalem pastu-*

it would seem that a custom (local at least) to dig sand or seaweed in the great waste of the shore might be prescribed for (as in the analogous cases), without its conferring a title to the shore itself. The statute of 7 James I. c. 18, (*d*) after reciting or taking notice that, " Whereas the sea-sand, by
" *long trial and experience*, hath been found to be very
" profitable for the bettering of land, and especially for the
" increase of corn and tillage within the counties of Devon
" and Cornwall, where the most part of the inhabitants have
" not *commonly* used any *other* manure for the bettering of
" their arable grounds and pastures ; notwithstanding divers
" having *lands adjoining* to the sea-coast there, have of late
" interrupted the bargemen and such others as have used
" of their *free wills and pleasures* to fetch the said sea-sand,
" to take the same *under the full sea-mark*, as they have
" *heretofore used to do*, unless they make composition with
" them at such rates as they themselves set down, though
" they have very small or no damage or loss thereby, to the
" great decay and hinderance of husbandry and tillage,
" within the said counties ;"—enacts—" That it shall and
" may be lawful to, and for *all persons whatsoever resident*
" *and dwelling* within the said counties of Devon and Cornwall, to fetch and take sea-sand at all places under the full
" sea-mark, where the same is or shall be cast by the sea,
" for the bettering of their land, and for the increase of corn
" and tillage, at their wills and pleasures. II. And that it
" shall and may be also lawful to and for all bargemen and
" boatmen, and all other carriers of sea-sand of the said
" counties, that shall fetch or take sand as aforesaid, *to land*
" *and cast* out of their boats and barges such sand as they
" shall so fetch or take at *such places* as sand hath at any
" time within the space of fifty years last past been used by
" such bargemen and boatmen *to be landed and cast ;* and

being Evidence of the Title to the Shore.

" also to fetch and carry the same by and through such
" ways as now be and by the space of twenty years last
" past have been used for the carrying and fetching thereof,
" paying for the taking, casting out and landing of every
" barge-load, boat-load, or sack of the said sand *upon the*
" *grounds of any man*, such duties as heretofore, within the
" said time of fifty years, have been used and accustomed
" to be paid for the same, and for passage by and through
" the *said ways*, such duties as have usually been paid by
" the space of twenty years, and in such manner and form
" as the same, within the said several times, have respectively
" been used and accustomed to be paid. And in such
" places where certain usual duties have not been paid, but
" uncertain compositions have from time to time been made
" by agreement with the owner of the soil there, to yield
" such reasonable compositions as, by agreement with the
" said owners, shall from time to time be made." (*e*)

This statute raises an inference against the presumption that the mere digging of sand, &c. may entitle either lords of manors or others to the *soil* of the sea-shore; for, by this statute, the sea-shore, throughout two of the largest maritime counties in England, is declared to be, and to have been heretofore *commonly* open to the spades and mattocks of all the *inhabitants* of those large counties. Now, if the lords of manors were actually entitled to the sea-shore in this district, the statute was unusually arbitrary, even in that arbitrary reign. But the statute does not take notice of any *ownership* of the lords of the manors; it states these lords, or rather " owners of lands adjoining," to have interrupted bargemen and others as *had used*, of their free wills and pleasures, to fetch sea-sand, and take the same under the full sea-mark, *as they had theretofore used to do ;*(*f*) and without

Comments on the statute.

(*e*) [Ierwood p. 87.]

noticing or regarding any ownership of the lords or others in the shore, enacts that *all* persons in the said counties should be at liberty, as theretofore, to take sea-sand at all places under the full sea-mark.

In the case of Bagott *v.* Orr (*g*) it was disputed at the bar, whether this statute was merely *declaratory* of the general right of the subject throughout the coasts of England, or an *enacting* of a *special* and peculiar privilege for the men of Devon and Cornwall, but the Court gave no opinion on the point. There was nothing in the privilege or benefit itself which peculiarly applied to the inhabitants of those counties; it was equally likely to be claimed and used in Sussex or Norfolk, and probably, had the other maritime counties made the same complaint of prevention, the same remedy would have been obtained. It is a right which is most likely to have grown up and been exercised in all maritime districts, immemorially, in like manner as the free fishery has been enjoyed. There are other instances where *general* rights *have* been confirmed to particular places, by special statute.

---

from the statute. He says, " This (the shore) *may* belong to a subject. " The statute 7 James c. 18 supposeth it, for it provides that those of " Devon and Cornwall may fetch sea-sand, for the bettering of their " lands, and shall not be hindered by those who have their lands ad-" *joining the sea-coast*, which appears by the statute, they *could not* " *formerly*." But the words of the statute expressly state, "That by " long *trial and experience* it had been profitable for the bettering of " land ;" and that " most part of the *inhabitants* had not *commonly* " used any other ;" and " that they had been of late prevented from " doing what they had been *used* to do at their free wills and pleasures," and " what they had *heretofore* used to do." So that it appears by the statute that they *could* do so formerly. The statute is directed mainly against the owners of " lands *adjoining to the coast*," and no sound inference is afforded by it, against the King, in favour of the right of the lords of manors of Devon and Cornwall to the sea-shore. [See Calmady *v.* Rowe, 6 C. B. 879.]

being Evidence of Title to the Shore. 97

At all events, it is certain, from the foregoing statute, that such right to dig, &c. may be claimed and enjoyed by thousands who have no ownership in the soil itself; and it also appears that one person may enjoy such right exclusive of all others, even of the admitted owner of the soil himself; and, if so, then such right exercised in the *shore*, does not *necessarily* involve title to such shore. In Devon and Cornwall an exclusive right to dig sand or weed on the shore, or to license others so to do, cannot now be set up by lords of manors; nor do the men of those counties stand in need of any licence other than the statute.

Admitting that an exclusive right of digging sand, &c. on the shore, may be exercised by some lords of manors; still it is necessary to *prove* such right, in the first instance, if it is to be used as a ground of title to the shore. Such right can only be proved two manner of ways—1st. By express grant exclusively to dig, &c. 2nd. By prescription or custom. Now, if we take a manor extending along *several miles* of sea-shore, such shore belonging clearly to the King, and he, by express grant, give to the lord of the manor a right to dig sea-sand, *without more words*, it would be strange to construe this into a grant of the whole of these several miles of sea-shore; and, if so, it would be still more strange to construe a prescriptive right or custom (*i.e.* one grown up by usage and encroachment), more liberally than the King's express grants, and beyond the terms even of the prescription. Every argument, indeed, which has been already applied to a several fishery, will equally apply to an exclusive privilege of digging sand, to shew that prescription for a mere liberty, profit, or privilege, is no title to land. The shore *may* be subject to a general or to a local right, claimed by others than the owners of the soil, of digging shells or sand, as well as to a right of fishing, or

As to an express grant of right to dig sand, &c.

Prescription ought not to have larger effect than an express grant of the right prescribed for would have.

can be established, the ownership of the soil—whether vested in the King, or in a subject by grant from him—is *entire;* but if such custom or usage be established, then one usufruct of the ownership, and no more, is detracted from it.

The lord of a manor claiming such profit *à prendre* out of the shore, might be considered in the same situation, in regard to the King, his lord paramount, as a copyhold tenant is in regard to the lord of the waste of a manor; and therefore, it is conceived, the right to dig gravel, &c. may exist as privilege in the lord, without carrying the ownership of the soil, as well as in a copyholder or freeholder without carrying the soil. If, indeed, such right were *prescribed* for by the lord, as a profit *à prendre* in the shore, the title to the soil of the shore would seem to be excluded by the very terms; for the ownership of the land is more than a mere privilege, or usage, or profit *à prendre.*

<small>Embanking and its evidence of title to the shore.</small>

With regard to the acts of the lord of a manor, or other owner of the old adjoining *terra firma,* in "embanking" against the sea or a tide-river, and enjoying what is so inned, and making grants to do the same, it is impossible, it must be owned, to construe this into a mere profit *à prendre,* like the digging for gravel, &c., for it is a positive and exclusive entry upon and taking possession of the land. Where no *grant* to the lord exists, such an act is an "intrusion" upon the King's prima facie title; and looking at such act *per se,* it would seem singular to construe an intrusion upon *one* piece of another man's land into evidence of a right to seize upon other parts of it, and even into evidence of title to that which has not yet been, but is liable to be intruded upon. (*h*)

and Embanking giving Title to the Shore. 99

But, in point of fact, the question, in this case, would seem to be one of *boundaries*. The title to the adjacent *terra firma* being admitted to belong to the claimant, the inquiry is directed to the boundary-line sea-ward. Acts of ownership down to the low-water mark are admissible evidence to carry the boundary-line so far. The *law* has fixed the high-water mark as the boundary, unless the contrary be shewn ; but the contrary *may* be shewn.

for that purpose : R. *v.* Pagham Commissioners, 8 B. and C. 355. As to embankments on rivers, see R. *v.* Ward, 4 A. and E. 384 ; Menzies *v.* Breadalbane, 3 Wilson and Shaw 235, S. C. 3 Bligh N. S. 414 ; R. *v.* Trafford, 1 B. and Ad. 880, S. C. 8 Bingham 204 ; Angell on Tide Waters, p. 95. But no encroachments can be made on the property of the Crown or its grantee : Todd *v.* Dunlop, 2 Rob. Scot. app. cases 333 ; Smart *v.* Council of Dundee, 8 Bro. Par. cases 119. The Crown has a title to prevent, by application for interdict, any encroachment, by the proprietors of grounds adjoining the sea-shore, upon the enjoyment of the shore by the lieges for the purpose of passage or relaxation. A proprietor of ground, described by his title as being of a specified extent, and as bounded by the sea-shore, has no right to enclose that part of the shore, which is covered by the sea only in ordinary spring tides, over which the public has been from time immemorial in the habit of passing, and over which he cannot prove any past use or possession by himself. Smith *v.* Stair, Earl of, 6 Bell's, app. cases 487.

Where the Crown seeks to recover lands alleged to have been reclaimed from the sea by encroachment or purpresture, if the defendant disputes the Crown's title to the soil, between present high and low water mark, the Court will direct issues to try that right, before inquiring how far in former times the ancient high-water mark extended inland ; and this course will be adhered to, notwithstanding the hardship it may impose upon the defendant, who, by admitting the soil, on which he has done acts of ownership, to be part of the foreshore, will in effect have proved the case of the Crown, in the event of his failing to satisfy a jury, that a grant must be presumed. Att.-Gen. *v.* Chamberlaine, 4 K. and J. 292. But if the defendant admits the Crown's title to the soil, between present high and low water mark, then, upon an inquiry what is the boundary of the foreshore, the onus would be thrown upon the Crown, of showing that the high-water mark in former times extended further inland than at present. Ibid. ; see also Lord Westbury's remarks in Bicket *v.* Morris, 1 L. R., H. L., Scot. 60 ; Att.-Gen. *v.* Lonsdale, Earl of, 7 L. R.

Thus if a series of "intakings," by the lord of the manor and his predecessors, or their grantees, should be proved, and although anciently and frequently exercised and repeated, should have been uniformly acquiesced in by the crown; and such intakings and grants should be regularly entered upon the court rolls of the manor (accompanied by the jurisdiction of "presentment and punishment of *purprestures*," (*i*) *i. e.* of inclosures attempted by others), a presumption is said to arise in favour of the lord's title to the *whole* shore, down to *low-water* mark, in proportion as these evidences are numerous, extensive, and unequivocal. These acts assert and involve the whole *seizin* and ownership, and not one profit only, like sand-digging. A presumption, therefore, if made at all, must confer a title akin to that involved or assumed by the acts on which it is raised. The *seizin* of the rest of the shore shall, it is said, be *presumed* from the repeated seizin taken of specific parts, so as to carry the boundary-line from that which bounds the *terra firma*, to that which bounds the *shore*. In such case, it is not the lapse of time which raises the presumption, but the acts of the party, and the acquiescence of the *prima facie* owner.

It might, perhaps, be thought that these "intakings" should be left to their own limits, and to stand or fall by their several titles, without adding the whole shore to them. For the principle which dictates these kind of presumptions is, the quieting possessions,—a principle not very applicable to the case in question, where a large extent of shore, never

(*i*) Query, whether the proof of jurisdiction to present and punish purprestures on the shore, in the Lord's Court, may not be deemed very decisive evidence of ownership of the shore. Purprestures are unlawful inclosures, and the right to put down and punish them seems strong evidence of ownership in the *locus in quo*. [See Calmady *v.*

yet reduced to possession, but daily under the dominion of the sea, is thus presumed to belong to *him* who has neither possession nor grant to plead. But it appears, that this kind of evidence in regard to boundaries is admitted in some cases of *inland* title, as well as in titles to the sea-shore.

The case of Hollis *v.* Goldfinch (*k*) turns partly upon this point. It was there contended, that certain acts of ownership exercised by proprietors of canal shares on *other* parts of the bank of the canal, were evidence of ownership of a particular spot in question. The Court, indeed, there held, that the plaintiff was *not* " at liberty to go into evidence " of the exercise of acts of ownership on *other* parts of the " bank, but ought to have been confined to evidence of acts " done on the *particular spot in question.*" See also Tyrwhitt *v.* Wynn, 2 B. and Ald. 554. But Mr. Justice Bayley's comment, in Hollis *v.* Goldfinch, on another case (Stanley *v.* White, 14 East, 332), would seem to draw a distinction as to the cases in which such evidence *aliunde* shall or shall not be admitted. " In all those cases," observes the learned Judge (Bayley), " where evidence of acts done in one spot " have been held admissible, in order to show a right in " another spot, a reasonable probability has been previously " made out, that the whole land had been formerly in one " owner, and had been all subject to one and the same " burden. The decided cases proceed on the ground of " *unity of ownership or character* between the spot in ques-" tion, and other places with respect to which the acts of " ownership given in evidence are adduced. Now, in the " present case, there was no such unity of ownership or " character established, *for the acts of ownership* are exer-

"cised *on different parts of a bank of a new cut which, in
" all probability, passed through the lands of many different
" persons.*" Mr. Justice Best also said, " The question be-
" tween the parties in this case was, to whom the right of
" soil in the bank belonged? Now how was that question
" to be decided? In the first place by title deeds, which
" must clearly relate to the *locus in quo,* or no inference
" whatever can be drawn from them. If title deeds cannot
" be produced, the next best evidence is possession; but
" then it will be the possession of the *locus in quo.* In this
" case there was no evidence of possession. The only other
" evidence must be acts of ownership: (*l*) now acts of owner-
" ship can only prove that which would be better proved
" by title deeds or possession. Acts of ownership when
" submitted to, are analogous to admissions or declarations
" by the party submitting to them, that the party exer-
" cising them has a right so to do, and that he is therefore
" the owner of the property upon which they are exercised.
" The declaration of A, who is in possession of land, that
" B is the owner of that land, is evidence in favour of B,
" and against A, as to that particular portion of land; but
" it is no evidence that B is the owner of the adjoining
" land, which is occupied by another person, unless, in-
" deed, A and the holders of the adjoining land all held
" by one and the same title. Generally speaking, there-
" fore, acts of ownership submitted to by the holder of one
" portion of land cannot be any evidence that the person
" exercising them has any right to the adjoining land. Be-

(*l*) *i.e.* Acts of ownership manifesting the animus possidendi, of the *locus* itself, and not a mere *animus* of taking or using some one *particular* profit, or easement. Actu externo opus est, unde *occupatio* potest intelligi. Seld. Mar. Clau. lib. 2, c. 2.—" Usus" et " occupatio" are not the same, as profits *à prendre* show ;—the " usus," if it have the import of " occupatio" or " possessio," must imply the usufruct in

"sides, one landholder might, from goodnature or other causes, permit acts which others would refuse; or he might lose his rights by negligence. It would be extremely hard, therefore, to construe the implied acknowledgment, arising from acts of ownership exercised over the lands of A, to be received as evidence of an acknowledgment of a similar right over the land of B, who has never submitted to any acts of the kind."(*m*) The above doctrine of the learned Judge (Bayley) seems to apply strongly to the acts of ownership alluded to in the shore of a manor; and it may be concluded that embankments, and intakings of portions of the shore, immemorially, repeatedly, and uninterruptedly exercised by the lord, or his grantees, will establish a presumption in favour of the lord, against the Crown. But it is not to be forgotten, that as the King's grants are always construed strictly, so presumptions of this kind are only to be admitted against the Crown on strong evidence, more especially in a case in which public utility sides with the Crown, as, indeed, is always assumed. (*n*)

The King's grants construed stricto jure.

If what has been urged be well founded, the conclusion to be drawn is,—that neither a fishery, nor a right to wreck, nor the franchise of royal fish, nor, *perhaps*, the usage or custom of digging of sea-weed, shells, or sand, ought to support a claim to the actual freehold and ownership of the soil of any tract of sea, or sea-shore, bounding a manor,—so long as it retains the character of sea-shore,—where presumption arising from the more decisive acts of ownership of intaking and granting the soil itself, and the presentment and punishment of purprestures are wanting. All

Conclusion that none of the beforementioned franchises or uses of the shore will give title to the soil.

(*m*) See Stanley *v.* White, 14 East. 332 ; Barnes *v.* Mawson, 1 Maule and Selw. 77 ; Child *v.* Winwood, 1 Taunt. 208.

(*n*) [Rex *v.* 49 casks of Brandy, 3 Hag. Adm. R. 271 ; see also ante, p. 20 ; and Forsyth's Constitutional Law, p. 175, et ante, pp. 21 (note), 65, and post 106.]

such *franchises* and *liberties* are distinct from the ownership of the soil, both in essence, in title, and in technical character; and the enjoyment of such rights does not, by any *necessary* presumption, involve the seizin and ownership of the soil in which they are exercised. And if this be not the case, between subject and subject, *a fortiori* it ought not to be against the King's ownership and title.

It may be here also noted, that Lord Hale himself, in one part of his work (see De Jure Maris, Appendix, post, xxix.), lays it down as law, that *custom* "cannot entitle the subject to *relicted* lands, or make such lands part of a manor." If so, it may, perhaps, be reasonably contended, that the enjoyment of mere customary privileges in the shore cannot " entitle the subject to the lands of such shore, or make " such lands part of the manor."(o)

Neither would there seem to be better ground in point of policy than at law for thus taking, by means of presumption alone, the ownership of the sea-shore from the King, and transferring it to individuals, whose private gains and petty profits may create frequent public inconvenience and illiberal extortion. In a commercial country, such as England, the free and unrestricted use of the sea-shore is of national importance, and no encouragement ought to be given to claims which have a tendency materially to interfere with the national welfare, and they ought therefore to be treated *stricto jure*.

It is well known, that by the Roman law the sea-shore was common to all, and incapable of ownership, even in the Emperor. "Littorum quoque usus publicus jure gentium " est, sicut ipsius maris ;—*proprietas* autem eorum potest " intelligi *nullius* esse; sed ejusdem juris esse cujus et

---

(o) [See Att.-Gen. *v.* Turner, 2 Mod. 107; Att.-Gen. *v.* Farmen, 2 Lev. 171; Callis, 48, 53.]

on the Ownership of the Shore.

"mare, et quæ subjacent mari, terra vel arena." (*p*) So also, Grotius (*q*) holds, that a man cannot have any property in the shores and sands of the sea ; these are all incapable of improvement, and can only be exhausted by the only uses to which they can be applied ; viz. of supplying fish and sand. And even our own early law writers did not hesitate to hold *nearly* the same doctrine as part of our own law. "Naturali vero jure," says Bracton, (*r*) "communia sunt "omnia hæc,—aqua profluens, aer et *mare*, et *littora* maris, "quasi maris accessoria. Nemo enim ad littora maris "accedere prohibetur, dum tamen a villis et ædificiis "abstineat, quia littora sunt de jure gentium communia, "sicut et mare." But he does not add the remainder of the sentence from the civil law, viz. "proprietas autem eorum potest intelligi nullius esse,"—by which it may be inferred, that he did not mean to deny that the "*ownership*" (such as it was) rested with the King, asserting only that the "*usus*" was common to all, as that of the sea was ;—and so far he will be found essentially right ;—for the uses to which the sea is applicable, and also common to all, are "navigation" and "fishing,"—and for these uses the shore is acknowledged to be equally applicable and common. Other common uses of the shore have been of late claimed on behalf of the public, viz. for the purpose of bathing in the sea, (*s*) and for digging and carrying away sand, shells, stones, and weed, for agricultural and building purposes. (*t*) The value and utility of these rights to the public, entitle them to the fullest consideration before the law is to be deemed settled *against* these enjoyments.

Bracton's doctrine.

(*p*) Inst. Lib. 2 tit. 1 sect. 5, lib. ii. sect. 2, c. 3.
(*q*) Grot. de Jur. Bell. ac. Pac. (*r*) Bracton, lib. ii. fol. 7, sect. 5.
(*s*) Blundell *v.* Catterall, 5 B. and Ald. 268.
(*t*) Bagott *v.* Orr, 2 Bos and Pul. 472. See these cases fully considered hereafter.

It might seem most desirable that the shore should remain vested in the King, whose policy it would be to leave it open to his subjects for useful purposes, and to be, as it were, the trustee thereof for the public use and benefit.(*u*)

Alienation of Crown lands prohibited. There was a time when the Crown could grant away to the subject the royal demesnes and landed possessions at pleasure ; but now, by statute law, (*x*) such royal grants are prohibited, and the Crown lands cannot be so aliened. So much, therefore, of the sea-shore as has not been actually aliened by grant, and bestowed on lords of manors and other subjects, still remains vested in the Crown, incapable of alienation. A King of England cannot be insensible of the value of this property, for it concerns, through him, the public advantage; and it is not going too far to say that the Crown ought, upon all occasions, to evince great jealousy in the preservation of this right against the encroachments of particular individuals, and to require the strictest proof of their exclusive ownerships, whensoever claimed. The law itself protects the property of the Crown with greater jealousy and strictness than the property of the subject. The rule, as before stated, being that the King's grants shall be construed *strictly*, and with a leaning in his favour as against the grantee ; (*y*) but that, as between subject and subject, the grant shall be construed most in favour of the grantee and against the grantor. But to support a title to the sea-shore in favour of the subject

(*u*) [See remarks on case of Dickens *v*. Shaw, post.]
(*x*) [1 Anne, ch. 7, sec. 5. Ruff ed. See Doe, d. R. *v*. York, Arch-

against the Crown, upon "presumption" drawn from the enjoyment of a prescriptive right,—is to open a wide door to individual claims against Crown lands. The King's right is a *jus publicum*, and it is not the rule of our Courts of Justice to assert or favour the *jus privatum* against the *jus publicum*; on the contrary, the *jus privatum* is to be tried *strictissimo jure*, whenever it offends or may offend against the public good or public rights. (*z*)

An express grant of so much sea-shore from the King, made at a time when such grants were not prohibited by statute law, cannot, of course, be set aside. But, as the other lands of the Crown cannot be taken from the Crown by a claim or presumption founded on prescription, and the sea-shore is as much land of the Crown as any other land in its possession,—there seems to be no better ground for admitting mere prescription to prevail in the one case than in the other; nor has a single case or decision presented itself wherein the learned writer of the treatise so much referred to has been confirmed in his doctrine, that a title to a prescriptive franchise, liberty, or easement, derivable from the sea or sea-shore, will, by presumption or construction of law, support a title to land; nor can it possibly do so, if the doctrine quoted in a former page (*a*) be law, viz. that prescription alone cannot give title to lands, because of lands more certain evidence of title may be had; viz. by grant;—or by adverse possession during the period prescribed by the statutes of limitation.

But although it may be deemed an object of no small importance to protect the right of the Crown to the seashore, against the encroachments of individuals; yet, where a claim is made on behalf of the *public*, and the King's

---

(*z*) [See remarks on the case of Dickens *v.* Shaw, post.]
(*a*) P. 22, ante.

right is opposed to the general right of the subject, the Courts of Law, which favour liberty, and have an anxious regard for public rights, and presume the King himself to be personally interested in the public good, will protect the claims of the public to the utmost verge of the law.(*b*) The *ownership* of the shore, as between the public and the King, has been settled in favour of the King; but, as before observed, this ownership is, and has been immemorially, liable to certain general rights of egress and regress, for fishing, trading, and other uses claimed and used by his subjects. These rights are variously modified, promoted, or restrained by the common law, and by numerous acts of parliament relating to the fisheries, the revenues, and the public safety, but a statement of which is not within the limited scope of our subject.

As to derelict and alluvion.

Let us now proceed to inquire how the law stands with regard to tracts of dry land adjoining the shore which are deserted by the sea, and become *terra firma* by new formation, and usually are interposed between the old *terra firma* and the ordinary high-water mark of the shore. It is for the most part barren and waste, but in some places (particularly in low and marshy districts) capable of pasturage and cultivation. This soil embraces not only that which is always dry, but that also which is subject to high spring tides and extraordinary inundations. It is all deemed land gained from the sea. (*c*)

Land gained from the sea is of three kinds:

1st. Per alluvionem, alluvion, or land washed up by the sea.

2nd. Per relictionem, derelict land, or land left dry by the shrinking or retirement of the sea.

(*b*) [See Dickens *v.* Shaw, Appendix, post, lxiv.]
(*c*) De Jure Maris, ch. iv. sec. 2; Appendix, post, xi. and ch. vi.;

3rd. Per insulæ productionem, *i.e.* islands and islets gradually or suddenly formed out of the sea, or at the mouths of rivers, &c. (*d*)

The law on this part of the subject is laid down by Blackstone, (*e*) in these words: "As to lands gained from " the sea either by *alluvion, i. e.* by the washing up of sand " or earth, so as in time to make *terra firma;* or by *derelic-* " *tion*, as when the sea shrinks back below the usual water   Alluvion.

(*d*) De Jure Maris, Appendix, post, xiv. xxxv. ; Callis, 43.
(*e*) 2 Black. Com. 261. [In Att.-Gen. *v.* Chambers, 4 De G. and J. 55, Lord Chelmsford, referring to the passage in Blackstone, says, " I am not quite satisfied that the principle 'de minimis non curat lex' " is the correct explanation of the rule on this subject; because, al- " though the additions may be small and insignificant in their progress, " yet, after a lapse of time, by little and little a very large increase may " have taken place which it would not be beneath the law to notice ; " and of which if the party who has the right to it can clearly show that " it formerly belonged to him, he ought not to be deprived. I am " rather disposed to adopt the reason assigned for the rule by Baron " Alderson, in the case of the Hull and Selby Railway Company, 5 M. " and W. 327,—viz. 'That which cannot be perceived in its progress is " taken to be as if it never had existed at all ;' and, as Lord Abinger " said, in the same case, 'The principle,' as to gradual accretion, 'is " 'founded on the necessity which exists for some such rule of law for " 'the permanent protection and adjustment of property. It must be " ' always borne in mind that the owner of lands does not derive benefit " ' alone, but may suffer loss from the operation of this rule ; for if the " ' sea gradually steals upon the land, he loses so much of his property, " ' which is thus silently transferred by the law to the proprietor of the " ' sea-shore.' If this be the true ground of the rule, it seems difficult " to understand why similar effects, produced by a party's lawful use " of his own land, should be subject to a different law ; and still more " so if these effects are the result of operations upon neighbouring lands " of another proprietor : whatever may be the nature and character of " these operations, they ought not to affect a rule which applies to a re- " sult and not to the manner of its production. Of course, an exception " must always be made of cases when the operations upon the party's " own land are not only calculated, but can be shown to have been in- " tended, to produce this gradual acquisition of the sea-shore, however " difficult such proof of intention may be." See Rex *v.* Lord Yarborough, 2 Bligh. N. R. 162 ; Emans *v.* Turnbull, 2 John's (N.Y.)

As to Alluvion

"mark, in these cases the law is held to be, that if this "gain be by little and little, by small and *imperceptible* "degrees, it shall go to the owner of the land adjoining, for "'de minimis non curat lex;' but if the alluvion or dere- "liction be sudden and considerable, the land shall go to "the King, as lord of the sea." His authorities are, Bracton, lib. ii. c. 2; Callis on Sewers, 48, 53; 2 Roll. Abr. 170; Dy. 326. (*f*)

The words of Bracton are,(*g*) "Item quod per alluvionem "agro tuo flumen adjecit, jure gentium tibi acquiritur. Est "autem alluvio latens incrementum, et per alluvionem adjici "dicitur, quod ita paulatim adjicitur, quod intelligere non "possis quo momento temporis adjiciatur, &c. si autem non "sit latens incrementum, contrarium erit." Lord Hale (*h*) observes upon these words, "Bracton follows the civil law "in this and some other following places; and yet, even "according to this, the common law doth regularly hold at "this day between party and party." And he further observes: "This jus alluvionis is, de jure communi, by the "law of England, the King's; viz. if by any marks or "measures it can be known what is so gained, and if the "gain be so insensible and indiscernible by any limits or "marks, that it cannot be known, idem est non esse et non "apparere, as well in maritime increases as in the increases "by inland rivers." (*i*)

(*f*) And see note to Dyer, 326; [and American Case Municipality No. 2 *v.* Orleans Cotton Press, 18 Louis R. 122.]

(*g*) Lib. ii. ch. 2. (*h*) Appendix, post, xxvi.

(*i*) [In the Att.-Gen. *v.* Chambers, *supra*, Lord Chelmsford, after quoting this passage, said : " Lord Hale clearly limits the law of gradual "accretions to the cases where the boundaries of the sea-shore and "adjoining land are so undistinguishable, that it is impossible to dis- "cover the slow and gradual changes which are from time to time "accruing, and where, at the end of a long period, it is evident that

and Derelict Land.

Although the doctrine is laid down by Bracton and Lord Hale upon the word "*alluvio*," yet there is no doubt that Blackstone is right in applying it also to gradual and imperceptible *derelictions* of the waters ; in both cases the owner of the soil adjoining is entitled by common law, for the reasons given by these writers; viz. "de minimis non curat lex,"—"idem est non esse et non apparere;" and because it is in compensation for land either actually or in danger of being lost. (*k*) Blackstone (*l*) says, that the soil so gained by the owner extends to "the USUAL water mark;" he does not explain what is the usual water mark, whether the high or low water mark; but from what is already said, it is clear that the *usual* water mark is the high-water mark.(*m*)

<small>Belong to the owner of the adjacent land</small>

" line, cannot be determined. But where the limits are clear and
" defined, and the exact space between these limits and the new high-
" water line can be clearly shown, although from day to day, or even from
" week to week, the progress of the accretion is not discernible, why
" should a rule be applied which is grounded upon a reason which has
" no existence in the particular case?" See also Stewart *v*. Greenock Harbour Trustees, 4 Scot. Session Cases, 283, 3rd series.]

(*k*) Callis, 48.   (*l*) Black. vol. 2, p. 261.
(*m*) P. 9, ante et seq.

[The materials accumulated from mining or manufacturing operations upon lands bordering the sea, or upon a public river, where there has been a gradual silting up of rubbish, slate, or other material, either upon the lands where the mines or manufactories are situated, or upon the neighbouring property, would seem to be subject to the ordinary rule, for the title to alluvion arising from artificial causes does not differ, as to the rights of the landowners, from the title to alluvion arising from natural causes, where the artificial causes arise from a fair use of the land adjoining the sea-shore, and not from acts done

As to what Ownership of the adjoining

What ownership of the adjacent land entitles to the alluvion, &c.

Now, the owner here intended is the absolute owner of *freehold;* it cannot mean a *leaseholder* or *copyholder*, for these are not looked upon by the law in the light of land-*owners*. If, therefore, the lord of the adjoining manor claim at all, he must claim in respect of his freehold, and he has the freehold,—

1st. Of the demesnes; *i.e.* the freehold lands in his own occupation.

2nd. Of the copyhold tenements; *i.e.* subject to the copyholder's interest.

3rd. Of the waste: *i.e.* subject to the tenant's right of commonage, &c.

And by consequence, if either the demesnes, the copyhold, or waste, constitute the land immediately adjoining, the lord, as freeholder, will be entitled to the alluvion soil on the coast, as far as high-water mark. By the same rule, any owner of the *freehold* of the land immediately adjoining to and in boundary limited by the sea, will be entitled as far as high-water mark; and if the lord of the manor part with his freehold to another, in any spot of land adjoining to the coast, such person, it is conceived, acquires all "alluvion," properly so called, from the sea.

As to the demesnes, or lands in the lord's own hands, viz. which are neither copyhold nor waste, such land being his own absolute freehold, clearly entitles him to the adjoining alluvial land gained gradually and imperceptibly

---

United States, 10 Peters, 717; Banks *v.* Ogden, 2 Wallace, 67; Saulet *v.* Sheperd, 4 Wallace, 502; Murray *v.* Sermon, 1 Hawks, N. C. Rep. 56; Adams *v.* Frothingham, 3 Mass. R. 352; Angell on Watercourses, 6th ed. p. 52; On Tide Waters, 249; Phear, 43; Houck, 147.

[And, on the other hand, if the sea, or an arm of the sea, by gradual and imperceptible progress, encroach upon the land of a subject, the

from the sea, as part of such demesnes; and on this point no more need be said. But his freehold title in the copyhold tenements, and in the wastes, is subject to certain rights and interests, which require further consideration; and it may be contended,

As to the nature of the interest the lord of a manor gains in alluvion which attached to a copyhold tenement,

1st. That if the adjoining land be a copyhold tenement, and its boundary is no otherwise limited than by the sea, then the copyholder acquires the same right to the alluvion as he had in the copyhold adjoining, and may claim to hold such new soil as copyhold, and part of his old tenement; and,

and the copyholder's interest therein.

2nd. That if the adjoining land be *waste* land of the manor, then all the copyholders have the same rights of common, &c. in the alluvion or new soil, that they had in such waste land adjoining, and as if it were part of such waste.

As to the right of the tenants, where such alluvion is part of the wastes.

As to the first point, viz. the copyholder's right, it must be very much a question depending upon the description of the "tenement" in the court rolls of the manor. If the tenement, to which the copyholder has been admitted, extend, either expressly or by fair implication, to the sea, or expressly or by implication to high-water mark, then it may be contended that the new alluvial soil is part of the copyhold tenement adjoining; but if the boundary of the tenement be fixed, on the side of the sea, to a particular demarcation, *other* than that made by the water mark for the time being, and short of it, then all beyond that line of demarcation is clearly no part of his tenement, and must either be part of the demesnes or of the waste.

As to the copyholder's right in respect of his tenement.

If the lord set up a claim to the alluvion against the copyholder, when the adjoining land is copyhold, it must be in respect of his interest in the land adjoining, which is a *freehold* interest, subject to a *copyhold* interest. He cannot claim it as part of his own private demesnes, be-

As to the lord's right as opposed to the copyholder's.

cause he cannot show the adjoining land to be such, it being copyhold; nor can he claim it as part of the waste, because the adjoining land is copyhold, and not waste land.

As to the lord's claim when the alluvion is waste.

Next, suppose him to claim the alluvion as part of the adjoining waste, by the same reasoning as last used, the new soil being adjacent to the waste, is part of it, and subject to all the rights claimable in or out of the old waste, and by consequence to the local customs, commons, &c. (if any) alleged or prescribed for by the tenants in respect of such waste.

Having stated, that in regard to the new alluvial soil gradually heaped up and deposited at and above the edge of high-water mark, the lord, if possessed absolutely of the adjoining land, is entitled to such new soil, absolutely; but if only of the freehold of the copyhold tenement, then subject to such copyhold interest; and if only of the wastes, then subject to the customary rights of the tenants for commonage, &c. in such waste.—It may be further observed, that land gradually and *imperceptibly* left " PER RECESSUM MARIS" is subject to the same kind of claim, both in respect of the person, the form, and the substance, as the *alluvion* or soil heaped up "PER PROJECTIONEM MARIS," and may, in like manner, assume the character of freehold demesnes, copyhold, or waste, according to the nature of the soil adjacent. (*n*)

The same doctrine as to land imperceptibly derelict.

The gradual and insensible *retreat* of the sea is, however, generally *the effect of its own action by the heaping up of alluvial soil, beach, or sand;* and the land thus acquired may rather be said to have been gained per alluvionem or projectionem, than per recessum or relictionem maris. Thus it is observed by Lord Hale, that "there is no alluvion without some kind of reliction, for the sea shuts out itself."

The gradual retreat of the sea, generally the effect of alluvion, and more properly so called.

Lakes and Marshes gained from the Sea.

When, therefore we speak of land acquired "*per alluvionem,*" we may be understood to mean all *imperceptible* additions made by the sea to the adjacent soil; and when we speak of "*derelict*" land, we intend thereby land suddenly, and by *evident marks and bounds*, left and become dry land. There may indeed be some cases wherein it is matter of doubt whether the acquest ought to be deemed insensible and gradual, or sudden and manifest. Such cases must be left to the common sense and judgment of the jury, and the nature of the evidence, always remembering *prima facie* and *jure communi*, the land gained is the King's, since it was clearly his so long as it remained seabottom, and it is only *not* given to him, in the case in question, because of the difficulty of drawing the line, and the unwillingness of the common law (in respect of its own dignity and the liberty of the subject) to be too nice in trifles, " de minimis non curat lex."

In marshy districts, however, a case might occur of some nicety; viz. where the sea gradually heaps up a bar to itself across a marshy arm or inlet of the sea; the communication between the sea and the inlet becoming gradually less, until at last the entrance is quite blocked up, and the inlet becomes a lake or pond, which also is capable of being drained, or gradually drains itself. Such an acquest from the sea may sometimes be of considerable extent and value. Now, if the lord of the adjoining manor can establish no title to the soil, as and when it was covered with water, the only question will be, whether it is a gradual and insensible or sudden and distinct acquest from the sea. On the part of the King it may be insisted that, until the sea was finally shut out, so much, at least, as was "aqua cooperta," continued part of the sea-bottom, and *as such* belonged to the King; and, consequently, that until the hour that the

[margin notes: The word "derelict" is import sudden and perceptible gains from the sea. Whether imperceptible or not must be left to the jury. Large acquests from the sea in marshy districts, by gradual exclusion of the sea, forming marshes, lakes, ponds, &c. As to the King's right therein.]

or storm, all the land covered with water was the King's; that the final exclusion of the sea was not a gradual but sudden effect, and that immediately thereupon the lake and its soil became, to the then edge of the still water, the King's own, and relieved from the common law rights of fishing, &c. That all subsequent diminution of the water by evaporation and drainage, natural or artificial, was for the benefit of the King, whether such drainage be gradual and imperceptible or not. It may also be insisted, that it is not the gradual or slow operation of nature in point of *time*, but the small and *imperceptible* nature of the daily addition of *soil* which governs the title in favour of the subject; and consequently, where the acquisition is not of that character, the reason for the rule against the King's right does not exist; and these, it is considered, are the grounds which would decide the case in favour of the Crown.

On the side of the owner of the adjoining soil, it may, however, be urged, that at least so much of the dry soil as had been added to his adjacent land, by the gradual and insensible decrease of the water, from the gradual closing of the communication with the sea and decrease of tide, becomes *de die in diem* his own "jure alluvionis," and that the King's claim can extend no farther than to that portion which is proved to have been subject to the tide at the time of the final exclusion of the sea. It may also be urged, with some plausibility, that the lake or pond which remains after the sea has shut out itself by a bar,—has become, in the eye of the law, "land,"—*i.e. in*-land, aqua cooperta; and that its gradual formation into a still water lake or pond, was tantamount to a gradual dereliction of so much land, *i.e.* an imperceptible addition, from time to time, of so much lake or pond of still water; and inasmuch as a lake

struction of law, so *this*, having become imperceptibly surrounded by land, and cut off from the sea by its own action, has imperceptibly become so much additional soil to the adjacent old terra firma. But the answer to this is, that so long as any communication continues open with the sea and its tides, the whole soil which the water covers must have the same character in point of title, and be treated as "pars maris." Such peculiar cases as these must depend on the circumstances in evidence, and upon the point "an graduatim an non?" A question determinable only by evidence, and the judgment and common sense of the Judge and Jury. The inquiry is a question at common law, between the King and the subject, on a matter of *fact;* the law being already well known and established, and as the fact may be found, the land will be disposed of by the law; viz. if it be a gradual and imperceptible acquest, to the subject; if otherwise, then to the King. The evidence on both sides will be deduced from eyesight and hearsay testimony, natural or artificial land marks, perambulations, records, and written documents, tending to show whether the events and alterations which have happened are of a nature to be rightly deemed sudden and distinct, or gradual and too minute to be distinguished by ordinary observation.

It is not, indeed, either the *sudden* or the *gradual* nature of the *event* which governs the law, but the *perceptible* or *imperceptible* nature of the *acquisition;* and therefore the direction of the evidence will be to show the greater or less degree of distinctness and certainty with which the *quantum* of soil claimed can be ascertained to have accrued within time of memory. Whatever reason and common sense denominates imperceptible and indefinable, or which, even if perceptible and definable, is still too minute and value-

It is not the gradual laps of the time, but the imp ceptible nat of the addition, which favours the subject.

ship, will be deemed part of the adjoining soil, and, as it were, to have grown out of it. In all other cases the King's right will attach. (*o*)

Lord Hale observes, that *custom* may, in the case of alluvion, "give the jus alluvionis to the land whereunto it accrues." (*p*) But if the *jus alluvionis* be a general common law right, it does not appear how it can be given by "custom," unless the word be used in the sense of the "general custom of the realm," which is the common law. The following cases are quoted by him.

<small>Abbot of Ramsey's case.</small> "Communia (*q*) Trin. 43 E. 3, Rot. 13, in Scaccario, which is that very record which is cited by Dyer, 326, out of the book of Ramsey. Process went out against the Abbot of Ramsey, ad ostendendam causam, quare 60 acræ marisci in manum Regis non debent sesiri, quas Abbas appropriavit sibi et domui suæ, sine licentia Regis, super quodam generali commissione de terris a Rege concelatis et detentis. Abbas respondit, quod ipse tenet manerium de Brancaster, quod *scituatur* est juxta mare, et quod est ibidem quidam mariscus, qui aliquando per influxus maris minoratur, aliquando per defluxus maris augetur, absque hoc quòd appropriavit sibi prout per præsentationem prædictam supponitur. And issue joined, and verdict given for the Abbot, by Nisi Prius, before one of the Barons. "Et judicium, quòd eat sine die, salvo semper jure Regis." The learned writer hereupon subjoins, "though there were "a verdict upon the issue, whether appropriavit an non, "yet it is plain that the title stood upon that which the "Abbot alleged by way of increment. And note, here is "*no custom* at all alleged; but it seems he relied upon the "*common right* of his case, as that he suffered the loss, so he

(*o*) [See Houck, 154, et seq.]   (*p*) Appendix, post, xxvi.

"should enjoy the benefit, *even by the bare common law*, in
"case of alluvion." (*r*)

The next case is stated, by Lord Hale, as follows:— Abbot of Peterboro's case.
"M. 23, E. 3, B. R. Rot. 26. Lincolnia. The Abbot of Peter-
"borough (*s*) was questioned at the King's suit for acquiring
"30 acras marisci in Gostrerkill, licentiâ Regis non obtentâ.
"The Abbot pleaded, quòd per *consuetudinem patriæ* est,
"et à tempore quo, &c., extitit usurpatum, quòd omnes et
"singuli domini, maneria terras seu tenementa super cos-
"teram maris habentes, particulariter habebunt marettum
"et sabulonem, per fluxus et refluxus maris, secundùm
"majus et minus, prope tenementa sua projecta. Et dicit,
"quòd ipse habet quoddam manerium in eâdem villâ, unde
"plures terræ sunt adjacentes costeræ maris, et sic habet
"per fluxus et refluxus maris circiter 300 acras maretti
"terras suas adjacentes, et per temporis incrementum se-
"cundùm *patriæ consuetudinem;* et absque hoc quòd ipse
"perquisivit, &c. And upon issue joined it depended many
"years before the issue was tried. But afterwards, P. 41.
"E. 3, B. R. Rot. 28, Lincolnia, Rex, viz. given, quòd se-
"cundùm consuetudinem *patriæ*, domini maneriorum prope
"mare adjacentium habebunt *marettum* et *sabulonem* per
"fluxus et refluxus maris per *temporis incrementum* ad
"terras suas costeræ adjacentes projecta, &c. Ideo Abbas
"sine die." Lord Hale then proceeds to observe, "1st.
"Here is *custom* laid, and he relies not barely upon the
"case without it. 2d. In this case it was per incrementum
"temporis et per mare projecta. It is not a sudden relic-
"tion or recessus maris. And though there is no alluvio
"without some kind of reliction, for the sea shuts out itself,

(*r*) [See Woolrych, p. 445; Jerwood, 56. *Re* Hull and Selby Railway, 5 M. and W. 331.]
(*s*) Abbot of Peterborough's case, Appendix, post, xxvi. [See also,

" yet the denomination is taken from that which predomi-
" nates. It is an acquest per projectionem, not per reces-
" sum or relictionem. 3d. That such an acquisition lies in
" *custom and prescription*, and it hath a reasonable intend-
" ment, because these secret and gradual increases of the
" land adjoining cedunt solo tanquam majus principali; and
" so by custom it becomes a perquisite to the land, as it
" does in all cases of this nature by the civil law."

It must be concluded that the "consuetudinem patriæ" is to be interpreted "the custom of the realm," which is the common law. It does not appear how a local custom of this kind can exist, as contradistinguished from the common right; for, by common right, imperceptible alluvions or derelictions belong to the owner of the adjacent freehold, throughout the coasts of England.

The words "secundum majus et minus," and "incrementum temporis," put this case upon precisely the same ground as the former one. All other writers agree that such a right as the one claimed and established in both these cases, is a common law right, and if so, it cannot correctly be pleaded as a local custom; and at this day, beyond doubt, it is quite enough to rely *barely* upon the common law, acting upon the evidence of the gradual and insensible acquisition. The foregoing doctrine regarding "alluvion" was very fully argued and considered in the recent case of the King v. Lord Yarborough.(*t*)

The King v. Lord Yarborough.

This was a record transmitted from the petty bag office into the Court of King's Bench, which sets forth an inquisition taken at *Cleathorps*, in the county of *Lincoln*, on the 12th day of *November*, 1818, by which, amongst other things, it was found that there is a certain piece of land,

(*t*) 3 B. and C. 91 [in error 2 Bligh, N. S. 147, S. C. 5 Bing. 163. See

and land Derelict.

being salt marsh, lying near or adjoining to the parish or lordship of *North Cotes*, in the said county, which piece of land is bounded towards the south and south-west by the sea-wall or sea-bank of the said lordship of *North Cotes*, and towards the north-west by part of the sea-wall or sea-bank of certain lands in the lordship of *Titney*, and on all other parts by the sea, and contain by estimation 453 acres or thereabouts, and is of the annual value of 4s. an acre, and was in times past covered with the water of the sea, but is now and has been for several years past by the sea *left*, and is not covered with water, except at *high* tides, when the sea doth flow to the said sea-walls or sea-banks; which said piece of land, from the time of such *dereliction*, hitherto has been and still is unoccupied, but the herbage thereof has been from time to time eaten and consumed by the cattle and sheep belonging to divers tenants or occupiers of lands situate within the said parish of *North Cotes*. And the inquisition then stated, that the said piece of land, together with other lands therein specified, the commissioners had taken and caused to be seized into the hands of our said lord the King. To this inquisition the defendant filed a traverse, which (after craving oyer of the commissioners' return and inquisition, and admitting the boundaries, quantity, and value of the land in question, and that the same piece of land is now and has been for several years past not covered with water, except at high tides, when the sea doth flow to the said sea-wall or sea-bank) states, that "from time whereof the memory of man " runneth not to the contrary, there hath been and still is " a certain manor called or known by the name of the " manor of *North Thoresby* cum *North Cotes*, situate in the " parish of *North Cotes* aforesaid, in the said county of " *Lincoln*, and that the defendant, long before the respec-

The King v.
Lord Yarborough.

"sition, to wit, on, &c., was seized in his demesne as of fee,
"of and in the manor of *North Thoresby* cum *North Cotes*,
"and the demesne lands thereof, and that the same piece
"of land heretofore, to wit, on the 1st day of January, 1300,
"and on divers other days and times between that day
"and the day of the finding the inquisition, by *the slow,*
"*gradual, and imperceptible projection, alluvion, subsidence,*
"*and accretion of ooze, soil, sand, and matter, being slowly,*
"*gradually, and by imperceptible increase in long time cast*
"*up, deposited, and settled by and from the flux and reflux of*
"*the tide and waves of the sea in, upon, and against the out-*
"*side and extremity of the demesne lands of the same manor,*
"hath been formed, and hath settled, grown, and accrued
"upon and against and unto the said demesne lands of the
"same manor, and the same and every portion thereof,
"when and as the same hath so there been formed, settled,
"grown, and accrued, hath thereupon and thereby at those
"times respectively in that behalf above mentioned, forth-
"with become and been, and from the same several times
"respectively have and hath continued to be, and still are
"and is part and parcel of the said demesne lands of the
"same manor, and the several owners and proprietors of
"the same manor for the time being during all the time
"aforesaid, until the time of the seizin of the defendant as
"aforesaid, and defendant, during the time he hath been
"so as aforesaid seized of and in the said manor, from the
"time of the formation and accretion of the same piece of
"land and every part thereof respectively, continually,
"until the time of the finding of the inquisition respectively,
"were and was seized in their and his demesne as of fee,
"of and in the same piece of land and every part thereof,
"when and as the same hath so been formed and accrued
"as aforesaid, as and for part and parcel of the demesne

and land Derelict.

" piece of land in the plea mentioned, and in the inquisition last above mentioned, or any part or parcel thereof, was or now is by the sea *left*, in the manner and form as in the inquisition is above supposed and found."—The replication of the Attorney General traversed part of the inducement to the defendant's traverse, as follows : " Without this, that the said piece of land in the inquisition lastly mentioned, being the piece of land before described, at the times in the said plea mentioned, by the slow, gradual, and imperceptible projection, alluvion, subsidence, and accretion of ooze, soil, sand, and other matter, being slowly, gradually, and by imperceptible increase in long time, cast up, deposited, and settled by and from the flux and reflux of the tide, and waves of the sea in, upon, and against the outside and extremity of the demesne land of the same manor, hath been formed, and hath settled, grown, and accrued upon and against and unto the said demesne lands of the same manor, in manner and form as the defendant hath above in his plea in that behalf alleged ;" and the defendant in his rejoinder took issue upon that fact.—The replication then took issue on the defendant's traverse, "that the said piece of land, in the plea of defendant mentioned, was and now is by the sea *left*, in manner and form as in the inquisition is above supposed and found ;" and thereupon also the defendant joined issue. These issues were tried at the then last assizes for the county of *Derby*, before *Park*, J., and a verdict found for the *defendant*. A rule *nisi* having been obtained to show cause why a new trial should not be had, the Court directed, at the time of showing cause against the rule, that the facts proved at the trial should be stated in a special case for the opinion of the Court, and that if judgment should be given for the King upon such case, the

The King v. Lord Yarborough.

a new trial had; and if judgment should be given for the defendant upon such case judgment should be entered for the defendant upon the verdict. The case was as follows:

The land in question consists of 450 acres of salt marsh called *fittees*, being the land covered with herbage, which, at the time of taking the inquisition set forth in the pleadings, lay between the sea-wall and the sea opposite to *North Cotes*, in the county of Lincoln. It was proved that this land had been formed in the course of time by means of ooze, warp, silt, sludge, and soil carried down by the *Humber*, and deposited and cast up by the flux and reflux of the sea, upon and against the adjacent land, whereby the land has been enlarged and increased, and the sea has receded. The matter thus deposited is at first soft and sludgy, but in the course of five or six years grows firm, and then produces herbage. With respect to the degree or rate of growth and increase of the land, the evidence produced on the part of the Crown was as follows:—The first witness proved that the sea had receded in parts 140 or 150 yards within twenty-six or twenty-seven years, and that within the last four years he could see that it had receded much in parts, but could not say how much; and in parts he believed that it had not receded at all. The alteration, he said, had been slow and gradual, and he could not perceive the growth as it went on, though he could see there had been an increase in twenty-six or twenty-seven years of 140 or 150 yards, and that it had certainly receded since he measured the land the year before. The second witness proved, that in fifteen years there had been an increase of the fittees on the outside of the sea-wall; in some parts from 100 to 150 yards; that it grows a little from year to year. That within the last five years there had been a

and land Derelict. 125

perceptible to the eye at the moment. The third witness said, there had been some small increase in every year; and the fourth witness said, the swarth increased every year very gradually, and that perhaps it had gathered a quarter of a mile in breadth in some places within his recollection, or during the last fifty-four or fifty-five years, and in some places it had gathered nothing. It was proved that the ground between the sea-wall above mentioned and another sea-wall still more remote from the sea, appeared to have been covered over with the sea formerly.

The judgment of the Court was delivered by Lord Tenterden, after the Court had heard Counsel and taken time to consider. "Upon this case the only question for the "judgment of the Court is, whether the evidence given at ". the trial was such as to justify the verdict of the jury upon "the issues joined. Whether the pleadings have been cor- "rectly framed on either side, or what may be the legal "consequence and effect of the verdict, supposing it to "stand, are points now before us. I notice this, because "some part of the argument at the bar was more properly "applicable to a matter of law upon admitted facts, than "to the question whether particular issues are maintained "by the evidence; or, in other words, whether particular "facts are found to exist. *Judgment of the Court.*

"The second issue upon the record arises upon a traverse "of the matter found by the inquisition. The matter thus "found is, that the land now claimed by the Crown was in "times past covered with the water of the sea, but is now, "and has been for several years *left* by the sea. Now, the "distinction between land derelict, or left by the sea, "acquiring a new character in consequence of the mere "subsidence and absence of the salt water, and land gained "by alluvion or projection of extraneous matter, whereby "the sea is excluded and prevented from overflowing it, is *Distinction between derelict land and alluvion.*

The King v. Lord Yarborough.

"easily intelligible in fact, and recognized as law by all the "authorities on the subject. Upon the evidence it is very "plain, that the land in question is of the latter description, "and therefore the issue joined upon this point was pro-"perly found for the defendant.

"The principal question arose upon the first issue, and "it is, as I have before intimated, merely a question of "fact. The defendant has pleaded, that the land in ques-"tion, by the *slow, gradual, and imperceptible projection,* "*alluvion, subsidence, and accretion of ooze, soil, sand, and* "*other matter, being slowly, gradually, and by imperceptible* "*increase, in long time cast up, deposited, and settled by and* "*from the flux and reflux of the tide and water of the sea,* "*in, upon, and against the outside and extremity of the* "demesne lands of the manor, hath been formed, and hath "been settled, grown, and accrued upon, against, and unto "the said demesne lands. This allegation has been denied "on the part of the Crown, and an issue taken upon it. "The allegation regards only the manner in which the "land has been formed: it contains nothing as to the "result of its formation, nothing as to the practicability of "ascertaining, after its formation, by any marks or limits, "or quantity previously existing and known, or by "measure to commence and be taken from such marks, or "with reference to such quantity, how much is now land "that once was sea. It is clear upon the evidence, that the "land has been formed slowly and gradually in the way "mentioned in the plea. The argument was upon the "word 'imperceptibly;' and for the Crown, two passages "were cited from *Sir Matthew Hale's* treatise, *De Jure* "*Maris,* wherein that very learned writer speaks of land "gained by *alluvion,* as belonging generally to the *Crown,* "unless the gain be *so insensible that it cannot be by any*

and land Derelict.

"*by any limits or marks*, according to the words of the
" other passage, found that the sea was there; idem est
" non esse et non apparere. In these passages, however,
" Sir Matthew Hale is speaking of the legal consequence
" of such an accretion, and does not explain what ought to
" be considered as accretion insensible or imperceptible in
" itself, but considers that as being insensible, of which it
" cannot be said with certainty that the sea ever was there.
" An accretion extremely minute, so minute as to be im-
" perceptible, even by known antecedent marks or limits,
" at the end of four or five years, may become, by gradual
" increase, perceptible by such marks or limits at the end
" of a century, or even of forty or fifty years. For it is to
" be remembered, that if the limit on one side be land, or
" something growing or placed thereon, as a tree, a house,
" or a bank, the limit on the other side will be the sea,
" which rises to a height varying almost at every tide, and
" of which the variations do not depend merely upon the
" ordinary course of nature, at fixed and ascertained
" periods, but in part also upon the strength and direction
" of the wind, which are different almost from day to day.
" And, therefore, these passages from the work of Sir
" Matthew Hale are not properly applicable to this ques-
" tion; and considering the word 'imperceptible' in this *Meaning of the word*
" issue as connected with the words 'slow and gradual,' we *"impercepti-*
" think it must be understood as expressive only of the *ble;" it im- ports the man-*
" manner of the accretion, as the other words undoubtedly *ner of the accretion.*
" are, and as meaning imperceptible in its progress, not
" imperceptible after a long lapse of time; and taking this
" to be the meaning of the word 'imperceptible,' the only
" remaining point is, whether the accretion of this land
" might properly, upon the evidence, be considered by the
" jury as imperceptible. No one witness has said that it
" could be perceived, either in its progress or at the end of

The King v. Lord Yarborough.

"a week or a month. One witness, who appears twice to "have measured the land, says, that within the last four ".years he could see that the sea had receded, but he could "not say how much; the same witness said, that it cer- "tainly had receded since he measured it last year, but he "did not say how much; and, according to his evidence, "the gain in a period of twenty-six or twenty-seven years, "was on the average about five yards and a half in a "year. Another witness speaks of a gain of from 100 to "150 yards in fifteen years; a much greater increase than "that mentioned by the first witness; and this second wit- "ness adds, that during the last five years there had been "a visible increase in some parts of from thirty to fifty "yards. Upon the evidence of this witness, it is to be "observed that he speaks very loosely, the difference "between 100 and 150 in fifteen years, and between thirty "and fifty in five years, being very great. The third "witness said, there had been some small increase in every "year. The fourth witness said, the swarth increases every "year very gradually, and *perhaps* it had gathered a "quarter of a mile in breadth in some places within his "recollection, or during the last fifty-four or fifty-five "years, and in some places it had gathered nothing. And "this was the whole evidence on the subject. We think "the jury might, from this evidence, very reasonably find "that the increase had not only been slow and gradual, "but also imperceptible, according to the sense in which, "as I have before said, we think that word ought to be "understood; and, consequently, we are of opinion, that a "new trial ought not to be granted, and the rule, therefore, "must be discharged."(*u*)

(*u*) A judgment of the House of Lords has since been reported [in the case of Gifford *v.* Lord Yarborough, 5 Bing. Rep. C. P. p. 163,

and land Derelict.

It remains to be observed, that with regard to derelict land left by any *sudden* and *violent* shrinking or retreat of the sea, whether upon the open coasts, or in creeks or arms or inlets of the sea, it *uniformly belongs to the King*, and may be claimed by him at any time within the period fixed by the statutes of limitation. *That*, also, must be regarded in the nature of derelict land, and as vesting in the Crown, which, although not *suddenly* left by or gained from the sea, is nevertheless, upon the evidence, perceptible in its acquisition and increase, in quantity and limits not to be mistaken by ordinary observation.

<small>As to sudden violent derelictions of land.</small>

In a note to Vaillant, ed. of Dyer, (*x*) p. 326 b, it is said, "the Prince [King] shall have all lands left by or gained "from the sea. I have seen and perused a treatise thereon "and therein many examples of Romney Marsh and "Bromhill, in Kent, of which there are farmers to the "King; and there is vouched a memorandum they came "to an agreement with the Lord the King. Trin. 43 Ed. "3, Rot. 13, ex parte of the Treasurer's Remembrancer. "If the sea-marks are gone, so that it cannot be known if "ever there was land there, the land gained from the sea "belongs to the King. But if the sea cover the land at "flux of the sea, and retreat at the reflux so that the sea- "marks are known, if *such* land be gained from the sea, it "belongs to the owner." 8th Eliz., Corporation of Rumney's case. This is an addition to Dyer, by the Editor, from Dyer's own notes. So Lord Hale lays it down, (*y*) that "if "a subject hath land adjoining the sea, and the violence of " the sea swallow it up, but so that there be yet reasonable " marks to continue the notice of it, or though the marks " be defaced, yet if by situation and extent of quantity, and

<small>If the sea-marks of land covered by the sea can be ascertained, it remains to the original owner, or returns when the water is gone.</small>

(*x*) Dyer, 326 b.
(*y*) [Appendix, post, xii. and Re Hull and Selby Railway Company,

Recovery of ground once terra firma but once flooded.
"bounding upon the firm land, the same can be known, "though the sea leave the land again, or it be by art and "industry regained, the subject doth not lose his property; "and accordingly it was held by Cooke and Foster, M. 7 "Jac. C. B. though the inundation continue forty years." For which he cites Dy. ub. sup. and "a notable case of an overflowing by the Thames," Rot. Parl. 8 E. 2. M. 23. Burnell v. the Bishop of Bath and Wells.(z) Callis(a) also, in his book on sewers, puts this case: "The sea overflows a "field where divers men's grounds lie promiscuously, and "there continueth so long, that the same is accounted par- "cel of the sea; and then after many years the sea goes "back and leaves the same, but the grounds are so defaced "as the bounds thereof be clean extinct, and grown out of "knowledge, it may be that the King shall have those "grounds; yet in histories I find that *Nilus* every year so "overflows the grounds adjoining, that their bounds are "defaced thereby, yet they are able to set them out by the " art of geometry." At this day it may be concluded that the former ownership may be identified by mensuration, so that if the sea suddenly swallow up ten acres, and after several years leave twenty acres dry, the ten acres may be reclaimed by admeasurement, but then the locality must be proved.

Sudden accession of land is not alluvion.
As soon as it is found by inquisition of office to be land *derelict*, the King's title attaches by the common law. "This accession of land," says Lord Hale, (b) "in this eminent and "sudden manner, by the recess of the sea, doth not come "under the former title of *alluvio*, or increase *per projec-* "*tionem;* and therefore, if an information of an *intrusion*

(z) Vin. Abr. title Prerogative, B, a, 2. Com. Dig. title Prerogative, D. 62.
(a) Callis, p. 51.
(b) De Jure Maris, Appendix, post, xxvii.; R. v. Lord Yarborough,

"be laid for so much land relict per mare, it is no good de-
"fence against the King to make title *per consuetudinem*
"*patriæ* to the *marettum*, or *sabulonem per mare projectum ;*
"for it is an acquest of another nature." And this was accordingly adjudged, H. 12, Car. Rot. 48, in the case of the King against Oldsworth and others, for Sutton Marsh, in Scaccario. And in that case it was likewise held and adjudged that lands acquired *per relictionem maris* are not *prescribable as part of a manor*, or as belonging to the subject; for that were to prescribe, in effect, that the narrow seas to the coast of France or Denmark were part of a manor. In that case the information, plea, and judgment, were in substance as followeth: viz. "Quòd cum 7,000 acræ
"marisci salsi vocati Sutton Marsh jacentes et existentes
"juxta Sutton Long in comitatu prædicto, videlicet, inter
"Sutton Long et mare ad refluxum ejusdem, fuissent parcella
"littoris marini, ac ad refluxus maris naturales et ordinarios
"aquis salsis et marinis inundatæ: cùmque eadem 7,000
"acræ marisei salsi nuper à mari undæ inundatæ fuissent,
"fuissent relictæ." Then the information sets forth a grant by King James, under the great seal, to Peter Ashton and others, and a regrant by them by a deed inrolled to the King, and that Michael Oldsworth, &c. intruded. The defendant, Oldsworth, came in, and as to part, pleaded as tenant, viz. "Quòd bene et verum est, quòd prædictæ
"7,000 acræ marisci salsi vocati Sutton Marsh, jacentes et
"existentes juxta Sutton Long; viz. inter Sutton Long et
"mare ad refluxum ejusdem, fuerunt parcellæ littoris marini,
"et ad refluxus maris naturales et ordinarios aquis salsis
"inundatæ, et à mari relictæ prout per informationem. But
"he further saith the King was seized, in right of the duchy
"of the manor of Sutton, et quòd plures terræ dicti manerii
"ante relictionem dictæ costeræ maris adjacebant; et quod

Derelict so
does not li
prescriptio

"manerlorum, terrarum, seu tenementorum super costeram
"maris adjacentium, particulariter habebunt marettum et
"sabulonem per fluxum et refluxum maris *secundùm majus*
"*et minus* prope terras seu tenementa sua projectum sive
"relictum ; quodque et prædictæ 7,000 acræ marisci salsi ad
"terram prædictam parcellam manerii de Sutton adjacent,
"et per fluxus et refluxus maris relictæ fuerunt à mari, et
"projectæ ad terram prædictam parcellam manerii de
"Sutton prædicti, ratione cujus relictionis prædictæ dominus
"rex fuit seisitus, &c. de prædictis 7,000 acris in jure duca-
"tus, &c." And then he entitles himself by a grant under the
duchy seal, and traverseth what he had not confessed.
Upon this there was a demurrer and judgment for the King,
upon solemn argument, and principally upon this reason,
that *custom cannot entitle the subject to relicted lands*, or *make
it part of a manor ;* (c) and it differed from the case of the
Abbot of Peterborough before cited, for there it was only
project, but here, *relict* is added to the plea, that it might
answer the information ; though the plea in the Abbot of
Peterborough's case was the precedent by which the plea
was drawn, and with which it agreed, saving the addition of
relict.

" And yet the true reason of it is, *because the soil* [*once*]
" *under the water, must needs be of the same propriety as it is*
" [*was*] *when covered with the water.* If the soil of the sea,
" while it is covered with water, be the King's, it cannot
" become the subject's, because the water hath left it.
" But in the case of *alluvio maris* it is otherwise, because

---

(c) This deserves notice. In a former page (85) we have seen, that Lord Hale considers prescription and usage time out of mind, to be sufficient to establish the ownership of the lord of a manor to the bed

" the accession and addition of the land by the sea to the
" dry land gradually, is a kind of perquisite, and an acces-
" sion to the land; and therefore, in case of private rivers,
" it *seems by the very course of the common law* such a
" gradual increase, cedit solo adjacenti; and though it
" may be doubtful whether it be so ex jure communi, in
" case of the King, yet doubtless it gives a reasonableness
" and facility for such right of alluvio to be acquired by
" custom; for although in every acquest per alluvionem
" there be a reliction, or rather exclusion of the sea, yet it
" is not a recess of the sea, nor properly a reliction." Lord
Hale then adds, " But this is to be carried along with us
" in the case of recessus, or relictio maris, vel brachii
" ejusdem; that where the land, as it stood covered with
" water, did by particular *usage or prescription*(d) belong to
" a subject, there the recessus maris, so far as the subject's
" particular interest went while it was covered with water,—
" so far the recessus maris vel brachii ejusdem belongs to
" the same subject."

" The King of England hath the propriety as well as
" jurisdiction of the narrow seas; for he is in a capacity of
" acquiring the narrow and adjacent sea to his dominion,
" by a kind of possession which is not compatible to a
" subject, and accordingly regularly the King hath that
" propriety in the sea, but a subject hath not, nor indeed
" can have, that property in the sea, through a whole tract
" of it, that the King hath; because, without a regular
" power, he cannot possibly possess it. But though a sub-

(d) But, according to this doctrine, derelict land *may* be *virtually*
prescribed for (a position denied ante p. 131).—For if a man may
prescribe for 1,000 acres of sea and the soil under it, the soil, whether
wet or dry, is equally prescribed for. Here also, there seems a dis-
crepancy in his Lordship's doctrine. There seems no reason why
portions of land under the sea may be prescribed for, and portions of

"ject cannot acquire the interest of the narrow seas, yet he may by *usage and prescription* acquire an interest in so much of the sea as he may *reasonably possess;* viz. of a districtus maris,(e) a place in the sea between such points, or a particular part contiguous to the shore, or a port or creek or arm of the sea. These may be possessed by a subject, and *prescribed* in point of interest, both of the water and *the soil itself*, covered with the water, within such a precinct; for these are manoriable, and may be entirely possessed by a subject." The learned writer then alludes to title by prescription:—

" The Civilians tell us truly, *nihil præscribitur nisi quod possidetur.* The King may prescribe the property of the narrow seas, because he may possess them by his navies and power. A subject cannot; but a subject may possess a navigable river or creek, or arm of the sea;—because these may lie within the extent of his possession and acquest."

" The consequence," says he, "of this is, that the soil relinquished by such arms of the sea, ports, or creeks,— nay, though they should be wholly dried or stopped up, yet such soil would belong to the owner or proprietor of that arm of the sea, or river, or creek, for here is not any new acquest by the reliction, but the soil covered with water was the subject's before, and also the water itself

(e) Along the coast, therefore, where none of these inlets or districts are found, the land under the water cannot, at all events, be prescribed for, being too open and indefinable, and, therefore, the shore, in such places, is not prescribable, even if a "districtus maris" may be, although neither the one nor the other would seem correctly to lie in prescription. It is difficult, also, to say what the quantity of sea is that a subject " may *reasonably* possess ;" that which the King has actually granted, we may suppose the subject may reasonably possess ; but

and Land Derelict.

"that covered it; and it is so now that it is dried up, or
"hath relinquished its channel, or part of it."(*f*)

"And such an acquest of a propriety in an arm or creek <small>As to the</small>
"of the sea may be as well within the precincts of a port, <small>right to the soil in ports</small>
"as without; and *that* though the King, or some subject
"hath the port, in point of franchise or privilege.(*g*) For,
"although the soil of all creeks and navigable rivers, *espe-*
"*cially within ports*, do originally belong to the King, in
"point of propriety, as well as in point of franchise, yet the
"subject may have so great and clear a possession of the
"soil lying under the water of that port, that it may belong
"to a subject in point of interest or propriety of the soil,
"though he have or have not the port in point of fran-
"chise;(*h*) and consequently, if the sea should relinquish
"the channel, or creek, or arm of the sea within such a
"port, it might and would belong to that subject who had
"the propriety of the soil, and water before it were so
"relicted."

"And this is an exception out of that generality, possi-

(*f*) Callis, p. 51, seems to deny this doctrine, as if the *change* produced a change of title; but there can be no difficulty in agreeing with the doctrine laid down in the text, *supposing the title to the soil when covered with water to have been good.*

(*g*) If the port has never been out of the hands of the Crown, and is an ancient port, q. if it be possible for the subject to be owner of its soil?

(*h*) Also, Since it is the King's undoubted right to originate new ports, and since he is also *prima facie* absolute owner of the sea-bottom and sea-shore, q. is it possible that the courts of law can allow a Lord of a Manor to make title to so essential a part of the new port as the soil (which may be of great extent), on mere prescriptive evidence? The shore within the precinct of ports, often extends *several miles* along the coast. A title interfering with the prerogative of originating new ports, ought not to be favoured. [As to the creation of new ports, see Nicholson *v.* Williams, 6 L. R., Q. B. 632; 40 L. J. N. S., M. C. 159, S. C.; Jenkins *v.* Harvey, 1 C. M. and R. 877; Exeter, mayor of, *v.* Warren, 5 Q. B. 773; 8 Jur. 441, S. C.; 9 and

"bly, that *terræ relictæ per mare* may not be prescribed. "But a certain creek, arm of the sea, *or districtus maris*, "*may be prescribed in point of interest;* and by way of "consequence or concomitance, the land relicted there, "according to the extent of such a precinct as was so pre- "scribed, will belong to the former owner of such *districtus* "*maris*. But otherwise it would be, if such *prescription*, "before the reliction, extended only to a liberty, or *profit* "*à prendre*, or jurisdiction only within that precinct; as "liberty of free fishing, admiralty jurisdiction, or the juris- "diction of a leet or hundred, or other court; for such may "extend to an arm of the sea, as appears by 8 E. 2, Co- "ronæ, for *these are not any acquests of the interest of the* "*water and soil, but leave it as it found it.*" (*i*)

"Therefore, the discovery of the extent of the prescrip- "tion or usage, whether it extend to the soil or not, rests "upon such evidence of facts as may justly satisfy the "court and jury concerning the interests of the soil." The learned author then proceeds to observe:—

1st. "That a subject may, by usage or *prescription*, be "owner or proprietor of such an arm of the sea, creek, or "particular portion of the sea contiguous to the shore, as *is* "*not a public port or haven*, and consequently if that part "be left dry, per recessum vel abstractionem maris, that "will belong to that subject that had such antecedent pro- "priety when it was covered with water."

"This will appear by a review of those cases that are in "the precedent chapter concerning the right of fishing in "the sea, many of which instances make it appear that there "may be a right of propriety in the soil aquâ coopertâ, and

(*i*) This seems to contradict the doctrine of the same writer quoted and controverted in former pages of this tract. For if such rights, when prescribed for, leave the water and soil where they found them,

As to the Soil of Ports.

"the right of fishing *resulting* not as a profit *à prendre*, but
"upon the very right of the soil itself."

2nd. "That a subject having a *port* of the sea may have,
"and, indeed, in common experience and presumption hath,
"the very soil covered with the water; for though it is true,
"the franchise of a port is a different thing from the propriety
"of the soil of a port, and so the franchise of a port *may* be
"in a subject, and the propriety of the soil may be in the
"King, or in some other, yet in *ordinary usage and pre-*
"*sumption* they go together." (*k*)

    A subject may have a port, and either with or without the soil.

"If the King at this day grant *portum maris de S.*, the
"King having the port in point of interest as well as in
"point of franchise, it may be *doubtful* whether at this day
"it carries the soil, or only the franchise, *because it is not*
"*to be taken by implication*. But surely, if it were an ancient
"grant, and *usage* had gone along with it, that the grantee
"held also the soil, this grant might be effectual to pass
"both, for both are included in it."

    q. Whether the grant of a "port," without more words, will carry the soil?

The learned author then proceeds to say, "*and so* if by
"prescription or custom, a man hath portum maris de S.;
"in ordinary presumption he hath not only the franchise,
"but the very water and soil within the port, for a '*portus*
"*maris*' is *quid aggregatum*, as a manor; and such a pre-
"scription may carry the soil as well as the franchise;
"and though this doth not always hold, yet most times it
"doth."

    If a man have a port, by prescription, will that carry the soil?

"Escaetria, 12 E. 1. n. 1. Portus et piscaria et mariscus
"de Topsham spectant ad Amiciam Comitissam Devon.
"She had not only the franchise of the port, but the soil of
"the port, and the fishing and salt marsh adjoining. And

(*k*) It may be argued, that if the franchise of a port be prescribed for, and the port be dried up, and no longer a port, the prescription is lost, and consequently cannot exist to give title to the *soil* so left dry.

As to the Soil of Ports.

" vide the case of the port of Plymouth, (*l*) parcel of the
" manor of Trematon, wherein it will appear that a subject,
" as he may be owner of a port in point of franchise, so he
" *may be* owner of the very soil of the haven in point of
" propriety. And so concerning the port of Poole: the
" Earl of Surrey was owner of it in point of propriety, as
" well as franchise, and had the anchorage of ships there,
" which seems to be ordinarily a perquisite in respect to the
" soil."

3rd. " That a man who is not owner of a port in point of
" franchise, but the franchise of the port belonging to the
" King, yet such a subject *may* by *usage* have the very
" propriety of a creek or arm of the sea, parcel of that port,
" and of the soil thereof; and may have, upon that account,
" the increase of land that happens by the recess of the
" water of that arm of the sea."

" Register, 252. The Prior of Christchurch Cantuariæ
" petitions the King, quòd cùm quædam antiqua trenchea,
" quæ se ducit à brachio maris vocata A, versus villam de
" B, *quæ est in solo* ipsorum Prioris et Conventûs, per sabu-
" lones et arenam maris jam de novo taliter sit obstructa,
" quòd naves per trencheam illam usque ad dictam villam
" de B venire nequeunt ut solebant; et quædam alia
" trenchea ducens ab eodem brachio maris usque ad eandem
" villam de B jam vi maritimâ facta existet, per quam
" naves et batelli à mari usque ad villam illam commodè
" et sine impedimento poterunt transire. An 'ad quod
" damnum' issues to enquire, 'si sit ad damnum vel præ-
" 'judicium nostri aut aliorum, seu nocumentum dictæ villæ
" 'de B, si eis *licentiam concedamus* quòd ipsi dictam anti-
" 'quam trencheam omnino obstruere et commodum suum
" 'inde facere possint.'" Lord Hale then observes: "Here

As to the Soil of Ports. 139

" the *common passage* for ships to a town *admitted* in point
" of *propriety* to belong to the Prior, and that they may
" make profit of the soil being stopt up."

This, however, it may be observed, does not seem to be a correct conclusion drawn from the case; the trenchea or common passage seems to have been *admitted* to belong to *the King*, whose *licence* was asked for the conversion of it to profit; there is no admission that the Prior could appropriate the soil of it without the King's licence.

Comments.

The learned author proceeds to inform us, "that though
" the subject may have the propriety of a navigable river,
" part of a port, yet these cautions are to be added, viz. :—

1st. " That the King hath yet a right of empire or
" government over it, in reference to the safety of the king-
" dom and to his customs, it being a member of a port." (*m*)

2nd. " That the people have a public interest, a jus pub-
" licum, of passage and repassage with their goods by
" water, and must not be obstructed by nuisances or im-
" peached by exactions. For the *jus privatum* of the
" owner or proprietor is charged with and subject to that

(*m*) An ancient survey of the King's ports is lodged in the Exchequer. Gilb. Evid. 69. The same, it is presumed, as that noticed by Selden, lib. 2, ch. 22, where he states that James 2d, in 1604, ordered 12 surveyors, "rerum maritimarum callentissimis," to survey the coasts of England, and to fix on certain headlands, or points, by drawing straight lines from point to point, to fix the limits of the King's chambers, "regias cameras, et portus regios." This map, or chart, was drawn on a plate of brass, and published by the King's proclamation. (Procl. 1, martii 2, Jac. 2d, 1604, in Rot. Pat. part 32.) The spaces in the sea, enclosed within the straight lines, are 27. These "regias cameras," King's Chambers, are named as follows,—Holy Island, the Sowter, Whitby, Flamborough Head, the Sporne, Cromer, Winterton-nesse, Easter-nesse, Layestoff, Est-nesse, Orfort-nesse, the North-foreland, the South-foreland, Dungenesse, Beach, Dune-

As to Islands.

"*jus publicum* which belongs to the King's subjects, as the
"soil of an highway is; which, though in point of property
"it may be a private man's freehold, yet it is charged with
"a public interest of the people which may not be preju-
"diced or damnified." (*n*)

The learned writer then observes as to Islands :—

Islands, these belong to the Crown. 3rd. "As touching Islands arising in the sea, or in the
"arms, or creeks, or havens thereof, the same rule holds
"which is before observed touching acquests by the relic-
"tion or recess of the sea, or such arms or creeks thereof.
"Of common right and *prima facie* it is true they belong

Unless formed out of a place the property of a subject. "to the Crown; (*o*) but where the interest of such dis-
"trictus maris, or arm of the sea, or creek, or haven, doth
"in point of propriety belong to a subject, either by charter
"or by *prescription*, the islands that happen within the
"precincts of such private propriety of a subject will
"belong to the subject according to the limits and extents
"of such propriety. And, therefore, if the west side of
"such an arm of the sea belong to a manor of the west
"side, and an island happen to arise on the west side of the

These will belong to the subject. "*filum aquæ* invironed with the water, the propriety of such
"island will entirely belong to the lord of that manor of
"the west side; and if the east side of such an arm of the
"sea belong to a manor of the east side *usque filum aquæ*,
"and an island happen between the east side of the river
"and the *filum aquæ*, it will belong to the lord on the east
"side; and if the *filum aquæ* divide itself, and one part
"take the east and the other the west, and leave an island
"in the middle between both the *fila*, the one half will
"belong to the one lord and the other to the other. But

(*n*) [R. *v.* Tindall, 1 N. and P. 723; Williams *v.* Wilcox, 8 A. and
E. 314, S. C. 3 N. and P. 616, et ante, p. 43; Mayor of Colchester *v.*

As to Islands.

" this is to be understood of islands that are *newly* made; for
" if a part of an arm of the sea, by a new recess from his
" ancient channel, incompass the land of another man, his
" propriety continues unaltered. And with these diversities
" agrees the law at this day. And Bracton, lib. 1, cap. 2,
" and the very texts of the civil law, (*p*) vid. Digest, lib. 41,
" de acquirendo rerum dominio legibus, 7, 12, 21, 29, 30,
" 38, 50, 56, 65, et ibidem, lib. 43, tit. 12, de fluminibus l. 1.
" and 6. Vide Bracton ubi supra, Habet etiam locum hæc
" species accessionis in insulâ natâ in flumine, quæ, si
" mediam partem fluminis teneat, communis eorum est qui
" pro indiviso ab utrâque parte fluminis prope ripam prædia
" possident, &c. For the propriety of such a new accrued
" island follows the propriety of the soil before it came to
" be produced." (*q*)

The foregoing pages of quotation from Lord Hale's treatise have been given at length, because they embrace all

(*p*) But by the Civil Law, islands formed in the sea " dantur primo occupanti." Just. Inst. [De rerum divisione, Britton, titulo Purchase, fol. 86 B.]

(*q*) [Appendix, post, xxxiv. Where a sand-bank has been formed in a tidal river, which at low water divided the river into two equal streams, a line drawn down the middle of the river at low water, taking the two channels together, is to be regarded as the limits of the respective rights : Wedderburn *v.* Paterson, 2 Scot. Sess. Cases, 3rd series, 902 ; Scot. Jur. vol. xxxvi. p. 452, S. C. And if a shifting island springs up in the channel, so as to impede or embarrass the fishings of one of the proprietors, he must submit, and hope for a change ; the law can give him no redress. But if the shifting island becomes fixedly annexed to, and incorporated with his bank, the permanent accretion will give rise to a new medium filum : Zetland, Earl, *v.* Glover; Incorporation of Perth, 2 L. R. Scot. App. 70. See also Hunt on Boundaries, p. 19 ; Jerwood, p. 89 ; Phear, pp. 11 and 44 ; Schultes, 118. As to the law in America, see Middleton *v.* Pritchard, 3 Scam. (Ill.) 519, 522 ; Stuart *v.* Clark's lessee, 2 Swan. 12 ; Jones *v.* Soulard 24, Howard 64 ; People *v.* Canal Appraisers, 13 Wendell, N. Y. Rep. 355; Hopkins' Academy, Trustees of, *v.* Dickenson, 63 Mass. (9 Cush), 548 ; Angell on Tide Waters, 267 ; Angell on Watercourses, 6th edit.

Comments on the foregoing quotations from Lord Hale.

that is generally laid down as *good law* upon this part of our subject, and also some other points, perhaps questionable. He first of all agrees with all other law authorities, that the *derelict* land belongs to the King. He further states it as law (and it is apprehended to be sound law), that *custom* or *prescription* cannot entitle the subject to *relict lands;* (r) and that it was decided by a case he quotes, that lands acquired "per relictionem maris" are not prescribable as part of a manor, or as belonging to the subject, (s) and we are also told "that the soil [which was] under the water, "must needs be of the same propriety [when left dry] as "when covered with water; (t) so that if, while it is covered "with water, it be the King's, it cannot become the sub- "ject's *because* the water hath left it." We are, however, soon after told (u) that the "subject may by *usage* and *pre-* "*scription* acquire an interest in so much of the sea as he "may reasonably possess, as a districtus maris, a place in "the sea between two points, or in a particular part con- "tiguous to the shore, or of a port or creek, or arm of the "sea. These," says he, "*may be prescribed* in point of "interest, both of the water, and the soil itself, covered with "the water."

Custom cannot entitle a subject to relict land.

Soil which was covered with water does not change ownership by becoming dry.

q. Whether a portion of land covered with sea, may be prescribed?

According to this doctrine, land which when aqua cooperta *can* be prescribed for by the subject, *cannot* be prescribed for when relict by the sea. If the soil covered with water was the subject's before (and according to Lord Hale's doctrine it may be so by *prescription*, so long as it is covered with water), then, says he, such soil when dried up would belong to him who was such owner. But it may be asked, how does he prove himself to have been such owner when it was under water? The answer is, by *prescription;* and yet it is insisted that he cannot prescribe for derelict

as to the Soil of Ports. 143

land at all! Surely this is *in effect* prescribing for the very same land. It may be fairly urged, that if land under the water may be prescribed for, against the King's *primâ facie* title, the *same* land when left dry may or rather must also be prescribed for,—because "it must needs be of the same propriety as it was when covered with water."

Suppose I have always claimed (but without having any actual *grant* to show) the ownership of a certain districtus maris, and have never had the title questioned, and it suddenly becomes dry land; can I *prescribe* that it was mine when under water, and thus acquire a title to it? If I can do so, this is virtually prescribing for the derelict land. The law of England, however, makes no distinction between land covered and land not covered with water; both are "*land*," technically speaking; and therefore, it seems a contradiction in terms to say that land covered with water can be prescribed for, and land relict cannot. Undoubtedly, if the subject had no legal ownership in the soil under the water, against the King's title, such subject can have no better title to it when it is relict and dry. This, however, does not explain why land covered with the sea may be prescribed for, and the same land left uncovered may not. Indeed, according to what has been before urged, neither the one nor the other can be made good, in point of title, by prescription; both being merely land, and therefore not lying in prescription.

Example.

The doctrine that if, by prescription, a man "hath "portum maris de S. in ordinary presumption he hath not "only the franchise, but the very water and *soil* itself "within the port," rests also on doubtful ground, if the author's distinction be sound, viz. that the *port* or *franchise*, and the *soil*, do not *necessarily* go together: "the franchise "of a port," says he, "is a different thing from the pro-

q. Whether prescription for the franchise of a port, will carry the soil?

"in a subject, and the soil in the King or some other." (*x*) Now, if this be the case, it does not appear why they should, in *ordinary* presumption, go together under one word, *portus*. The learned writer doubts (*y*) whether the *express* grant of a *port* would, at his time of day, without more words, carry the soil; but conceives that an *ancient* grant of the port, coupled with ancient usage, would carry the soil. All grants of ports are now to be deemed ancient grants; no modern grants (at least including the soil) can be made: are we then to construe every ancient grant of a port, without more words, as giving inclusively a title to the soil? Undoubtedly, if the mere prescription for a port will carry not only the franchise, but the soil, by reason that "*portus*" is *quid aggregatum*, (*z*) like a manor, then indeed there can be no just reason why the word "portus," in a *grant*, should not also have the effect mentioned.

Whether the word "Portus" in a grant will pass the soil as well as franchise?

But, it may be asked, why in any case should the mere word "*Portus*" carry the soil, as well as the franchise, if the soil and the franchise are (as they are stated to be) separate ownerships, and capable of being possessed by different persons, and are sometimes so held? The franchise should rather be deemed an adjunct to the soil, than the soil to the franchise, and yet it is nowhere said that the ownership of the soil carries the franchise. It is not intended to be denied that one person *may* have *both;* but it may be doubted whether the word "*Portus*" will, in any case, carry more than the *franchise;* and consequently it is presumed that the grant must contain sufficient words of grant of the soil. It would be singular, in such a case, to allow the *soil* to be *prescribed* for, when the *port* only is actually *granted;* and if an express grant of the port, without more words, will not carry the soil, it is difficult to admit that the mere prescription for a *port* will give the soil also. Prescription, or presumption, ought not to give more than the express grant (supposed to have had existence) would have given; especially against the Crown. (*a*)

There can be no good reason of policy for thus construing the grant beyond its letter, or conferring the soil of a port on a subject by presumption or prescription. Where the port had better have been, the soil may as well remain. There can be no occasion to strain points of legal doctrine, the effect of which will be to deprive the King of that which was vested in him for the good of the public. The cases quoted by Lord Hale, in support of this doctrine, do not seem to warrant the conclusions drawn from them. Thus we find the words of the first case, "*Portus* et *pis-* "*caria* et mariscus de Toppesham spectant ad Comitissam "Devon," are deemed sufficient to prove that not only the *franchise* of the port, but the *soil* of the port also belonged to her. Now, the "piscaria" is not the soil of the port; nor is the "mariscus" *adjoining*, the soil of the port; and therefore all that the words *per se*, give, is the franchise of the port, the fishery, and the adjacent marsh; and the word "port," even in his own admission, may, or may not, carry the soil. Nothing appears to warrant a construction beyond the franchise, the fishery, and the adjacent marsh; yet, in a subsequent part of his work, (*b*) he draws similar conclusions more fully from this case; where, after quoting the case of the port of Toppesham in the same short form as above, he adds,—it appears,

" 1st. That the Earls of Devon had the propriety of the "soil of the port by *prescription;* *for* they had all the "profits that arise by reason of the property of the soil;

(*a*) [Jerwood, p. 50.]
(*b*) [Appendix, post, xxxii. and De Portibus, p. 55.]

" viz. the *fishery* and the salt marsh, which possibly might
" be an 'incrementum maritimum.' But upon this it may
" be observed, that the salt marsh was *adjoining*, and
" might well pass *eo nomine;* and there is no more ground
" for construing 'mariscus' into a grant of the soil of the
" *port*, than for holding the grant of the 'portus' to be a
" grant of the 'mariscus.' As for the 'piscaria,' it seems
" impossible to convert *that* into a grant of the soil itself,
" for a piscaria, it is admitted on all hands, often exists
" independent of the soil, where the soil is clearly in the
" King, or another; this has been already shown. Besides,
" the words 'spectant ad C, D,' prove nothing on the point
" of *prescription*. But he proceeds,—

" 2nd. They had also the franchise of the port, by prescription, and all the incidents thereof, viz.

1. Applicatio navium,
2. Exoneratio navium,
3. Mercatum et venditio mercandisarum et per retail,
4. Victualling of mariners and ships,
5. Lodging and entertainment of mariners.

" All which are privileges in a special manner belonging
" to ports, and cannot be had without that liberty legally
" vested."—All which may be true enough, and yet not
prove the *soil* to pass by the word " portus."

The next case cited by the same learned writer is that of
Plymouth and Sutton Pool. (*c*) " P. 10. Ed. 3, B. R. Rot.
" 73, dorso, it appears, that Willielmus Denlarena Comes
" Surrey, had the port of *Pool* and anchorage and other
" duties belonging to it."

" It appeared among the charters of the Duchy of Corn-
" wall, the transcripts whereof remain in the receipt of the
" Exchequer, that Rogerus de Valletort-avantort, gave to

(*c*) [De Portibus, p. 56; Jerwood, p. 63; Appendix, post, xxxii. and

as to the Soil of Ports. 147

" Richard King of the Romans and Earl of Cornwall, and
" the heirs of his body, *Castrum* [castle] de Trematon, et 59
" feoda militum, in Cornwall et Devon, ad idem *castrum*
" pertin. ac etiam *manerium de Trematon*, et villam de esse,
" CUM AQUA." (*d*)

" To this castle of Trematon belong a certain petty manor
" called Sutton Vantort, and also the water and port of
" Sutton; for so appears by the close roll, Claus. 17, E. 2,
" m. 14, Sutton *cum aqua* et *portu* spectat ad castrum de
" Trematon."

" By the death of Edmond, his son, without issue, the
" earldom and this castle came to the Crown. Possibly
" Richard, Earl of Cornwall, after issue had, made some
" alienation before the statute of Westminster, 2d, whereby
" the reversion to the heirs of Vantort was barred."

" The earldom of Cornwall and this castle of Trematon
" descended to King Edward the 3d. He, by *charter*, in
" parliament, grants the earldom of Cornwall to his eldest
" son, 'et castrum et manerium de Trematon, cum villa de
" Saltash, et parco ibidem cum aliis pertinentiis.' See the
" Charter, 8 Rep. 8. The prince's case."

" By this grant," says Lord Hale, " without any special
" mention of the *water* or *port* as belonging to it, the port
" and water of Sutton, now Plymouth, was annexed to the
" duchy of Cornwall, for though the charter grants 'prisas
" ' et custumas vinorum necdum proficua portuum nostro-
" ' rum, intra eundem Comitatum Cornub. simul cum

(*d*) Nothing passes by the word " aqua," save a fishery. " If," says
Lord Coke, " a man grant aquam suam, the soil shall not pass, but
" the piscary within the water passeth therewith." Co. Litt. 4 b.
Plowd. 154, says, that by " aqua, a piscary shall pass ;" and he adds,
that " by a grant of a piscary, the soil shall pass ;" by which it might
be inferred that " aqua" will carry the soil. But in a former page it
has been contended, under strong authority, that a grant of a " piscary"

" 'wrecco maris, et balena, et sturgeono,' yet that did not
" extend to the *water of Sutton,*(e) which was in Devon, but
" it [the water] passed by the strength of its being parcel
" of, and appendant to the castle of Trematon."

" The *town of Plymouth,* which is indeed caput portus
" from whence the port now takes its denomination, *was not*
" *part of Trematon,* but built upon the *manor of Sutton*
" *Prior,* and was incorporated, and its jurisdiction settled
" by act of parliament. Rot. parl. 18 H. 6, n. 32, and con-
" firmed by rot. parl. 3 E. 4, n. 45. But always in both,
" whatever was *parcel of Trematon* was *excepted;* and con-
" sequently the haven [portus] itself (which was parcel of
" Trematon) was not annexed thereby to Plymouth, but
" stood upon the same foot of interest as before."

" There lies adjacent to this town [of Plymouth], within
" the barbican thereof, a space of about thirty acres, which is
" covered *every* tide with the sea, and ships ride there, and
" come to unlade at the keys of Plymouth, commonly called
" *Sutton Poole;* for the interest of the soil of these thirty
" acres, being parcel of the port, an information of *intrusion*
" was, as directed out of the Exchequer chamber, preferred
" against the Mayor and Commonalty of Plymouth. The
" defendants pretended title to it as parcel of the town of
" Plymouth, and showed *usage* to have had certain customs,
" called land leave, terrage, &c. But these referred to the
" *shore* rather than to the place in question.(*f*) They allege
" that it was also within the limits of their charter, and that
" they exercise *jurisdiction* of their courts there; both
" which were admitted. But it was insisted upon, on the
" other side, that the *soil itself was excepted,* as *parcel of the*
" *castle of Trematon;* and it was showed that the King

(*e*) But see last note.
(*f*) Sed quære, if it was regularly covered by the ordinary tides, this

"had used to have in right of his duchy in the place in
"question, anchorage, basselage, fishing, and the rents of
"fishers, and divers other port duties that savoured of the
"soil; as appears by divers accounts of the duchy; divers
"records mentioning Pola de Sutton was parcel of Tre-
"maton; several leases made by the King's progenitors of
"*aqua* et *Pola* (*g*) de Sutton; and some to the town itself,
"or some in trust for them; and divers other weighty
"evidences for the propriety of the soil of Sutton Pool;
"being the very harbour itself, and belonging to Tre-
"maton: and accordingly a verdict given for the King."
The learned writer then adds, "I have mentioned this the
"rather because,—

"1st. Here the very interest of the port, the water, and
"*soil*, and port duties themselves, were claimed and re-
"covered by the Crown, not upon any prerogative title;
"for if it had been so, it would have passed to the town
"of Plymouth, being within the precincts of their incorpo-
"ration, and *grant*; and then the exception of Trematon
"had not been available, but as parcel of and belonging to
"a manor that was formerly a subject's."

"2nd. That the King, primâ facie, hath a right to ports
"of a royal franchise, yet the accession of this manor to the
"Crown did not sever the interest of the port from the

(*g*) Although, as before observed, "aqua" will not pass the soil
(see note to p. 147, ante), yet the words "stagnum," or pola (forsan?), a
pool,—"gurges," a deep pit of water,—"palus," and "mariscus," a
marsh, will pass the soil, being *quid aggregatum*, see Co. Litt. 4 b. So

" manor, no more than in case of a fair or market ap-
" pendant by prescription; for if, by the accession to the
" Crown, it had been divided from the castle, or manor,
" it could not have passed, without special words, to the
" Prince, as it plainly did here. As the *port* was *by pre-*
" *scription* parcel of the manor of Trematon, so it con-
" tinued parcel, notwithstanding the accession thereof to
" the Crown, by the death of the Earl of Cornwall without
" issue; and it passed, together *with the castle, by the general*
" *grant of it*, as a leet or market, or any other parcel or
" appendant; and so, not like those flowers of the Crown
" which are rendered disappendant by the accession to the
" Crown, as waifs, strays, &c."

With regard to this last cited case, the result undoubtedly was, that the King retained both the soil and the port
of Sutton Vantort; but it does not seem so clear that he
retained it as appendant by *prescription*. As to the franchise
of the port, it is not meant to deny that a franchise may
be appendant to a manor by prescription; but the case by no
means proves that the *soil* of the sea, or an arm, or port
thereof, *may* be in like manner *appendant, by prescription, to
a manor*. It is to be remembered that *the soil of the port*
belonged to the King, before it was a port, and does not
appear to have ever been divested from the Crown at all; (*h*)
and even if his ancestors had granted it away as parcel of
the land of the manor, yet when the whole fell again to
Edward 3, he became possessed of the soil in his ancient
title. His descendant, King Charles 2 (for whom the
verdict was given),(*i*) was, in the present case, entitled to

(*h*) The first grant quoted is that to the King of the Romans, and
unless the soil in question was "*parcel of the castle* and manor of
Trematon," at the time of this grant, by metes and bounds,—(and
nothing appears to show whether it was or was not),—it was still in

as to the Soil of Ports.

it in a double right, if possible; for all that his ancestors had once granted away with Trematon and the manor, fell to him again by descent; and if they had never granted the soil, then it was his *ab origine*. The town of Plymouth must have produced either the King's grant of the soil in question, or some tantamount evidence of right to it: and as they failed so to do, even on the disputed ground of prescription, the *soil* necessarily remained to the King, and the franchise of the *port* remained *appendant* to the manor. It does not appear that the evidence adduced on the King's side was necessary to his case, further than concerned the franchise, although it was also used to rebut the claim to the soil. The grant to the King of the Romans was of the castle and manor of Trematon, and the town, *cum aquâ* [and "aqua" carried the fishery only], and the manor of Sutton Vantort, and also the *water* and *port* of Sutton Vantort, were admitted to belong to the *castle;* i.e. to be appendant to it. The castle, the manor, the town *cum aqua*, all fell to King Edward by descent, and he, by a somewhat different form, granted "castrum et manerium de Trematon " cum villa de Saltash et Parco ibidem cum *aliis perti-* " *nentiis*," without any mention of the *port* or *aqua* of Sutton Vantort. The town of Plymouth being built on another manor, viz. Sutton Prior, was no part either of the manor of Trematon or of the manor of Sutton Vantort; and the soil in question was clearly part of the port or pool of Sutton Vantort, which was parcel of the greater.manor and castle of Trematon.(*k*) The *charter* of the town contained *an express exception of whatsoever was parcel* of the *castle and manor of Trematon;* and therefore, clearly Sutton Vantort, both pool and manor, were doubly excepted; first, if parcel of Trematon; and secondly, from being within a different manor from Sutton Prior, viz. Sutton Vantort, which, at all events, was not belonging to Plymouth. If the pool and soil of Sutton Vantort did not pass by the grant of King Edward, as a *less* within a *greater* manor, then it remained in King Edward, and subsequently, by succession, vested in King Charles; and if it *did* so pass to the Prince of Wales, then, through him, it came also to the Crown, and by the Crown it was *excepted* by the words of exception in the charter, so that quacunque, &c. the town of Plymouth had no title. But surely this is no evidence that land covered with the sea may be *prescribed for*. It was admitted on all sides that Sutton Vantort,(*l*) cum aqua et Portu, spectant ad [belong to] castrum de Trematon; and it was clear that Trematon was excluded, totidem verbis, from the Town Charter, and was vested in the King. The King, therefore, did not prescribe at all, for he produced written evidences of his title, and had his *original common law right besides*. In fact, all that did not pass from the Crown by the original grant to the King of the Romans, in the first instance, was the King's soil by common law; all that *did* pass by that grant came afterwards to King Edward, by descent; and all that King Edward granted to the prince, and also all that did *not* pass in the grant to him, but was crown property *ab origine*, became ultimately vested in King Charles; so that in him, at the time of the dispute, all title centered, save what the town possessed by their charter, and there it was not to be found. Lord Hale also cites in this place, in support of the same doctrine, the case of the Barons of Barclay (*m*) already quoted; but which case, if referred to, will not appear to establish the point, that he who prescribes for a *port* thereby also acquires the soil of it; for in that case the King was admitted to be owner of the franchises of the ports both of Bristol and Gloucester, within the precincts

As to the Soil of Ports.

of which the land claimed by the Barons was situate, and yet the land was adjudged to the Barons, whilst the ports remained in the King. The King was, prima facie, the lawful proprietor of the soil, and was also the owner of the port; and according to Lord Hale, the port and the soil ordinarily go together; and yet, it seems, these badges of ownership were not sufficient to outweigh the claims of the Barons, specially proved, to the land.

There seems to be this material difference when we speak of "Portus" in the crown,—and the same in a subject. In the crown, the soil and the port are ordinarily united, because the soil is the property of the crown by common law; but it is not so in the case of a subject, whose right to the soil is adverse to the ownership of the King. It is matter of course that the soil belongs to the King, until the contrary be proved. So also the franchise of the port. But in the case of a subject, each of these distinct rights is set up against the King's prima facie acknowledged ownership, and it does not seem correct to take the one from the King by implication, because the other is substantiated against him. It is well known, that the *portus* often extends over *several miles of shore*, on both sides of the actual harbour, as happened in the last cited Barclay case; and it would seem unreasonable to construe the word "Portus" into a title to such an extent of land, where the franchise alone will satisfy the word, and the franchise and land are fairly and technically distinguished from each other by the law itself. No other cases, save those quoted by the learned writer, present themselves to give colour to such construction: and with regard to the cases or records alluded to, it is not too much to say, that from the manner in which they are reported, it is not easy to collect out of the mass of evidence adduced, what was, and what was not the true

margin: Distinction between "Portus" in a subject and in the Crown.

Summary of the principal

The principal points of law discussed in the foregoing pages are these :—

1. That the dominion and ownership of the British Seas, and of the creeks, bays, arms, ports, and tide rivers thereof, are vested, by our law, in the Crown.
2. That this ownership includes *aquam et solum;* both the water, its products and uses, and the land or soil under the water.
3. That such ownership includes the shore, as far as the reach of the high-water mark of the [medium high tide between the springs and the neaps].
4. That the land subject to spring tides, and high spring tides, is no part of the sea, or sea-shore; but belongs to the title and ownership of the *terra firma*.
5. That by grant from the Crown, a subject may have a lawful ownership of a certain portion of the sea, its creeks, bays, arms, ports, or tide-rivers, and of the shores thereof, *tam aquæ quam soli.*
6. But that such grants must have a date anterior to the statutes restraining the alienation of Crown lands.
7. That no distinction exists at law, between the title or proofs of title to such land covered with water, and the title to *terra firma*.
8. That where the ownership claimed by a subject in any such *districtus maris*, or tide-river, or shore cannot be proved by the production of the grant, such ownership can *no otherwise* be established than by adverse possession, under the Statutes of Limitation.
9. That such ownership cannot be supported by "prescription," properly so called, against the King, and never could, at any period, be so supported under the feudal law.
10. That the proofs of title, where the grant itself is not forthcoming, to such *districtus maris aut littoris* must be *paris materiæ* with those required to prove title to inland estates.
11. That proof, by prescriptive evidence, of a right to a franchise, liberty, or easement in or out of the soil, is no sufficient evidence of title to the freehold and inheritance of the land itself, whether such land be *terra firma* or *pars maris*.
12. And consequently, that the ownership of a several fishery, or of the franchises of wreck, of flotsan, jetsan, and ligan, or of royal fish, or of ports, or the liberty of digging for sand, or shells, &c., will not be sufficient to establish an absolute ownership over the soil itself, where such rights are enjoyed against the Crown.
13. And, therefore, neither the express *grant* of a franchise, or liberty, nor "prescription" for such (which supposes a grant) can be con-

Points discussed. 155

14. That "alluvion," properly so called, belongs to the ownership of the freehold of the adjacent *terra firma*, subject to such interests in others as such ownership is liable to.
15. That "derelict" land, properly so called, belongs to the Crown, as land suddenly and by manifest marks left by the sea.
16. That islands produced out of the British Seas, and the creeks, bays, arms, ports, and tide-rivers thereof, belong, like derelict land, to the Crown.
17. Unless the soil under the water out of which such islands are produced, previously belonged to a subject.
18. That the title of a subject to the soil of a *districtus maris*, viz. to the soil of any creek, bay, arm, port, or tide-river, or to the shore, in no substantial respect differs from a title to *terra firma*.
19. That it is more for the public advantage that the ownership of subjects should be limited to the *terra firma;* and consequently, that by the rule of law, as well as of public policy, claims set up to tracts of sea, or of ports, or tide-rivers, or of the shore, ought not to be *favoured* against the Crown.

SUPPLEMENTAL CHAPTER

ON THE PUBLIC RIGHT TO USE THE SHORE

FOR BATHING,

AND FOR DIGGING AND TAKING SHELLS, SAND, ETC.

As to the Right to use the Shore for Bathing.

As to the right of bathing on the shore.

THE general right to frequent the shore for sea-bathing was made the subject of legal question, for the first time, in the case of Blundell *v.* Caterall.(*a*) The plaintiff, who resisted the right, "was the lord of the manor of Great "Crosby, which is bounded on the west by the river "Mersey, an arm of the sea." It is stated in the report of the case, "that as lord of the manor he was *owner* of the "*shore*, and had the exclusive right of *fishing* thereon *with* "*stake nets*. The defendant was the servant at an hotel "erected in 1815, upon land in Great Crosby, fronting the "shore, and bounded by the *high-water mark* of the river "Mersey, the proprietors of which hotel kept *Bathing* "*Machines* for the use of persons resorting thither, and

Right to use the Shore for Bathing.

"who were driven by defendant in machines across the
"shore into the sea for the purpose of bathing; and the
"defendant received a sum of money from the individuals
"so bathing, for the use of the machines, and for his ser-
"vice and assistance. No bathing machines were ever used
"upon the shore of Great Crosby before the establishment
"of this hotel; *but it had been the custom for people to cross
"it on foot for the purpose of bathing*. There was also a
"common highway for carriages along the shore, and it
"was proved that various articles for market were occa-
"sionally carted across the shore, although the more common
"mode of conveyance for such things was by a canal, made
"about forty years ago. The defendant contended for a
"*common law right* for all the King's subjects to bathe on
"the sea-shore, and to pass over it for *that* purpose on foot
"and with horses and carriages." It was decided by *three* Decided in
of the learned judges against one,(*b*) that no such *general* Blundell *v*. Caterall, that
right in the subject to frequent the shore, *for the purpose of* the public have *no* com-
bathing, existed, whether on foot or in carriages. mon law right
   This was the first case in which the public right to use to bathe on the sea-shore.
the sea and sea-shore for bathing, was ever *judicially* either Remarks on
claimed or opposed, as was remarked by Mr. Justice Bayley. the case of Blundell *v*.
The case was very fully argued, and the judges gave their Caterall.
opinions at considerable length. The learned counsel who
argued against the right, opposed it on *three* several grounds.
"*First*, from the silence of the authorities. *Secondly*,
"because such a right was contrary to analogies. *Thirdly*,
"because it was contrary to acknowledged and established
"rights;" and the three judges, by whom the case was
decided, seem to have been governed, principally, by the
first and *last* of these several grounds of argument.
   It is to be observed, that the title of the lord of the Remarks con-
manor to the absolute ownership of the shore itself was tinued.

supposed to be proved; and not only the soil of the shore, but also "an exclusive right of fishing thereon with stake nets," was taken for granted to be the private property of the lord; and, therefore, the particular question was *not* whether the shore was subject to such *general* customary right of bathing, but whether the *private ownership* of such shore, coupled with an exclusive private fishery with stake nets, was subject to such general customary right of bathing. The Court, however, did not confine themselves to the narrow ground of the incompatibility of the bathing with carriages, or on foot, in a place where a private fishery with stake nets existed; on the contrary, they decided upon the broad ground, that a general common law right did not exist at all, by ancient custom and usage, of frequenting the sea-shore for bathing. It was taken for granted, on all hands, that the original ownership of the shore is in the Crown; and that even the King's ownership was subject to the common law rights of fishing and navigation; and also, that the subject who became owner of the shore by the King's grant, was as liable as the King to those customary rights; but it was denied that either the King's or a subject's ownership of the shore was subject to a like general common law usage of bathing.

With regard to the *silence of the books*, the Court said, " that no trace of such a right was to be found in the " books." But it seems to have been admitted that " the books" were not the *only* authorities for or against such right; for the Court also said, " that the existence or the " extent of the subject's right was to be collected in this, " as in other instances, from the *manner in which* the sea-" shores throughout the kingdom have been from time to " time immemorially used; as well as from legal authorities." Now the silence of the books may, in some cases, be alleged in a right. The custom in question would seem to be a right of all others the least likely to become the subject of legal dispute. The silence of the books in respect of a custom so natural and universal, may be thought to make as much *for* as *against* the usage : (c) nor can the mere silence of the books be deemed a sufficient negative of a custom. If, indeed, the practice of bathing has generally prevailed, time out of mind, throughout the realm, the silence of the books gives consent rather than denial. The right in question was a case of *custom*, and by the *dicta* of the judges themselves, we are permitted, in the absence of all book authority, another distinct ground for decision, viz. " immemorial usage," which is the very essence of the common law itself.

It is not easy to point out a custom more universal, more natural, or more ancient on the sea-coasts not of England only, but of the whole world, than that of bathing. We know that the natives of the British Islands have been from time immemorial famous for their skill and intrepidity in the art of swimming. The most barbarous and the most

Antiquity of the custom, and its universality.

(c) It is admitted, that in some cases, "the silence of the books may be eloquence," as Lord Ellenborough expressed it in Aubrey *v.* Fisher, 10 East. 456. But *that* is where some singular custom differing from, or opposite to the general custom, is set up, and no mention or allusion made in the books to the opposite and particular custom. Thus in the case alluded to, the general custom of the *realm* was that trees under twenty years' growth were, if cut, to be deemed underwood and titheable, but trees of twenty years' growth and upwards were deemed *timber* trees, and not titheable. A custom was set up *in one county* that if the tree did not contain ten feet of solid timber, it was underwood ; and his Lordship's remark was applied to this alleged custom, which was deemed not to be good accordingly. In the principal case the custom to bathe is general ; and a custom set up, in one district, of limiting the bathing to one class of persons, or to persons of a certain age, or to a certain hour, would be a singular exception to a general rule ; and if the books were silent about it, might well be denied. But it would be strange to construe the silence of the books into a denial of a custom *which has actually existed universally* civilized nations in all parts of the globe have equally practised bathing and swimming. So far from the silence of our books being a good authority for the non-existence of this right, it would have been the more singular circumstance of the two to have found the point in any way disputed. The constant enjoyment of this privilege for ages without dispute, would, it might be supposed, have proved sufficient to establish it as a common law right, similar to that of fishing in the sea. It is difficult, indeed, to imagine a general and public right of fishing in the sea, and on the shore, unaccompanied by a general right to bathe there.

Distinction between the custom as claimed in respect of the sea, &c., and inland waters.

It is true, that if the natural instinct or habit of man to bathe be *alone* sufficient to establish such right, it would confer a right to bathe in rivers, streams, lakes, &c., which not being subject to the tides, are no part of the sea. But it is not the inclination alone, but the universal and habitual practice which is necessary to establish such a right; due regard being also had to the nature of the ownership in the *locus in quo*. Rivers and lakes, &c. not subject to the tides, being no part of the sea, are no public highway, no "great waste," subject to public use for fishing, navigation, &c. They are, by our law, private property to all intents and purposes. The analogy, therefore, does not fully hold; but even in this case it may be doubted whether a custom, proved to have existed time out of mind, of bathing at a particular place, in any river or lake, by the inhabitants of the adjacent parish, town, or district, especially where a common of piscary exists, may not be reasonably supported as an easement or liberty, on the same principle as a right of way. However this may be, the nature and degree of these habits amongst a maritime people, dwelling on the sea-coasts, and addicted to naviga-

the Shore for Bathing.

same footing as the habits of an inland people. We are, nationally, a maritime people, and general customs should be tried by the national habits and pursuits of such a people.

In the case before us it was argued, that although no express mention is made of bathing as a general common law right, yet the common right to frequent the shore (*littus*), without limitation of purpose (so that it be legal), is expressly asserted by Bracton. The learned judges, however, who decided the case, considered Bracton not only to have *quoted*, but to have *interpolated* this doctrine from the *Civil* law, and that the Civil law and our law do not agree. Mr. Justice Best (who dissented from the decision of the Court) replies to this reasoning, "that Bracton "has not *stated* this right as civil law; he has made it part "of his book '*de legibus et consuetudinibus Angliæ.*'" It appears, in fact, that the passage actually referred to and contradicted by the three learned judges, as being a mere transcript from the civil law, relates *not* to the *sea-shore*, but to the *banks of rivers*. There is a *separate* section in the Institutes relating to the sea-shore, which says, " LIT- " TORUM *quoque usus publicus juris gentium est, sicut et* " *ipsius maris ;*"(*d*) and *this* passage, nearly in the same words, Bracton has also;(*e*) although the learned judges commented on the text relating to *river banks*, viz. "*Riparum* etiam *usus publicus est, jure gentium, sicut ipsius fluminis*,"(*f*) which, at this day, is certainly not deemed, in its fullest extent, good law.(*g*) The reasoning, therefore, seems to have been this, Bracton is wrong in his law that " RIPARUM *usus communis est*," &c. therefore, "*littorum usus non est communis.*" But this is certainly a "*non*

The text of Bracton as favouring the right.

(*d*) Just. Inst. lib. ii. Tit. 1, sect. 5. (*e*) Bracton, lib. i. ch. 12, sect. 5.
(*f*) Bracton, lib. i. ch. 12, sect. 6.

sequitur;" and although the Court, from authorities, proved Bracton to be wrong, to a certain extent, in his law respecting particular uses made of banks of rivers (as for towage), yet no authorities were adduced showing that the *"communis usus"* of the *sea-shore* for bathing is not a good custom. It has been before shown that Bracton does not copy or follow the civil law in certain points relating to the sea and sea-shore. For whereas the language of the Institute (*h*) is, *"proprietas autem eorum potest intelligi nullius esse,"* the text of Bracton contains no such doctrine. Thus it is evident he did not merely copy the Institutes, since he has wholly omitted a most important sentence, which, as we have amply shown in former pages, is not law with us, whatever it might have been with the Romans.

Distinction between "ripa" and "littus."

The *ripa* or bank, and the *littus* or shore, are not one and the same. The *ripa* is *terra firma*, and generally cultivable, and therefore damageable in its crops and produce. But the *shore* is covered twice every twenty-four hours by the "tide," and partakes of the nature of sea-bottom, and is by Lord Hale himself distinguished from *"terra firma,"* and classed rather with sea-bottom. In legal parlance, indeed, shore, sea-bottom, and *terra firma* are all technically *land;* still, however, with this further technical distinction, that a grant of so many acres of *land*, without more words, will include no more than the "ripam," and will not include the "littus," nor any portion of land covered with water, unless so specially described. Wherefore, it is evident that the two words, *ripam* and *littus*, are not quite identified with each other; nor does a negative applied to a right claimed in respect of the one, *necessarily* touch or disaffirm a right claimed as to the other.(*i*)

(*h*) Instit. lib. ii. tit. 1, sect. 5.

the Shore for Bathing.

It may be safely admitted, that the banks of rivers not subject to the tides are not so open as *Bracton* represents, without admitting any mistake, to the same extent, as to the sea-shore. Few (if any) of our *old* law-writers are deemed better authority than Bracton; and if we are to assume, that because he is wrong in one case, and the law is since altered in another, therefore, in a third and different case he must also be wrong, what law-writer have we who can pass such an ordeal? Mr. Justice Buller, in the case of Ball *v.* Herbert(*k*) (which related to towage on the *banks* of a navigable river)(*l*), observes on the passage of Bracton, "riparum usus," &c.,—" It plainly appears to have " been taken from Justinian, and is only part of the Civil " law; and whether or not it has been adopted by the " Common law is to be seen by looking into our books, " and there it is not to be found."(*m*) But, it may be asked, what are "our books" if Bracton be not one? and if Bracton be not contradicted by other authorities or customs, he is, *prima facie*, an acknowledged law-writer of authority.

The text of Bracton as bears on th distinction.

Now, as the books are totally silent in regard to *bathing*

" that 'bank' more properly refers to hard, dry land. This is so of
" the word 'ripa,' according to the proposition in Hale's treatise; but
" the bank of the bay may include a sand-bank or mud-bank, though
" alternately covered and uncovered by the flux and reflux of the sea,
" and so be equivalent to 'shore.' The American courts have held
" that a 'bank' of a river is that space of rising ground above low-
" water mark, which is usually covered by high water, and the term,
" when used to designate a precise line, may be somewhat vague and
" indefinite:" Howard *v.* Ingersole, 17 Ala. U. S. 780; 13 How (U. S.) 426, per Curtis J.; Stone *v.* Augusta, 46 Maine, 127, 137. See also Child *v.* Starr, 4 Hill 369, per Cowen J. as to " Shore ;" Angell on Watercourses, p. 32, 6th edit.]

(*k*) 3 T. R. 253, post, 176, n.   (*l*) Quære, tide river?
(*m*) The judges, in the principal case, quoted the words of Judge Buller, as applicable to Bracton's doctrine relative to the sea-shore; although they were not so applied by Judge Buller himself, but to

(which is one part of the "communis usus littorum"), and silent also as to several other common uses to which the shore may be applied, the authority of Bracton, as to the right of the public to *make use* of the sea-shore, might be deemed good authority for all such customary uses made of it as are uncontradicted by the books, and not incompatible with other unquestionable rights, or the known laws of the land. There is nothing singular in the laws of two different nations agreeing in their permission of a custom so natural as bathing. The habit of bathing is as natural to a native of Britain as to a Roman; much more so, indeed, if the effect of insular habits (and habit is second nature) be considered. It would have been more singular if the *Civil* and *British* laws had not agreed in throwing open the seashore for purposes of public use common to all mankind.

The coincidence of phrase adopted in expressing such legal right, can be no sufficient ground for rejecting the law. The phrase may be borrowed, and yet speak the law of the land. If the law were as singular as the phrase, that might be a rational ground for doubting whether the law, as well as phrase, be not *foreign;* but in a case where it is so natural that all nations should think, and act, and legislate alike, it seems not reasonable to hold that the law is foreign because one of our jurists, writing in Latin, borrows a Latin phrase or sentence. Our early law writers wrote in the language of the Civil law, and not in their native tongue; the language of the Civil law was the language of our Courts in early times, though the law itself might differ; and many sentences in our early Latin writers might be pointed out, which lay down the undeniable Common law of England in the same words by which the Civil law expresses the same rule. Natural reason alone has made the Civil law and Common law to coincide in many points,

[margin: does not necessarily allow that because Bracton's text is taken from the Civil law, that the doctrine may not be good at common law.]

the Shore for Bathing. 165

be used to declare both codes, what wonder if the like words and phrases of one and the same language be used to express similar laws.

There are several points of the Roman law, delivered by Bracton in the language of the Institutes, which are allowed to be part of our Common law at this day, as Lord Hale himself admits. It is clear that our law has either *actually* adopted the Civil law in some points, or has, from the nature of things, coincided with it. The only true question is, whether the matter in dispute be or be not a part of *our* laws and customs? The Common law of England *may* adopt, and certainly has adopted, some detached portions of the Civil law; and it is not strange or difficult to suppose both these systems of law to have agreed in sanctioning a natural right and habit, coexistent with the earliest habits of the human race. Had the Roman law *first* declared that to bathe in the sea was *not* a common right, but must be asked or hired from the owner of the shore, and the English law had followed in the same words, it might then, indeed, be imagined that so strange a restraint in the law of England upon so natural a use of the sea-shore, expressed in the words of the Roman law, was interpolated from that law. But as regards the point in question, it is a custom common to all nations, and foreign to none.

<small>The Roman law and our Common law agree in som points.</small>

To say that the law was borrowed, is to infer that the custom did not exist before the time of borrowing. But will it be said that the shore was not as much frequented for bathing *before* that time as *after*? Men were used to bathe and swim long prior to the written codes of Rome or England. The *custom* preceded the *law*, and that which Roman law may have sanctioned by book, may have been already custom, *i.e.* Common law, in England. It must be admitted that our law and the Roman law do also *dis-*

<small>The custom of bathing preceded the law both of England and Rome.</small>

sea-shore; this was, at some length, proved by Mr. Justice Holroyd; but this is no evidence that they do not *agree* in other points. They *do* agree in the common right of fishing; why may they not agree in the common right of bathing? In those points wherein they differ, our books and Common law cause the difference; but do our books and customs create any difference as to bathing? It is admitted that not one expression in our books is to be found *contradictory* to the common right to frequent the sea-shore for bathing; and that bathing is, and ever has been, a *general* custom and practice will hardly be denied; for the habit is coeval at least with fishing and navigation, two acknowledged "*communes usus*" of the sea-shore.

The Court seem to have construed the words of Bracton, "*communis usus*," in an extreme sense, viz. as denying *all* ownership over the shore, even in the King. But it does not appear that the words were intended by Bracton to be understood further than as importing common rights of *usage*, distinct from the "*jus proprietatis ;*" nor is it *necessary* to interpret him to mean that the ownership of the soil was *not* (as now held to be) in the King. Indeed, we have just now shown that he wholly omits the doctrine of the Institutes, as regards the "*proprietas.*" He must, therefore, be taken to have meant no more than that the shore was a public *common*, open to public resort, and convertible to various public uses, as is the sea. It is in every day's experience that the shore *is* open " to common use." It is difficult to say what other common uses the shore can be converted to by the public, besides those of a "highway for the exercise of the fisheries and navigation," "digging " of the soil for manure, and for materials for building, " ballast, &c.," and, lastly, " bathing." The first three of these uses are confirmed by the law; and the digging and

Statute law to all the inhabitants of two of the largest maritime districts (*n*) in England, but has been disputed as a general right. (*o*)

Thus the language of Bracton would seem to be warranted alike by law and practice in every use to which the *sea* can be applied; whilst one disputed instance (the digging of sand, &c.) will not apply to the *sea*, and therefore does not come strictly within his words, which are "*sicut et ipsius maris.*" The sea is a public highway,—so also is the shore. The sea is subject to the public right of fishing and navigation,—so also is the shore; and to what other purposes is the *sea* applied, by *common right*, to which the *shore* has not been at least *equally* applied by common *use*, digging for sand, &c. not excepted? So far, therefore, as relates to the "communis usus" (exclusive of the barren *ownership* of the soil) the text of Bracton is borne out by matter of fact. (*p*) Callis also, quoting from an old text-writer, says,

<small>Uses of the sea and seashore.</small>

(*n*) Devon and Cornwall. See p. 94, ante.
(*o*) In Bagott *v.* Orr. 2 Bos. and Pull. 472.
(*p*) In the case, the King *v.* Commissioners of Sewers, for Pagham, Sussex, 8 B. and C. 355, it is laid down by the Court, "that every landowner exposed to the inroads of the sea, has a right to protect himself, and is justified in erecting such *works* as are necessary for that purpose." This was said in regard to *groynes*, a kind of work which takes permanent possession of the soil, and is only effectual when constructed upon the "shore." These groynes are piles of wood carried out from high-water mark, at right angles from the coast, towards the sea, across the "shore." The effect is to accumulate the beach and shingles on the one side into heaps, and which accumulation constitutes the protection sought for. The sea is thus made to shut out

As to the general Right to use

"*Rex habet proprietatem sed populus habet usum ibidem necessarium.*"(*q*) The practice of bathing and swimming may justly be termed "necessary" to a maritime people. It is true the shore may be converted to other uses than those independent of the ownership of the "shore," or as a right inherent only in the ownership of the shore. Presuming the "shore" to belong to the Crown (as is to be presumed until the contrary be shown), the question is, whether all owners of lands on the coast have a right *so* to use the shore, such shore being the property of the King? or whether the Court intended to apply the doctrine only to *those* who were *owners* of both the land and the "shore?" Such works are, in fact, an *embanking* against the sea, and do not only protect the land from further inroads, but recover lost land from the sea. The question is of importance, as regards evidence of title to the "shore;" for if the right be *general*, and independent of the ownership of the shore, such acts cannot be evidence of *private* right to the shore. And if the ownership of the shore will alone give the right to do such acts, the ownership of the shore, in point of title, must have existed *before* any such act; and if so, then such act can only be proved *lawful* by proving a pre-existing title to the shore. If the title to the shore must be *first proved* to make any such act *lawful*, the title to the shore must be proved by evidence *dehors* the act itself. Presumption, in this case, is no good title against the Crown. Such acts as these, done by private individuals, are independent of acts done by Commissioners under the Statute of Sewers, 23 H. 8, ch. 5. It will hardly be held that the erection of *one* groyne, by the lord of the adjacent manor, will, after a lapse of twenty or more years, be *per se* sufficient evidence of title to the soil of the shore against the King. One or two groynes will often prove adequate to the protection of several miles of coast; and even occasion very considerable additions to such extent of coast. If, however, the right to erect such works upon the shore be held to be a general Common law right, it is no slight argument in favour of Bracton's doctrine. It may also be remarked, that if by the construction of such works such rapid *additions* are obtained from the sea as the law will *take notice of*, they will belong to the Crown, *unless* those additions have been taken possession of by sufficient acts of ownership for the period of time required by the Statutes of Limitation, to negative the King's title. See p. 120, ante; and 2 Anst. 614, Attor. Gen. *v.* Richards. [It is not competent for the proprietors of land on either side of a river to disturb the ordinary course of the stream to the prejudice of the opposite proprietor: Menzies *v.* Breadalbane, 3

the Shore for Bathing.

just mentioned, but not such as are in their nature *open* and *common;* therefore, an *appropriation* or *in-taking* of it is not a "*communis usus.*" Now, in the case of a common within a manor, it is well known that the lord of the manor is owner of the soil of the common; but that the tenants have a certain "communis usus" of such common, so as to render the "soil" of comparatively trifling value to the lord. He cannot infringe upon the rights of the "commoners," by any in-taking or inclosure of the common. Why cannot this analogy serve for the sea-shore? The common uses to which it has *generally* and immemorially been applied by the public, might as reasonably be supported, as are similar uses of the soil of inland manors, so long as such uses are beneficial to the public; and the ownership of the soil might be available only in cases where the "common rights" are not injured. The soil of the shore would seem to deserve no better protection on behalf of private owners, than the soil of a common within a manor; on the contrary, a private ownership of the sea-shore, if asserted and acted upon, is very likely to prove a public nuisance; and therefore deserves no encouragement or support against any public uses which are laudable and beneficial, and have ancient usage in their favour.

But the Court seem to have denied the *continued* and *immemorial* custom of bathing on the sea-shore. Lord

As to the immemorial custom of bathing.

Bli. N. S. 414; 3 W. & Shaw, 235. In Rex *v.* Trafford, 1 B. and Ad. 888; Lord Tenterden, distinguishing between a right to embank against the sea and against a river, says: " In the one case, if the works be success-
" ful, the water is prevented from coming where, within time of memory
" at least, it never had come; in the other it is prevented from passing
" in the way in which, when the occasion happened, it had been always
" accustomed to pass."

It is no defence to an indictment for a nuisance for embanking in the water-way, that although the work be in some degree a hindrance to navigation, it is advantageous in a greater degree, to other uses of the

Tenterden declared, "that if the right exist now, it must "have existed at all times; but we *know*," he adds, "that "sea-bathing was, until a time comparatively modern, a "matter of *no frequent* occurrence;" and he adds, "that he "was not aware of any practice in this matter sufficiently "extensive or uniform to be the foundation of a judicial "decision." But, with great deference, it seems singular to deny the uniformity, universality, and frequent occurrence of bathing and swimming in the sea; a practice known to exist habitually wherever man and sea-water are to be met with. There is not a village on the coast where the practice will not be found to have uniformly prevailed. Cleanliness, health, amusement, and utility, have all operated to make the custom general on the sea-coast.

It is true that the *manner* of bathing in "machines," (*r*) (as his Lordship remarked) may not be either *ancient* or extremely uniform; but the *right*, and the precise *manner* of exercising that right, are not the same questions. The right of bathing, and not the right of bathing in "*machines*," is the true question, and was, in fact, the question decided by the Court. It is another question whether the right of way to the sea be open for carriages in some *particular spot* of the *ripam* in regard to the private ownership there. If the public have a convenient approach to the shore, it is enough, without their being allowed to make as many ways as they please, and from mere caprice, over the grounds of others. That the public, in every parish, manor, &c. on the coasts, have a right to one or more convenient ways of approach to the shore, according to the wants, extent, and localities of the district, is not to be denied, since without this, fishing and navigation would be valueless. Nor is it sufficient that such way should be a mere foot-way; and if it be a way for horses and carriages, and I thus have a right to drive down to and along the shore in a machine or carriage, to get into a boat to float on the sea, why may I not do so to get into the sea itself? (*s*) The right of way to the sea was never yet contended to be a mere *footway;* the same mode of approach to and from the sea as is allowed for fishing or embarkation, is all that is desired on behalf of bathing. As to denying the right to bathe, on the ground that the "machines" are a "modern invention," it may be thought that they are rather a recommendation than otherwise in support of a custom, which, in its more ancient practice, was not so decent, or so well adapted to modern refinement.

But it was further declared, by Mr. Justice Holroyd, that " such right of bathing is inconsistent with the nature of " permanent private property, as well as inconsistent with " the fishing on the sea-shore being also an exclusive right." Now, with regard to the sea-shore being private property, this does not seem to be a species of ownership worthy of being *favoured* either against the Crown or the public. It was also well and truly said, by the learned counsel for the defendant, " that no subject, claiming under the King, can claim a greater right than the King had in the shore;" and the true question all along is, whether the King's ownership in the shore is not itself subject to this usage? The ownership of the Crown in the shore has always been subject to the public right of using it as a road for fishing and navigation. It is evidently not the *sea* alone, but the *shore* also which is subject to these two Common law rights. Thus, the frequenting the shore is claimed and enjoyed as an accessary to these rights, which are the principals. It is like a grant by A, of a piece of ground to B, in the midst of the ground of A, which grant were useless unless B had a right of way over A's ground to the piece of ground granted to him; therefore, the law implies and gives to B a right of way over A's other ground. So the shore lies between the fishery or navigation and the public, but the public have a right to the fishery and navigation, and a convenient way is presumed over the shore for carrying them on; such as for launching boats, carriage and footway for the conveyance of the fish, goods, &c. to and from the boats, &c., and for exercising whatever other conveniences common sense and usage point out as *essential* to these rights; in short, whatever obstruction would render the fishery or navigation nugatory, must be deemed unlawful and incompatible with those rights. But to build houses or docks on the shore, or to form permanent quays or wharfs by the fishermen or traders themselves (not being owners of the soil), will be going beyond the essentials of their rights. All such permanent appropriations of the soil are no part of the public rights of fishery or navigation, and should therefore be matter of private bargain. The temporary purpose for which the shore is used must be essentially and necessarily subservient to the right claimed, and so far such temporary purpose, it is apprehended, is not inconsistent with private property in the shore. To this extent the Common law right to use the sea-shore, does, it is conceived, prevail throughout the coasts of England, whether such "*locus*" be a port, or not; or whether it be the King's property or the property of a subject.

But if, in addition to his ownership of the soil of the shore, the subject claim a private fishery, such claim, if allowed, is paramount to the public fishery; and therefore no accessory to the public fishery (such as a right of way) can be allowed to injure the private right; for if the public fishery itself yield to the private, the incidents to such public fishery must yield also. Now, assuming the right to bathe to be coeval in antiquity of usage with ancient modes of fishing which require the fisher to immerse himself in the water), the same evidence which will support the private fishery against the public fishery, and its incidental right of way, will also support the private fishery against the "bathing" and its incidental right of way, so far as it may interfere with such private fishery; and if the bathing, in the case of Blundell *v.* Catterall, under consideration, did injury to the private fishery, and such private fishery was good in title, then the decision of the case was just, *quoad hoc.* Of two incompatible rights, if one be allowed to be good, the other cannot be so ; but then the case we have put is similar to the case of a private fishery, excluding the general and public fishery.

It was expressly allowed by the learned Judge, "that, as "incident to the fishery, the public *must* have the means of "getting to and upon the water for those purposes ;" but he adds, " that it will appear, that it is by and from such "places only as necessity or usage have appropriated to such "purposes." Is it then meant to be laid down as law, that the "sea-shore" is only accessible for the purpose of fishing, in old fishing villages, or sea-ports? Suppose a village on the sea-coast, whose inhabitants never yet launched a boat, are the cottagers precluded from turning fishermen, and approaching and exercising on the shore their Common law right of fishery? It would seem that the whole sea-coast of the realm is the *place* appropriated by "usage and necessity" to the public common of piscary. The right is attached to the person, to every individual of the public body. It is the birth-right of the subject, and he is not bound to exercise his right in one place more than another. All that he has to do is to pay regard to rights declared by the law paramount to his own ; but the mere ownership of the soil is no such private right as can bar the *jus publi-*

is subject to such right, and the ownership of individuals derived from the Crown is not greater.

As to the right to land from boats, &c., on the shore.

It is said, by Mr. Justice Holroyd, " that it is not by the " Common law, nor by statute, lawful to come with, or land, " or ship customable goods in creeks or havens, or other places " out of ports, unless in cases of danger or necessity, nor fish, " or land other goods not customable, where the shore or " land adjoining is private property."(*t*) Undoubtedly, customable goods cannot lawfully be landed except in the ports assigned for their reception, and the payment of duties. The *jus regium* of the King, which entitles him to levy the customs, entitles him, as *custos portuum*, to appoint the places for the landing and shipping of customable goods; but it is difficult to consider the law as granting the public fishery, and yet denying the right to land the fish upon the *ripam*, as well as *shore*, so far as such *temporary* use of the *ripam* or of the shore is reasonably *necessary ;* such fish to be forthwith removed, and not left or marketed there, to cause permanent or unreasonable obstruction to the ownership of the soil.

The public have a right to fish on the

There can be no doubt whatever but that the public have a right to fish on the *shore*, although the soil thereof may

(*t*) " If one has piscary in any *water*, he has no power to land without the assent of the tenants of the frank-tenement." Savil, xi. pl. 29, inhabitants of Ipswich *v.* Brown, 23 Eliz. See Vin. Abr. title Piscary, D. But the fishery here meant is a *several* or *private* fishery. In Ward *v.* Cresswell, Willes 265, Vin. Abr., Piscary B,—Defendant in replevin, avows taking six boat oars (from boats hauled above high-water mark) as damage feasant, for that the *place where* was his freehold. Plaintiff pleads in bar of the avowry,—1. A common of fishery in the sea there, *as appurtenant to certain tenements* there,—2. A liberty of landing and putting on shore their boats upon the place, for the use of the fishery. It was held that fishing in the sea, being matter of common right, a prescription for it, as appurtenant to a particular township, is void. Accord : the plea in bar was held to be ill. Here the landing and putting up their boats (which was the damage)

the Shore for Bathing. 175

happen to be private property. To exclude the public there must be proved a *several* fishery, as well as an ownership of the soil. The public fishery extends over sea and shore, and there are many kinds of fish which can only be caught on the shore. The case of Bagot v. Orr, (*u*) has expressly decided that the public have a Common law right to take *shell fish* on the "shore," without reference to the person to whom the soil belongs; and, it is presumed, the "fishery" includes all kinds of fish (royal fish excepted) wherever their haunts may be, whether in the great waste of the sea, or upon the shore. With regard to the fish taken at sea, it would be difficult to contend that it would be *necessary* to carry fish to a *port*, before it is landed. (*x*) The right to land the fish upon the strand nearest where it is caught, would seem to be an essential adjunct of the fishery ; the fishery is for the sustenance of the fishermen, their families, and others dwelling on the spot whence they embark; and to require the fish to be landed at a port perhaps twenty miles off, with all the delays of winds, and tides, and office, and land carriage, &c., is utterly destructive of the fishery. It must be presumed, that the Common law right of fishery includes the right to land the fish at the places where it may be most conveniently sold and used for food. Half the fisheries in the kingdom would be ruined if a contrary doctrine prevailed.

shore, as well as on the sea.

The public no compellable to land fish caught at sea at the port.

It is difficult to regard the fishery as a *public* and *general* right, and the necessary way and passage for its exercise as a *local* and *partial* privilege. The public right to navigate the seas, and to fish therein, is not limited to particular places; it is not a local right, but pervades the whole coast of England. The right of way for the exercise of these

As to the rig of way along the "ripa" above high-water mark.

(*u*) Bagott *v.* Orr, 2 Bos and Pull. 472. See this case more fully,

public rights would seem to be commensurate. But the fisherman or navigator must be ruled by the law, through the verdict of a jury, as to what shall be *sufficient* in the *locus in quo*. The law (for instance) will compel him to take the usual and public road down to the sea-side, if there be one within reasonable and convenient distance; but when there, how is he to reach his boat, which may be a mile off along the shore, at the time of *high water*, unless he can go along the edge of the coast on the *terra firma*,(*y*)

(*y*) Callis, p. 74, says, "I cannot more aptly compare a *bank* of the "sea, or of a navigable river, than to a high way;" and he extends this right of way to a right "to tow the boats to and fro." But more recent authority has decided that "towage along the banks of navig- "able rivers is not a common right." Ball *v.* Herbert, 3 T. R. 253, post, p. 215. This would not seem to be a "necessarium usum" for navigation, properly so called. But for every "necessarium usum," affecting the public fishery and navigation, the bank would seem to be open to the public. Whether the fishermen and others have a *right* to drag up their vessels above the reach of the tides, upon the banks, for security and for repairs, as is the universal *practice*, does not seem ever to have been decided; this would appear to be *essential* to the protection of the fishery, and perhaps be supported. [See Appendix, post, p. lxiii.] See note to p. 174, ante. So the practice of drying nets on the adjacent land, as well as on the shore, does not seem to have ever been sanctioned by a judicial decision, as a common right. Callis, however, states it as such, p. 73. It might be considered, perhaps, a practice of too vague a character to be supported as a general right, or even local easement or liberty. In some places such a privilege might prevent the cultivation and usufruct of many acres of valuable ground. Nets are said often to extend more than a mile when spread out, belong- ing to one boat only. See what is said by Holroyd, J. in Blundell *v.* Caterall, 5 B. & Ald. pp. 295, 296, and cases cited there, which seem opposed to such privilege. [See Gray *v.* Bond, 2 B. and B. 667, 5 J. B. Moore, 527 S. C. It was there held that it is not lawful for fishermen, merely as such, to dry their nets on a part of the shore which belongs to private persons, or to use such shore land for any purpose accessory to fishing; but the case shows that, by user, the owner of a fishery in a public navigable river may acquire a right to draw to land and land nets, used in the fishery, at certain places on the banks of a river, the property of private persons unconnected with the fishery. See also Hoyle *v.* McCunn, 31 Scot. Jur. 63; S. C. 10 Dec. 1858: 21 Court of

to his boat? It would be a serious obstruction to the fishery if he must bring his boat where the old road runs into the sea, and nowhere else. So, when on the sea, if he desire to land his fish, his merchandise (not customable) or himself, at the time of high water, unless he is allowed a way along the *terra firma*, to the next public road, he cannot land at all; wherefore, in all such cases, at the time of high water, either there must be a Common law right of way, along the dry land to the nearest inland road, and consistent with the public right of fishing and navigation, or at the time of high water no man can embark or disembark at other places than where the inland road meets the sea. Such a rule, in regard to the fishery, and to all the boat and small craft navigation, would be very injurious to the common right, and prejudicial to the public.

The Common law does not seem to control, in such manner, the general rights of fishing in and navigating the seas. It does not compel the subject to embark or disembark his person or his goods (not customable) at one place more than another; and it is conceived, that in order to the full, complete, and unimpeded exercise of these great public rights, a right of way, above and along the edge of high-water mark, is involved in the existence of those other public rights, and annexed to them; but subject (for the due protection of *private* rights) to the control of a jury, as to what shall be deemed *sufficient*, in the place of exercise. _{The law do not compel goods not customable be landed a port.}

The object of these remarks has been to shew, that if a right of common, or to a liberty, or easement be established, the essential means of enjoying that right are established with it. If there be a customary right to bathe in the sea, the use of the sea-shore, so far as such use is essential to the custom, must accompany it, but no further. The general doctrine of Bracton, that the sea-shore is "common

right of bathing, or any other common use of such shore, until it be shewn that such general doctrine is contradicted by law, or custom, or both, as to that particular use of it; but no custom, no authority whatever has been adduced to *contradict* Bracton's general doctrine, so far as it is considered to include sea bathing.

If this usage of bathing be rejected as not founded in law, it must be rejected by arguments grounded on "the " incompatibility with private rights, or with public con- " venience" of the custom. (*z*) The Court, indeed, in their decision, seem to have addressed themselves most particularly to the points of the inconsistency of *this* right with *other* rights, and its public inconvenience. Its incompatibility with other rights was strongly insisted upon by all three of the learned judges. It was said by Mr. Justice Holroyd to be "inconsistent with the nature of permanent private property." By Mr. Justice Bayley it was asked, " If the soil be vested in an individual, is he to be deprived " of the right of saying how that soil shall be used, and the " privilege of making any regulations he may think fit?" And by Lord Tenterden, " every public right to be exercised " over the land of an individual is, *pro tanto*, a diminution of " his private right:" and Mr. Justice Bayley and Lord Tenterden urged, that "it would prevent the owner of the " soil from building quays, wharfs, or private houses, as " well as from making embankments, &c.; for all such " would be obstructions to this public right of bathing " (if allowed), and, therefore, abateable as nuisances." (*a*)

(*z*) [See Appendix, post, p. lxv.]
(*a*) This argument, as well as that used by the Court, p. 171, ante, rests upon the assumption that the sea-shores throughout the kingdom are for the most part in the hands of private owners, and are *not* the property of the Crown. This, however, seems to be not only a gratuitous presumption, but a presumption against the King's title. The

the Shore for Bathing. 179

But it is to be remembered, that any such appropriations of the shore, even by the owner, are liable to be abated as nuisances, if they interfere with the public rights of *fishing* and of *navigation*. Whether they are or are not nuisances is a question for the jury. Thus then the private property of the shore (such as it is) is already, in two material instances, under the check of a jury, by which the owner is plainly interdicted from doing with the shore "as he pleases;" and why should it be thought *hard* to leave it to a jury to protect any other beneficial public custom (as bathing), by determining whether the obstruction be or be not, in reason and common sense, a public nuisance? that is,—such an obstruction of the bathing as ought to be put down. Quays, wharfs, and embankments in general, *below* high-water mark, convert that which was shore into *terra firma*, being, in fact, so much land gained from the sea, and therefore no longer shore. If any ground be left on the *other* side, towards the sea, that may be shore, and subject as before; but no one can suppose that an embankment by which the soil is rescued from the sea by the owner of the shore, would be abateable as a nuisance, in favour of bathing or fishing, whilst the shore, beyond and around, is still open to the public, and these rights may be enjoyed as easily as

As to its compatil with priv rights.

Quays, v &c. on t shore.

the Crown, and that individual subjects have no right, except by ancient grant from the Crown, to build houses, or construct wharfs, &c. on the shore. It is not to be *assumed* that the Crown has granted away *all*, or the *principal* part of the shores of the kingdom. But if these private ownerships are only *partial*, and not *general*, it does not seem a legitimate ground of argument to object to a *general* custom, as such, *because* it might stand opposed, in a few places, to the *particular* ownerships of a *few* individuals. The question ought to be considered as one between the King's ownership in all the "shores" of the realm, and the uses claimed therein by his subjects, in diminution of such absolute ownership. The custom of bathing on the shores of the realm has always been as fully acquiesced in by the Crown as the fishery, and from times as remote and immemorial. See Appendix, before. Nor was it ever contended that the supposed owner of the soil of the shore has not a right to convert it into *terra firma*, at his own risk and expense, unless in so doing he created a public or local nuisance. (*b*)

There is no law which makes a conversion of the seashore into *terra firma*, *always* and *necessarily* a nuisance; it must be proved to be a nuisance in its consequences,—and if it prove so to the public, it is better put down. If a road have been used, time out of mind, in a particular direction down to the sea, and by my in-taking of the shore I interpose dry land between the water and the place where the water before met the road, where is the difficulty of prolonging the road down to the new-formed high-water mark? A road existed heretofore over the shore to the sea, and is not lost by the shore's being now dry land; the said land, when wholly dry, is not altered in title, but is still subject to the right of road to the sea. Why, therefore, are not these rights reconcileable with each other? Suppose the sea to have suddenly retired from a tract of land, and the old road, instead of ending in the sea, to be thrown back a mile from the water, will not the law carry it on into the water? And why not also if the land become *terra firma* by the act of the party? If I have a way to the shore, am I, when arrived there, to ask leave of the Crown, or other owner, to walk, or ride, or drive into the water? In launching boats, and disembarking when the tide is low, it is frequently necessary to wade some distance through the water,—and it is to be presumed that it is lawful so to do. When I have reached the shore, how can any line of road be prescribed to me which the next tide will not obliterate? The right of way on the sea-shore is bounded by the water's edge, which is never stationary between high-water and low-water mark. But if that which was shore be made

the Shore for Bathing.

dry land, one road may then be set out for general use over it, in continuation of the road which before led to the shore, and so into the sea, or along the new shore. The right of bathing would seem to be nothing more than a right of way down to the shore, along the shore, and into the sea.

Every permanent occupation of the shore by exclusion of the sea is an embankment or in-taking; and every owner of the soil, whether the King or a subject, proving his ownership, has a right to appropriate such soil; but subject and without prejudice to existing rights of others. If the law of Bagott v. Orr (c) be good, and a general Common law right of fishing on the shore at ebb tide exist, then *any* exclusive appropriation of the soil of the shore is in derogation of the public common right of piscary, and abateable as a nuisance, *if a jury shall decide it to be so* in the disputed place. So any appropriation or obstruction of the shore, or of the customary public approaches to the shore, injurious to the public right of navigation, is abateable as a nuisance. (*d*)

Right to ba a right of w into the sea

The learned Judges, however, doubted whether, if they admitted the use of the shore for *bathing* to be a public liberty or privilege, all useful appropriations of the shore would be prevented. But if the appropriation in any given case would be a nuisance not to the bathing only, but to the fishery and navigation also, the sooner it is abated the better, whether the bather, or the fisherman, or the navigator effect it; and if it be no obstruction, no nuisance, to navigation or fishing, but actually auxiliary and beneficial towards those national purposes, where is the probability that *such* an appropriation will, in its extent or locality, be adjudged a nuisance by a jury, on behalf of the bather alone? On the other hand, if the appropriation prove of

The right t bathe will occasion o more benefi uses to be down as nuisances.

(*c*) 2 Bos. and Pull. 472.

no advantage to fishing and navigation, whilst it materially interferes with the custom of bathing, a custom which may have become essential to the local interests of the place, the sooner such an appropriation is declared a nuisance the better. (*e*)

*ional ad-
:ages re-
.ng from
present
om of
ting in the*

The custom of bathing is not the less ancient or wholesome, because in the present age it has become a *fashion;* and it is now too late to deny that this fashionable custom, freely exercised, has caused a great resort of people to the sea-coasts, and has raised into existence many large and beautiful towns, and produced a spirit of industry and speculation, in furtherance of this bathing custom, which has added greatly to the wealth, population, and strength of the country. Millions of capital have been expended for the accommodation of those who frequent the shores of the realm, for the purpose of exercising their supposed right of bathing; and the fortunes of thousands are dependent on this "custom;" and yet, by the decision of the above case, it has been thought good to place all this great expenditure and risk of industry and capital at the mercy of a private owner of the sea-shore, out of regard to the barely possible case of a jury's interfering with the appropriation of such shore by the owner to the national purposes of fishing, navigation, and commerce, on the ground that it is *nevertheless* an obstruction to bathing. If the interests of these national purposes clash, it might be left to the Jury to decide which shall prevail.

*: custom of
ting in the
too general
e construed
cal custom.*

It is said by Mr. Justice Holroyd, that "where there is, " or has hitherto been, a necessity, or even urgency, for " such a right, there, as far as such necessity has existed, " some usage must have prevailed." This admits that there possibly *may* be a *local* usage or custom of bathing. Now every manor on the coast has its inhabitants, and it were an assertion easily disproved were it said, that bathing in the sea is *not* customary with these inhabitants; and it would be impossible to arrive at the precise degree of necessity or urgency which introduced or continued the practice. Assuming that the inhabitants for the time being of the sea-coasts of England, are and have ever been accustomed to frequent the shore for bathing, it would be singular to denominate this a collection of *local* customs. The inhabitants of the sea-coast are, in fact, the only class of the community who *fish* in the sea, or on the sea-shore, and yet it is not a *local* but a public and *general* Common law right of fishing; and the custom of bathing is as general amongst the inhabitants of the sea-coast as fishing. It would be strange, therefore, to denominate the one custom a *general*, and the other custom (which is at least equally general amongst the same class of persons) a *local* custom. But if the right to frequent the shore for bathing by means of *carriages* be denied, then, indeed, every watering-place (as they are now called) in the kingdom may be wholly dependent upon the owner of the soil of the shore.

Lord Tenterden observes, that the "machines are of comparatively modern invention." It certainly is not handed down to us, by any records, by what various means our ancestors approached the sea for the purpose of bathing. But the question does not depend upon the inquiry as to what "machines" they employed to transport themselves *to* and *into* the sea;—but whether the sea-shore be, or be not, subject to a right of road or way for footmen, horses, and carriages to pass over and along it to the sea. Has not the subject a right of *carriage*, as well as *foot* way along the shore, to his fishing-boat, yacht, or trading vessel? And if he have, it would seem singular to deny his further right to drive or wade into the sea.

over a man's *stake-nets*, wears, or private fishing-place; *that is a case sui generis*, and an exception to the general rule; but it is considered that no book, or authority, or custom whatsoever, denies the right of way *ad libitum*, over and along the "shore," so long as it is *shore*, whether the soil be the King's, or belong to a subject by grant from the Crown. Such right of way is allowed for fishing; (*f*) and, when the case was *res integra*, it might have been expected that the Courts would have allowed the shore to be used as a highway as much for the one purpose as the other, instead of thus virtually declaring the same man a trespasser for bathing, who was no trespasser when up to his knees or neck in water, in search of a lobster, a crab, or a shrimp.

It was further said by the Court, that in the exercise of this right (if allowed), "one man might make his own " special profit of conveying persons over the shore, the soil " of another; and that such man had no reason to complain " if the owner of the soil shall participate in the profit." (*g*) But the profit made by the bathing-assistant is upon the use of the "machine," and the labour of his driving it, and his attendance; and it might as well be urged, that if I am driven in a hired carriage across the soil of the lord of an inland manor, along a public parish road, the lord can, reasonably, stop the driver, and insist upon "participating in his profit" or hire. According to this view of the case, the ownership of the sea-shore may, by a rapacious indi-

(*f*) [See Dickens *v.* Shaw, Appendix, post, p. xlvii.]
(*g*) This also seems to be an objection raised to a *general* custom, upon the ground of its interference with some *few partial* ownerships. But the ownership to which this general custom stands properly opposed, is the general ownership of the *Crown* in the sea-shores of the realm, and not to the ownerships of a few scattered individuals. It is not to be assumed, nor is it presumed by the law, that the subject

of Bathing considered. 185

vidual, be made, in many places of public resort, a most lucrative source of exaction.

The Court, moreover, decided against the liberty of bathing, not only from the silence of the books, and its supposed "inconsistency with certain private rights," but were also of opinion, that "in sea-bathing, as it now prevails, "particular regulations are desirable; and yet the exist- "ence of this common law right would be a great obstruc- "tion to any such regulation." But it can scarcely be deemed a public benefit to subject this right of bathing to the superintendence of the owner of the soil of the sea-shore, (*i.e.*) the lord of the manor, or his grantee, who may be a hundred miles off; and who is under no obligation, by law, to concern himself about it at all. It is to be remembered, too, that so far as *decency* is concerned, the public are perfectly able to protect themselves; for the *indecency* of bathing in too public places, and in too exposed a manner, is indictable as an offence, and punishable at common law, by the local magistrates, without paying any tax to the lords of the sea-shore. The idea of denying this ancient, universal, and healthful custom the support of the Courts of Law, *with a view* that the lord of the manor may superintend the bathing (not without charging his own price for it), or in order that "some contests" between the bathing men and women may be prevented thereby, seems singular. It is not probable that the owner of the soil will ever interfere in these matters, unless for the purpose of making a profit thereby. The public are not likely to be the gainers by his services, especially if they may be taxed for the use of the shore, at the will of the owner. The decision in the case of Blundell *v.* Catterall has, however, put it in the power of every owner of the soil of the sea-shore to levy a tax *ad libitum* upon the bathers, not only at fashionable

As to the public Right to dig

wherever such ownership of the shore can be proved. If the public are laid open to such a tax, they will do well to try with a closer scrutiny the claims set up by lords of manors to the "sea-shore;" and not to take it for granted that, because A or B is lord of the manor *on the coast*, that he is *therefore* owner of the *shore*, now that such ownership involves a question most important to the property of thousands, the prosperity of numerous towns and districts on the coast, and the general health, convenience, and enjoyment of the public. (*h*)

As to the public right to dig for Sand, Shells, &c. on the Shore.(*i*)

The case of Bagott *v.* Orr, 2 Bos. and Pull. 472, turned upon two points; 1st, whether the subjects of the realm had a general Common law right to catch and take *shell-fish* on the sea-shore, *between the flux and reflux of the tides*?

(*h*) [See Angell on Tide Waters, 32. Where there is a local board, see as to Bathing 10 and 11 Vict. c. 89, s. 69; 21 and 22 Vict. c. 98, s. 44; and the Town Police Clauses Act, containing provisions as to bathing. Powers conferred upon local commissioners, or local boards of health under 10 and 11 Vict. cc. 34 and 89; or under any special Act, for the regulation of the mode of bathing on the seashore, and licensing bathing machines there, do not warrant the licensees of such machines in placing them on any part of the foreshore which is private property: Mace *v.* Philcox, 15 C. B. N. S. 600; 33 L. J. N. S. C. P. 124.]

(*i*) [See Dickens *v.* Shaw, Appendix, post, p. li. It has been held in America that there is a public right to dig for shell-fish in a part of the shore which had become private property: Peck *v.* Lockwood, 5 Day (Conn.) R. 22. And there is a common right, in legal presumption, to take shell-fish on the shore between high and low water mark. Martin *v.* Waddell, 16 Peters (U.S.) R. 367; Arnold *v.* Munday, 1 Halst. (N. Y.) R. 1; Fleet *v.* Hegeman, 14 Wend. (N. Y.) R. 42; Cornfield *v.* Coryell, 4 Wash. (Cir. Co.) R. 371; Parker *v.* Cutler, Mill Dam Corp. 20 App. (Me.) R. 353; Hall *v.* Whillis, 14 Sc. Sess. Cases, 2nd series, 324; Angell on Watercourses, p. 73; and Angell on Tide

for Sand, &c. on the Shore.

2dly, Whether the subjects of the realm had a general Common law right of digging, collecting, and carrying away for use sea *shells*, and, by consequence, any other portion of the *soil* of the sea-shore? It was an action of trespass, brought by Bagott against the defendant Orr. The first count was, the breaking and entering the plaintiff's closes, called &c. [names] *and the sea-shore* in the parish of Keysham, and plaintiff's *shell-fish* and *shells* there finding, catching, taking and carrying away, and converting and disposing thereof to defendant's own use. The second count was for breaking and entering the same closes, and with defendant's feet, and the feet of his servants, in walking, treading up, trampling upon, subverting and spoiling plaintiff's soil, earth, and sand, and with the feet of cattle, and with the wheels of carriages, and the keels of boats treading up, trampling, &c.; and the plaintiff's *shell-fish* and *shells* breaking, crushing, and destroying, and with spades, &c. digging, and making holes, pits, and turning up, &c. plaintiff's earth, soil, and sand, and digging up, raising up, and getting up divers large quantities of plaintiff's *shell-fish* and *shells*, and carrying away the same, and converting and disposing thereof to defendant's own use. There were several other counts for breaking and entering plaintiff's *several fishery*, and his *free fishery*; on which issues in fact were joined. The defendant pleaded, 1st, the general issue. 2dly, as to the trespasses mentioned in the two first counts, that the closes therein severally mentioned were the same, and that the said closes in which, &c. at the said several times when, &c. were and still are, and from time immemorial have been, *parcel of a certain arm of the sea*, in which every subject of this realm, at the said several times when, &c. of right had, and of right ought to have had, and now hath, and of right ought to have, the liberty and

2. As to the public right dig for and t shells, sand, &c. on the shore.

Case stated.

getting, taking, and carrying away *shell-fish* and *shells* there, and therefore, defendant being a subject of this realm, at the said several times when, &c. entered into the said closes in which, &c. so being part and parcel of the said arm of the sea, to fish therein, and to catch, dig for, raise, get, take and carry away the *shell-fish* and *shells* there, and did then and there fish, and caught, took, and carried away the said *shell-fish* and *shells* in the second count lastly mentioned, as it was lawful for him to do, and for the digging up and carrying away of the said *shell-fish*, he entered the said closes in which, &c. by himself and with other persons, and with the said cattle, carts, waggons, and other carriages, and with the said boats, lighters, and other vessels, the same being reasonable, and proper, and necessary in that behalf, and in so doing, he necessarily, and unavoidably, with his feet, &c. in walking, a little trod up, &c. the earth and sand in the second count mentioned, and with the feet of the said cattle, &c. a little trod up, &c. other the soil of plaintiff's last-mentioned closes, and the said *shell-fish* and *shells*, in the second count first mentioned, necessarily and unavoidably a little broke, crushed, and destroyed, and with the said spades, &c. the same being useful, proper, and necessary in that behalf; and in digging up, raising, and getting the said *shell-fish* and *shells*, in the second count lastly mentioned, necessarily and unavoidably made the said holes, and pits, in plaintiff's said closes, and necessarily and unavoidably with the spades, &c. dug up, &c. a little of the earth, soil, and sand, in the said closes, doing as little damage on that occasion as he could, which are the same, &c. whereof, &c. and this, &c. whereof, &c. Upon this the plaintiff new assigned, alleging that defendant, on the days in the first count mentioned, broke and entered plaintiff's closes in the first count mentioned, "being certain

for Sand, &c. on the Shore. 189

"*sea*, in plaintiff's manor of Keysham,(*k*) and the said
"*shell-fish* and *shells* there found, caught, took, and carried
"away, and converted and disposed thereof when the same
"closes in which, &c. were left dry, and not covered with
"water." And also that defendant, on the days and in the
manner in the second count mentioned, broke and entered
into plaintiff's closes, being certain closes lying between
the flux and reflux of the tides of the sea, within plaintiff's
said manor of Keysham, and with his feet, &c. trod up, &c.
the earth, soil, and sand, in the second count mentioned,
and with the feet of the said cattle, &c. trod up the said
other soil in plaintiff's last-mentioned closes, in the said
second count mentioned, and plaintiff's said other *shell-fish*
and *shells*, in the second count mentioned, broke, crushed,
&c. and with spades, &c. dug and made holes, &c. and
raised up, and got up the said *shell-fish* and *shells*, &c. and
took and carried away the same, and converted and disposed
thereof, &c. when the said last-mentioned closes in which,
&c. were left dry, and were not covered with water, as plaintiff in the first and second counts of the said declaration
complained against him, which several trespasses so above
new assigned are other and different trespasses, &c. wherefore, &c. To the new assignment the defendant pleaded,
first, the general issue ; secondly, that the said closes, first
above newly assigned, and the several closes secondly above
newly assigned are, and at the several times, &c. were the
same closes, and not other or different closes, and are, and
at those times when, &c. *were certain rocks and sands of the
sea ;* lying within the *flux and reflux* of the tides of the sea ;
and that the said *shell-fish* and *shells* in the said closes, &c.
were certain *shell-fish* and *fish-shells* which, at the said
several times when, &c. were in and upon the said rocks

(*k*) Thereby *claiming* the shore as parcel of the manor ; but whether

and sands of the sea, and which but a little before the said times when, &c. were, by the ebbing of the tides of the sea, left there in and upon the said closes in which, &c. and that in the said closes in the said declaration mentioned, *every subject of this realm*, at the said several times when, &c. of right had, and of right ought, &c. the liberty and privilege of getting, taking, and carrying away the *shell-fish* and *fish-shells* left by the said ebbing of the tides of the sea, in and upon the said closes in which, &c. wherefore the defendant, being a subject of this realm, at the said several times when, &c. entered into the said closes in which, &c. to get, take, and carry away the *shell-fish* and *fish-shells* left by the ebbing of the tides of the sea, in and upon the said closes in which, &c. and then and there got, took, and carried away, the said *shell-fish* and *shells*, in the said first count mentioned, and also got, and for that purpose, with spades, &c. necessarily dug up and raised up, and took and carried away, the other *shell-fish* and *shells* in the second count lastly mentioned, and for the getting, taking and carrying away of the said *shell-fish* and *shells*, the defendant, at the said times when, &c. entered the said closes in which, &c. as it was lawful for him to do, by himself and with other persons, and with the said cattle, carts, &c. and the said boats, &c. the same being reasonable and proper and necessary in that behalf, and in so doing he necessarily and unavoidably, &c. broke, crushed, and destroyed, and with the said spades, &c. dug up, &c. a little of the said earth, soil, and sand, in the said closes, as it was lawful for him to do, for the causes aforesaid, doing as little damage on that occasion as he could, which are the same, &c. whereof, &c. and this, &c. wherefore, &c. To this plea there was a replication traversing the right of every subject to take *shell-fish* and *shells*, and a special demurrer thereto, because it traversed

replication was clearly bad, it was abandoned by the plaintiff's counsel, who relied upon objections to the plea.

It appears that the plaintiff asserted the said closes "were lying *within the flux and reflux of the sea*, WITHIN " the plaintiff's manor;" and his *ownership* of these closes (being part of the sea-shore) *was not disputed*. In virtue of this ownership, he (Bagott) denied the right of the defendant (Orr) to catch *shell-fish*, and also his right to carry away for use sea *shells*. The Report says, "the Court were " of opinion that, if the plaintiff had it in his power to " abridge the Common law right of the subject to the *shell-* "*fish*, he should have replied that matter specially; and " that not having done so, the defendant must succeed " upon his plea, as far as related to the taking of the *fish;* " but observed that, as no authority had been cited to support his claim to take *shells*, they should *pause* before they " established a general right of that kind." *Remarks upon the case of Bagott v. Orr.* *Judgment of the Court.*

It is to be regretted that a fuller report of the judgment in this case has not been given (if more was said); but it seems to be understood, that the Court affirmed the general Common law right of the subject to take or catch "*shellfish*," but doubted whether any such general Common law right existed for the subject to take *shells;* meaning, it is presumed, shells of fish destroyed by natural causes before capture, and not the shells of the shell-fish caught by the fishermen, otherwise the decision would have much of the character and effect of that recorded in the "Merchant of Venice."

With regard to the catching of *shell-fish* on the sea-shore, it would seem to constitute an integral part of the public *common of piscary*, and to be subject only to the same occasional exclusion, by a prescriptive *several* fishery, as the public fishery in the sea itself, and creeks and arms thereof, *The catching and taking shell-fish on the shore is of common right.*

lobsters, crabs, prawns, shrimps, oysters, and various other shell-fish, besides certain other kinds of fish, such as eels, &c. is carried on in every fishing village on the coast, and is one very useful and valuable branch of the fishing trade. The catch of these fish is, therefore, part of the public common of piscary, however the fisheries may be regulated (as many are) by act of parliament. Acts of parliament for the regulation of the fisheries are very numerous, and would form a large volume in themselves; and they regulate, in many instances, private as well as public fisheries. But such acts of regulation do not concern the ownership of the soil. The *oyster* fisheries are especially subject to the most jealous enactments, and many of them belong to private owners, or to corporations.(*l*) But whether to one indi-

(*l*) [In an action of trespass, quare clausum, &c., the defendant justified an entry for the purpose of taking oyster spawn in the locus in quo, being a public navigable river, the plea must shew that he took it under circumstances, that made the taking legal within the provisions of the several acts for its preservation: Maldon, Mayor of, *v.* Woolnet, 12 Ad. and E. 13. But the person who is entitled to fish for oysters is not now restricted from taking the spawn: see Bridger *v.* Richardson, 2 M. & S. 568. The statute therein cited has been repealed by 24 and 25 Vict. c. 109, sect. 39.

[By the Oyster and Mussel Fisheries Act, 29 and 30 Vict. c. 85, the Board of Trade may make a provisional order for an oyster fishery, on application by a memorial in that behalf, under certain conditions contained therein, but not for a longer period at once than sixty years; and where any portion of the sea-shore proposed to be comprised in the order belongs to the Crown, in right of the Crown, or forms part of the possessions of the Duchy of Lancaster or Cornwall, the consent, respectively, of the commissioners, the chancellor of the Duchy of Lancaster, and the Duke of Cornwall, or other person empowered to dispose of the lands, must first be obtained. See also 30 Vict. c. 18; 31 and 32 Vict. c. 45; and 32 and 33 Vict. c. 31.

The salmon fishings in the open sea around the coast of Scotland, unless parted with by grant, belong exclusively to the Crown, and form part of its hereditary revenue. This right of the Crown is not merely a right of fishing for salmon, but " a right to the salmon fishings around the sea-coast of Scotland; it is not to be regarded simply as

the Shore part of the public Fishery. 193

vidual, or to a corporate body, it would seem that the title to such exclusive privilege must be supported, as against the *prima facie* public right, by the same kind of evidence as already mentioned in regard to a private fishery in the sea and tide rivers, viz.—grant from the Crown, or prescription. There is no distinction (in regard to the nature of evidence required to substantiate the right of a corporation) between a *separate fishery* claimed by a corporate body, or by one individual. The same remark applies to the ownership of the *soil* itself of the sea-shore in corporate bodies, or in individuals. It has already been contended, that the ownership of the soil of the shore does not necessarily confer a right to a several fishery, nor a right to a several fishery necessarily confer the ownership of the shore. Although, in regard to the latter, the cases incline to annex the soil to the ownership of a several fishery. But the *onus* of proof lies upon the individual, or corporate body, who would claim the exclusive right of fishery against the *general* Common law right of all the King's subjects to catch shell and other fish upon the sea-shore, as well as in the sea itself.

Now, if this be good law, and the King's subjects have a general Common law right of frequenting the shore (whether belonging to a lord of a manor or not, and so that there be no prescriptive several fishery) " on foot and with cattle, carts, and carriages," for the purpose of catching these kinds of fish, there can be no doubt that the shore is a highway for fishing at least, as public as the sea itself.

interest constituting part of the regal hereditary property." Salmon fishings in the open sea around the coast of Scotland may not only become the subject of a royal grant, but they may be feudalized ; the assertion that the sea is common to all, and that there can be no appropriation of it, except where it adjoins the shore, is an erroneous assertion : Gammell *v.* Commissioners Woods and Forests, 3 Macq.

No part of the shore, from the extremest lines of the flood and ebb tides, can be free from public use and resort for the fishery. The shore is, in this sense, part and parcel of the sea, and although an ownership is more frequently claimed in the shore by grant from the King, than in the sea itself; yet, as it was in the Crown as part of the sea, so it is granted to the subject as part of the sea, and therefore liable to the public common of piscary.

<small>As to the public right to dig for shells, sand, &c. on the shore.</small>

With regard to the question of right to dig for shells, &c., a technical distinction is to be noted between a mere right of egress and regress, or *way*, and a right to dig and take away the soil. The first is, in law, a mere *liberty*, or *ease-*

<small>Distinction between easements and *profits-a-prendre*.</small>

ment; but the carrying away the soil is called a *profit-a-prendre*, being the conversion of the soil into profit; the one takes more of the substance from the owner of soil than the other, and diminishes the value of the ownership of the soil in proportion. Blackstone, J., in his Commentaries, (*m*) after stating that "common" is "a profit which one man hath in the land of another," and after describing the commons of pasture, piscary, and turbary, adds, "there is " also a common of digging for coals, minerals, stones, and " the like, all these bear a resemblance to common of pas- " ture in many respects; though in one point they go much " farther—common of pasture being only a right of feeding " on the *herbage* and *vesture* of the soil, which renews an- " nually; but common of turbary, and those afore men- " tioned are a right of carrying away the *very soil* itself." Nevertheless, a right to pasture cattle on the lord's common waste, and a right to dig turves or marl, are both *technically* the same, viz. *profits-a-prendre;* but a right of *way* over the soil is a mere *liberty* or *easement*. It is clear, however, that the subjects of the realm may enjoy a *profit-*

for Sand, Shells, &c. on the Shore. 195

a-prendre by general right, as well as an easement, because the public right of fishing is a profit-a-prendre.

Now as the treatise ascribed to Lord Hale has compared the "great waste" of the sea (of which the shore is part) to the waste lands of a manor, it will be well to explain the point in question by shewing, that the wastes of a manor may be, and often are, subject to rights similar to that of digging and carrying away the materials of the "sea-shore;" and then to inquire how such right ought to be supported (if the point be not yet settled *contra*) in regard to the sea-shore, as well as inland manorial wastes. It must be remembered, however, that manorial customs are *local* and not *general* rights. Thus a copyhold tenant of an inland manor may dig for marl for manure, and for turf for fuel. (*n*) So he may dig for gravel and sand, (*o*) and notwithstanding these acts of the copyholder, the soil and freehold of the waste is in the lord of the manor. But these are local customs of the manor, and in some manors do not at all exist.

As to taking *profits-a-prendre* in the wastes of inland manors.

The cases referred to in favour of taking sand and stones, &c. in an inland waste of a manor, which were expressly stated to be for building and repairs, and the case of taking marl for manure, are perfectly analogous to the uses to which the soil of the sea-shore is most capable of being applied, and which, together with the fishing and navigation, constitute its essential value. Since, then, the custom or usage to dig and carry away for use the materials of the soil of another in *inland* titles is (as a local custom) well known and admitted, the question remains, whether a custom to dig shells, or sand, or stones, &c. on the sea-shore, which shore is either owned by the King, or by the lord of

They are analogous to digging for shells &c. on the shore.

(*n*) Gilb. Ten. 327 ; 2 Atk. 189 ; [Hall's Profit à Prendre, p. 316.]
(*o*) Duberly *v.* Page, 2 T. R. 391 ; Shakspear *v.* Peppin, 6 T. R. 741.

the manor adjacent, can be claimed and maintained as a *local* custom? or, if not, then whether as a *general* custom for all the subjects of the realm?

First, can it be claimed as a *local* custom or usage? for, if it can, *that* will be inconsistent with a *general* custom. As a local custom it must be claimed by the parties, either as *tenants* of the adjacent manor, under the manorial custom, and as if the *shore* were part and parcel of the *wastes* of the manor, and therefore within the manor; or it must be claimed by them as "*inhabitants*" of the adjacent hamlet, town, parish, hundred, or county. If it be claimed in right of the manorial customs, the "sea-shore" of the *locus in quo* must be admitted or proved to be part and parcel of the waste lands of the manor. As waste of the manor, the shore, it is conceived, *may* be subject to such commons as waste lands in inland manors are usually subject to; and all that will be necessary in such case will be, to prove the usage or right of *common-à-prendre* by the usual evidence resorted to in the case of similar claims in inland manors. But if, from circumstances, the claimant cannot support such right by the custom of the manor, either because he is no tenant, or because the shore does not appear to be within the manor, in such case he must support his right as an "inhabitant" of the adjacent hamlet, vill, parish, hundred, or county, which is also a *local* claim; or, lastly, as a subject of the realm, which is a public and *general* claim. Neither the local claim, as "inhabitants of the adjacent hamlet," &c., nor the general right make it *necessary* that the "shore" should be *extra manerium.* Whether it be or be not within the manor, it *may* yet be subject either to a *local* or to a *general* right. (*p*)

for Sand, Shells, &c. on the Shore.

There is, however, a distinction taken at law, between "inhabitants" of a particular place or district, and "owners" of estates or tenements in such place or district, as to making title by prescription to these kind of customs. In the *latter* case, the custom is, as it were, attached to the *estate*, and the owner claims in respect of his estate; but in

<small>Distinction between prescription in the *que* estate, an as an "inhabitant."</small>

custom to take shingle, &c. from the sea-shore above high-water mark is void, because it is a claim to take a profit in alieno solo : Pitts *v.* Kingsbridge Highway Board, 19 W. R. 884. See Constable *v.* Nicholson, 32 L. J. C. P. 240 ; S. C. 14 C. B. N. S. 230 ; Blewitt *v.* Tregonning, 3 A. & E. 554 ; Race *v.* Ward, 4 E. and B. 702 ; Post *v.* Pearsall, 22 Wend. (N. Y.) R. 425 ; Perley *v.* Langley, 7 N. Hamp. 233 ; Sale *v.* Pratt, 36 Mass. (Pick.) R. 191 ; Angell on Watercourses, p. 71 ; Angell on Tide Waters, 273.

[A profit à prendre in another's soil cannot be claimed by custom, however ancient, uniform, and clear the exercises of that custom may be ; neither can a right to carry away the soil of another, without stint, be claimed by prescription, for a prescription to be good must both be reasonable and certain : Att.-Gen. *v.* Mathias, 27 L. J. Ch. 761 ; S. C. 6 W. R. 780, 4 K. and J. 579. The Court of Queen's Bench, in Rogers *v.* Brenton, 10 Q. B. Rep. 26, S. C. 17 L. J. Q. B. 34, expressed an extra-judicial opinion that the custom of tin bounding in Cornwall, which involves the taking of a profit in alieno solo, might have been good, if coupled with an obligation to work ; but assuming, says Byles, J. in Att.-Gen. *v.* Mathias supra, "that opinion to be correct, I am not aware that it has ever been extended to any other case," and so difficult did the learned counsel for the plaintiff feel their position to be, that they desired to treat the custom which they were bound to support as the lex loci of a province. See Macnamara *v.* Higgins, 4 Ir. Com. Law R. 326.

In Padwick *v.* Knight and Others, 7 Ex. 854, it was held that a surveyor of highways cannot justify a trespass under a prescriptive right, or a custom to take stones from the waste, whether adjoining the seashore between high and low water mark, or otherwise, for the purpose

the *other* case it is merely *personal*, claimed in a personal character, as an "inhabitant." Lord Coke (*q*) lays it down, that a custom, such as gavel-kind or borough-english, cannot be alleged in an upland town, (*r*) but such town may allege a custom to have a way, or to well order commons, &c. "But," he adds, "in special cases, a custom may be "alleged within a hamlet, or town, or burgh, or city, manor, "an honor, an hundred, and a county." It is said, in Vin. Abr. tit. "prescription," (*s*) that "inhabitants, *unless incor-* "*porated*, cannot prescribe to have any *profit* in the *soil* of "another; but in matters of *easement* only, as in a *way*,

may take shingle from the sea-beach for the purpose of such repair, the custom not being a matter relating to ratio or cesses within the meaning of the Act: Oxenden *v.* Palmer, 2 B. and Ad. 236. See also remarks of Erle, C. J. in Le Strange *v.* Rowe, 4 F. and F. 1048.

In the case of Constable *v.* Nicholson, 14 C. B. N. S. 230, the pleas claiming a right in the inhabitants to take the gravel, &c. to be used for the cultivation of their land, and in the parish officers for the necessary repairs of the highway, were all held bad; for that, so far as they were capable of being construed as justifying under such a custom, such custom would be void, being a claim of a profit à prendre in alieno solo, which can only exist by grant or prescription; and if the claim be founded on prescription it would be equally bad, inasmuch as it was a claim by persons who, not being a corporation, were incapable of taking by grant and not being claimed in a *que* estate. See also Dyce *v.* Lady James Hay, 1 McQueen, H. L. 305.

By sect. 52 of the Highway Act, 5 and 6 Wm. 4, c. 50, materials are not allowed to be taken away from the shore for the repair of highways, where any danger of an encroachment by the sea will be increased by such removal: see Pitts *v.* Kingsbridge Board, supra. As to the relief equity affords by injunction, see Clowes *v.* Beck, 13 Beav. 347; Chalk *v.* Wyatt, 3 Meriv. 688; Earl Cowper *v.* Baker, 17 Ves. 128; Youl on Waste, 186, 189.

As to the removal of shingle from the shore or bank of a port or harbour, see Nicholson *v.* Williams, 6 L. R. Q. B. 632. It has been held that a grant by the Crown, to a class of persons previously unincorporated, of a profit à prendre to be taken out of the Crown's soil is valid: Willingale *v.* Maitland, L. R. 3 Eq. 103; S. C. 36 L. J. Ch. 64.]

for Sand, Shells, &c. on the Shore.

"&c., but not in matters of interest." Cro. Jac. 152, and Gateward's case (*t*) are cited.

This case is a leading case on the subject of pleading, alleging, or prescribing for customs. The point in the case was a common of pasture, claimed by the defendant in a close of land belonging to the plaintiff, as a customary right enjoyed time out of mind by the *inhabitants* dwelling and residing in an ancient messuage, in the ancient town of Stixwold, adjoining to the close. "It was resolved, that the custom was against law, for several reasons. 1. There are but four manner of commons, *i.e.* common appendant, appurtenant, in gross, and by reason of vicinage: and this common, *ratione commorant'*, and resident', is none of them; and *argumentum a divisione est fortissimum in jure.* 2. What estate shall he who is 'inhabitant' have in the common, when it appears he hath no estate or interest in the house (but a mere habitation and dwelling), in respect of which he ought to have his common? for none can have interest in common in respect of a house in which he hath no interest. 3. Such custom will be transitory, and altogether uncertain; for it will follow the person, and for no certain time or estate, but during his *inhabitancy*, and such manner of interest the law will not suffer, for custom ought to extend to that which hath certainty and continuance. 4. It will be against the nature and quality of a common, for every common may be suspended or extinguished, but such a common will be so incident to the person, that no person certain can extinguish it, but as soon as he who releases, &c. removes, the new inhabitant shall have it. 5. If the law should allow such common, the law would give an action or remedy for it; but he who claims as an 'inhabitant' can have no action for it. 6. In these words

Gateward's case. Prescription for a *profit-a-prendre* by "inhabitants," not good.

(*t*) 6 Rep. 59. [See Macnamara *v.* Higgins, 4 Ir. Com. Law R. 326,

'inhabitants' and 'residents' are included tenant in fee simple, tenant for life, for years, tenant by elegit, &c. tenant at will, &c., and he who hath no interest but only his habitation and dwelling; and by the rule of all our books, without question, tenant in fee-simple ought to prescribe in his own name, tenant for life, years, by elegit &c., and at will, &c., in the name of him who hath the fee; and as he who hath no interest can have no common, so none that hath no interest, if he be but at will, ought to have common, but by good pleading he may enjoy it. 7. No improvements can be made in any wastes, if such common [custom] should be allowed; for the tenants for life, for years, at will, tenant by elegit, statute staple, and statute merchant of houses of the lord himself, would have common in the wastes of the lord himself, if such prescription should be allowed, which would be inconvenient. But two differences were taken and agreed by the whole Court. 1. Between a charge in the soil of another, and a discharge in his own soil. 2. Between an *interest* or *profit* to be taken or had in another soil, and an *easement* in another's soil; and, therefore, a custom that every inhabitant of a town hath paid a *modus decimandi* to the parson in discharge of their tithes, is good; for they claim not a charge or *profit-à-prendre* in the soil of another, but a discharge in their own land. So of a custom, that every inhabitant of such a town shall have a *way* over such land, either to the church or market, &c., *that* is good, for it is but an easement, and no profit; and a way or passage may well follow the person, and no such inconvenience as in the case at bar. 8. It was resolved, that copyholders in fee, or for life, may, by custom of the manor, have common in the demesnes [wastes] of the lord of the manor, but then they ought to allege the custom of the manor to be '*quod quilibet tenens customarius cujus-*

for Sand, Shells, &c. on the Shore.

libet inhabitans infra aliquod antiquum messuagium cus-
'*tomar*,' &c. For a copyholder hath a customary interest
in the house, &c., and therefore he may have a customary
common in the lord's wastes; and in such case he cannot
prescribe in the name of the lord, for the lord cannot claim
common in his own soil, and, therefore, of necessity such
custom ought to be alleged. Vide 21 E. 3, 34, Foiston's
case, 4 Rep. 31, 32. (*u*) Another difference was taken and
agreed, between a *prescription*, which is always alleged in
the *person*, and a *custom*, which always ought to be alleged
in the land; for every prescription ought to have, by
common intendment, a lawful beginning, but otherwise it is
of a custom, for that ought to be reasonable, and *ex certâ
causâ rationabili* (as Littleton saith) *usitata*, but need not
be intended to have a lawful beginning, as custom to have
land devisable, or of the nature of gavel-kind, or borough-
english, &c. These, and the like customs, are reasonable,
but by common intendment they cannot have a lawful
beginning by grant, or act, or agreement, but only by
Parliament. See also, for this matter, Foiston's case. Also,
it was agreed, that the custom of a manor that *dominus pro
tempore* shall grant lands customary, is good, and tenant at
will may do it; and so 20 H. 6, 8, b. by the custom of the
Court of Common Pleas, the Chief Justice grants divers
offices for life, and these customs are good; but, in such
cases, he who grants them hath an interest in the manor or
office, and their grant is made good by the custom; and
19 R. 2, action sur le case, 52, a beadle of the hundred shall
have three flagons of beer of every brewer who sells within
the hundred, *causâ quâ supra*. But a custom, that an
inhabitant or 'resident' shall grant or take any profit, is
merely void. 9. It was resolved, that if the custom had

<small>Gateward's case.</small>

been alleged, that *quilibet paterfamilias infra aliquod antiquum messuag'*, &c., it would also be insufficient for the causes and reasons aforesaid; and if he hath any interest he may be relieved as aforesaid. Vide reported by Spelman that such custom is not warranted by law, and so it was adjudged in this Court. Trin. 33 Eliz. Rot. 422. See the Book of Entries, Trespass, Common, 6. Vide 9 H. 6, 62 b, 7 E. 6, Dyer, 70, Iseham's case." (*x*)

The case of Grimstead *v.* Marlowe (*y*) follows Gateward's case; and it is there laid down by Lord Kenyon, that a man must prescribe in a *que estate* for a *profit-a-prendre*, which a mere "inhabitant" or "resident" cannot do; and it seems settled, that where an *inhabitant of a town* would claim a *profit-a-prendre*, he must prescribe that "he and all "those whose *estate* he hath in his house have used to have "common," &c., as in Mellor *v.* Spateman, 1 Saund. 339, 343. (*z*)

The case of Grimstead *v.* Marlowe (*a*) was a right of common of pasture, claimed by an inhabitant of the parish of Leatherhead. It was pleaded in virtue of a custom, "that every 'inhabitant' occupying, residing, and dwelling "in any ancient messuage or tenement within the parish of "Leatherhead, for the time being, &c., had been used and "accustomed," &c. But the Court held that such plea was bad, because it was a *profit-a-prendre*, which could not be pleaded but in a *que estate:* here the plea was mere *habit-*

(*x*) [See Lloyd *v.* Jones, 6 C. B. 81; Bland *v.* Lipscombe, 4 E. and B. 713, n.; Hudson *v.* McRae, 4 B. and S. 585; Att.-Gen. *v.* Mathias, 4 K. and J. 579; S. C. 27 L. J. Ch. 761; Waters *v.* Lilley, 21 Mass. (Pick.) R. 145.]

(*y*) 4 T. R. 717.

(*z*) [See Lockwood *v.* Wood, 6 Q. B. 50; Post *v.* Pearsall, 22 Wend.

for Sand, Shells, &c. on the Shore. 203

ancy, or occupancy, not ownership; but the Court did not object to its being prescribed for by the party, "that he and all those whose estate he hath, &c., in his house" had enjoyed such *profit-a-prendre*, and gave him leave to amend accordingly. Here it is to be observed, that no distinction was taken that he could not (if he would) prescribe in a *que estate* in a parish or town, in contra-distinction to a borough, or city, or county, inasmuch as the prescription, in such case, would be in respect of the *estate* he had in his tenement, and not in respect of its being in this or that place. It was immaterial where the *que estate* was situated, provided he could establish his prescription by the usual proofs, " that he and all those who owned, or had owned before " him that *estate*, had been used to have the *profit-a-prendre* " in question." (*b*)

It would seem, therefore, that every one who would claim a *local* custom or usage to dig marl, or sand, &c. in *inland* manors must (on account of its being a *profit-a-prendre*) plead in the *que estate*, (*c*) *i.e.* in respect of his interest in the tenement which he holds; which prescription, however, must be laid in the person of him who is *seized in fee-simple*, and not in the person of one who holds any lesser interest; who is not, in the eye of the law, owner of the estate. But tenant for life, for years, or at will, may prescribe in the name of the tenant in fee-simple. A copyholder is allowed to prescribe in his *own* estate for the reason given in Gateward's case. Thus far, however, seems clear, that by due form of pleading, in respect of his ancient tenement situate within a town, and by consequence, in other *loci* known to the law, as honors, manors (parishes), hundreds, boroughs,

_{How the custom to dig shells, &c. must be prescribed for as a local custom.}

and counties, all these persons before named may, by good evidence of immemorial usage, substantiate such *profits-a-prendre* as before mentioned.

Such being the law in regard to *profits-a-prendre* in *inland* titles, there would seem to be no objection in law to prevent the owners, or their lessees, of any ancient tenement in any such district or place before named, *situate on the coast* (as the defendant Orr in the case in question), from pleading in the *que estate*, and prescribing for a customary right or usage of taking shells, sand, or other portions of the soil of the *shore*, and if supported by the usual evidence, making good such local usage. There would seem to be no *technical* reason why this might not be done, in respect of the "great waste" of the sea-shore, where the party has an ancient tenement on the coast, as well as in respect of inland wastes.

Whether the Courts would permit any such customary profit, derivable from the *sea-shore*, to be pleaded as a *local* custom, *without* the *que estate*, *i.e.* as "easements" are pleaded, does not seem to have been ever mooted. The reasons given in Gateward's case would seem to preclude any such proposition; at least where the "shore" is part of the manor, and in the lord's ownership. Where the shore is not within the manor it is the property of the Crown, and whether, as such, it will admit of a different form of laying the local custom or profit in question, viz. in the *person* as "inhabitant," does not appear. It is concluded that it will not; but it is remarkable, that the men of Devon and Cornwall have immemorially enjoyed the custom of taking the *soil* of the shores of those counties for use, either in the character of "*dwellers*" and "*inhabitants*"- *locally*, or else by the *general* Common law right, and not in the *que estate*. For this appears from the preamble of

for Sand, Shells, &c. on the Shore.

"*sand*, by long trial and experience, hath been found to be
"very profitable for the bettering of land, and especially
"for the increase of corn and tillage within the counties of
"Devon and Cornwall, where the most part of the *inha-*
"*bitants* have not used any other worth for the bettering
"of their arable grounds and pastures; notwithstanding,
"divers having lands adjoining to the sea-coasts there, have
"of late interrupted the *bargemen* and such others *as have*
"*used of their free wills and pleasures* to fetch the said sea-
"sand, to take the same *under the full sea-mark*, as they
"have *heretofore* used to do;" the statute then goes on to
confirm the right of "all persons whatsoever *resident* and
"*dwelling* within the said counties of Devon and Cornwall,
"to fetch and take sea-sand at all places under the full
"sea-mark," &c. (*d*)

Statute of 7 Jac. 1, c. 18, declaring the right in the "inhabitants" of Devon and Cornwall, to take sand on the shore.

Now this statute, it is to be observed, asserts a pre-exist-ing custom, commonly used by the *inhabitants*, at their free wills and pleasures, to take a *profit-a-prendre* upon the shores of the counties of Devon and Cornwall. But if they were entitled to such custom as a local custom, *prior* to the statute, it must have been by "prescription," and a pre-scription *not* founded on the "*que estate*," but enjoyed as "inhabitants;" and if the "inhabitants" of the counties of Devon and Cornwall could have so claimed, at law, the profits in question, then the "inhabitants" of other coun-tries, or districts, might set up a custom, *so pleaded*, to enjoy the like profit. It may be, and probably is the fact, that the inhabitants of other maritime counties have been used to take sand, shells, &c. for similar or equally useful pur-poses as those referred to in the statute of James; and yet it is evident, that unless the rule be relaxed so as to permit them to prescribe otherwise than in the *que estate*, they, the

Remarks on the statute.

(*d*) See the statute fully cited, p. 94 and 196, ante, [and remarks

inhabitants of other counties, cannot maintain such custom as a local custom, except by similar aid of Statute law, or as a general right, however it may have been heretofore acquiesced in by the King, or mesne lord of the soil, and is further recommended by its public utility. It is also manifest, that if those persons only who possess "ancient tenements" can maintain such right by pleading in the *que estate*, it will be confined to a comparatively limited number of persons, and very different from that enjoyed by the men of Devon and Cornwall. It must be allowed, however, that regarding Gateward's case as good law, it would seem to compel the Courts to put the claim to dig and use the soil, &c. of the sea-shore (if pleaded as a *local* custom) upon the same footing as an inland claim to dig, &c. in the waste of a manor, and to confine the right in question to those persons only who can plead in the *que estate*, *i.e.* who are owners of an ancient tenement on the coast. (*e*)

<small>Whether the custom to dig for shells, &c. on the shore is of common right.</small>

With regard to the custom as a *general right* in all the subjects of the realm, as pleaded in the principal case, it is obvious that if the Courts could support the right upon the same footing as the public right to fish, no technical difficulties would arise as to the pleading. The defendant Orr, in the case referred to, seems to have felt the difficulty of pleading a local custom for a *profit-a-prendre* as an "inhabitant," and therefore grounded his case on the general right. As the Court *hesitated* before it decided on the general right, and did not use any very decisive language against it, there may perhaps be room for a further discussion of the question. The point, as regards the "sea-shore," and the public right so to use it, was *quæstio nova* in Bagott *v.* Orr.

<small>The custom or practice is general through-</small>

It certainly is not necessary to plead a *general* custom in the *que estate*, whether such custom be a *profit-a-prendre* or

for Sand, Shells, &c. on the Shore. 207

not. Looking at the general claim as *res integra*, it must be admitted that there is reason to presume that the "inhabitants" of all the districts bordering on the sea-coasts of England, have *actually* (whether now allowed to be *lawfully* or not) been in the *habit* of resorting to the "shore" for the materials in question, for manure and other useful purposes, without asking the consent of the owner of the adjacent *terra firma;* and it would be difficult to find a cultivated and inhabited spot, on or within reasonable distance from the coast, where it has not been the practice of the inhabitants to resort to the shore for materials for manure, for ballast, for building, road mending, &c. It is the natural, if not the necessary result of their locality and wants. (*f*) It is not to be looked at as a want confined to those persons only who are *immediately* dwelling on the sea-side, but may be reasonably extended to all within convenient reach of it; to all such, in fact, as have, by a like immemorial usage, established a general right to fish. It may also be remarked, that where such general inducement exists everywhere along the coasts of England to use such materials, and yet no case is to be found *supporting* the practice as a local and limited custom, or *denying* it as a general right (if we except Bagott *v.* Orr), the presumption is in favour of it as a general custom. out the maritime counties

In the case of Bagott *v.* Orr, after quoting the statute of James I., before noticed, the learned Counsel in favour of the right contended, (*g*) that "the statute was, in fact, a full "recognition of the right of the subject to use the shore of "the sea in every way in which it could be serviceable to Whether the statute of 7 James I., ch. 18, be declaratory of the common righ or not.

(*f*) Lord Hale mentions " ballastage" or a toll " for liberty to take up ballast *out of the bottom of the port*," as a *port duty,* arising " from the propriety of the soil," de Portibus maris, 74. Qy. As to any toll

"him." On the other side it was contended, that "it was "an enacting, and not a declaratory law; and that a pecu-"liar privilege is thereby granted to the men of Devon and "Cornwall, which peculiar privilege it would have been "absurd to have granted, if *all* the people of England had "been entitled thereto at Common law." The Court offered no argument upon this statute, or upon the reasoning on either side. Now, it may perhaps be insisted in favour of the public, that the statute is both a declaratory and an affirmative statute. It states a long existing usage, without throwing a doubt upon its legality, and affirms that such use shall be continued. It forbids the owner of the soil "adjoining the *coast*" to molest those who frequented the *shore* for the purposes of digging sand, &c. but allows such owners to take a reasonable toll, or composition, for the damage done, *not* to the *shore*, but to their "adjoining grounds," and for casting sand there, and for way, passage, &c. in places where no general right of way existed to the shore. The toll was not for *digging* and *appropriating* sand, &c. *under the full sea-mark*.

There is not a word in the statute intimating a right in the owner of the land adjoining to a property in the sand, &c. itself, *under full sea-mark*. The words are, "paying "for the taking, casting out, and landing of every barge-"load of sand *upon the grounds of any man*, such duties, "&c., and for passage by and through such ways, &c., such "duties, &c. as had been used and accustomed." (*h*) There

---

(*h*) Payments to the owner of the adjacent ground or bank, immediately above high-water mark, for *depositing* timber, stone, &c. there, are very common. But this is not for the *landing* the goods,—but for the use of the ground so appropriated. According to Lord Hale, de Portibus maris, 51, it was resolved, in a case he cites, that "though a "man may take amends for the *trespass* in unlading upon his ground, "yet he might not take it as a certain common toll." [See Dickens *v*.

for Sand, Shells, &c. on the Shore.

may have been abundance of the same materials worth taking *above* high-water mark, and the soil above high-water mark belonged to the adjoining land. The owners of the adjoining grounds, above the full sea-mark, appear to have also refused to permit sand to be heaped upon or carried over their land, which the statute, for the public good, compels them to allow; but this does not show or prove a right in such persons to the *shore*, under the full sea-mark. The first section of the statute seems to be *declaratory* of the custom of the counties, viz. to dig and fetch away sand under full sea-mark. The second section is *remedial*, and mandatory, confirming and enforcing the *ancient custom*, and directing that the sand shall be unloaded and landed, &c. upon such adjoining places as have been used within fifty years, and be carried away by such ways as have been used within the last twenty years, saving to the owners of such places and ways, their reasonable right of toll and charge for such easements.

Here then is a customary right of common, or *profit-a-prendre*, recognized and confirmed by statute law as belonging to all the inhabitants of Devon and Cornwall; (*i*)—not merely to the "owners of ancient tenements in their *que estate*," but to all the "residents and dwellers" in those counties. It is manifest, therefore, that, according to the statute, a right of common *a-prendre* for digging sand existed, as an ancient custom, or usage, by *prescription* in two of the largest and most populous maritime counties of England. This custom *so* allowed would seem to be in opposition to the doctrine of Gateward's case, decided in the fourth year of the same reign, only three years prior to the statute, if it be regarded as a *local* custom. Therefore, in order to support the doctrine in Gateward's case, it must be assumed (in opposition to the positive words of the statute) that no such *profit-a-prendre* existed in the inhabitants of those counties prior to the statute, on the ground that such custom could not, according to law, be in "inhabitants," as such.

Yet the language of the statute certainly authorizes us to assume it to have been either a good general, or good local custom, independent of and prior to that statute; whilst Gateward's case decides that, considered merely as a *profit-a-prendre*, it could not have been a good *local* custom, *causa qua supra*. It would seem to follow, therefore, that if it could not be good as a *local* custom, it can be good *no otherwise* than as a *general* custom, in the same manner as the common of piscary in the sea and shore is a good custom (although a *profit-a-prendre*) as a general custom of the realm. That which is a good general custom of the realm, is good alike for Cornwall and Sussex, or any other maritime county. It cannot be supposed that such a custom, or such use of the shore, did not prevail as much in Dorset, Hants, or Sussex, and other maritime counties, as in Devon and Cornwall. All these were and are agricultural counties; and their farmers were then, and are now in the habit of manuring their lands, as well as the men of Devon and Cornwall; and it must be supposed knew as well the value and use of sand, or shells, or sea-weed, &c. for manure. There is every reason to believe that what the statute affirms to have been the old customary right of the Devonshire and Cornish men, was equally a practice in the other maritime counties. If so, the statute could not have set up a new, or merely local privilege.

But although the statute is not silent, the books certainly are; for the general right in question cannot be specifically traced in any of them, as a Common law privilege; neither is it *denied* by the books. In this view it resembles the regarding the right to bathe in the sea. It also resembles it, in that it is as difficult to say, that the practice of resorting to the sea-shore for materials, for the uses just mentioned, has *not* prevailed, time out of mind, throughout *all* our maritime counties. In this respect, also, it resembles the public right to catch fish on the shore. In some places on the coast it would be impossible to prove that any one had *actually* been accustomed to catch shell-fish upon the "shore;" but this will not invalidate the general right. Common sense and experience entitle us to assume, that fishing on the shore is far *more* general than the *not* fishing there at all. Yet it would be difficult to say, that *shell-fish* fishing is a custom more frequent or general than the digging and taking materials from the shore for useful purposes. The presumption is in favour of *both*, as general and immemorial practices. It may reasonably be doubted, whether the men of Devon and Cornwall have not carried away from the shore as much shells, sand, &c., and from as many places, as they have carried away shell-fish. Nor would it be easy nor reasonable to contend, that the men of Dorset or Hants have not exercised, in an equal degree, these several privileges. If it be admitted that the *presumption* is in favour of it, as a general *practice*, and that the practice is a great public benefit to the agriculture of the kingdom, why should not that suffice to warrant it as a lawful public *custom?*—our *books* being *silent* alike as to the negative or affirmative of the point, but, *in general language*, favouring it.

That it is a privilege very beneficial and important to the general advancement of agriculture and for other public purposes, cannot be denied: these are interests not *local* but *general*. Now it appears, that as a *local* custom it cannot be supported at law in favour of the "inhabitants" of

<small>Importance of the custom to agriculture and the general interests of the realm.</small>

nical objection (*k*) to its being so pleaded. In this respect it is in a worse situation than the right to *bathe;* for *that*, not being a *profit*, might, perhaps, be pleaded as a *local* custom by the "inhabitants," and as an "easement." But there is no mode by which the inhabitants of the maritime counties can maintain a right to manure their lands from the materials cast upon the shores of their coasts, except *that* which supports the public fishery, viz. the general custom of the realm. The men of Devon and Cornwall indeed may plead their statute, but the Statute law has done nothing for the other counties. This statute of James, however, can scarcely be construed into evidence that the general Common law right did *not* exist before; although such construction was attempted. If it *did* exist before, the statute certainly could not have abrogated it; for it is an affirmative and declaratory statute; and also in its operation *local*. No just or fair inference can be drawn from this partial statute to negative the right of other inhabitants of other maritime districts to a like privilege by common law. The statute did not confer this right as a *new* privilege, even upon these two counties, as appears by the very words of the statute itself. (*l*)

e custom :val with culture of d.

It will not be denied that agriculture is as ancient and as important a pursuit as fishing or navigation. The public interests are as much concerned in the one as in the other. It would also be difficult to contend, that the agricultural interests of *all* the maritime counties in the kingdom are

d as gene- *not* to be regarded as the general public interests of the realm. The right in question partakes of the character of the interests to which it is made subservient. It is sub-

(*k*) Gateward's case, 6 Co. Rep. 59 B.
(*l*) If it be a fact, that in nine-tenths of the maritime districts, this

servient to the agricultural interests of all the maritime counties of the realm ; a range large enough to entitle it to be called a *general* public benefit, even as the fishery is a general right and benefit, although actually limited to the maritime districts. There seems no substantial reason why the one "*communis usus*" of the shore might not be supported by the Courts, on public grounds and general usage, as well as the other. The *practice* is in favour of it ; the public interests are in favour of it ; and the Statute law, as far as it goes, is in favour of it. The silence of the "books" is neutral. There was a time when the books were equally silent in regard to the fisheries ; yet the fisheries subsisted at that time by the Common law. At that time, also, agriculture subsisted in the same districts where the fisheries were carried on. Probably agriculture was the *most* ancient of the two pursuits ; and unless it be assumed that agriculture is a *modern* invention, as bathing was assumed to be, then, so far at least as regards the application of the several useful manures furnished *spontaneously* by the sea and sea-shore, the taking and using such manures must have prevailed in the very manner by law required to establish a general Common law custom, viz. immemorially and generally.

It is reasonable to conclude, that the use of these natural manures, so plentifully offered and so accessible, was more ancient than of those more artificial kinds which require greater science and skill than was anciently in vogue.(*m*)

Antiquity of the practice of using marine manures in agriculture.

It may be supposed that some of these artificial kinds of manure have superseded, in some places, the frequent use of the soil of the shore; and perhaps it would appear that in other places the natural products of the shore have been more than ever resorted to for manures, where modern research has detected new soils, or new modes of combining such soils so as to increase the productive powers of land in tillage. In the same manner alterations and improvements have occurred in the fisheries. And when it is considered, that such common right to use the shore of the realm would include within its range not the open shores of the sea only, but the shores of all creeks and arms of the sea, and of tide-rivers, the value and utility of such a privilege to the public cannot be questioned. Every species of natural manure is to be found within this extensive range, as well as other products capable of conversion into rich manures by artificial processes. Some (such as chalk) are used both in the natural state, and also after being improved by artificial processes. (*n*)

times; and this is an artificial preparation of a manure to increase its powers. There is no doubt too but that the coming of the Romans into Britain introduced their improved modes of tillage; and at that time, the Romans had studied agriculture as a science, and it was held in particular honour by that great and wise people.

(*n*) In a book of agriculture of great authority (Sir John Sinclair's Code of Agriculture) it is said, p. 40, " an object deserving considera-" tion is the situation of the farm regarding manures; for an easy " access to lime, chalk, marl, sea-weed, &c. is of essential advantage " to cultivation." In various parts of the same work, the manures furnished by the " shore" are spoken of in the highest terms. Thus in p. 242, " sea-ooze" is mentioned as " of a most enriching nature." In p. 243-4, sea-weed is described as good for arable lands; and the late Duke of Richmond is stated to have used it in *Sussex*. Tangle, or drifted sea-ware, is extolled p. 243-4, as having " several advantages over other sorts of manure." Sea-shells are said " to abound in various

for Sand, Shells, &c. on the Shore.

In the case of Ball *v*. Herbert,(*o*) a right to use *towing-paths*, along the *banks* of navigable rivers, was contended for, as a general public privilege for all the subjects of the realm. But it was decided by Lord Kenyon and other judges (and it is conceived most reasonably) that no such general custom existed at law. The naturally navigable rivers, subject to the tides, are so very *few* in these kingdoms, that the practice of towing could not be regarded as *general*. The character of the right partook of the limited nature of the custom. It was, accordingly, decided by the court, that as a *local* custom it might be good, but not as a general right. The public right to navigate the seas and tide rivers is a right of way, *not* upon the *terra firma*, but upon and over those seas and tide rivers.—Even granting a right to use the *ripam* along the coast, so far as it is reasonably essential to fishing and navigation, still such right must be general in its quality, and such only as is *necessary* to the fishing and navigation, as *generally* carried on. Towing, in fact, seems to begin where navigation, properly so called, ends. It is very limited both in place and practice, so far as tide rivers are concerned. (*p*)

Now, in this case,(*q*) Lord Kenyon, addressing himself to the question of general Common law rights, says, "Com-"mon law rights are either to be found in the opinions of "lawyers, delivered as axioms, or to be collected from the "universal and immemorial usage throughout the country." It seems, then, that *either* of these grounds will suffice. It

The right towing-pa is not a ge ral right a navigable rivers.

---

shire, and in *Scotland.* It is also remarked, that "farmers prefer taking it as near the low-water mark as possible," p. 238. Indeed, the books written upon this interesting subject of agriculture, uniformly allude to the use of sea-shore manures as quite common and universal throughout the kingdom.

(*o*) 3 T. R. 253.   (*p*) Ante, p. 176.
(*q*) Ball *v*. Herbert, 3 T. R. 261, Lord Kenyon's doctrine as to

may, it is conceived, be "collected from universal and immemorial usage," that the sea-shore has been resorted to for the purposes in question, not in a few places, or in two counties only, but *generally* throughout the realm. It is a custom quite in contrast with that of towage: it is, in fact, essentially, and in its nature *general;* as agriculture is general, and the manuring of lands general, and the products of the shore are also as generally applicable and available in one part of the kingdom as another.

It is, therefore, on all accounts desirable, that the custom in question should be supported, if possible, as a general Common law right. As a *local* custom it is liable to be limited in extent and utility; the materials, in such case, cannot be legally carried away, used, or sold for use out of the precincts of the manor; besides, local customs may be *lost* by disuse, and cannot be revived. Ignorance, prejudice, want of capital, or of enterprise, or of means of conveyance, may, for a time, induce a neglect of the advantages afforded by the "sea-shore," in particular districts, until the right is lost by disuse, to the no small injury of the agriculture of those places. If the custom, as a local custom, cannot be proved to have existed within the memory of the inhabitants, it may be lost for ever; and however inclined, or capable, the next generation may be to use those advantages which their predecessors neglected, it is too late. It is well known, that in many places on the coast which had long been supposed destitute of good materials for manure, the finest manures have been ultimately found, either by accident, or scientific research. But the memory of man may not warrant its being taken, as a *local* privilege. So, the daily alterations which take place along the coast, by the action of storms and tides, will bring or lay open the finest manures, where there had been none for use before.

prejudice a general Common law custom. It cannot be lost by local disuse; and it may, at any time, be revived into use for the public good. Such is the case with the "fishery;" and, nationally speaking, so it should be with the custom in question.

REMARKS ON THE CASE OF DICKENS *V.* SHAW.

(APPENDIX, post, p. xlv.)

HIS case has decided, that a right to "wreck" will not *alone* confer a title, by presumption or construction of law, to the ownership of the soil of the "shore," against the Crown. So far, therefore, the doctrine contended for in former pages has been judicially supported. But the learned judges did not explicitly state, what *other* additional or cumulative evidence might suffice to establish such ownership. The exclusive right to take sand is alluded to, as *one* badge of ownership; and we are also told, that "the proper thing is to look to "the exercise, and see how the lord of the manor has, from "time to time, acted." There can be no doubt but that this must be the general rule, if *presumption of law* be allowed, at all, to confer a title to the "shore." Still, however, this case does not enable us to determine, out of all the badges of ownership alluded to by Lord Hale, how many may, and how many may not, be dispensed with. Whether wreck and royal fish together will suffice? Whether wreck and an exclusive fishing, or an exclusive taking of sand, will suffice? Whether to these must be added jurisdiction of "purpres-

and taking rent, embanking and in-taking from the sea, or some or one of these must also be brought into the scale? (a)

This case, however, furnishes a strong illustration of Bracton's doctrine regarding the *communis usus* of the sea-shore. For it appears that, in the shore of the manor of Brighton, between high and low-water mark, the public have immemorially exercised and enjoyed every useful privilege of which such shore seems capable. They have resorted to, and used it for the following purposes, viz. for the fisheries, for navigation, for free-way and passage, for bathing, for digging and taking sand, shell, stones, sea-weed, and other materials of the soil. And all this they have done, without restraint or hindrance from the Crown or the lord of the manor. These rights do not appear to have been confined or limited to the *tenants* of the manor, or to the *inhabitants* of the town; but have apparently been exercised by all men who dwelt within convenient reach of the shore. The franchise of wreck, or royal fish, could not be the subject of *common* use; but, for all uses capable of *common* and general enjoyment, the whole shore seems to have been, immemorially, perfectly free and open.

If the manor of Brighton should be found to represent, in these respects, the prevailing practice in the *great majority* of the sea-coast manors of the kingdom, it would be difficult *à priori* to controvert Bracton's assertion, "that the sea-shores are, *jure communi*, as open to common resort, and common use, as the sea itself." (b) There are, no doubt, many exceptions grown up; some by actual grant from the Crown, and more by gradual encroachment; but, with these exceptions, the general rule and presumption seems to be, that the Crown has immemorially held its ownership of the shore, subject to these common uses, in like manner as its

(a) See Phear, p. 89.

dominion over the seas is open to the common use of all the subjects of the realm. It must be acknowledged, however, that such does not seem to be the prevailing doctrine of recent authorities, as regards the sea-shore. Yet the learned Judge, in the foregoing case, declared, that "the " right of the Crown is not, in general, for any beneficial " interest to the Crown itself, but for securing to the public " certain privileges in the spot between high and low-water " mark." And if this be so, it might, perhaps, be conceded, that all those common uses of the shore which have been immemorially acquiesced in by the Crown, and enjoyed by the public, are, by this time, established of common right, in the same manner as the public fisheries have been enjoyed and established. Nothing more is wanted for the public than those common uses of the shore, which, as it seems, have been immemorially enjoyed in the shore of the manor of Brighton.

It is a question of some interest and importance, how far the present state of the law, upon the subject of the foregoing pages, is susceptible of alteration and amendment. Possibly it may form one of the topics for the consideration of those to whom the reform of the "laws of real property" has been entrusted. The Crown, on behalf of the public, has an interest in the shores of every sea-coast manor within its dominions; and the public are still more directly and continually concerned in the clearness and certainty of this portion of our law. The only parties who profit by its existing uncertainty, are the lords of manors themselves, whose individual interests are, for the most part, opposed alike to the Crown and to the public. The prevailing mode of making title to the sea-shore, by *prescription* and *presumption of law*, has a tendency to favour "intrusions" and "encroachments" upon the ownership of the Crown, and the

whether it ought ever to have been in the power of the Crown to alienate, by grants to individuals, any portions of the sea-shores of the realm; and it may be still more questionable, whether such alienation ought ever to have been *presumed* by a court of law, when no grant whatever could be produced. It may be thought, that prescription, or presumption of law, ought, in no case, to be allowed to prevail against the title of the Crown to so important a trust, confided, by the law, to its charge, for the good of the commonwealth. If the King were to make the sea-shores of the realm a source of private sale and profit, he would, according to what is said before by the Judges, be acting contrary to the trust for which the ownership of the shore was vested in the Crown by the Common law. Still less, therefore, ought private individuals to be aided by presumption of law, in their claims upon the shore, when the Crown and public are both thereby greatly impoverished." (c) "Our "common law of England," says Callis, "doth much surpass "in reason, either the imperial or civil law; for, by our law, it "is said, *Rex habet proprietatem, sed Populus habet usum ibid-* "*em necessarium.*" In the manor of Brighton, this doctrine seems to have been fully exemplified, and it may be doubted whether every judicial decision, which has diminished this *proprietatem* of the Crown, and narrowed this *usum necessarium* of the public, has not been a departure alike from the reason and the principles of the Common law.

(c) Jerwood, 125, 126.

APPENDIX.

A TREATISE

DE JURE MARIS ET BRACHIORUM EJUSDEM.

FROM A MANUSCRIPT (ASCRIBED TO)
LORD CHIEF-JUSTICE HALE.

CAP. I.

Concerning the interest of fresh rivers.

RESH rivers of what kind soever, do of common right belong to the owners of the soil adjacent; so that the owners of the one side have, of common right, the propriety of the soil, and consequently the right of fishing, *usque filum aquæ;* and the owners of the other side the right of soil or ownership and fishing unto the *filum aquæ* on their side. And if a man be owner of the land of both sides, in common presumption he is owner of the whole river, and hath the right of fishing according to the extent of his land in length. With this agrees the common experience.

Vide Mich. 18. 19. *Ed.* 1. *B. R. Rot. Nott.* in an assize by Robert Baker against Hugh Hercy for hindering his fishing in the water of Idell.

Juratores dicunt, quod prædictus Hugo non tenet prædictam piscariam in separali suo, simul cum Roberto Mortayn; quia dicunt, quod omnes, qui tenent terras abuttantes super aquam illam, in ea

ex parte orientali, et illi de Stratford ex parte occidentali. Dicunt etiam, quod quædam pars villæ de Stratford est de feodo de Lancastria, abuttans se super aquam prædictam, et ipsi de feodo illo piscantur usque filum aquæ. Hugo in *Misericordia.*

And so it was accordingly agreed upon evidence, Tr. 2. Jac. B. R. Owen et Dunch. Vide 8. H. 7. 5. 22. Ass. 93. Rastall's Entries, 666, *et sæpius alibi.*

But special usage may alter that common presumption; for one man may have the river, and others the soil adjacent; or one man may have the river and soil thereof, and another the free or several fishing in that river.

If a fresh river between the lands of two lords or owners do insensibly gain on one or the other side; it is held, 22. Ass. 93. that the propriety continues as before in the river. But if it be done sensibly and suddenly, then the ownership of the soil remains according to the former bounds. As if the river running between the lands of A and B, leaves his course, and sensibly makes his channel entirely in the lands of A, the whole river belongs to A; *aqua cedit solo:* and so it is, though if the alteration be by insensible degrees, but there be other known boundaries as stakes or extent of land. 22. Ass. pl. 93. And though the book make a question, whether it hold the same law in the case of the sea or the arms of it, yet certainly the law will be all one, as we shall have occasion to shew in the ensuing discourse.

But yet special custom may alter the case in great rivers. For instance, the river of Severn, which is a wild river, yet, by the common custom used below Gloucester bridge, it is the common boundary of the manors of either side, what course soever the river takes; viz. the *filum aquæ* is the common mark or boundary, though it borrow great quantities of land, sometimes of one side, sometimes of the other, and gives them to the opposite shore.

Though fresh rivers are in point of propriety as before *primâ facie* of a private interest; yet as well fresh rivers as salt, or such as flow and reflow, may be under these two servitudes, or affected with them; viz. one of prerogative belonging to the king, and another of publick interest, or belonging to the people in general.

Of these in the ensuing chapters.

CAP. II.

Of the right of prerogative in private or fresh rivers.

HE king by an ancient right of prerogative hath had a certain interest in many fresh rivers, even where the sea doth not flow or reflow, as well as in salt or arms of the sea; and those are these which follow.

1st. A *right of franchise* or *privilege*, that no man may set up a common ferry for all passengers, without a prescription time out of mind, or a charter from the king. He may make a ferry for his own use or the use of his family, but not for the common use of all the king's subjects passing that way; because it doth in consequent tend to a common charge, and is become a thing of publick interest and use, and every man for his passage pays a toll, which is a common charge, and every ferry ought to be under a publick regulation; viz. that it give attendance at due times, keep a boat in due order, and take but reasonable toll; for if he fail in these, he is fineable. And hence it is, that if a common bridge be broken, whereby there is no passage but by a boat or ferry, it hath been anciently practised in the Exchequer to compel that ferryman, that ferries over people for profit without a charter from the king or a lawful prescription, to accompt for the benefit above his reasonable pains and charge. *Communia Paschæ,* 20. E. 3. *in Scaccario.* Vide *Claus.* 36. E. 3. *m.* 10. The bridge called Heckbeth bridge being in decay, neither was it well known who should repair it; the king grants a temporary ferry and certain particular rates for passengers, appoints the profits to be taken in the first place for defraying of the charge of the barge and bargemen; and if it can appear who is by tenure to repair it, then surplusage of the profits of the ferry to be answered to the king; and if that cannot be known, then *charitatis intuitu* the king allows it to the repair of the bridge.

And this, that is said in reference to a fresh or private river, holds place much more in a publick river or arm of the sea; and therefore it need not be repeated when we come to that subject.

2dly. An *interest,* as I may call it, of *pleasure* or recreation. Before the statute of *Magna Charta cap.* 16. it was frequent for the king to put as well fresh as salt rivers *in defenso* for his recreation; that is, to bar fishing or fowling in a river till the king had taken

ripariæ, which anciently was directed to the sheriff to prohibit riviation in any rivers in his bailiwick. But by that statute it is enacted, *quòd nullæ ripariæ defendantur de cætero, nisi illæ quæ fuerunt in defenso tempore Henrici regis avi nostri, et per eadem loca et per eosdem terminos, sicut esse consueverunt tempore suo.*

After this statute the *Ripariorum defensiones* ran thus, as appears *Claus.* 20. *H.* 3. *m.* 3. *dorso.* *Claus.* 22. *H.* 3. *m.* 2. *dorso, et sæpius alibi.*

Rex Vicecomiti Wigorniæ salutem. Præcipimus tibi, quòd sine dilatione clamari facias et firmiter probiberi ex parte nostrâ, ut nullus de cætero eat ad riviandum in ripariis nostris in ballivâ tuâ, quæ in defenso fuerunt tempore Henrici regis avi nostri; et scire facias omnibus de comitatu tuo, qui ab antiquo facere debent pontes ad riparias illas, quòd provideant sibi de pontibus illis, ita quòd prompti sint et parati in adventu nostro quando eis scire faciemus.

And thus it was written to most counties.

But because this left the country in a great uncertainty in the writs of 22. H. 3. so afterwards it mentioned some one particular river.

Et *in alijs riparijs in ballivâ tuâ, quæ in defenso esse consueverunt tempore Henrici regis avi nostri;*

As Avon in Worcestershire, Bladen in Oxfordshire, Mules in Surrey, &c.

This hath been long disused; for it created a great trouble to the country; and little benefit or addition of pleasure to the king.

3rdly. An *interest of jurisdiction;* viz. in reference to common nuisances in or by rivers; as where the sewers were not kept, which gave the rise to the commission of Sewers, as well for fresh rivers as for salt. *Vide* Stat. 23. H. 8. cap. 5. The Commission thereby enacted recites this part of the king's jurisdiction, viz.

"We therefore, for that by reason of our royal dignity and prerogative royal we are bound to provide for the safety and preservation of our realm," &c.

And another part of the king's jurisdiction in reformation of nuisances, is, to reform and punish nuisances in all rivers, whether fresh or salt, that are a common passage, not only for ships and greater vessels, but also for smaller, as barges or boats; to reform the obstructions or annoyances that are therein to such common passage: for as the common highways on the land are for the common land passage, so these kind of rivers, whether fresh or

De Jure Maris et Brachiorum ejusdem. v

highways by land are called *altæ viæ regiæ* so these publick rivers for publick passage are called *fluvii regales*, and *haut streames le Roy;* not in reference to the propriety of the river, but to the publick use; all things of publick safety and convenience being in a special manner under the king's care, supervision, and protection. And therefore the report in Sir John Davys, of the piscary of Banne, mistakes the reason of those books, that call these *streames le roy*, as if they were so called in respect of propriety, as 19. Ass. 6. Dy. 11. for they are called so, because they are of publick use, and under the king's special care and protection, whether the soil be his or not. And this leads me to the third chapter.

CAP. III.

Concerning publick streams.

THERE be some streams or rivers, that are private not only in propriety or ownership, but also in use, as little streams and rivers that are not a common passage for the king's people. Again, there be other rivers, as well fresh as salt, that are of common or publick use for carriage of boats and lighters. And these, whether they are fresh or salt, whether they flow and reflow or not, are *primâ facie publici juris*, common highways for man or goods or both from one inland town to another. Thus the rivers of Wey, of Severn, of Thames, and divers others, as well above the bridges and ports as below, as well above the flowings of the sea as below, and as well where they are become to be of private propriety as in what parts they are of the king's propriety, are publick rivers *juris publici*. And therefore all nuisances and impediments of passages of boats and vessels, though in the private soil of any person, may be punished by indictments, and removed; and this was the reason of the statute of *Magna Charta cap.* 23.

Omnes kidelli deponantur per Thamisiam et Medwayam, et per totam Angliam nisi per costeram maris.

These kinds of nuisances were such, as hindered or obstructed the passage of boats, as wears, piles, choaking up the passage with filth, diverting of the river by cutts or trenches, decay of the banks,

And they were reformed.

Sometimes by indictments or presentments in the leets, sessions of the peace, oyer and terminer, or before justices of assize.

Oftentimes in the king's bench; as *Hil*. 50. *E*. 3. *B. R. Rot*. 23. for nuisances in the river of Trent; *H*. 23. *E*. 3. *B. R. Rot*. 61. in the river Ouse; *H*. 21. *E*. 1. in the river Severn; *Tr*. 28. *E*. 3. *Rot*. 29. in the river Leigh; and generally in all other rivers within the bodies of counties, which had common passage of boats or barges, whether the water were fresh or salt, the king's or a subject's, *Rot. Parliamenti* 14. *R*. 2. *n*. 34. *Mich*. 36. *E*. 3. *B. R. Rot*. 65. *Mich*. 18, 19. *E*. 1. *B. R*. and infinite more.

Sometimes by special commission; as for the river of Leigh, 19. Ass. 6.

And sometimes by the parties, that were prejudiced by such nuisance, without any process of law.

More of this we shall see when we come to consider of common nuisances in havens and ports.

But if any person at his own charge makes his own private stream to be passable for boats or barges, either by making of locks or cutts, or drawing together other streams; and hereby that river, which was his own in point of propriety become now capable of carriage of vessels; yet this seems not to make it *juris publici*, and he may pull it down again, or apply it to his own private use. For it is not hereby made to be *juris publici*, unless it were done at a common charge, or by a publick authority, or that by long continuance of time it hath been freely devoted to a publick use. And so it seems also to be, if he that makes such a new river or passage doth it by way of recompence or compensation for some other publick stream that he hath stopped for his own conveniency; as in the case of the Abbot of St. Austin's Canterbury, mentioned in the Register. So likewise if he purchaseth the king's charter to take a reasonable toll for the passage of the king's subjects, and puts it in use, these seem to be devoting and as it were consecrating of it to the common use. As he, that by an *ad quod damnum*, and licence thereupon obtained, changeth a way, and sets out another in his own land; this new way is thereupon become *juris publici*, as well as a way by prescription. For no man can take a settled or constant toll even in his own private land for a common passage without the king's licence.

CAP. IV.

Concerning the king's interest in salt waters, the sea and its arms, and the soil thereof: and first, of the right of fishing there.

HUS much concerning fresh waters or inland rivers, which, though they empty themselves mediately into the sea, are not called arms of the sea, either in respect of the distance or smallness of them.

We come now to consider the sea and its arms: and first, concerning the sea itself.

The sea is either that which lies within the body of a county or without.

That arm or branch of the sea which lies within the *fauces terræ*, where a man may reasonably discerne between shore and shore, is or at least may be within the body of a county, and therefore within the jurisdiction of the sheriff or coroner. 8. E. 2. *Corone* 399.

The part of the sea which lies not within the body of a county, is called the main sea or ocean.

The narrow sea, adjoining to the coast of England, is part of the wast and demesnes and dominions of the king of England, whether it lie within the body of any county or not.

This is abundantly proved by that learned treatise of Master Selden called *Mare Clausum;* and therefore I shall say nothing therein, but refer the reader thither.

In this sea the king of England hath a double right, viz. a right of jurisdiction which he ordinarily exerciseth by his admiral, and a right of propriety or ownership. The latter is that which I shall meddle with.

The king's right of propriety or ownership in the sea and soil thereof is evidenced principally in these things that follow.

1st. The right of fishing in this sea and the creeks and arms thereof is originally lodged in the crown, as the right of depasturing is originally lodged in the owner of the wast whereof he is lord, or as the right of fishing belongs to him that is the owner of a private or inland river. I shall not give many instances of this, because they are abundantly done to my hand in the book I formerly

Pat. 23. *E.* 1. *m.* 6. The king grants liberty to the Hollanders to fish *in mari nostro prope Jernemuth.*
Rot. Parliamenti 3. *H.* 5. *pars.* 1. *n.* 33. The king by proclamation made a general inhibition of fishing upon the coasts of Ireland to the prejudice of the English. Desired to be recalled, but was not.
Rot. Parl. 8. *H.* 5. *n.* 6.

Item pry le Commons, que come nostre Seigneur le Roy et ses noble progeniteurs de tout temps ont estre Seigneurs de le mere, et ore per le grace de Dieu est si venus, que nostre Seigneur le Roy est Seigneur de costs de ambe parties de le mere d'ordeiner sur touts estrangers passants permy le dit mere tiel imposition al oeps nostre Seigneur le Roy apprendre que a luy semble reasonable pur le salve gard del dit mere.

Responsio, " *Le Roy s'avisera.*"

But though the king is the owner of this great wast, and as a consequent of his propriety hath the primary right of fishing in the sea and the creeks and arms thereof; yet the common people of England have regularly a liberty of fishing in the sea or creeks or arms thereof, as a publick common of piscary, and may not without injury to their right be restrained of it, unless in such places or creeks or navigable rivers, where either the king or some particular subject hath gained a propriety exclusive of that common liberty.

Mich. 19. *E.* 3. *B. R. Rot.* 127. *Lincoln.* The commonalty of Grimsby impleaded the fishermen of Ole, which is within five miles of Grimsby, for lading and unlading their fish and other victuals at Ole;

Custumâ non solutâ, quæ est debita dictæ villæ Grimsby juxta cartas regis contra prohibitionem regis.

The defendants plead,

Quòd ipsi sunt liberi tenentes in hamletto de Thrusco, qui est infra præcinctum villæ de Ole, et quòd ipsi tanquam piscatores juxta costeram maris à tempore quo, &c. usi sunt piscari cum retibus et battellis suis, et pisces captos ad terram apud Thrusco et alibi in partibus ibidem venditioni exponere, absque hoc quòd blada victualia bona aut mercimonia carcarunt aut discarcarunt aut venditioni exposuerunt. Ideo veniat jurata.

Vide Statutum 2. *E.* 6. *cap.* 6. 5. *El. cap.* 5. *Bracton, lib.* 2. *cap.* 12. *Jus piscandi omnibus commune in portu et in fluminibus.* It must be taken to be rivers, that are arms of the sea, and *primo intuitu;* for *de facto* there doth fall out in many ports and arms of

De Jure Maris et Brachiorum ejusdem.

IId. The next evidence of the king's right and propriety in the sea and the arms thereof is his right of propriety to
The shore; and
The *Maritima Incrementa.*

(1.) The shore is that ground that is between the ordinary high-water and low-water mark. This doth *primâ facie* and of common right belong to the king, both in the shore of the sea and the shore of the arms of the sea.

And herein there will be these things examinable.

1st. What shall be said the shore, or *littus maris.*

2nd. What shall be said an arm or creek of the sea.

3d. What evidence there is of the king's propriety thereof.

1. For the first of these it is certain, that that which the sea overflows, either at high-spring tides or at extraordinary tides, comes not as to this purpose under the denomination of *littus maris;* and consequently the king's title is not of that large extent, but only to land that is usually overflowed at ordinary tides. And so I have known it ruled in the Exchequer-chamber in the case of Vanhaesdanke on prosecution by information against Mr. Whiting, about 12. *Car.* 1. for lands in ———— in the county of Norfolk, and accordingly ruled 15. *Car. B. R.* Sir Edward Heron's case, and *Pasch.* 17. *Car.* 2. *in Scaccario*, upon evidence between the Lady Wandsford's Lessee and Stephens, in an *ejectione firmæ* for the town of Cowes in the isle of Wight. That therefore I call the shore, that is between the common high-water and low-water mark, and no more.

2. For the second, that is called an arm of the sea where the sea flows and reflows, and so far only as the sea so flows and reflows; so that the river of Thames above Kingston and the river of Severn above Tewkesbury, &c. though there there they are publick rivers, yet are not arms of the sea. But it seems, that, although the water be fresh at high water, yet the denomination of an arm of the sea continues, if it flow and reflow as in Thames above the bridge.

22. *Ass.* 93. Nota *que chescun ew, que flow et reflow, est appel bras de mere cy tantavint come il flow.*

3. For the third, it is admitted, that *de jure communi* between the high-water and low-water mark doth *primâ facie* belong to the king, 5. Rep. 107. Constable's case. Dy. 326. Although it is true, that such shore may and commonly is parcel of the manor adjacent, and so may be belonging to a subject, as shall be shewn,

And as the shore of the sea doth *primâ facie* belong to the king, viz. between the ordinary high-water and low-water mark, so the shore of an arm of the sea between the high-water and low-water mark belongs *primâ facie* to the king, though it may also belong to a subject, as shall be shewn in the next chapter.

In the case between the town of Newcastle and the prior of Tinmouth, 20 E. 1. which is afterwards, in the Second Part, chapter the 6th, more fully recited; one of the charges against the prior is, that he had built houses at Sheles upon the river of Tyne between the high-water and low-water mark. The prior pleads that it was built on his own soil.

Ubi dominus rex nullum habet solum, neque liberum tenementum, eo quòd solum dictæ domus et liberum tenementum extendit se usque ad filum aquæ Tyne, ultra terram suam siccam, et inter quod quidem filum aquæ et terram prædictam domus prædicta habet piscariam suam liberam in longitudinem terræ ejusdem in eâdem aquâ.

The king's attorney replied,

Quòd, qualescumque mansiunculæ ibidem fuerunt temporibus prædecessorum prioris, idem prior, qui nunc est, tempore suo fieri fecit ibidem 26 domus super solum quod domino regi esse debet, eo quòd fluxu et inundatione maris comprehenditur.

Afterwards judgment was given against the prior, but not in express termes for the soil, but implicitly. See the judgment afterwards in the Second Part, 6th chapter.

And consonant to this there was a decree *Paschæ* 8. *Car.* 1. in the Exchequer, entered in the Book of Orders of that term, fol. 66. whereby it was decreed, that the soil and ground lying between Wapping-wall and the river of Thames is parcel of the port of London; and therefore and for that the same lies between the high-water and low-water marks of the river of Thames, all the houses built between the Hermitage-wharfe unto Dickshore eastward, and between the old wall of Wapping-wall on the north and the river of Thames on the south, are decreed to the king; and the same were accordingly by commission seized into the king's hands.

The title of the bill or information was laid, viz. 1st. That the river of Thames flowed and reflowed. 2d. That consequently it was an arm of the sea. 3d. That it was the king's river. 4th. That it was the king's port.—And upon all these it was concluded, that the land between the high-water and low-water mark was the king's land, and accordingly decreed.

De Jure Maris et Brachiorum ejusdem.

or rivers that are arms of the sea, viz. the land lying between the high-water and the low-water mark at ordinary tides.

(2.) The king hath a title to *maritima incrementa*, or increase of land by the sea; and this is of three kinds, viz. 1. Increase *per projectionem vel alluvionem*. 2. Increase *per relictionem vel desertionem*. 3. *Per insulæ productionem*.

1. The increase *per alluvionem* is, when the sea by casting up sand and earth doth by degrees increase the land, and shut itself out further than the ancient bounds went; and this is usual. The reason why this belongs to the crown is, because in truth the soil, where there is now dry land, was formerly part of the very *fundus maris*, and consequently belonged to the king. But indeed if such alluvion be so insensible, that it cannot be by any means found that the sea was there, *idem est non esse et non apparere ;* the land thus increased belongs as a perquisite to the owner of the land adjacent.

2. The increase *per relictionem*, or recess of the sea. This doth *de jure communi* belong to the king; for as the sea is parcel of the wast or demesne, so of necessity the land that lies under it, and therefore it belongs to the king when left by the sea; and so also it regularly holds in lands deserted by a river, that is an arm of the sea or a creek of the sea *primâ facie*, especially if the creek or river be part of a port.

Claus. 10. *E.* 3. *m.* 18. Upon an inquisition finding that half an acre in the suburbs of Canterbury,

Crevit in cursu ripæ Cantuariæ per alluvionem et diluvionem dictæ ripæ,

this half acre was seized into the king's hands. But it is true, it was afterwards restored to the Abbot of St. Austin's; because by another inquisition it was found,

Quòd non est solum nostrum, nec accrevit per alluvionem et diluvionem dictæ ripæ, sed extitit solum abbatis, &c. à tempore cujus memoria, &c.

Car. primi, Upon an information against Oldsworth and others for that which is now called Sutton Marsh, that 300 acres of land was *relictum per mare,* and that the defendants had intruded into it; the defendants pleaded specially, and entitled themselves by prescription to the lands project by the sea; and upon a demurrer adjudged against them. That 1st, by the prescription or title made to lands project, which is *jus alluvionis,* no answer is given to the title of information for lands relict, for these were of several natures. 2d, *mare;* for so if the channel between us and France should dry up, a man might prescribe for it, which is unreasonable; for

Nihil prescribitur nisi quod possidetur.

But this hath some exceptions, besides these that follow in the ensuing chapter.

If a subject hath had by prescription the property of a certain tract, or creek, or navigable river, or arm of the sea, even while it is covered with water, by certain known metes or extents; this, though it should be relicted, the subject will have the propriety in the soil relicted. For he had it before, though covered with water; and although the sea is a fluid thing, yet the *terra* or *solum subjectum* is fixed; and by force of a clear and evident usage a subject may have the propriety of a private river; though the acquest of the former be more difficult, and requires a very good evidence to make it out, as shall be said in the ensuing chapter.

If a subject hath land adjoining the sea, and the violence of the sea swallow it up, but so that yet there be reasonable marks to continue the notice of it; or though the marks be defaced; yet if by situation and extent of quantity, and bounding upon the firm land, the same can be known, though the sea leave this land again, or it be by art or industry regained, the subject doth not lose his propriety: and accordingly it was held by Cooke and Foster, *M.* 7. *Jac. C. B.* though the inundation continue forty years.

If the mark remain or continue, or extent can reasonably be certain, the case is clear.—Vide Dy. 326.—22. Ass. 93. See for this a notable case in the case of an overflowing by the Thames, which is an arm of the sea, *Rot. Parliamenti* 8. *E.* 2. *m.* 23. *pro Willielmo Burnello.* Phillip Burnell, father of William, being seized of the manor of Hacchesham near Greenwich, died his heir within age during his minority.

Aqua Thamissæ magnam partem terræ et prati manerij prædicti ac aliarum terrarum contiguarum superundavit.

The bishop of Bath and Wells, by agreement with the king, was to stop the breach at his own charges, and was to hold the land for seven years to reimburse his charges. This he did, and the land was regained, and the bishop held the land for his seven years, and three years over them. Burnell desired relief for his land in parliament against the Bishop. The answer was,

Sequatur versus episcopum ad communem legem;

De Jure Maris et Brachiorum ejusdem. xiii

P. 18. E. 2. Rot. 174. B. R. upon the like account a considerable quantity of marsh ground, containing 100 acres, parcel of the manor of Stebunhith, was regained from the Thames, and enjoyed accordingly. I think it is the same that is now called Stepney Marsh, or at least some part of the manor now built upon and contiguous to the Thames. The record is worth the reading, but long.

Claus. 18 *H.* 3. *m.* 21. *pro Villata de Shinberge* in Gloucestershire.

Rex Vicecomiti, &c. Quia accepimus per inquisitionem, quam fieri precipimus, quòd illa pars terræ, quam utraque villata de Shinberge et Aure sibi vendicant, eo quòd aqua Sabrinæ eam occupavit super campum de Shinberge versus campum de Aure, et postea processu temporis eam rejecit ad campum de Shinberge, antequam sic rejecta esset per aquam Sabrinæ; de jure pertinuit ad villam de Shinberge, et in parte fuit terra arabilis, et in parte pastura, ad eandem villam de Shinberge pertinens per divisam fossati, quod vocatur Hedgewood: precipimus tibi, quòd eidem villatæ de Shinberge plenam seisinam de prædictâ parte terræ habere facias. Teste Rege apud Gloucesteriam.

The river of Severn had gained upon Shinberge so much, that its channel ran over part of Shinberge lands, and lost part thereof unto the other side, and then threw it back again to Shinberge. It shall not belong to Aure. Neither was it at all claimed by the king, though Severn in that place be an arm of the sea. But it was restored to Shinberge as before.

But the truth is, that there the *maritima incrementa* of that river belong to the barons of Barclay, as shall be shewn. Yet the property of the soil was not lost to the owners that had it before.

And the truth is also, that river, which is a wild unruly river, and many times shifts its channel, especially in that flat between Shinberge and Aure, is the common boundary between the manors of either side, viz. the *filum aquæ*, or middle of the stream. And this is the custom of the manors contiguous to that river from Gloucester down to Aure, which was not taken notice of in that record. Yet it serves for this purpose to shew, that the king gained not the propriety against the town by such inundation.

It is true, here were the old bounds or marks continuing, viz. the Hedgewood. But suppose the inundation of the sea deface the marks and boundaries, yet if the certain extent or contents from the land not overflown can be evidenced, though the bounds be defaced,

xiv *Appendix.*

and extents that it formerly had. Only if any man be at the charge of inning of it, it seems by a decree of Sewers he may hold it till he be reimbursed his charges, as was done in the case of Burnell before alledged. But if it be freely left again by the reflux and recess of the sea, the owner may have his land as before, if he can make it out where and what it was; for he cannot lose his propriety of the soil, though it be for a time become part of the sea, and within the admiral jurisdiction while it so continues.

3. The third sort of maritime increase are islands arising *de novo* in the king's seas, or the king's arms thereof. These upon the same account and reason *primâ facie* and of common right belong to the king; for they are part of that soil of the sea, that belonged before in point of propriety to the king; for when islands *de novo* arise, it is either by the recess or sinking of the water, or else by the exaggeration of sand and slubb, which in process of time grow firm land invironed with water; and thus some places have arisen, and their original recorded, as about Ravensend in Yorkshire.

And thus much of the king's right of propriety which he hath in the sea, and also *primâ facie* and in common presumption in the ports and creeks and arms of the sea.

CAP. V.

The right which a subject may have in the creeks or arms of the sea, and how it may be acquired.

LTHOUGH the king hath *primâ facie* this right in the arms and creeks of the sea *communi jure*, and in common presumption, yet a subject may have such a right.

And this he may have two ways.

1st. By the king's charter or grant; and this is without question. The king may grant fishing within a creek of the sea, or in some known precinct that hath known bounds, though within the main sea. He may also grant that very interest itself, viz. a navigable river that is an arm of the sea, the water and soil thereof. He may also grant a manor *cum littore maris eidem adjacente;* and the shore itself will pass, though in gross and not parcel of the manor. He may also grant a manor or land contiguous to the sea, *unà cum*

De Jure Maris et Brachiorum ejusdem. xv

before. *Vide Cartæ Antiquæ*, G. 15. Grant 6. *Johannis* to the abbott *de Bello loco, viz. alveum super quem abbatia fundata est à vado de Hartford cum fluctu maris in ascendendo et descendendo inter utramque ripam.*

Vide ibidem, I. 17. *Carta Willielmi primi abbati sancti Augustini de totâ terrâ Estanore et totum littus usque medietatem aquæ.*

Vide ibidem, Carta Knuti monachis sancti Augustini de terrâ insulâ Thanet, tam in terrâ quàm in mari et littore.

Vide ibidem. F. 17. A grant by king William the first to the monks of Trinity, Canterbury, of divers liberties in their possessions *in terrâ et in mari.*

Vide Cartæ Antiquæ, O. 1. A grant by Edward the Confessor to the abbey of Hulm, *videlicet, wreccum in mari et in littore maris et in portubus maris. Cartæ Antiquæ*, D. D. 24.

But it seems the grant of *incrementa maritima* will not pass lands that often happen to be relict by the sea; because that is not so properly *maritimum incrementum*. And besides, the soil itself under the water is actually the king's, and cannot pass from him by such an incertain grant as *maritima incrementa;* but it must pass a present interest.

But if the king will grant land adjacent to the sea, *unà cum mille acris terræ aquâ maris coopertis eædem terræ secundum consuetudinem, &c. adjacentibus;* such a grant, as it may be penned, will pass the soil itself; and if there shall be a recess of the sea leaving such a quantity of land, it will belong to the grantee.

2d. The second right is that which is acquired or acquirable to a subject by custom or prescription; and I think it very clear, that the subject may by custom and usage or prescription have the true propriety and interest of many of these several maritime interests, which we have before stated to be *primâ facie* belonging to the king. I will go over them particularly, and set down which of these interests are acquirable by usage or prescription by a subject.

A subject may by prescription have the interest of fishing in an arm of the sea, in a creek or port of the sea, or in a certain precinct or extent lying within the sea: and these not only free fishing, but several fishing.

Fishing may be of two kinds ordinarily, viz. the fishing with the net, which may be either as a liberty without the soil, or as a liberty arising by reason of and in concomitance with the soil, or interest or places, *borachiæ, stachiæ,* &c. which are the very soil itself, and so frequently agreed in our books. And such as these a subject may have by usage either in gross, as many religious houses had; or as parcel of or appendant to their manors, as both corporations and others have had; and this not only in navigable rivers and arms of the sea, but in creeks and ports and havens, yea and in certain known limits in the open sea contiguous to the shore.

And these kinds of fishing are not only for small sea fish, as herrings, sprats, pilchers, &c. but for great fish, as salmons, which, though they are great fish, are not royal fish, as the report of Sir John Davys in the case of the fishing of Banne would intimate. And not only for smaller fish, and salmons, but even royal fish, as whale, sturgion, porpoise, which, though they are royal fish, and *primâ facie* and of common right do belong to the king, yet a subject may prescribe even for these as appurtenant to his manor, as is unquestionably agreed by our books.

Now for precedents touching such rights of fishing in the sea and arms and creeks thereof belonging by usage to subjects, the most whereof will appear to be by reason of the propriety of the very water and soil wherein the fishing is, and some of them even within the ports of the sea.

P. 4. *E.* 1. *B. R. Surrey.*—The prior of Stoke brings trespass for the fishing in *aquâ de Sturmer* against Hamon Clever.—The defendant justified, *quòd piscavit in communi aquâ ipsius Hamonis ex parte comitatûs Suffolchiæ, ubi ipse et antecessores sui semper solebant piscare.*—The prior *dicit, quod Michael avus ipsius Hamonis dedit totum jus, quod dicebat se habere in piscariâ mars de le Sturmer Deo et sancto Johanni de Stoke, &c.*

P. 34. *E.* 1. *B. R. Rot.* 14. *Kancia.*—*Prior de Coningshed implacitat abbatem de Furneys pro prostratione gurgitis in aquâ de Ulverstone.* The defendant justified; because each end of the wear was fastened upon the abbot's land. The abbot replies, *quòd Willielmus de Lancaster dominus de Kendal dedit prædecessori domûs suæ prædictæ aquam et piscariam ex utrâque parte ejusdem quantum impetus maris fluit et refluit.*

Vide Rastall's Entries, trespass in piscary, pl. 4. Prescription pur several fishing *in aquâ maritimâ fluente et refluente in seisonabili tempore cum 7 stallis separatis separalis piscariæ fixis pro retibus.*

P. 35. *E.* 1. *B. R. Rat.* 18. *Suffolchiæ.*—*Willielmus Braham im-*

De Jure Maris et Brachiorum ejusdem. xvii

suâ apud Braham. Defendens dicit, quòd prædicta piscaria est quoddam brachium maris et communis piscaria eorundem et aliorum, et non separalis piscaria. Ideo veniat jurata.

Whereby it is admitted, though *primâ facie* an arm of the sea be in point of propriety the king's, and *primâ facie* it is common for every subject to fish there, yet a subject may have by usage a several fishing there, exclusive of that common liberty which otherwise of common right belongs to all the king's subjects.

Trin. 10. *E.* 2. *B. R. Rot.* 83. *Norfolchiæ.* The abbot of St. Benedict Hulm impleads divers for fishing *in ripariâ, quæ se extendit à ponte de Wroxam usque quandam lacum vocatam Blackdam.*— Pending the suit the king's attorney came in, and alledged for the king, *quòd prædicta riparia est brachium maris, quæ se extendit in salsum mare, et est riparia domini regis salsa fluens et refluens, ubi naves et battelli veniunt et applicant extra magnum mare carcati et discarcati quietè absque tolneto seu custumâ alicui dando, et est communis piscaria quibuscumque; et dicit, quòd presentatum fuit in ultimo itinere coram Solomone de Roffa et socijs suis justiciarijs itinerantibus in comitatu isto, quod prædecessor prædicti abbatis fecit purpresturam super dominum regem in ripariâ prædictâ, gurgites plantando in eâdem et appropriando sibi prædictam piscariam tenendo tanquam sepâralem; per quod consideratum fuit, quòd gurgites illæ amoverentur, et quòd prædicta aqua remaneret communis piscaria. Et petit, quòd non procedatur ad aliquam inquisitionem inde capiendam, quousque præfati justiciarij super recordo et processu prædictis certiorentur.* Thereupon search is granted, and the record certified. And afterwards a *procedendo* was obtained; and issue being joined, it was found for the abbot, and judgment and execution given against the defendants for the damages, viz. £200.

Upon which record these things are observable.

1st. That *de communi jure* the right of such arms of the sea belongs to the king.

2d. That yet in such arms of the sea the subjects in general have *primâ facie* a common of fishing, as in the main sea.

3d. That yet a subject may have a separate right of fishing, exclusive of the king and of the common right of the subject.

4th. That in this case the right of the abbot to have a several fishing was not a bare right of liberty or *profit à prendre;* but the right of the very water and soil itself, for he made weares

Escœtria, 12. *E.* 1. *n.* 1. The earls of Devon had not only the port of Toppesham, *de quo infra;* but the record tells us, that *portus et piscaria et mariscus de Topsham spectat Amiciæ comitissæ Devon.*
Mich. 13, 14. *E.* 1. *B. R. rot.* 10. The abbot of Tichfend impleaded the burgesses of Southampton, *quòd diripuerunt gurgitem suam apud Cadeland. Burgenses respondent, quòd ipsa gurges levata fuit ad nocumentum domini regis et villæ Southampton, et quòd batelli et naves impediuntur, quo minus venire non possunt ad portum villæ prædictæ. Juratores dicunt, quòd à tempore quo, &c. non fuit ibi aliqua gurges, sed antiquitùs solebant stare pali, per quod credunt, quòd tunc fuit prostrata gurges eâdem occasione quâ modo, eo quòd fuit ad nocumentum transeuntium.*

Upon which record these things are observable.

1st. That a subject may by prescription have a wear in the sea, and consequently have an interest below the low-water mark ; for probably weares be such.

2dly. That, yet if it be a nuisance to the passage of ships, it may be abated.

7th *Rep.* 15. It appears, that the abbot of Abbotsbury before dissolution had not only a game of swans, but the fishing, yea and the soil of an arm or creek of the sea called a meere or fleete, *in quam mare fluit et refluit;* and it came to the king by the dissolution of the monastery.

And in many considerable arms of the sea that were navigable rivers, and flowed and reflowed with salt water, divers persons had weares and local fishing sluices. As for instance, in the river of Severn the earls of Lancaster had certain weares called Radley weares, part of his manor of Radley. *Clause* 10. *E.* 3. *m.* 29. The like for others in the river of Tese, *Patentes* 32. *E.* 3. *pars* 1. *m.* 15. *dorso in Twede, fines* 2. *E.* 3. *m.* 1. *in Trent. Pat.* 18. *E.* 2. *pars* 1. *m.* 3. *dorso. Pat.* 43. *H.* 3. *m. dorso in Severn. Pat.* 2. *E.* 4. *pars* 3. *m.* 15. *dorso. Pat.* 32. *E.* 3. *pars* 2. *m.* 15. *dorso in Ose. Pat.* 12. *E.* 2. *pars* 1. *m.* 3.

Trin. 50. *E.* 3. *B. R. rot.* 2. *Essex. Walterius filius Walteri monstrat domino regi, quòd cùm piscaria vocata le Reysand ab antiquo ut parcella manerij sui de Burnham appendebat, dominus rex per cartam suam eam concessit durante minore ætate suâ cuidam Bartholomeo Stigoune, qui prædictam piscariam detinet ad præjudicium et exhæredationem dictæ Walteri.* And thereupon a *scire facias* awarded. The defendant prayed aid of the king ; and after a *procedendo* they

De Jure Maris et Brachiorum ejusdem. xix

manerij prædicti. Ideo consideratum est, quòd prædicta piscaria, cum gurgitibus eidem pertinentibus, dicto Waltero liberentur.

Infinite more of this kind might be produced. I shall add no more here; but in the subsequent parts of this and the next chapter some other instances of this nature will occur, which be applicable to the prescription of the right of fishing in navigable rivers; and I have added the more, because there are certain glances and intimations in the case of the piscary of Banne, in Sir John Davys's reports, as if the fishing in these kinds of royal rivers, were not acquirable but by special charter, which is certainly untrue; for they are acquirable by prescription or usage, as well as royal fish may be.

It is true, that by the statute of *Magna Charta, cap.* 23. *Omnes kidelli deponantur de cetero penitùs per Thamisiam et Medwayam per totam Angliam, nisi per costeram maris.*

And this statute was seconded with others that were more effectual, viz. 25. E. 3. cap. 4. 1. H. 4. 12. 12. E. 4. cap. 7.

And by force of these statutes, weares, that were prejudicial to the passage of vessels, were to be pulled down; and accordingly it was done in many places. But that did no way disaffirm the propriety, but only remove the annoyance, which, as before is shewn, was not to be allowed in an inland river, if it be a common passage.

The exception of weares upon the sea-coasts, and likewise frequent examples, some whereof are before mentioned, make it appear that there might be such private interests not only in point of liberty, but in point of propriety, on the sea-coast and below the low-water mark; for such were regularly all weares. But as by the statutes of 25. E. 3. cap. 4.—45. E. 3. cap. 2.—1. H. 4. 12.—4 H. 4. cap. 11. and other statutes, the erecting of new weares and inhancing of old is provided against in navigable rivers; and by other statutes particular provision is made against weares new or old erected in particular ports (as in the port of Newcastle, by the statute of the 21. H. 1. cap. 18.; in the port of Southampton, by the statutes of 11. H. 7. cap. 5. 14. H. 8. cap. 13.; in the rivers of Ouse and Humber, by the statute of 23. H. 8. cap. 18.; in the river and port of Exeter, by the statute of 31. H. 8. cap. 4.; in the river of Thames, by the statutes of 4. H. 7. cap. 15. 27. H. 8. cap. 18. 3. Jac. cap. 20. and divers others); so by the statute of 3 Jac. cap. 12. all new weares erected upon the sea-shore, or in any haven harbour or creek, or within five miles of the mouth of any haven or creek, are prohibited under a penalty. But in all these statutes,

be such an interest lodged in a subject, not only in navigable rivers, but even in the ports of the sea itself contiguous to the shore, though below the low-water mark, whereby a subject may not only have a liberty but also a right or propriety of soil. But yet this, that I have said, must be taken with this allay, which I have in part premised.

1st. That this interest or right in the subject must be so used as it may not occasion a common annoyance to passage of ships or boats; for that is prohibited by the common law, and these several statutes before mentioned, viz. erecting new weares, inhancing old, fixing of pikes or stakes, and the like, in order to fishing: for the *jus privatum*, that is acquired to the subject either by patent or prescription, must not prejudice the *jus publicum*, wherewith public rivers or arms of the sea are affected for public use.

2d. That the fishing, that a subject hath in this or any other private or public river, or creek fresh or salt, is subject to the laws for the conservation of fish and fry, which are many.

And this gives me an occasion to divert to the examination of those commissions, that have been granted in common rivers, commonly called commissions of conservancy or water-bailiffs; which commissions have of late time especially been granted in all the great rivers in England, and under which the patentees have exercised a jurisdiction irregularly enough and to the damage of the people, and under the disguise of a publick good have filled their own purses with the money exacted from the people. Therefore touching their office,

1st. The office of a water-baillie or *scrutator* is a bare ministerial officer, which the king doth or may appoint in those rivers or places that are his in franchise or interest. And his business was, to look to the king's rights, as his wrecks, his flotson, jetson, water-strays, royal fishes. And he had no jurisdiction at all *quâ talis;* but his office was only ministerial, to receive and account for the casualties belonging to the king upon publick or great rivers, which did or in common presumption might belong to the crown. Such was that office of searcher, *scrutator*, or baillie of the river of Severn *usque ad pontem Wigorniæ*. Pat. 27. H. 6. parte 2. m. 20. Pat. 8. E. 4. parte 1. m. 22.

2d. The office of conservator of rivers and fish in rivers; and of these patents of conservancy we find mention in the statute 1. Eliz. cap. 17. And by a grant made to the city of London, and confirmed

De Jure Maris et Brachiorum ejusdem. xxi

This office of conservancy is of two kinds, or rather there are or may be two branches thereof.

1st. The conservancy in order to nuisances in rivers. This is grounded upon the statute of 1. H. 4. cap. 12. whereby it is enacted, that there shall be commissions granted to survey and keep the waters and great rivers, and to correct and amend the defaults. And this for Thames is annexed to the mayor of London also by the statutes of 4 H. 7. cap. 15. 27. H. 8. cap. 18.

2d. The conservancy in order to fishing. And this is that which is mentioned in the statute of 1. Eliz. cap. 17. And this is grounded upon the stat. of Westminster 2. cap. 47. which enacted, That the waters of Humber, Owse, Trent, Dove, Aire, Darwent, Wherf, Niddiore, Swale, Tese, Tyne, Eden, *et omnes aliæ aquæ in regno, in quibus salmones capiuntur, ponantur in defenso, &c. Et in partibus ubi hujusmodi ripariæ fuerint, assignentur conservatores istius statuti, qui ad hoc jurati sæpius videant et inquirant de hujusmodi transgressoribus. Et in primâ transgressione puniantur per combustionem retium, &c.* By the stat. 13. R. 2. cap. 19. the former statute is confirmed, and the river of Thames added; and the rivers of Lone, Wyre, Merse and Ribbell, and all other waters in the county of Lancaster be put in defence as to the taking of salmons, &c. and in parts where such rivers are, there shall be assigned and sworn good and sufficient conservators of this statute, as of the statute of Westminster.

But neither of these statutes extended to any rivers but such wherein salmon be. And inasmuch as such a commission could not be without the warrant of an act of parliament, as is observed truly by my Lord Coke upon the statute of Westminster 2. cap. 47. consequently their commission cannot extend further than that act warrants, viz. to none but to those that are particularly named, or at least wherein salmon are.

By the statute of 17. R. 2. cap. 9. the justices of the peace are appointed conservators of these statutes, except only as to the conservancy of the river of Thames and Medway annexed to the mayor of London.

By the stat. of 1. Eliz. cap. 17. there is a farther and more extensive provision against the destruction of other fish as well as salmon; and it limits, that the lord admiral, the mayor of London, lords of leets, &c. and all other persons, &c. which by grant or other lawful jurisdiction to inquire of, by the oaths of twelve men, and to hear and determine such offences.

This indeed doth enlarge the power of these conservators in respect of the offences, but not in respect of the limit of their jurisdiction.

Upon all this it follows,

1st. That these commissioners of conservancy have no power in reference to fishing, but in such places where salmons are or the rivers mentioned in the acts, though in those rivers they have jurisdiction as to other fish as well as salmon; and that the conservators have no power except in reference to nuisances in common or public rivers, and not in private nuisances between party and party.

2d. Consequently, not in the small rivers that fall into those rivers; for such small rivers as they, are not named in the acts of Westminster 2. nor 13. R. 2. and they have not any salmons in them, and so not within their jurisdiction.

3d. But yet in those rivers particularly named in the statutes of Westminster 2. and 13. R. 2. or in such rivers where salmons are, they have power to inquire of all offences contrary to the statute of 1. Eliz. because committed within the precinct of their jurisdiction.

4th. But then they must not convict nor fine men barely upon a presentment without a tryall; for such conviction without tryall is against law in any case, but a leete or swanmote court.

And therefore all those offences that are against the statute of 1. Eliz. within small rivers, are only punishable by the leete, or by the justices of the peace at their sessions, who are general conservators by the statute of 17. R. 2. cap. 9. and not before these conservators by commission, except as to the offences in Thames, which are inquirable by the mayor of London.

And thus much by the way concerning conservatorships and water-baillies; and also concerning the right of fishing in the sea or arms thereof belonging to a subject, either by grant or prescription, either as a liberty or in respect of ownership of soil.

CAP. VI.

Concerning the ownership or propriety which a subject may have in the sea-shore and maritime increments, &c.

COME now to those other parts of propriety which a subject may have by prescription or usage, viz. the sea-shore and maritime increases; which, though we have before stated to belong *primâ facie* to the king, yet they may belong to the subject in point of propriety, not only by charter or grant, whereof there can be but little doubt, but also by prescription or usage.

I. The shore of the sea.

There seem to be three sorts of shores, or *littora marina*, according to the various tides, viz.

(1st.) The high spring tides, which are the fluxes of the sea at those tides that happen at the two equinoxials; and certainly this doth not *de jure communi* belong to the crown. For such spring tides many times overflow ancient meadows and salt marshes, which yet unquestionably belong to the subject. And this is admitted of all hands.

(2d.) The spring tides, which happen twice every month at full and change of the moon; and the shore in question is by some opinion not denominated by these tides neither, but the lands overflowed with these fluxes ordinarily belong to the subject *primâ facie*, unless the king hath a prescription to the contrary. And the reason seems to be, because for the most part the lands covered with these fluxes are dry and maniorable; for at other tides the sea doth not cover them; and therefore touching these shores some hold, that common right speaks for the subject, unless there be an usage to entitle the crown; for this is not properly *littus maris*. And therefore it hath been held, that where the king makes his title to land as *littus maris*, or *parcella littoris marini*, it is not sufficient for him to make it appear to be overflowed at spring tides of this kind. P. 8. Car. 1. *in Camerâ Scaccarii*, in the cafe of Vanhesdanke for lands in Norfolk; and so I have heard it was held, P. 15. Car. B. R. Sir Edw. Heron's case, & Tr. 17. Car. 2. in the case of the lady Wandesford, for a town called the Cowes in the Isle of Wight,

(3d.) Ordinary tides, or nepe tides, which happen between the full and change of the moon; and this is that which is properly *littus maris*, sometimes called *marettum*, sometimes *warettum*. And touching this kind of shore, viz. that which is covered by the ordinary flux of the sea, is the business of our present enquiry.

1st. This may belong to a subject. The statute of 7. Jac. cap. 18. supposeth it; for it provides, that those of Cornwall and Devon may fetch sea-sand for the bettering of their lands and shall not be hindered by those that have their lands adjoining to the sea-coasts, which appears by the statute they could not formerly. *Vide Cartæ Antiquæ D. D. n.* 24. the charter of Alan de Percey to the monks of Whitby, and the bounds thereof, viz. *totam marinam à portâ de Whitby usque Blowick, &c. et usque Terdiso, et usque in mare, et per marinam in Whitby*, confirmed by king Henry I. And the bounds of that abbey's possessions take in many creeks of the sea, yet are given by a subject, viz. Derwent, Muse, Ese, &c.

2d. It may not only belong to a subject in gross, which possibly may suppose a grant before time of memory, but it may be parcel of a manor. And thus it is agreed 5. Reports, 107. in Sir Henry Constable's case, and the book of 5. E. 3. 3. cited accordingly. And according to this was the resolution cited Dyer 316. to be between Hammond and Digges, *P.* 17. *Eliz.* And accordingly it was decreed in the Exchequer-chamber, *P.* 16. *Car. inter l'* Attorney General *et* sir Samuel Roll, sir Richard Buller, and sir Thomas Arundell, *per omnes barones*. And the evidences to prove this fact are commonly these; constant and usual fetching gravel and sea-weed and sea-sand between the high-water and low-water mark, and licensing others so to do; inclosing and imbanking against the sea, and enjoyment of what is so inned; enjoyment of wrecks happening upon the sand; presentment and punishment of purprestures there in the court of a manor; and such like.

And as it may be parcel of a manor, so it may be parcel of a vill or parish; and the evidence for that will be usual, perambulations, common reputation, known metes and divisions, and the like. And upon this account the parson of Sutton about 14. Car. had a verdict for the tithes of Sutton-Marsh in Lincolnshire, upon a long and a great evidence; though it appeared, that within time of memory it was the mere shore of the sea covered at ordinary tides, and without the old sea-bank.

3d. It may not only be parcel of a manor, but *de facto* it many

De Jure Maris et Brachiorum ejusdem. xxv

as by prescription have royal fish or wrecks of the sea within their manor. For, for the most part, wrecks and royal fish are not, nor indeed cannot be well left above the high-water mark, unless it be at such extraordinary tides as overflow the land: but these are perquisites, which happen between the high-water and low-water mark; for the sea withdrawing at the ebb leaves the wrecks upon the shore, and also those greater fish which come under the denomination of royal fish. He therefore that hath wreck of the sea or royal fish by prescription *infra manerium*, it is a great presumption, that the shore is part of the manor, as otherwise he could not have them. And consonant to this is the pleading of Sir Henry Nevill's case, 5. E. 3. 3. and Rastall's Entries 634, transcribed out of the record *M.* 14. *E.* 1. *Rot.* 432. where an abbot, prescribing for wreck belonging to his manor, doth it in this form: *Ipseque et omnes prædecessores sui abbates monasterii prædicti et domini ejusdem manerii, per totum tempus prædictum, habuerunt, et habere consueverunt, ratione manerii prædicti, omnimodo bona wreccata super mare et ut wreccum super terram projecta per costeram maris in quodam loquo ubi mare secundùm cursum suum pro tempore fluxit et refluxit, à quodam loco vocato M. in parochiâ de L. &c.* And in the following plea, an abbot prescribes to have *wreccum maris infra præcinctum manerii sive dominii sui projectum et flotesan maris infra præcinctum manerii deveniens, quodque prædictum dolium vini fuit wreccum maris per mare projectum super littus maris apud S. infra præcinctum manerii sive dominii illius.*

And with this agrees the Register 102. Yet I find the earl of Cornwall had *wreccum maris per comitatum Cornubiæ ;* and thereupon being questioned for wreck, adjudged, *quod eat sine die.* P. 14. *E.* 1. *minus B. R. Rot.* 6. *Cornubia.* But that was in a contest between the king and him; for possibly the inferior lords might have it by usage against the earl.

Thus much shall suffice concerning the shore or space between the high-water and low-water mark, which may belong to a subject and be parcel of his manor.

II. Let us now come to the *maritima incrementa*, viz.

  Alluvio maris ;
  Recessus maris ; et
  Insula maris.

(1st.) For the *jus alluvionis,* which is an increase of the land

Appendix.

and slubb to the adjoining land, whereby it is increased, and for the most part by insensible degrees, Bracton, *lib.* 2. *cap.* 2. writes thus: *Item quod per alluvionem agro tuo flumen adjecit, jure gentium tibi acquiritur. Est autem alluvio latens incrementum. Et per alluvionem adjici dicitur, quod ita paulatim adjicitur, quod intelligere non possis quo momento temporis adjiciatur, &c. Si autem non sit latens incrementum, contrarium erit, ut vis fluminis partem aliquam ex tuo prædio detraxit, et vicini prædio appulit, certum est eam tuum permanere, &c.* But Bracton follows the civil law in this and some other following places. And yet even according to this, the common law doth regularly hold at this day between party and party. But it is doubted in case of an arm of the sea, 22. Ass. 93.

This *jus alluvionis*, as I have before said, is *de jure communi* by the law of England the king's, viz. if by any marks or measures it can be known what is so gained; for if the gain be so insensible and indiscernible by any limits or marks that it cannot be known, *idem est non esse et non apparere,* as well in maritime increases as in the increases by inland rivers.

But yet custom may in this case give this *jus alluvionis* to the land whereunto it accrues.

This is made out very plainly by these ensuing records.

Communia Trin. 43. *E.* 3. *Rot.* 13. *in Scaccario,* which is that very record which is cited by Dyer 326. out of the book of Ramsey.—Process went out against the abbot of Ramsey *ad ostendendam causam, quare* 60 *acræ marisci in manum regis non debent sesiri, quas abbas appropriavit sibi et domui suæ sine licentiâ regis, super quâdam generali commissione de terris à rege concelatis et detentis. Abbas respondit, quod ipse tenet manerium de Brancaster, quod scituatum est juxta mare, et quod est ibidem quidam mariscus, qui aliquando per influxus maris minoratur, aliquando per defluxus maris augetur, absque hoc quod appropriavit sibi prout per præsentationem prædictum supponitur.* And issue joined and verdict given for the abbot by *Nisi prius* before one of the barons. *Et judicium quod eat sine die, salvo semper jure regis.*

Though there were a verdict upon the issue, whether *appropriavit* or not, yet it is plain, that the title stood upon that which the abbot alledged by way of increment. And note, here is no custom at all alledged; but it seems he relied upon the common right of his case, as that he suffered the loss so he should enjoy the benefit, even by the bare common law in case of alluvion.

De Jure Maris et Brachiorum ejusdem. xxvii

was questioned at the king's suit for acquiring 30 *acras marisci in Gosberkile, licentiâ regis non obtentâ*. The abbot pleaded, *quòd per consuetudinem patriæ est et à tempore quo, &c. extitit usurpatum, quòd omnes et singuli domini, maneria terras seu tenementa super costeram maris habentes, particulariter habebunt marettum et sabulonem per fluxus et refluxus maris secundùm majus et minus prope tenementa sua projecta. Et dicit, quòd ipse habet quoddam manerium in eâdem villâ, unde plures terræ sunt adjacentes costeræ maris, et sic habet per fluxus et refluxus maris circiter* 300 *acras maretti terras suas adjacentes, et per temporis incrementum secundùm patriæ consuetudinem; et absque hoc quòd ipse perquisivit, &c.* And upon issue joined, it depended many years before the issue was tried. But afterwards, *P.* 41. *E.* 3. *B. R. Rot.* 28. *Lincolnia, Rex.* viz. given, *quòd, secundùm consuetudinem patriæ, domini maneriorum prope mare adjacentium, habebunt marettum et sabulonem per fluxus et refluxus maris per temporis incrementum ad terras suas costeræ maris adjacentes projecta, &c. Ideo abbas sine die.*

Observe,

1st. Here is custom laid, and he relies not barely upon the case without it.

2d. In this case it was *per incrementum temporis* and *per mare projecta*. It is not a sudden reliction or *recessus maris*, as I shall have occasion to mention hereafter. And though there is no *alluvio* without some kind of reliction, for the sea shuts out itself; yet the denomination is taken from that which predominates. It is an acquest *per projectionem* or *alluvionem*, not *per recessum* or *relictionem*.

3d. That such an acquisition lies in custom and prescription; and it hath a reasonable intendment, because these secret and gradual increases of the land adjoining *cedunt solo tanquam majus principali;* and so by custom it becomes as a perquisite to the land, as it doth in all cases of this nature by the civil law.

(2d.) Now as touching the accession of land *per recessum maris*, or a sudden retreat of the sea, such there have been in many ages. Sometimes the ocean, especially the narrow sea lying between us and France and the Netherlands, leaves the English shore in a great considerable measure; possibly by reason of some superundation on the other eastern shore, or by some other reason we know not.

This accession of land, in this eminent and sudden manner by the recess of the sea, doth not come under the former title of *alluvio*, or

intrusion be laid for so much land relict *per mare*, it is no good defence against the king to make title *per consuetudinem patriæ* to the *marettum*, or *sabulonem per mare projectum;* for it is an acquest of another nature. And this was accordingly adjudged, *H.* 12. *Car. Rot.* 48. in the case of the king against Oldsworth and others for Sutton Marsh, *in Scaccario*. And in that case it was likewise held and adjudged, that lands acquired *per relictionem maris* are not prescribable, as part of a manor or as belonging to the subject; for that were to prescribe, in effect, that the narrow seas to the coasts of France or Denmark were part of a manor. In that case the information plea and judgment were in substance as followeth, viz.

Quod *cùm* 7000 *acræ marisci salsi vocati Sutton Marsh, jacentes et existentes juxta Sutton Long in comitatu prædicto, videlicet, inter Sutton Long et mare ad refluxum ejusdem, fuissent parcella littoris marini, ac ad refluxus maris naturalis et ordinarios aquis salsis et marinis inundatæ: cùmque eædem* 7000 *acræ marisci salsi nuper à mari, unde inundatæ fuissent, fuissent relictæ*. Then the information sets forth a grant by king James under the great seal to Peter Ashton and others, and a regrant by them by deed inrolled to the king, and that Michael Oldsworth, &c. intruded. The defendant Oldsworth came in; and as to part pleaded as tenant, viz. *quòd bene et verum est, quòd prædictæ* 7000 *acræ marisci salsi vocati Sutton Marsh, jacentes et existentes juxta Sutton Long, viz. inter Sutton Long et mare ad refluxum ejusdem, fuerunt parcella littoris marini, et ad refluxus maris naturales et ordinarios aquis salsis inundatæ et à mari relictæ prout per informationem*. But he further saith, the king was seized in right of the duchy of the manor of Sutton, *et quòd plures terræ dicti manerii ante relictionem dictæ costeræ maris adjacebant; et quod consuetudo patriæ est et à tempore quo, &c. quòd domini maneriorum, terrarum, seu tenementorum super costeram maris adjacentium, particulariter habebunt marettum et sabulonem per fluxum et refluxum maris secundùm majus et minus prope terras seu tenementa sua projectum sive relictum: quodque et prædictæ* 7000 *acræ marisci salsi ad terram prædictam parcellam manerii de Sutton adjacent, et per fluxus et refluxus maris relictæ fuerunt à mari, et projectæ ad terram prædictam parcellam manerii de Sutton prædicti, ratione cujus relictionis prædictæ dominus rex fuit seisitus, &c. de prædictis* 7000 *acris in jure ducatûs, &c.* And then he entitles himself by a grant under the duchy seal, and traverseth what he had not confessed. Upon this there was a demurrer and judgment for that custom cannot entitle the subject to relicted lands, or make it part of a manor: and it differed from the case of the abbot of Peterborough before cited; for there it was only *project*, but here *relict* is added to the plea, that it might answer the information; though the plea in the abbot of Peterborough's case was the precedent by which the plea was drawn, and with which it agreed, saving that addition of *relict*.

And yet the true reason of it is, because the soil under the water must needs be of the same propriety as it is when it is covered with water. If the soil of the sea, while it is covered with water, be the king's, it cannot become the subject's because the water hath left it. But in the case of *alluvio maris*, it is otherwise; because the accession and addition of the land by the sea to the dry land gradually is a kind of perquisite, and an accession to the land; and therefore, in case of private rivers, it seems by the very course of the common law, such a gradual increase *cedit solo adjacenti;* and though it may be doubtful whether it be so *ex jure communi* in case of the king, yet doubtless it gives a reasonableness and facility for such right of *alluvio* to be acquired by custom; for though in every acquest *per alluvionem* there be a reliction or rather exclusion of the sea, yet it is not a recess of the sea, nor properly a reliction.

But this is to be carried along with us in the case of *recessus* or *relictio maris vel brachii ejusdem;* that where the land, as it stood covered with water, did by particular usage or prescription belong to a subject, there the *recessus maris*, so far as the subject's particular interest went while it was covered with water, so far the *recessus maris vel brachii ejusdem* belongs to the same subject.

The king of England hath the propriety as well as the jurisdiction of the narrow seas; for he is in a capacity of acquiring the narrow and adjacent sea to his dominion by a kind of possession which is not compatible to a subject; and accordingly regularly the king hath that propriety in the sea: but a subject hath not nor indeed cannot have that property in the sea, through a whole tract of it.

covered with the water within such a precinct; for these are manoriable, and may be entirely possessed by a subject.

The civilians tell us truly, *nihil præscribitur nisi quod possidetur.* The king may prescribe the propriety of the narrow seas, because he may possess them by his navies and power. A subject cannot. But a subject may possess a navigable river, or creek or arm of the sea; because these may lie within the extent of his possession and acquest.

The consequence of this is; that the soil relinquished by such arms of the sea, ports, or creeks; nay, though they should be wholly dried or stopped up; yet such soil would belong to the owner or proprietor of that arm of the sea, or river, or creek: for here is not any new acquest by the reliction; but the soil covered with water was the subject's before, and also the water itself that covered it; and it is so now that it is dried up, or hath relinquished his channel or part of it.

And such an acquest of a propriety in an arm or creek of the sea may be as well within the precinct of a port, as without; and that, though the king or some other subject hath the port in point of franchise or privilege. For though the soil of all creeks and navigable rivers, especially within ports, do *primâ facie* belong to the king in point of propriety as well as in point of franchise, yet the subject may have so great and clear a possession of the soil lying under the water of that port, that it may belong to a subject in point of interest or propriety of the soil, though he have or have not the port in point of franchise: and consequently, if the sea should relinquish the channel or creek or arm of the sea within such a port, it might and would belong to that subject, that had the propriety of the soil and water before it were so relicted.

And this is an exception out of that generality, possibly, that *terræ relictæ per mare* may not be prescribed. But a certain creek, arm of the sea, or *districtus maris*, may be prescribed in point of interest; and, by way of consequence or concomitance, the land relicted there, according to the extent of such a precinct as was so prescribed, will belong to the former owner of such *districtus maris.* But otherwise it would be, if such prescription before the reliction extended only to a liberty, or *profit à prendre*, or jurisdiction only within that precinct; as liberty of free fishing, admiral jurisdiction, or the jurisdiction of a leet or hundred or other court; for such may extend to an arm of the sea, as appears by 8. E. 2. *Corone;* for these are not any acquests of the interest of the water and soil, but

De Jure Maris et Brachiorum ejusdem. xxxi

Therefore the discovery of the extent of the prescription or usage, whether it extend to the soil or not, rests upon such evidences of fact as may justly satisfy the court and jury concerning the interest of the soil.

That which I have to say concerning creeks or havens or arms of the sea, and the propriety of them, will be contained in these following assertions.

1st. That a subject may, by usage or prescription, be owner or proprietor of such an arm of the sea, creek, or particular portion of the sea contiguous to the shore, as is not a public port or haven; and consequently, if that part be left dry *per recessum vel obstructionem maris*, that will belong to that subject, that had that antecedent propriety when it was covered with water.

This will appear by the review of those cases that are in the precedent chapter concerning the right of fishing in the sea, many of which instances make it appear, that there may be a right of propriety in the soil *aquâ coopertâ*, and the right of fishing resulting not as a *profit à prendre*, but upon the very right of the soil itself. And those instances, that follow in this chapter, will farther make out the propriety of the soil of such places as these compatible to a subject.

2d. That a subject having a port of the sea may have, and indeed in common experience and presumption hath, the very soil covered with the water; for though it is true, the franchise of a port is a differing thing from the propriety of the soil of a port, and so the franchise of a port may be in a subject, and the propriety of the soil may be in the king or in some other, yet in ordinary usage and presumption they go together.

If the king at this day grant *portum maris de S.* the king having the port in point of interest as well as in point of franchise, it may be doubtful whether at this day it carries the soil, or only the franchise; because it is not to be taken by implication. But surely, if it were an ancient grant, and usage had gone along with it, that the grantee held also the soil, this grant might be effectual to pass both; for both are included in it.

And so if by prescription or custom a man hath *portum maris de S.* in ordinary presumption he hath not only the franchise, but the very water and soil within the port; for a *portus maris* is *quid aggregatum*, as a manor; and such a prescription may carry the soil as well as the franchise; and though this doth not always hold,

Escaetria 12. *E.* 1. *n.* 1. *Portus et piscaria et mariscus de Topsham spectant ad Amiciam comitissam Devon.* She had not only the franchise of the port, but the soil of the port, and the fishing and salt-marsh adjoining. *Vide infra,* when we come to the rights of ports. And *vide infra, par.* 2. *cap.* 4. the case of the port of Plymouth, parcel of the manor of Trematon, wherein it will appear, that a subject, as he may be owner of a port in point of franchise, so he may be owner of the very soil of the haven in point of propriety. And see in the same chapter concerning the port of Poole. The earl of Surrey was owner of it in point of propriety as well as franchise, and had the anchorage of ships there, which seems to be ordinarily a perquisite in respect to the soil.

3d. That a man who is not owner of a port in point of franchise, but the franchise of the port belonging to the king, yet such a subject may by usage have the very propriety of a creek or arm of the sea parcel of that port, and of the soil thereof; and may have upon that account the increases of land that happen by the recess of the water of that arm of the sea.

Register, 252. The prior of Christ Church *Cantuariæ* petitions the king, *quòd cùm quædam antiqua trenchea, quæ se ducit à brachio maris vocata A. versus villam de B. quæ est in solo ipsorum prioris et conventûs, per sabulones et arenam maris jam de novo taliter sit obstructa, quòd naves per trencheam illam usque ad dictam villam de B. venire nequeunt, ut solebant; et quædam alia trenchea, ducens ab eodem brachio maris usque ad eandem villam de B. jam vi maritimâ facta existet, per quam naves et batelli à mari usque ad villam illam commodè et sine impedimento poterunt transire.* An *ad quod damnum* issues to inquire, *si sit ad damnum vel præjudicium nostri aut aliorum, seu nocumentum dictæ villæ de B. si eis licentiam concedamus, quòd ipsi dictam antiquam trencheam omnino obstruere et commodum suum inde facere possint.*

Here the common passage for ships to a town admitted in point of propriety to belong to the prior, and that they may make profit of the soil being stopt up.

In Scaccario Car. —— upon the prosecution of Sir Sackville Crow, there was an information against Mr. John Smith, farmer of the lord Barclay, setting forth, that the river of Severn was an arm of the sea, flowing and reflowing with salt water, and was part of the ports of Gloucester and Bristol, and that the river had left about 300 acres of ground near Shinberdge, and therefore they

De Jure Maris et Brachiorum ejusdem. xxxiii

Upon not guilty pleaded, the tryall was at the exchequer bar, by a very substantial jury of gentry and others of great value.

Upon the evidence it did appear by unquestionable proof, that Severn in the place in question was an arm of the sea, flowed and reflowed with salt water, was within and part of the ports of Bristol and Gloucester, and that within time of memory these were lands newly gained and inned from the Severn; and that the very channel of the river did within time of memory run in that very place where the land in question lies; and that the Severn had deserted it, and the channel did then run above a mile towards the west.

On the other side, the defendant claiming under the title of the lord Barclay alledged these matters, whereupon to ground his defence, viz.

1st. That the barons of Barclay were from the time of Henry the second owners of the great manor of Barclay.

2d. That the river of the Severn *usque filum aquæ* was time out of memory parcel of that manor.

3d. That by the constant custom of that country, the *filum aquæ* of the river of Severn was the common boundary of the manors on either side of the river.

When this statute of the evidence was opened, it was insisted upon, that the river in question was an arm of the sea, a royal river, and a member of the king's port, and therefore lay not in prescription to be part of a manor. But the court overruled that exception; and admitted, that even such a river, though it be the king's in point of interest *primâ facie*, yet it may be by prescription and usage time out of mind parcel of a manor.

Thereupon the defendant went to his proofs, and insisted upon very many badges of property or ownership; as, namely,

That the lords of the manors adjacent to this river, and particularly those of that manor, had all royal fish taken within the river opposite to their manor *usque filum aquæ:*

That they had the sole right of salmon fishing:

That they had all wrecks cast between high-water and low-water mark:

That the lords of the manors adjacent had ancient rocks or fishing-places, and weares, or such as were of that nature, within the very channel:

That they had from time to time granted these fishing-places, some by lease, some by copy of court roll at their several manors, by the names of rocks, weares, staches, boraches, putts; and that they were constantly enjoyed, and rent paid by those copy-holders and lease-holders:

That by common tradition and reputation, the manors on either side Severn were bounded one against another by the *filum aquæ*, and divers ancient depositions produced, wherein it was accordingly sworn by very many ancient witnesses:

That the increases happening by the reliction of the river were constantly enjoyed by the lords adjacent.

These and many other badges were opened, and were most effectually made good by most authentical evidences and witnesses. But before the defendant had gone through one-half of his evidence, the court and the king's attorney-general sir John Banks, and the rest of the king's counsel, were so well satisfied with the defendant's title, that they moved the defendant to consent to withdraw a juror, which though he were very unwilling, yet at the earnest desire of the court and the king's counsel he did agree thereunto.

So that matter rested in peace, and the lands, being of the yearly value of two hundred pounds and better, are enjoyed by the lord Barclay and his farmers quietly and without the least pretence of question to this day. This I know; for I was thoroughly acquainted with this case, and attended at the bar at the tryall.

This great and solemn tryall for the right of a royal river, in a port and part of it, doth fully prove that which I have to say touching this matter.

But though the subject may thus have the propriety of a navigable river part of a port, yet these cautions are to be added, viz.

1st. That the king hath yet a right of empire or government over it, in reference to the safety of the kingdom and to his customs, it being a member of a port, *prout inferiùs dicitur*.

2d. That the people have a publick interest, a *jus publicum*, of passage and repassage with their goods by water, and must not be obstructed by nuisances or impeached by exactions, as shall be shewn when we come to consider of ports. For the *jus privatum* of the owner or proprietor is charged with and subject to that *jus publicum* which belongs to the king's subjects; as the soil of an highway is, which though in point of property it may be a private man's freehold, yet it is charged with a publick interest of the people, which may not be prejudiced or damnified.

De Jure Maris et Brachiorum ejusdem.

creeks or havens thereof, the same rule holds, which is before observed touching acquests by the reliction or recess of the sea, or such arms or creeks thereof. Of common right and *primâ facie*, it is true, they belong to the crown, but where the interest of such *districtus maris*, or arm of the sea or creek or haven, doth in point of propriety belong to a subject, either by charter or prescription, the islands that happen within the precincts of such private propriety of a subject, will belong to the subject according to the limits and extents of such propriety. And therefore if the west side of such an arm of the sea belong to a manor of the west side, and an island happen to arise on the west side of the *filum aquæ* invironed with the water, the propriety of such island will entirely belong to the lord of that manor of the west side; and if the east side of such an arm of the sea belong to a manor of the east side *usque filum aquæ*, and an island happen between the east side of the river and the *filum aquæ*, it will belong to the lord on the east side ; and if the *filum aquæ* divide itself, and one part take the east and the other the west, and leave an island in the middle between both the *fila*, the one half will belong to the one lord, and the other to the other. But this is to be understood of islands that are newly made ; for if a part of an arm of the sea by a new recess from his ancient channel incompass the land of another man, his propriety continues unaltered. And with these diversities agrees the law at this day, and Bracton, *lib.* 2. *cap.* 2. and the very texts of the civil law. *Vide Digest. lib.* 41. *de acquirendo rerum dominio, legibus* 7, 12, 21, 29, 30, 38, 50, 56, 65. *et ibidem, lib.* 43. *tit.* 12. *de fluminibus, l.* 1. § 6. *Vide Bracton ubi supra. Habet etiam locum hæc species accessionis in insulâ natâ in flumine, quæ, si mediam partem fluminis teneat, communis eorum est, qui pro indiviso ab utrâque parte fluminis prope ripam prædia possident, &c.* For the propriety of such a new accrued island follows the propriety of the soil, before it came to be produced.

And thus much shall suffice to have been said concerning these *incrementa maritima,* and how they may in point of propriety belong to a subject. It remains, that a few words be said touching some other prerogatives, that have a cognation with this matter we are about, viz.

Wreck of the Sea ; and
Royal Fishes ;
which shall be the business of the next chapter.

CAP. VII.

Concerning the prerogative and franchise of wreck and its kinds, and royal fish.

S touching wreck of the sea, in the first place, it is sometimes called *wreccum maris*, sometimes *warettum*, which is sometimes in records applied to the accession of lands by alluvion. The record of the abbot of Peterborough, cited in the former chapter, is, *domini habuerunt warettum et sabulonem.* Though I have used the word *warettum*, in the old French it is called wreck, and sometimes *varech*.

The kinds of it are two, viz.

1st. Such as is called properly so, the goods cast upon the land or shore.

2d. Improper for goods that are a kind of sea-waifs or stray, *flotson, jetson,* and *lagon*.—Of both these briefly.

I. Touching wreck of the sea. It is not properly wreck, till it be cast upon the shore or land; and therefore by the statute of 15. R. 2. cap. 3. wreck of the sea is declared to be determinable by the laws of the land, and not before the admiral in any wise; and it was one of the articles anciently within the inquiry and jurisdiction of the coroner. *Vide* stat. 4. E. 1. *officium coronatoris,* viz. concerning wreck of the sea, wheresoever found; and if any lay hands on it he shall be attached by sufficient pledges, and the price of the wreck shall be valued and delivered to the towns. This power was annexed to the coroner by the statute of 3. E. 1. called Westminster 1. And therefore as long as the goods are floating upon the sea, they are not wreck; and according is the resolution 5. Reports, sir Henry Constable's case.

But all goods cast upon the shore are not therefore *ipso facto* wrecked so as to entitle the king or lord of a liberty to them; but it must have these qualities, viz.

1st. It must be such goods or ship that is wrecked or perished at sea. For if the goods were taken by pirates, and then they come or be brought or left upon English ground by any means, they are not wreck to be forfeit, but provision is made for resti-

De Jure Maris et Brachiorum ejusdem. xxxvii

which is cited in the comment upon Westminster 1. cap. 4. viz. that if enemies or pirates take a ship, and take out all the passengers and goods, and turn the hull to the sea, and it is cast upon the land, though no living thing come in her, she is not wrecked so as to give the forfeiture. Yet though the law may be such, the case, that is cited, warrants it not, which is *Clause* 5. R. 2. *m*. 24.; for there the mariners got all to land in Norfolk in the long-boat, and left the ship to the enemies, and so within the following rule.

2d. Though the ship or goods be wrecked and cast upon the shore, yet if any living thing escape alive to land out of the ship, it is not such a wreck as gives a forfeiture And this was the ancient law before the statute of Westminster 1. cap. 4. as is resolved and made evident by the resolution of Constable's case, *ubi supra*, and the lord Coke's comment upon that statute; for though the common law give the king *bona wreccata*, as shall be shewn; yet, because it was *lex odiosa* to add affliction to the afflicted, it was bound up with as many limits and circumstances and to as narrow a compass as might be.

3d. That these goods be cast upon the shore or land, and not brought thither in a ship or vessel. *Vide inter placita* Gersey 2. et 3. E. 2. A ship was broken at sea; and the goods floating in the high sea, certain mariners took them up and put them on shipboard, and they came with their ship into the land of Geffry Carteret, who by charter had wreck of the sea; and before he seized, the vessel went to the shore of the abbot of Chirburgh, who had likewise wreck. The goods being seized by the king's officer, these two interpleaded for the goods as wreck.

Et Willielmus le Mareis, qui sequitur pro domino rege, dicit, quòd nullus eorum petere possit bona prædicta ut wreccum; quia dicit, quòd ea tantùmmodo sunt wreccum, quæ fluctus maris projiciunt ad terram, vel infra portum, aut tam prope terram, quòd à stantibus in terrâ possunt perpendi, et sic ducantur vel trahantur ad portum; sed quæ reperta sunt in alto mari, unde certum non existit, quòd fluctus maris ea vellent projicere, si non per laborem marinellorum levantium à mari, et ponantur in navi vel batello, et sic in vasi ducantur ad terram et non tangunt terram alicujus pertrahentium, nec alio modo non possunt dici wreccum, sed tantùmmodo de adventuris maris, de quibus nullus potest aliquid clamare, nisi salvatores et dominus rex, vel ille, cui rex concesserit libertatem percipiendi hujusmodi adventuras. Et petit judicium pro domino rege, et prædicti, &c. non dedicere possunt. Consideratum est, quòd prædicta vina remaneant domino regi, et prædicti Petrus et alij in misericordiâ pro falso clamore. Postea prædicta vina de prædictis doliis concessa sunt prædicto priori pro 60s. *de quibus solvit prædictis salvatoribus* 40s. *pro parte suâ, et de* 20s. *residuis respondet regi.*

This, though it were a proceeding in Gersey, who were heretofore and yet are guided by the customs of Normandy, yet even, these customs as to the point of wreck are very near if not altogether the same with those of England, as appears by the 17th chapter of the *Grand Custumier, de Varech*. And this resolution above cited is consonant to that of sir Henry Constable's case, 5. Reports, though differing in terms and names.

And thus much of the nature of wreck, and this by the laws of England is forfeit; and the propriety of the first owner is, by the seizure of the king, or his officer, or lord of the liberty having his franchise, wholly divested.

But if goods are cast upon the shore, though they have not all these properties, they may be seized by the king, or the lord that hath the liberty of wreck, and lawfully detained, till the right owner come and claim them, and make it appear that they are his; and the common law allowed him a year and a day for the making his claim. And therefore as to this also the statute of Westminster 1. cap. 4. was but an affirmance of the common law, as it seems; for the very same time is allowed for the claim of goods so seized by the *Custumier* of Normandy.

And the time, from whence the day and the year is to be accompted, is from the time of the seizure, as appears by the comment upon that statute; and if not claimed within that time, they were lost.

But if there were a seizure by persons that had no right to seize, the elapse of the year and the day, as it is conceived, did not bar the right owners.

The statute of the 27. Ed. 3. cap. 13. provides more expedition for the restitution of the merchant, where the goods are not lawful wreck; but it seems the generality of that statute takes not away the loss of the goods by non-claim by a year and day after seizure.

35. H. 6. 27. If goods of a common person be seized as wreck, if he claim not in a year and day, they are lost; but if the king's goods were wrecked, he need not claim.

And *nota*, this claim is available only where the goods are cast

De Jure Maris et Brachiorum ejusdem. xxxix

living thing escaped to the land. But where the goods are a legal wreck, this claim signifies nothing; for the goods are *ipso facto* forfeit by being wreck and seized; for the provision of the statute of 3. E. 1. as to the claim and proof within the year and day refers only to such goods as are cast upon the shore, but are not lawful wreck.

But yet in such case, where the goods are not wreck in law, the merchant must allow salvage, or the charge that the taker up of the goods is at for their saving. *Pat.* 14. *E.* 4. *m.* 12. *dorso.*

Thus much for the nature of wreck. Now concerning the propriety of it.

The statute of *Prerogativa Regis*, cap. 11. tells us to whom wreck doth of common right belong in England. *Rex habebit wreccum maris per totum regnum, balenas et sturgiones captas in mari vel alibi infra regnum, exceptis quibusdam privilegiatis locis per regem.*

This was the common law before this statute; and this statute as to this point, and most if not all other points of prerogative in that statute called *Prerogativa Regis*, is but declarative of the common law, and rather a repetition or collection of the king's prerogatives than any enacting law.

And the same was the prerogative of the duchy of Normandy, as appears in the *Grand Custumier, cap. de Varech.*

See Spelman *in Glossario,* title *wreck,* several charters mentioned by king William the first, yea and by Edward the Confessor, of *wreck* and *jactura maris.*

King R. 1. in the second year of his reign released wreck through all England, as the same author cites it out of Hoveden. But his successors resumed the prerogative again, and that before the statute of 17. E. 2. called *Prerogativa Regis;* and frequent instances thereof are long before that statute in the times of E. 1. H. 3. and king John.

But though wreck of the sea doth *de jure communi* belong to the king, yet it may belong to a subject.

1st. By charter; and this is without question.

2d. By prescription; and although this was doubted in the time of Bracton, yet the law is settled and unquestionable at this day.

Sometime wreck hath belonged to an honour by prescription; as to the honour of Arundel, though the *caput baroniæ* were in the county of Sussex; being another county from the place where the

Sometime to the owner of a county. The lords of all counties palatines regularly had *wreccum maris* within their counties palatines, as part of their *jura regalia*. But yet inferior lords might prescribe for wreck belonging to their several manors within a county palatine. The earl of Cornwall, which though it were not a county palatine it had many royalties belonging to it, had *wreccum maris per totum comitatum Cornubiæ*, viz. as against the king, though particular lords might prescribe for it against the earl. *P*. 14. *E*. 1. *B. R. Rot.* 6 & 29. *Cornubiæ*.

And thus much concerning wreck, and the right of it.

II. Somewhat is fit to be mentioned concerning *flotson, jetson*, and *lagon*.

These are not wreck of the sea, but of another nature; neither do they pass by the grant of *wreccum maris*, as is resolved in that case of sir Henry Constable, and the case of the 3. *E*. 2. where they are stiled *adventuræ maris*.

And as they are of another nature, so they are of another cognizance or jurisdiction, viz. the admiral jurisdiction.

The right of flotson, jetson, and lagon, and other sea-estrayes, if they are taken up in the wide ocean, they belong to the taker of them, if the owner cannot be known.

But if they be taken up within the narrow seas, that do belong to the king, or in any haven port or creek or arm of the sea, they do *primâ facie* and of common right belong to the king, in case where the ship perisheth, or the owner cannot be known; which is also one of the resolutions of sir Henry Constable's case. But if the owner can be known, he ought to have his goods again; for the casting them overboard is not a loss of his propriety.

Although the right of these adventures of the sea within the king's seas belongs to him, where the owner cannot be known, yet the king hath little advantage of it; for by the custom of the English seas, the one moiety of what is so gained belongs to him that saves it. And accordingly the custom is recited in a letter by the king of England to the French king, *Claus*. 7. *E*. 3. *parte* 1. *membrana* 23. *dorso*, to satisfy him of the usage, that if the merchant's goods, that are floating in the sea, be saved, though the merchant made out his property, yet the goods were usually divided, the one moiety to the merchant, and the other moiety to them that save them for salvage. But it seems by the statute of 27. *E*. 3. cap. 13. that hard custom was mitigated as to the merchant; and a reason-

De Jure Maris et Brachiorum ejusdem.

adventure of them that saved it. But whether anything hath altered that custom as to the king, I find not.

The other moiety of these *bona vacantia* taken upon the narrow seas was anciently, and I think at this day, taken by the admiral as his fee; which yet he takes in *jure regis*.

And this appears by the old articles of the admiralty entered in the black book of that court, wherein, though there be many extravagant articles, that no way belong to their jurisdiction, yet those that concern these things in question are good evidence what the usage was.

Among which this was one: *Item soit inquise de touts neifes vesseux et bateux, que sont troves waife sur le mere, dont l'admiral ne ad sa part à lui due d'office, c'est à dire la moiety.*

And again: *Item soit inquise de touts ceux, que ont trove sur le mere flotesan tonne ou pipe de vyne ou doyle ou bales de madder drape coffres ou autres choses dont l'admiral ne ad sa part à lui due d'office.*

And thus much for the *jus commune* of these *adventuræ maris*.

But yet a subject may be entitled to these, as he may be entitled to wreck, viz.

1st. By charter.

2d. By prescription. And that is agreed in that case of sir Henry Constable, viz. that a man may have flotson, &c. by prescription between the high-water and low-water mark. Some of the west country prescribe to have it as far as they can see a Humber barrell. And much more may be had by prescription in an arm of the sea; and accordingly the barons of Barclay have ever had it in the river Severn, of the east side of the *filum aquæ*, over against their barony of Barclay.

These liberties of wreck, flotson, jetson, and lagon, and that also of royal fish, may be parcel of or belonging to an hundred. But enough of this.

Now touching royal fish, therefore called so, because of common right such fish, if taken within the seas parcel of the dominion and crown of England, or in any creeks or arms thereof, they belong to the crown; but if taken in the wide sea, or out of the precinct of the seas belonging to the crown of England, they belong to the taker. 39. E. 3. 35. *per* Belknap.

Touching the kind of these fishes that are called royal fish, there is usually rendered a whale. *Claus. 5. R. 2. m.* 29. *de pisce vocato* whale *jam noviter ad terram in solo prioris de Merse alienigenæ in manu regis existente ad opus regis deferendo.*

But because they may be great fish that come under no known denomination, we find the claim of such under the name of *piscis regius*, or sometime *grand pisce*, without any certain denomination. *Vide Claus.* 20. *H.* 3. *M.* 3. *dorso.* A controversy between the king's bailiff and the prior of St. Swithen *de quôdam pisce regio* claimed by each without any distinct name. The prior procures the king's bailiff to be thereupon excommunicated, and the king commands his absolution. But salmon or lamprey are not royal fish.

By the common right of the king's prerogative these belong to the king, if taken within his seas or the arms thereof.

Anciently the entire sturgeon belonged not to the king; but only the head and the tail of the whale, according to Bracton, cited by Stamford upon this chapter of the prerogative.

According to the custom used in the admiralty, these great fish, if taken in the salt water within the king's seas, they were divided, and a moiety was allowed to the taker, the other moiety to the admiral in right of the king: one of the articles of the admiralty above cited being, *Item soit enquise de ceux, que ont prise ou trove sur le mere whales, balens, sturgeon, porpoise, ou grampise, dont l'admiral n'a sa part pur le roy, c'est à scavoire la moitie.*

Where observe these two things:

1st. That these royal fish extended to other than whale and sturgeon, viz. to porpoise, and *grampise*, or great fish.

2. The admiral is to be answered for the king the moiety, which seems to expound Bracton as to the division of the whale. The king had the head, and the queen the tail, which countervailed a moiety; and the taker had the body, which countervailed the other moiety.

Thus much for the right of the king to these royal fish.

A subject might and may unquestionably have this franchise or royal perquisite,

1st. By grant.

2d. By prescription within the shore between the high-water and low-water mark, or in a certain distinct *districtus maris*, or in a port or creek or arm of the sea; and this may be had in gross, or as appurtenant to an honour manor or hundred, as appears by infi-

De Jure Maris et Brachiorum ejusdem. xliii

And this shall suffice concerning the rights of the sea and the creeks thereof according to the laws of England, as far forth as it is necessary to be known in order to what follows, viz. the havens ports and creeks of the sea within the dominion of the crown of England, which shall be the business of the second part of this discourse, as a necessary *præcognitum* to the customs and right thereof according to the laws of England.

The following note by Francis Hargrave is prefixed to the "*De Jure Maris et Brachiorum ejusdem,*" first printed in Hargrave's Collection of Law Tracts, 1787.

[The manuscript, from which this treatise is printed, was part of the valuable present to the editor from GEORGE HARDINGE, Esquire, Sollicitor-General to the Queen; for which acknowledgement is made in the preface to this volume. There cannot be the least doubt of its being written by lord chief-justice HALE; though it is not in his hand-writing, but appears to be a fair copy by some transcriber. The contents agree with the article No. 20. and 21. in the list of lord chief-justice HALE's manuscripts at the end of his life by bishop BURNET. The title of the manuscript is *verbatim*, as here given by the words between the marks of quotation.]

SUSSEX SUMMER ASSIZES, 1822.

Lewes, Tuesday, August 6th; before Mr. Justice Park and a Special Jury.

DICKENS AND ANOTHER v. SHAW.

HIS was an action of trespass brought by the lords of the manor of Brighton, against the defendant Shaw, for digging and taking away sand from the sea-shore of Brighton. The defendant pleaded *not guilty,* putting it upon the plaintiffs to prove their title to the *locus in quo.*

Mr. Courthope, counsel for the plaintiffs, lords of the manor, attempted to prove their title to the soil of the shore, down to low-water mark, by the following badges of ownership:—1st. The right of the lord to wreck. 2nd. Grants made by the lord of portions of the shore, as part of the waste of the manor. 3rd. A toll, or payment of mackarel, to the lord, from every mackarel-boat landing mackarel. 4th. The interference of the reeve, from time to time, in settling disputes between the fishermen, bathers, and others using the shore.

The evidence produced to prove grants of the shore, failed; the grants appearing to have been of ground *above* high-water mark, and no part of the "shore," with one modern exception only, and that equivocal. The toll of mackarel was proved to be, *not* for the use of the "shore," but a "capstan rent," and for the use of ground for a fish market; both capstans and market being *above* high-water mark. No other boats or vessels but the mackarel boats paid this or any other toll. The interference of the reeve, in adjusting disputes, proved to be merely occasional, and of a nature too indeterminate to afford any badge of ownership of the soil. No toll, or

proved to have been paid at any time, either to the reeve, for the lord, or otherwise;—but by the plaintiff's own evidence it appeared *that sand, stones, &c. had been immemorially dug, and taken away by all mankind that pleased, without interruption or payment.* Evidence was also gone into by the plaintiffs to show that the holes made by those who took the sand, had of late occasioned some obstruction and nuisance to the bathers and fishermen; but this of course, could not be construed into evidence of ownership of the soil. The only assumed badge of ownership, therefore, proven in the present case, was *the right to wreck.* There was no private fishery. No grants of portions of the shore. No payments or tolls for taking the soil. No grant from the Crown, nor other documentary evidence of ownership, nor any substantiated jurisdiction. The argument of the counsel (Mr. Marryat) for the defendant, was in substance as follows:—

"It is conceded by the plaintiff, that, by the rule of law, the space between high and low-water mark belongs to the King. But in this particular manor, we are told that the *lord* has a property in the soil, between high and low-water mark. The evidence amounted to this,—1st. The right in the lord to wrecks of the sea. 2ndly. Certain grants, which, it is contended, show that the lords have made grants between high and low-water mark, which is not borne out on the evidence. 3rdly. It is said they have exercised *jurisdiction* between high and low-water mark; because when a man has come with a cart in front of the bathing machines, the reeve has interfered. 4thly. It is said that there are *capstans* fixed on the beach, above high-water mark; and that persons, who have come with the mackarel boats, land them with the assistance of these capstans; and that those who have had the privilege of landing their mackarel, and selling them in the fish-market, have paid six out of a hundred, or six out of a thousand, for the privilege of so landing them, and for the use of the capstans. But the payment of the mackarel is for the use of the capstans, and for the privilege of the fish-market. This has been proved. The fish-market is always above high-water mark, and the fish are always sold above high-water mark, though not always in the same place; for, occasionally, the high tides have obliged them to remove the market to some other spot; but according to the usual rise of the tide, the market is always above high-water mark."

" If the lord of the manor claimed to take this portion of mackarel as a tax upon the fish, for the privilege of *landing* on the beach, *it would be an illegal claim ;* for every man has a right to fish in the sea : and it would be useless to give a right to fish in the sea, unless he had the privilege of landing them. It is incidental to the right of fishing, to bring the fish on shore."

" But if this toll is a compensation for the use of the capstans and fish-market, which are on the lord's soil, then the payment is legal,[1] and intelligible."

" That wrecks have sometimes been taken is not denied,—but wrecks are generally thrown up at the top of the tide ; if the property come ashore in a gale, it will be thrown up considerably above high-water mark."

Mr. Justice Park.—" That depends upon the weight of it."

Counsel.—" Generally speaking, in violent gales of wind the property will be thrown up above the ordinary high-water mark ; or at the summit of the tide. Now a man may have a right to wreck, and yet not have a right to the soil ; for nothing is more common, (as is well known to those conversant with such subjects,) than to find the grant of a manor, with a right to wreck of the sea, without any grant of the soil, between high and low-water mark, included in it."

" The digging for sand is assumed to be an injury, for a tide or two, to the boatmen coming on shore in the night, who may be ignorant of the removal of the solid sand, and may get into lighter sand. We are not contending whether the inhabitants of Brighton shall be supplied with sand or not, on account of this assumed nuisance. Brighton must be supplied with sand, and as Brighton has increased ten times in extent, it must be supplied with ten times the quantity of sand. But this injury, or nuisance, would be precisely the same if a payment were made to the lord of the manor for his permission to dig, (as is now claimed,) as it would be if they dug without the payment ; but the truth is, this claim is now brought forward for the private pecuniary advantage of the lord of the manor. But the people have dug there, according to the testimony of a witness of fourscore, during all his time, without any such claim or interruption till within the last three years ; and the question is—if these men shall be shut out from doing that which persons have done

---

[1] Grants of the shore are noticed by Lord Hale as *singular*, rather than as common or *general* cases.

at all times, and which the inhabitants of Brighton have done at all times; for, as the old witness said, if any body interfered, they only got some impertinence for their trouble. If it has been done at all times, and exercised at all times, in defiance of the lord, by what right is it that the lord now seeks payment for his permission, which is a new assertion of a claim made by him in the total absence of any such right, as far back as the memory of any living witness can reach? And there is not any reason to believe that sand was not dug at all times."

"The increase of the practice has been with the increase of the town,—for they must dig for the convenience of the town; and the lord of the manor, who has permitted this practice so long, has *now* no right, even if he *originally* had a right to interpose. He has no jurisdiction over the soil, nor any right to derive a profit for his consent to dig there. He has not interposed with respect to *shingle*."[1]

"Under these circumstances, the question is a very important one; for, if the lord of this manor be proprietor of the soil between high and low-water mark, not a cart could go down without his consent, and paying toll, to unload a vessel. But no such claim has ever been made. But if the lord were proprietor of the soil, and if he has a right to require money for his permission to dig sand, he might require something from the owners of carts coming to unload the merchant ships. If the plaintiffs should succeed to-day, not only might such claim be made, but the whole use of Brighton, as a bathing-place, will be done away with: for if it is once established, that the lord is proprietor of the soil, no person will have a right to cross the sand, without his permission, with bathing-machines, which have been there as long as memory can go, but for which no claim has ever been made."

"All the various uses of the beach, in the various modes stated, must all be affected by the verdict. These people have been in the habit of taking sand perpetually, without interruption, except that the reeve says, he has interfered when a cart went in front of the bathing-machines. It is said that these gentlemen are only desirous

---

[1] Shingle, or the "beach," has immemorially been taken as freely as the sand, for "ballast" for the fishing-boats, and ships resorting to the shores, and for road mending, and other useful purposes. So sea-weed, or tangle, when thrown up in any quantity, has been taken, and carted away for manure, without toll or payment of any kind.

Dickens and another v. *Shaw.*

to prevent injury to the mariners and fishermen, as if the injury would be much diminished if they took a compensation; but there would not be any difference whatever as to the danger, nor would it be at all diminished in consequence of any payment to the lords—the consumption would be quite the same. It appears that the flux and reflux of the tide extends to five or six hundred feet."

Mr. Justice Park.—Gentlemen of the Jury,—This is an action of trespass, which is brought by two gentlemen who appear, by the evidence, as well as the record, to be lords of the manor of Brighton: and the action is brought against the defendant for digging in a certain close of the plaintiffs, on the sea beach. The defendant does not put in any plea on the ground of jurisdiction, as he might have done, but he contents himself with saying, that he is not guilty, which is quite enough to put it on the plaintiffs to show that the soil is theirs. The learned counsel for the defendant has stated, in very strong language, the danger that would ensue by your giving a verdict for the plaintiffs: he thinks the natural consequence would be, that all the bathing would be stopped, and that all the persons who get coals from the ships would not be able to continue to do so, and that these and other consequences would follow. To me this case does not seem fraught with such difficulty; for if you establish that these gentlemen are not only lords of the manor, as they *are*, undoubtedly, *above* high-water mark—but whether they are between high and low-water mark is for you—it is not because a person is owner of the land, that he is to shut out me, or any other man, from that which we have been in the constant exercise of for years; *that* does not follow. The learned counsel for the plaintiffs has put in my hand an Act of Parliament, which I am bound to take judicial notice of. It is an act of the 50th of Geo. III. chap. 38, which is about 1810; and there is this clause found in it:—" Pro-
" vided always, that this act, or any thing herein contained, or in
" any bye-law, rule, order, or regulation, to be made by the said
" commissioners as aforesaid, shall not extend, or be construed to
" extend, to authorize or empower the standing or using of any
" bathing machine upon any part of the beach or coast of the sea,
" adjoining to the said town, or in any wise to authorize or em-
" power the said commissioners, in any manner, to dig away, dis-
" turb, or remove the soil, chalk, sand, or other materials of the
" cliff, or the rock, stone, beach, or sand on the sea-shore, within
" the said town, without the consent of the lords of the manor of

Appendix.

"Brighthelmston, or the consent of any person or persons who, by reason of property in the soil or otherwise, may legally be entitled to prohibit or prevent the same." This is a very strong clause certainly, and therefore certainly it did contemplate that, by possibility, other persons than those who have a general legal right by law, had a right there.

Gentlemen, you have been truly told by the counsel on both sides, that, generally speaking, a lord of the manor, which manor has a beach adjoining it, is not necessarily thereby entitled to the land under the flux and reflux of the sea. That is so; the king is lord of all the land between high and low-water mark; but, at the same time, it is not only possible, but is often proved to be the case, that grants have been made from the king, of this soil to his subjects. And there are instances in which this right is obtained, not from grants from the king, but by long prescription. Lord Hale, in his book de jure Maris, lays down the law upon this subject in a manner which is very striking; and he refers to that sort of evidence as is required by judge and jury, as to the high and low-water mark. He says, "The ordinary neap tide is the boundary of that which is properly called the *littus maris;* and touching this kind of 'shore,' viz. that which is covered by the *ordinary* flux of the sea, (and we must look to what it is in ordinary times,) this may belong to a subject, the statute of the 7th of James I. chap. 18, supposeth it; for it provides that those of Cornwall and Devon may fetch sea-sand for the bettering of their lands, and shall not be hindered by those who have their lands adjoining to the sea-coast, which it appears by the statute they could not formerly." Then he goes on to show what the proof should be in such cases; and he says this, amongst other things, "enjoyment of wreck, happening upon the sand; presentment and punishment of purprestures[1] there, in the court of a manor, and such like." Why then, this particular species of pro-

---

[1] Where there is a house erected, or an inclosure made, upon any part of the king's demesnes, or of an highway, or common street, or public water, or such like public things, it is properly called a "*purpresture,*" from the French word "*pourpris,*" an inclosure. Blac. Com. vol. 4. Thus, then, if the lord of a manor, on the coast, has enjoyed the jurisdiction in his manor court, of presenting, punishing, and putting down inclosures and nuisances upon the "shore," it is a badge to show that the "shore" is within and part of the

Dickens and another v. *Shaw.*

perty, which we are now considering, has not the same means of enjoyment as a man has over land of another description, because it is impossible it should be enjoyed in the same way.[1] The question is, if there has not been in this manor, for a considerable number of years, all that enjoyment [by the lord], of the "shore," which has been pointed out by Lord Hale. William Murrell says, he has been reeve for the manor of Brighton, to the plaintiffs, for seventeen years; and, in the course of that employ, has seized *wrecks* whenever they were found between high and low-water mark, and he never seized any wreck above. Upon that subject Lord Hale says—"For the most part, wrecks and royal fish are not, and, indeed, cannot be well left above the high-water mark, unless it be at such extraordinary tides as overflow the land; but these are perquisites which happen generally between the high-water mark and the low-water mark; for the sea, withdrawing at the ebb, leaves the wreck upon the shore." The reeve says, "the last seizure he made was of four top-masts:" he says, "I have seized different pieces of timber during this period, but nothing of any particular value. Three different times I have seized. When I have seized, I have always carried them up to Mr. Kemp (the lord). Upon all occasions this has been accounted for to the lord." Then he goes on to speak of paying for the mackarel. I agree, to a certain extent, with what has been said upon that by the learned counsel for the defendant. I do not think much weight is to be placed on that circumstance, except this, that it is a strong confirmation to show these gentlemen are lords of the soil *above* the high-water mark. They (the fishermen) put down the capstans all over the place; nobody trouble themselves about it; but whenever the reeve saw it, he gave them leave, if he was down near the spot; if not, he has sanctioned it. But the mackarel are evidently paid for the use of the capstans, for taking care of them, and keeping them in order, and to prevent people misusing them; therefore I do not think much reliance can be placed on that circumstance. "Sometimes," says the reeve, "the fishermen dis-

---

[1] There may be a difference in the *quantum* of enjoyment, profit, or use; but both the soil of the shore, and of the *terra firma*, must be enjoyed the *same way;* the one being capable of *fewer* uses than the other. The inclosing, digging sand, stones, &c., and otherwise converting the *soil itself* to profit, are the same modes of enjoyment as may be had in inland estates. There is much barren soil far from the sea, the only uses of which are such as the "shore"

agree about boats coming ashore before the capstans; and they send for me, and I have gone several times with my horse, and drawn the boats away. The capstans are removed from time to time." He says, " when there have been disputes among the bathing people, I am sometimes referred to, the same as with the fishermen; I have removed carts from before bathing-machines, where they have been digging, as it prevented them getting the machines down." One witness says, one of his men was *nearly* lost by their having made a hole, by digging for sand, which had not been filled up by the tide; so, persons going to bathe, not knowing of these holes, might be, *perhaps*, drowned. It is said, that the taking of sand from the beach has been done at all times. I have no doubt but where people wanted a *few spades* of sand, they have taken it from the beach, and nothing has been said; and if it had been but a *few spades*, it is probable that nothing would have been said now. But it is a very different thing from taking loose sand which has floated up, and scraping it up, to digging it and carrying it away by carts-full. If, however, the defendant has this right, he has a right to retain it. The witness says, "I had a conversation with Shaw (the defendant) on the subject of taking the sand; I have gone two or three times before the 22nd of February; the defendant spoke to me first; he said he had been served with a notice, and he was afraid he should get into trouble; that there had been a subscription amongst the tradesmen, and they had advised him not to pay, until such time as they had had their meeting, as they meant to stand a trial with the lords of the manor." However, gentlemen, though this was said by the defendant, if the plaintiffs cannot make out their case to your satisfaction, the defendant must have a verdict. It lies on the plaintiffs to make a good case. Then the witness (the reeve) is questioned as to the situation of the fish-market, and he says, "it is *above* high-water mark;" and he says, "the fishermen send their fish on shore, in *wherries*, when the water is not sufficiently high to let the fishing-boats come up to the beach; when *it is*, they come up to a particular part of the beach, and, as soon as they have unloaded, they go to sea again." It is supposed, that the wrecks which this man spoke of, are of no great value, there being but very few instances that any living witness speaks to. One of them, which this witness speaks of, sold for eight or nine pounds, reduced by the expenses of bringing it to him for the lord, to the real profit of two

lord got about four pounds. He says, all the wrecks between high and low-water mark, he has always appropriated to the use of the lord. Then Samuel Carden is called; he says—"I am turned of fourscore: I have resided at Brighton all my time, and am a fisherman. He always understood the lord of the manor took the wrecks. He cannot speak of any particular instance. He remembers last winter a man of his had like to have been lost, by, falling into one of the holes which had been dug in the sand." He is then asked as to the payment of the mackarel, and as to the capstans, and does not vary from the evidence given by Murrell (the reeve). Other witnesses spoke to the same effect. Then James Blunden is called, and he produces the court rolls of the manor, to show that grants of part of the waste have been made by the lord. The use of these entries is to show, that this has been a manor from all times; at least, from 1662 we have entries. Then, as to the taking of wreck, what has been said by the witness is confirmed by two or three instances, which are recorded in the rolls of court. Now, as to these *grants;* I will mention the case of John Williams, amongst others. This appears to be a very strong instance, *as far as it goes*.[1] The witness then goes on to show, that on the 31st of March, 1743, there was a presentment of a piece of a mast, which was taken up and disposed of to the use of the lord, according to the custom of the manor. And also a small cask of brandy, containing about six gallons, taken up on the coast as a wreck of the sea, and which was seized (as they say) for the use of the lord. And, also, at the same court, there is an entry of a piece of east-

[1] The grant to Williams was as follows:—May 27, 1813. "To John Williams of a piece of land, containing in length, from east to west, at the south end, twenty-two feet and nine inches, *abutting to the* SEA-BEACH *on the south* and west, and the ground of the said John Williams on the north, and the ground in the occupation of Richard Russel Kemp on the east, by the year's rent of three guineas, on the feast of St. Michael, the archangel, without deduction." There is nothing in this grant to show that it was a grant of ground *below* high-water mark. The abutment to the south is on the "sea-beach," which, in common understanding, means to the *high*-water mark. There is no measurement of the *depth*, southward; if it was meant to be to the *low*-water mark, it would have been so said. The sea-beach is the ground between the "flux and reflux of the tide," and extends here to from six to seven hundred feet. There is now a high road formed *between* Williams's premises and the sea. This road is protected, towards the sea, by a wall, and, at ORDINARY tides, this wall is not washed by the sea. Williams's title, under

country oak, which was taken and disposed of for the use of the lord. So that here we have three instances of wreck, eighty years ago, in the very place. This is, certainly, a very strong fact in favour of the plaintiffs; *at least,* it shows that it was never questioned that they had *this* right. On the 29th of January, 1746, there is a presentment of two small casks of brandy and a piece of pipe of oil; these are both taken and appropriated to the use of the lord. Now, gentlemen, *these are all very strong instances in favour of the right contended for.* The learned counsel for the defendant has stated, with truth, that there has been no instance, until of late years, of any prevention of taking *sand.* I have no doubt of it: for, as we know, a few years back the demand for it was not very great; and, when they took but little, there being no demand for it, then there was no interruption; but when a man comes down constantly, and when a *variety of men* come down and dig holes in the sand, in a manner which must be very inconvenient, it then well became those who are the lords of the soil (if the plaintiffs *are* lords of the soil) to interfere, even if they propose to themselves to derive an emolument from giving permission to take it.

Gentlemen, this is the whole of the case. If this case had been met by *other* evidence, it *might* have been a *very difficult* thing for the plaintiffs to have made out their rights. It is, however, to be observed, that all the evidence, such as it is, *is all one way.* The whole must depend on the nature of the property, and the use of it. The nature of it is such, that there can have been but very little use of it. If they had been in the habit of taking money for the use of the bathing-machines, or for the landing of coals, then the evidence would have been very strong; but you must take it as it is: it is for you to say, if there has been an exercise of the right, such as from the nature of the property admitted of. If the evidence, such as it is, and uncontradicted, is not sufficient, in your opinion, to entitle the plaintiffs to a verdict; if you think it too slight, and if you think that this thing has been in the habit of being constantly done without any complaint or interruption, you will find for the defendant; if not, you will find a verdict for the plaintiffs, with one shilling damages.

Juror.—My lord, admitting that the lord is entitled to wreck, between high and low-water mark, does it follow that he is entitled

Dickens and another v. Shaw.

to that. The lord of the manor *may* have the grant of the soil between high and low-water mark; but, by the law of England, the king has a right to the soil between high and low-water mark; yet the subject may be in possession of it by *grant* or *prescription*, and that is evidence from which you may draw an inference.

Juror.—If the lord is entitled to wreck, should your lordship think he would be entitled to the soil?

Mr. Justice Park.—If uncontradicted.

Juror.—I was in hopes we should have seen the original grant.

Mr. Justice Park.—That, from the nature of things, cannot be, but in a very few instances.

Verdict for the defendant.

The counsel for the plaintiffs having obtained a rule to show cause why a new trial should not be granted, the case was argued in Hilary Term, 1823, February 13th, in the King's Bench, and the same printed report is in substance, as follows:—

Mr. Justice Best read the report of the learned judge who tried the cause.

At the conclusion of the report, Mr. Justice Park observed:—
" The jury debated some time; then they said, they should like to see the grant; I told them there was none produced, and probably none could be produced. I explained to them the law, as to the prescriptive right. On their return they found their verdict for the defendant, with which I was not satisfied."

Mr. Marryat (against the rule).—This was a verdict by a special jury. The question was decided conformably to the common law presumption, and there was nothing to affect or turn that presumption, unless the circumstance of the plaintiffs having taken the wreck of the sea can be so considered; for I shall not dispute, nor did I dispute at the trial, that there was sufficient evidence that the plaintiffs, as lords of the manor, had the right of wreck.

Mr. Justice Bayley.—We will hear you, Mr. Courthope.

Mr. Courthope (for the rule).—It was said there was nothing to answer the common law right, except the circumstance of wrecks being claimed by the lord. As to the common law right being unquestionably in the king, that, of course, I cannot dispute. I am not here to dispute the common law right; but this is a case where all the evidence, whatever evidence there was, was all on one side.

Mr. Justice Best.—It is stated, that, till lately, all mankind that

Mr. Courthope.—That does not establish the right of all mankind to the soil.

Mr. Justice Bayley.—No; but it has a tendency to show that the soil was not where you say it was.

Mr. Courthope.—All mankind taking it cannot establish the right; the right to the soil would still be vested in the king, or in his grantee. The question is—whether all persons, and every person who please, at his or their own will and pleasure, has a right to deal with this soil. That is the only question; and I contend the evidence, as to *that*, is all one way; for no evidence was given to show any right being elsewhere. There is no claim made on the part of the crown; there is no right set up on the part of the crown.

Mr. Justice Best.—If the crown had any occasion to make use of this soil for any purpose of navigation, then the question would be—whether there was any thing to preclude the crown from that.

Mr. Courthope.—The inquiry is—whether this is a verdict against evidence. I submit that the evidence was decidedly in our favour; and I not only rely upon that, but also I should have thought that the expression of my Lord Hale, and not of Lord Hale only, but in Constable's case, reported in Coke, which is to the same effect, would have put this matter beyond all doubt. I think the expressions are—" I observe three things," &c. &c.—" *thence it follows* that it was part of the manor."—Perhaps your lordships could not go so far as to say, " thence it follows." I do not go so far as that; but after such an authority, and after the expression of Lord Hale, I may be permitted to say, it was very important evidence to show that the right was in that party who had the right of wreck.

Mr. Justice Best.—My Lord Hale *does not put it on wreck only;* there is the constant fetching of sand.—*Prima facie*, the soil is in the crown, and *prima facie* the right of wreck is in the crown; but the crown may grant the privilege of wreck to the lord of the manor without granting a right in the soil; or the crown may grant a right in the soil without granting the right of wreck; or the crown may grant *both* rights to the lord of the manor; but the person who claims the right in the soil, must make out that right to the satisfaction of a jury.

Dickens and another v. Shaw.

weight of evidence is to be considered with reference to the evidence which is given in answer. I have always understood this was considered,—that "wreck," in the absence of all other evidence, is very important evidence. I by no means contend that a proof of wreck is decisive on the subject, but only what weight the evidence of wreck ought to have, where there is no evidence on the other side. I would contend with great deference, after the expressions which have dropped from the court, that the taking of sand is no evidence of a right elsewhere. I do imagine that where sand was taken by a variety of individuals, having no claim to the soil, that it generally went to establish that the soil was not in any of those individuals, because they take it as the right of all mankind—who can have no such title; therefore it shows a general right in some individual;—and therefore I should think the question fairly to be between the crown and its grantee, whether it were in one or the other. I certainly feel *that* was a very important piece of evidence, in the absence of all evidence to the contrary;—but I am anxious not to be considered as resting on the right of wreck alone; the circumstance of wreck being in the grantee of the crown, is important evidence in the absence of all evidence on the other side. The court will not consider *all* the instances mentioned by Lord Hale, as instances which are all to be taken *conjointly*,—he merely mentions them as instances of cases by which the right may be established. It is a *species* of evidence—and how is it confirmed in the instance here of a grant to Williams, which is, unquestionably, on part of the property in question?—property which is below the high-water mark. The lord is here exercising that most important of all rights, dealing with the soil, by making a grant of it at court—making a grant of it to another individual.

Mr. Justice Bayley.—What is the date of that grant?

Mr. Marryat.—1813.

Mr. Courthope.—I admit that 1813 is a late date; but still it is undisputed. All I contend for is—that, as the crown has not disputed it, here are individuals who undoubtedly are exercising a right, which I am sure must be felt by the court as very important, and *which it is fit some person should regulate*. There are large holes dug, endangering the lives of the fishermen.

Mr. Justice Best.—I should think the proper remedy would be, by *indicting* them for it;—certainly, it is a very abominable nuisance.[1]

Mr. Courthope.—But it has been tried as a private right; and, suppose it was the only piece of evidence, there is this, which on such a subject, I think, is a most important piece of evidence,—it is the constant and invariable interference of the reeve for regulating all disputes; it shows that, instead of being a subject of public regulation, a private right has always been considered as existing in the lord. If when these instances had occurred, some public proceeding, some application to the crown to remedy the nuisance, had been adopted,—it would have been evidence that the right was in the crown: but the universal application has been to the reeve, the lord's representative.

Mr. Justice Bayley.—You mean about removing the carts?

Mr. Courthope.—No; filling up the holes. These holes are great nuisances, as they are considerably below high-water mark. They are nuisances to bathers, and to persons bringing up their boats,—both these descriptions of persons, whenever these nuisances have occurred, have applied to the reeve, instead of applying to the crown; which would have been done, if, as has been suggested, the crown, for the public purpose of navigation, has this property vested in it; and then some public inquiry would have taken place, and some public prosecution would have been instituted.

Mr. Justice Bayley.—Are not you overstating that?—What instance of application did any witness speak of, except one, which was an application two years ago to Mr. Murrell?

Mr. Courthope.—I do not affect to state the exact number of times;—I am making only a general observation—not as applicable to any particular interference—that when these nuisances have occurred, application has been made to the reeve, to remedy them.

Mr. Bolland.—Murrell himself says, (I have this from my own note,) that he had removed the sand people a great many times. He was a very old witness—eighty years of age. He says, he has sometimes been applied to about these holes, by the people belonging to machines,—that they were nuisances, as they prevented the getting down the machines.

Mr. Justice Bayley.—They *were* nuisances; and when there was

dangerous; and one instance of punishment, as a nuisance, might restrain it. The Act of Parliament cited by the learned judge (Park) at the trial, an act vesting various powers in commissioners, for the regulation of the town (it not being incorporated), would probably have provided an effectual remedy for all disputes and nuisances affecting the shore, had the Act been framed *after*.

Dickens and another v. Shaw.

any nuisance, they always applied to Murrell, and he remedied it.[1]

Mr. Courthope.—Therefore, by the application to the reeve, who is the representative of the lord of the manor, he was treated and recognized as the person who had the superintendence of and the interest in the soil.

Mr. Justice Best.—I suppose this was all very strongly pressed on the jury; and, if we were to grant you a new trial, you would hardly get more than one shilling damages, and you would have to pay the costs for a new trial.

Mr. Justice Bayley.—This does not conclude any thing.

Mr. Courthope.—We had no opportunity of observing on any of the remarks made by my learned friend.

Mr. Justice Bayley.—You may hereafter, in any other action, if they should venture to repeat the thing again;—you will have a right to bring another action, and you may then be able to show that, in some other instances, in which sand has been got, and stones have been got, (and there are a great many stones got in that beach,) to show that there have been applications to the lord of the manor for leave to do so.[2]

Mr. Courthope.—It has been truly said, that until of late years the subject has been of very little importance, for undoubtedly, till of late years all mankind might have taken this thing—but nobody hardly thought of taking it. Now, undoubtedly, it has become a great object.

[1] The learned judge, no doubt, means here to assent to the matter of fact, viz., that the reeve's interference was attended to. But how did he remedy it? There is no evidence of "presenting and punishing purprestures" in the manor court. But this was the only *official* way that the reeve could interfere. It was in evidence, that at the times when he interfered, "the sand people resisted it, and were saucy;" but no jurisdiction was exercised to punish them.

[2] These things are usually taken by the lowest and most ignorant of the people. The mere fact of such persons asking *leave* of the lord, or of his bailiff, may arise, and probably does in general arise, from their fear "of getting into trouble," as was said by one of the poor "sand people," in this very case. Such poor people will often ask leave for what they have a perfect right to do without leave; and rather than be prevented from earning a pittance to supply their immediate wants, will consent to pay to an interfering bailiff a modicum of their earnings, and thus compromise the public right, as well as the title of the crown. This mere asking and giving leave, therefore, or paying for it, deserves, perhaps, not much weight where no "presentment and punishment of purprestures" exist, as evidence of regular jurisdiction, savouring of owner-

Mr. Justice Bayley.—Great quantities have been taken away within the last twenty years, undoubtedly; and if you look at many of the houses, and, I believe, at some of the streets in Brighton, they show that it has not been a *modern* practice only,—for an immense number of the houses in Brighton are built with the round stones which are thrown up by the sea.[1]

Mr. Courthope.—It is acknowledged that the right of the soil, where these stones lie, is the property of the lord of the manor.

Mr. Justice Bayley.—They are sometimes washed up *above* high-water mark, and sometimes they are not.

Mr. Courthope.—The greater part of them are *above* the high-water mark;—the mass of these stones have, undoubtedly, been taken from time to time, *below* the high-water mark.[2]

Mr. Justice Best.—If they were taken from time to time without paying for them, I should think that would be very strong evidence against the lord.

Mr. Courthope.—That would be to show that all his majesty's subjects have a right in this soil.

Mr. Justice Bayley.—I do not think that it proves the right is not in the *crown ;* for, in general, the crown has the right,—not with a view to the private reservation to collect the stones for itself, or to collect the sand for itself, but *for the general interest of the public ;*[3] and, if you can, without interfering with and prejudicing the interest of the public, remove the sand and the stones, the crown will not interfere. But if you do that which amounts to a *nuisance*, then you may be *indicted* for it; or, if that which is done does not

---

[1] This is perfectly correct,—the old town is principally built of stones taken from the beach; the new portion of the town is principally of brick, or walls cased in brick or tile. Others are faced with the round "boulders," noticed by the learned judge. There is not a house or wall in Brighton which is not composed, more or less, of materials taken from the shore; including sand, and fine and coarse gravel, or beach, for mortar, and the manufacture of bricks.

[2] The "boulders," are almost always collected below high-water mark; being the larger stones, they are not borne so far up as the common beach, by the ordinary action of the tides. No toll was ever taken for them on the Brighton shore.

[3] In Blundell *v.* Caterall, the court seem to have been disposed to favour the vesting of the shore in the lords of manors, in order that the uses of the shore might be under "particular regulations;" but, from what is here said by the learned judge, it seems the court inclines to the ownership of the crown, and that the public are likely to be most benefitted, and sufficiently protected by such ownership. *Vide* 5 Barn. and Ald. 268.

Dickens and another v. Shaw.

extend to an absolute nuisance, as if it is *purpresture*, the crown may remove it.[1]

Mr. Courthope.—There have been grants.

Mr. Justice Bayley.—They are grants on that which is avowedly the property of the lord of the manor, *above* high-water mark.

Mr. Courthope.—In the grant to Williams he has gone beyond it.

Mr. Justice Bayley.—That is one instance, and a very modern instance that.

Mr. Justice Holroyd.—There are only three instances of grants—1743, 1802, and one in 1813.

Mr. Walford.—And only one of them above high-water mark.

Mr. Justice Bayley.—Two above high-water mark.

Mr. Courthope.—My observation on that was merely to show, that the taking of stones would be very weak evidence to establish the right, where that which is unanswered is an important right, as that of dealing with the soil.

Mr. Justice Bayley.—Are there no acknowledgments paid to the lord of the manor for *carriages* which go from time to time down to the sea-shore?—Do the bathing-machines pay any rent to the lord of the manor?[2]

Mr. Marryat.—No; it was proved that they did not.

Mr. Justice Bayley.—These are very strong things.

Mr. Courthope.—That would only go to show some prescriptive right of passage over it.

Mr. Justice Bayley.—All this is evidence for the jury. I do not say that the jury might not have found a verdict for you; but the question is, whether the verdict is so much against the weight of evidence as that we ought to grant a trial, where the injury, which the defendant has done, is certainly of very comparatively trifling consideration.

Mr. Courthope.—The great object is, the setting of this question at rest.

Mr. Justice Bayley.—Then, if that is the real object, it may be tried at any other time, by any other person;—the lord has been acquiescing in this for a century.

[1] See Jerwood, p. 67.
[2] These machines are numerous, and, when ranged above high-water mark, take up a considerable space of ground. But the right to drive in one of these, or any other vehicle, down to the shore, and into the sea, or by the usual approaches to the shore, has, in a former page, been contended for, with great deference, as of common right, not liable to toll of any kind.

Mr. Courthope.—There is a subscription for trying the right.

Mr. Justice Bayley.—That is said by the defendant.

Mr. Bolland.—I will not trouble your lordships long on this, more than to call the attention of the court to this circumstance, which I think makes this subject differ from many others,—viz. that, with respect to these grants, one of which is very modern, undoubtedly; but your lordships know the situation of this place: except the part where the baths are, there is no other part of the beach of Brighton that could be properly the subject of a grant, than the part between the east and west cliff. It would be idle to go beyond the jetty, or the eastern side of the bathing-machines, and to go on the *western* side, or the Shoreham side; for if the lord was to make a grant to enable a man to build a house *there*, the sea is making such encroachments on that side, that, in all probability, it would take it away from him in a very short time. So that, the part where Mr. Williams's baths are, was the only part which could be serviceable to make a grant for the purpose of building. The encroachments of the sea on one side would make buildings out of the question.

Mr. Justice Bayley.—The sea gains on the east, and leaves on the west.

Mr. Justice Best.—You might leave the lord of the manor and the sea to settle that question.

Mr. Justice Bayley.—Very likely Williams might be inclined to take that grant, for this reason,—he thought that by paying a small sum of money, he might have it in peace.

Mr. Bolland.—The crown would be naturally watchful of its own privileges; and if the lord had no right to make this grant, it is not very likely that the crown would have let it remain without inquiry. But there was also an *important* fact, and one which made a very great impression on the learned judge; it was this—that they formerly *scraped* the sand from the surface, not making any *large holes.*

Mr. Justice Bayley.—When the lord complained, (through the reeve,) they were saucy;—therefore, if the lord of the manor was the person who had the right to control them, the reeve might have complained to the lord of the manor, who naturally, one would think, would have stopped them.

Mr. Bolland.—If we take the whole of the sea-shore, from one part of Great Britain to another, people no doubt do, in places which are unfrequented, not only take sand, but dig holes also, where the

Dickens and another v. Shaw.

which the sea restores the next tide, without causing any complaint. But there was other evidence; for your lordships will find that it is reported by the learned judge, from the mouth of the witness, that there is a payment of mackarel, taken for all boats that land.

Mr. Justice Best.—That is capstan rent:—it is a very common thing.

Mr. Justice Bayley.—It was admitted to be capstan rent.

Mr. Bolland.—There was no evidence of its being so at the trial; nor is it necessary they should pay any rent for the use of the capstans.

Mr. Justice Best.—I should be glad to know how, in point of law, you can support a prescription against fishermen, compelling them to pay a toll for what they have no advantage from. They pay this all over the coast.

Mr. Bolland.—It was shown that the fishing vessels never could land, for they were a large kind of boat; but the mackarel is landed in smaller boats: the larger ones stand off.

Mr. Justice Best.—You know the larger boats never could be got on shore without the capstans, though the smaller ones can. It is very important that there should be capstans, that large boats may be drawn up in safety on a gale coming on.[1]

Mr. Justice Bayley.—I have seen them drawn up a hundred times.

Mr. Bolland.—But, my lords, we say this verdict is erroneous, and that it should be corrected. Your lordships will see the finding of the jury will appear to be *sanctioned*, by its not going down to a new trial; so that, in the event of another action, it will operate to our prejudice in this way,—it will be thought the right has been established in this action.

Mr. Justice Bayley.—If this case is worth the expense of a new trial, and a fresh action is brought against any person who shall commit a similar trespass, the jury would be told by the judge who tried the cause,—that very little reliance was to be placed, to the prejudice of the lord, upon the verdict in question;—that it was only the inference of the jury drawn from the evidence *then* laid before them;—and if, before another jury, *other* evidence be laid,

---

[1] It did not appear, in this case, that any boat, small or large, paid for their safety, in being laid up, when not in use, above high-water mark. Yet the practice not only here, but everywhere, is, and must be, to use the strand, bank, or *terra firma*, above high-water mark, for this purpose; and so far as is

or even the same evidence, and such a statement made, which shall induce the jury to come to a different conclusion, there is nothing to prevent them from so doing. It does not appear to me, that we are at liberty to say the verdict was wrong, or that the matter in dispute is of that value that we ought to grant a new trial. The law, as it seems to me, was very properly laid down by the learned judge at the trial; the right, up to the high-water mark, is in the lord of the manor of the adjoining land, as manorial. *Prima facie*, the lord of the manor is entitled up to high-water mark; but between high and low water-mark,—the *ordinary* high and low water-mark,— the right is *prima facie* in the crown; and the crown has, likewise, the right of wreck. The right of wreck, and the right of soil, being both in the crown, the crown may grant both the one and the other to one and the same individual;—or it may grant the soil without the right of wreck;—or it may grant the right of wreck, without granting the right of soil. And, in forming a judgment, whether in any particular spot, as in the boundary of any particular manor, whether there has been a grant to any, and what particular extent,— the proper thing is, *to look to the exercise, and see how the lord of the manor has from time to time acted.* The right of the crown is not, in general, for *any beneficial interest to the crown itself, but for securing to the public certain privileges in the spot between high and low-water mark.* And if any nuisance is committed on that spot, then the crown has the power of proceeding to rectify such nuisance. Now, in forming a judgment in this case, up to what extent there had been a grant by the crown to the lord of the manor, there is a great deal of evidence on the subject of wreck, and there would be no difficulty in saying,—if this were a question of the right of wreck,—that there is abundant proof that the crown had granted *this* right to the lord of this manor. But "wreck" is not the only act of ownership which the lord may exercise, or which the person to whom the soil belongs may exercise. *There are many rights to be exercised on the spot between high and low-water mark,*—amongst others, that of getting sand is one, and sometimes also the power of getting stones is another,[1] particularly that kind of stone, which, I believe, at Brighton, is called a "boulder." And then, if I show that, as far back as memory can go, the lord of the manor has constantly exercised the right of wreck; and, if I find *that* is *almost* the only right he has been in the habitual exercise of, and that

[1] Query, if these are not one and the same, as matter of right, involving one

other persons, from time to time, have exercised an opposing right, and to an extent which must have come to the knowledge of the lord, and exercised it with a degree of temper which shows they were standing on something like a right of their own,—a right in opposition to the lord,—I think *that* was a species of evidence which was very proper for the consideration of the jury, to enable them to judge to what extent the crown had granted the soil. Now, according to the testimony of the second witness, Carden—" Till lately, all mankind used to take sand, and when he has remonstrated with them on the subject, they have been saucy."—Why, that is the conduct of persons who think there is nobody on the spot who has the power to interfere, to prevent that which they are doing;— assuming, that, formerly, they did not dig *so much* as now, but they were in the habit of digging. Now, there is an instance in May, 1813, of a grant taken from the lord of the manor for the purpose of doing something[1] between high and low-water mark; but that is one instance, and one instance only, and it was for the jury to form their judgment, what weight was to be placed on that instance;— the right would be either in the lord of the manor, or in the crown. The crown might not know any thing of the grant;—or the crown might see what was doing was not a thing which interfered with public purposes, or with navigation, or with the rights of the public,— as far as the rights of the public were to be exercised for the benefit of the public, between high and low-water mark; and, therefore, the crown would not interfere. Then, how is it to be known to any body else, except the lord of the manor?—Then Murrell (the reeve) says, from time to time he has removed carts, and that complaints have been made to him respecting persons who have taken sand. And with reference to those holes:—those holes were, in many instances, *nuisances*, and might have subjected the parties, not to an action of trespass at the suit of the lord, but to a prosecution on the part of the crown, for the injury they did to the general rights, which, in such places, the public might have thought were nuisances. With respect to the instances in which Murrell interfered, they are not specifically pointed out, nor are the places as to which he from time to time interfered. Whether he had a proper cause for his interference is not made clear. But all this was for the consideration of the jury, in opposition to the other evidence on the part of Carden. I cannot say that, looking to the whole of this case, there was such a preponderance in the weight of evidence on the part of the plaintiffs, as made it imperative on the jury to find a verdict for the plaintiffs; on the contrary, I think the weight of evidence, from the constant exercise of persons unconnected with the manor, without leave of the lord of the manor, in taking sand, from time to time, was strong evidence to warrant the jury in coming to the conclusion they have come to. It does not appear to me, in this case, that the right is of any great value [to the lord]; indeed, of so little value is the subject matter which is taken, that the lord for many, many years, never thought it of the least value at all, and never thought it worth his while to interfere. For these reasons I think we ought not to grant a new trial.

Mr. Justice Holroyd.—I think there is not sufficient ground, in this case, to say that the verdict was wrong—to authorize us to set it aside, and grant a new trial. It is true, Lord Hale instances *wreck* as *one* of the species of right, which *tends* to show a right to the soil. In one place, in his treatise " De Jure Maris," he intimates, that if it were otherwise, the party could not get down to take the wreck. I think it *may* be evidence of ownership, particularly if coupled with *other* acts of enjoyment of the right of soil. Where the crown grants the right of wreck, it is *probable* the crown grants the right of soil also; but if the crown grant the right of wreck alone, by *that grant the party would have a right to come and take the wreck, as incidental to the grant,* otherwise the grant of the right could not be a grant of anything whatever. Every thing necessary for the enjoyment of a right, passes incidentally with the grant. The jury may have considered this, not merely on the few acts of enjoyment which were proved to show this was a part of the rights of the lord, and not of the rights of the crown; but they may have proceeded as well on the evidence which was actually given, and the few acts of enjoyment on the part of the plaintiffs, as on what further evidence might have been expected to be given, if the right had been in the lord, and not in the crown. The circumstance

Dickens and another v. Shaw.

public, yet it is a sort of property which the crown would be less likely to interfere with, and to take away the right from the subject, who is likely to derive a benefit from it. I think there was not such a weight of evidence as to authorize us to grant a new trial. This verdict will not be binding on the party, or have, probably, any such effect in a case having *further* evidence, (if further evidence can be given,) as to prevent the further evidence having its due weight, if it shall be thought right to agitate the question again. I think, therefore, this rule must be discharged.

Mr. Justice Best.—I do so entirely concur with what has been said by my learned brother, that I should not think it necessary to say a word, if it were not for some observations which have been made, at the bar, by counsel, and which, perhaps, might be misunderstood at Brighton, if they remained unnoticed. Let it not be understood, that because the lord has not sufficiently made out his right to the beach, that persons may, without subjecting themselves to punishment, dig holes so as greatly to endanger the lives of those who have occasion to land. There cannot be a doubt, that persons who dig holes of that kind, are liable to be indicted for a most dangerous nuisance. This cause has been tried by a special jury; a description of persons not likely to be unfriendly to the rights of the lord. They have thought that the lord has not satisfactorily made out his right to the spot in question. I entirely agree with them. By the common law,[1] the right to the spot in question is in the king, and, therefore, *a lord must make a strong case*, and, if he pleases, he may produce a grant from the king, to show that the right, originally in the king, has been transferred to the lord. What Lord Hale says, is, that a party having one right is *some* evidence to show that he has another; but not that it is sufficient to show, by having the right of wreck, that he is the owner of the soil. The case here is nothing like that which he puts: he should show that he has continually taken sand, and licensed others to do so;— is there any evidence of that kind in this cause? It appears that, in ancient times, whoever thought proper to carry away sand, did so. It appears that, in more modern times, the lord has interrupted the parties; but it does not appear that he has, in any other instance, either licensed others to exercise this right, or exercised it himself. I think this was an extremely weak case on the part of the lord of the manor; and, in my judgment, certainly not sufficiently strong

lxviii   *Appendix.*

to beat down the common-law right which exists in the king. It has been argued, that these acts were done by individuals, at Brighton, who gave no proof of right: if the right is in the king, it is not necessary they should have given that proof, because he has the common-law right. Is there any evidence to show that the common-law right has, or has not, been transferred to the lord? It is to be presumed, that, while the right is in the king, he would permit these things to be done, if they were not injurious to the navigation. For these reasons, I am of opinion, that we ought not to send this down to another trial.

Rule discharged.

THE
SPEECH OF MR. SERJEANT MEREWETHER,
IN THE COURT OF CHANCERY,

SATURDAY, DECEMBER 8, 1849.[1]

Upon the claim of the Commissioners of Woods and Forests to the Sea-Shore, and the Soil and Bed of Tidal Harbours and Navigable Rivers; the nature and extent of the claim, and its effect upon such property.

THE ATTORNEY-GENERAL AGAINST THE MAYOR AND CORPORATION OF THE CITY OF LONDON.

*R. Serjeant Merewether.*—My LORD, Mr. Bethell having so forcibly and conclusively stated to your Lordship the grounds upon which he apprehends that this Judgment is erroneous,[2] and having also stated so very distinctly the manner in which the present question comes before your Lordship, has relieved me from addressing my arguments to any point but that which he has specifically left to me. I will therefore confine myself to the discussion of the proposition to which Mr. Bethell last referred, and which is contained in the information; that " by the Royal prerogative the ground and " soil of the Coast and Shores of the Sea round this Kingdom, and " the ground and soil of every Port, Haven and Arm of the Sea, " Creek, Pool, and navigable River thereof, into which the Sea ebbs

[1] Reprinted by the kind permission of Henry A. Merewether, Esq., Q. C.
[2] The Judgment was by the Master of the Rolls; confirming the Master's

"and flows, and also the shore lying between high-water mark and
"low-water mark, belong to Her Majesty :" and it will be my duty
to submit to your Lordship the authorities, which I think will be
abundantly satisfactory, to show that such a proposition cannot be
supported.

I am not insensible to the difficulty I have to meet in discussing
the proposition; because I am fain to admit that it has been asserted again and again; nor could I fail to allow, that learned
Judges upon the Bench have asserted it, but in all instances merely
as *obiter dicta;* and I will venture to say that on no occasion has
that proposition been supported by any legal decision. My Lord, I
am also of course aware that I am attempting to support a negative
proposition—a difficult task at all times—but the difficulty of which
is greatly removed by the consideration, that if this opinion, though
so long entertained, is wrong, it must be abandoned. My Lord,
I am much encouraged in this attempt by a case a few years ago
in the Court of Exchequer,[1] in which a deep-rooted practice in
pleading (the very marrow of the law) was terminated, after it had
been acted upon for a period of 200 years:—right reason and common sense required that it should be overruled; and the learned
Judges who presided in that case, recognizing nevertheless that it
had been adopted for so many years,—recognizing nevertheless that
they had themselves been most strongly inclined to adopt it as a
rule of practice, having in the first instance, without hearing the
other side, called upon Mr. Serjeant Manning to support the plea:
yet after full discussion, it was expressly decided upon the plea of
the Statute of Limitations, which, though in the negative, had always
been pleaded with a verification, that prayer of judgment was the
proper form; and the Court set aside the practice, though so long
pursued. My Lord, I must say also that I cannot help bearing in
mind the sound and cogent observation made by Lord Denman, that
" a large portion of that *legal opinion,* which has passed current for
" *law,* falls within the description of law *taken for granted.*"[2] There
are undoubtedly many points, turning upon minute and careful in-
vestigation of the foundation of the English law, which are taken,
too hastily, for granted.

My Lord, out of respect to your Lordship,—and to this general
opinion which has been so long entertained—and more especially
out of respect to those learned Judges who have adopted it, I have

[1] Bodenham *v.* Hill, 7 Meeson and Welsby, 274.

Speech of Mr. Serjeant Merewether. lxxi

not ventured hastily upon the denial of this proposition, but have felt it my duty to look fully into all the cases, and authorities, and documents, which can bear upon the subject:—and I will now, with as much brevity as I can, lay before your Lordship those authorities which have led me to the conclusion I trust I shall be able to maintain.

It will be familiar to your Lordship that there are no records of any kind in this country from which we can expect to derive any certain information, and still less any information upon such a subject as is now submitted to your consideration, earlier than the Saxon period of our history; and your Lordship is probably aware that very lately a large collection of the charters of that time has been made by Mr. Kemble, with extreme assiduity, including many hundred charters of the Saxon period ; and of course, when venturing to deny a proposition of law of this extent, spreading all round the kingdom, such documents ought to be examined, to see if there were any trace of any right of this kind existing in the Crown, or anything from which it might be inferred. *Saxon Charters.*

Lord Chancellor.—Do I understand that the answer of the Corporation of London denies the right in the Crown?

Mr. Solicitor-General.—No, my Lord, it leaves it in obscurity, how they derive their title.

Mr. Serjeant Merewether.—The question is, whether the soil and bed of the river belong to the Crown.

Mr. Randell.—It does not, my Lord, admit a right in the Crown, but asserts an immemorial title in the Corporation.

Mr. Solicitor-General.—They neither admit it nor deny it ; they leave it in obscurity.

Mr. Serjeant Merewether.—Your Lordship will observe that the question depends upon the allegation of title by the Crown.

Lord Chancellor.—No: all this depends entirely upon the pleadings, whether the Corporation raise it, or state it in their defence. When we are beginning with the Saxon era, it is a long way off in point of time, and will take a long time to determine; I do not see that it is material, till we first ascertain with certainty that it does arise.

Mr. Solicitor-General.—One of the points put, my Lord, in the Court below, was, that even as between two subjects, strangers, where there was no fiduciary relation at all between them, it was the duty of a defendant to plead what he said issuably: to say what the case was which he intended to make ; and that was one of the

Lord Chancellor.—I presume the information claims the original right to the bed of the river in the Crown.

Mr. Solicitor-General.—Yes, my Lord, the office of Conservator.

Lord Chancellor.—What does the answer say as to the original title of the Crown?

Mr. Serjeant Merewether.—The answer, my Lord, is full as far as the Conservancy is concerned.

Lord Chancellor.—I mean as to the bed of the river.

Mr. Serjeant Merewether.—It does not answer as to the soil and bed of the river; and I am contending before your Lordship, that we are not called upon to answer in that respect, because the person requiring us to answer, has no title which justifies his so doing.

Lord Chancellor.—The information alleges that the Crown has the title?

Mr. Serjeant Merewether.—Yes, my Lord.

Lord Chancellor.—And the answer does not deny that; it is not denied by the answer, and is asserted by the information.

Mr. Serjeant Merewether.—My learned friend, the Solicitor-General, says, my Lord, that we are to plead issuably upon that point; but it is a proposition of law and not an issue of fact. The question is one which cannot be disposed of by your Lordship in supporting these exceptions, without causing great prejudice to the Corporation of London, by assuming that there is such a principle of law.

Lord Chancellor.—If the Corporation of London had said, "We " deny the right of the Crown; the Crown never had a right to the " bed of the river Thames;" then it would have been altogether their case to show whence they derived their title; but what strikes me at present is, that they have not denied that title.

Mr. Randell.—We certainly have denied it.

Mr. Solicitor-General.—I will read the passage to your Lordship, that there may be no discussion about it; my learned friends will admit that this is the only passage of the sort in the answer:—

" The Defendants deny that Her Majesty and her progenitors,
" time out of mind, is or have been seised, in right of the Crown of
" England, of and in the port and haven of London, or of the river
" of Thames, and Defendants make out the contrary as herein is
" mentioned; but except the port and haven of London, and except
" so much of the bed and soil of the river Thames as lies within the
" limits aforesaid, and which belong to and are vested in the said

Speech of Mr. Serjeant Merewether.

" Defendants submit to the judgment of this honourable Court,
" whether by the Royal prerogative, or otherwise, the ground and
" soil of the coasts and shores of the sea round this kingdom, and
" the ground and soil of every port, haven, and arm of the sea,
" creek, pool, and navigable river thereof into which the sea ebbs
" and flows, and also the shore lying between high-water mark and
" low-water mark at ordinary tides, belong to Her Majesty; or
" whether Her Majesty hath a right of empire or government over
" the navigable rivers of this kingdom; but Defendants admit that
" the said river Thames is an arm of the sea into which the sea has
" always flowed and reflowed; and that the said river is and has
" been from time immemorial an ancient and navigable river and
" king's highway for all persons, with their ships, vessels, boats and
" craft, to pass and repass and navigate, at their free will and
" pleasure, and to moor their vessels in convenient parts of the said
" river, not impeding the navigation thereof, subject to such regula-
" tions as Defendants, within the limits of their rights of ownership,
" have from time to time prescribed."

Mr. Serjeant Merewether.—My Lord, I imagine that is a direct denial of the principle of law which is laid down in the information; and when my learned friend, the Solicitor-General, says that we should plead issuably upon that point, it is not an issuable fact, but a proposition of law, upon which the title of the Crown rests; and if that is not maintainable, they have no right to ask for a discovery in this respect. As far as the Conservancy is concerned, that is a matter of jurisdiction,—a matter derived from the Crown as the fountain of justice.

Lord Chancellor.—I think the exception rests upon the title to the bed of the river.

Mr. Serjeant Merewether.—Exactly so; we have fully answered as to the Conservancy; the only point is, that we have not answered as to the soil and bed of the river; to which my answer is, that we are not called upon to do so.

My Lord, I was observing that in these most valuable documents —I shall pass over many shortly—because my object will rather be to draw your Lordship's attention to them than to enforce them by any laboured argument;—for I am confident that the result of their mere enumeration will be, that there is no foundation for the proposition of law now asserted—I was saying that in these numerous documents there is no trace whatever of any such prerogative in <small>Saxon Charters.</small>

lxxiv *Appendix.*

to the sea-shore as belonging to the lands adjoining; there are grants of charters giving in express words the sea-shore, and salt marshes, and other things of the same kind upon the sea-shore, as appurtenant to the lands granted by the charters.

Lord Chancellor.—Accompanying the grant of the lands?

Mr. Serjeant Merewether.—Accompanying the grant of the lands, and amongst the appurtenances. From the earliest times it appears to have been a part of the land, and passing with the land, and adjunctive to the land; and there is no prerogative right of the Crown as interposing between the sea and the owner of the adjoining land.

Saxon laws.

My Lord, the next documents, which will be familiar to your Lordship, will be the Saxon laws, in which the rights and prerogatives of the Crown are alluded to—Theftbote, Treasure-trove, and other rights of that description; but there is no reference whatever to such a prerogative right as the one now claimed.

I ought here to draw your Lordship's attention to the extent to which this right would apply if it could be established; and to the value of property of that description at that period, when the knowledge of machinery not being so advanced as at present, mills were chiefly upon the sea-shore, fish were ordinarily caught by weirs upon the banks of rivers and on the shores of the sea, and salt obtained by a mode now almost in disuse—those things at that period were of great value.[1]

Domesday.

The next document to which I shall claim your Lordship's attention will be one to show that such a right as this now insisted upon could hardly by possibility have existed. I allude to that great fiscal document the *Domesday Book.* Your Lordship is well aware that there all the land of the Crown is set out. The *Terra Regis* precedes the entry of the general property in each county; but there is no trace in that document, from the beginning to the end, of any such right belonging to the King. On the contrary, in the first page of the book there is mention of a tide-mill at Dover in the possession of the Bishop of Baieux: so that not only is that document totally silent as to any such right of the Crown, but in the instance to which I have referred, as well as in many others where salt-pans and places on the sea-shore are referred to, they are treated as belonging to the owners of the adjoining land, and not to the Crown.[2]

Speech of Mr. Serjeant Merewether. lxxv

One word will dispose of the next document, the laws of William the Conqueror, as well as those of Henry I.: they also are like the Saxon laws: there are prerogatives of the Crown alluded to, but no reference whatever to any peculiar right in the Crown to the sea-shore. *Laws of William the Conqueror and Henry I.*

I would not willingly pass by any of the books most known as the earliest text-books in our law, and the next authority in order of time is Glanville.[1] As your Lordship will probably be aware, that author has a passage expressly upon *Purprestures*, being encroachments upon the Crown or the public, which, when proved, subject the land to forfeiture. That matter is mentioned in Glanville; but from the beginning of the book to the end, and in the *Regiam Majestatem* (a work I believe nearly the same), there is not, in the one nor in the other, the slightest reference to the prerogative of the Crown as affecting the sea-shore. *Glanville.*

In order of time, *Magna Charta* will be the next document to which I shall draw your Lordship's attention. The first charter of King John mentions nothing with regard to the sea-shores; but it is a curious fact, that in the second charter,[2] that of Henry III., an exception as to the sea-shores is introduced; for in that charter, which speaks of the destruction of kidells and weirs upon the rivers, there is an express exception "*nisi per costeram maris:*" so that kidells are not to be removed from the sea-shore. It appears to me, my Lord, that it is impossible to doubt that the exception was introduced for the protection of those owners upon the sea-shore who had weirs there; that weirs in the rivers were necessary to be removed with a view to their free navigation, but that they were not equally so on the sea-shores: and as it has been laid down, that supposing there were an Act of Parliament which required the removal of weirs, it would not operate upon weirs belonging to the King; so this exception seems to be solely for the protection of those rights on the sea-shore which the owners of the adjoining land at that time possessed, and which are so recognized in this great charter. *Magna Charta.*

I have now to advert to a treatise which I am well aware has led to much of the misconception respecting this supposed principle of law. It is a treatise, familiarly called Lord Hale's: but I have every reason for thinking, as far as regards the book published by Mr. Hargrave, that it is not Lord Hale's—at least I would venture *De Jure Maris.*

so far as to say, that there is no sound reason for assuming that it is. I have looked at the manuscript in the British Museum; the writing is beyond all question not Lord Hale's; it is the writing of a clerk, evidently copied from some book; and there is nothing in it to show that it is Lord Hale's, excepting that in one corner of the first leaf there is put at the top " Chief Justice Hale," but in a modern handwriting. That Mr. Hargrave had no information that it was Lord Hale's—and that he himself was scarcely satisfied that it was so—seems to be plain; because, for his authority that it is Lord Hale's, he refers only to an observation of Sir Thomas Parker, in his reports, quoting "a manuscript of Lord Hale's," which Mr. Hargrave assumes to be this—" De Jure Maris." But, my Lord, when that matter is investigated, it will be found that in the British Museum there is another manuscript, in Lord Hale's handwriting, and which is probably the one alluded to by Sir Thomas Parker; Mr. Hargrave therefore himself seems rather to have proceeded upon that imperfect evidence than any precise knowledge of his own. And I say this, my Lord, because it will be a matter of considerable importance whether this is really a work of Lord Hale's or not; and I cannot help thinking, that out of regard to the character of that very learned Judge, the proper conclusion is that it is *not;* on account of the apparent contradictions and inaccuracies which are to be met with on the face of the treatise itself. Therefore as an authority I imagine it cannot be relied upon, though it has been hitherto treated as a book of authority. In a future stage of the observations which I have to make, I shall state to your Lordship how it ought to be treated as bearing upon this point.[1] At present I am only, in the course of the argument, treating the records quoted in it chronologically, in which manner alone I imagine that these authorities and documents can be made to explain each other and be rendered intelligible.

Henry III.   I am about to draw your Lordship's attention to the *Shinberge* case[2] which relates to the river *Severn*, and is mentioned in that treatise. In other parts of this work it is assumed that when the sea once flows over land (and I am sorry to say that view seems to have been entertained and acted upon lately in a case near Hastings. *Hastings*), such land belongs to the King. The river of Severn had gained upon Shinbridge, so much so that its channel ran over

---

[1] See Jerwood, p. 32, *et seq.*

Speech of Mr. Serjeant Merewether. lxxvii

Shinbridge lands, and had lost part thereof unto the other side, though it was afterwards thrown back again to Shinbridge; the decision was, " It shall not belong to Aure " (the opposite village); " neither was it at all claimed by the King, though Severn in that " place is an arm of the sea." Now the proposition in this information is that an arm of the sea, the shores and all belonging to an arm of the sea, are the property of the Crown. It appears to me that this doctrine was at least unknown in the reign of King Henry III. I shall have occasion also afterwards to draw your Lordship's attention to another case much of the same kind, commonly called *Lord Barclay's* case, which arose upon the same river a little higher up.

The next books of authority in our law which might be consulted upon this subject are, Bracton, Fleta, and Britton. Now *Bracton* is often quoted upon this subject; but there is no authority whatever in Bracton, my Lord, to support this prerogative of the Crown. There is a learned disquisition as to the right to property acquired by occupancy, and as a portion of that branch of the inquiry, the cases of *alluvion* upon the sea-shore are referred to. But I am quite satisfied that your Lordship will see at once that no doctrine of alluvion can be used for the purpose of showing that the whole of the sea-shore is vested in the Crown; because alluvion is founded in point of fact upon the *absence* of any occupation in anybody else, and the burthen of proof by the doctrine of alluvion is rather thrown upon the Crown than upon the subject;[1] contrary to the proceedings which are meditated in this case, the burthen of proof is there thrown upon the Crown, because the doctrine of alluvion is this; that if there is land which grows on, as it were, from the sea to other land, the owner of the adjoining land shall have it, unless it can be shown by metes and bounds that it does not belong to his land; and then it belongs to the Crown by the most obvious title, which I readily admit, namely *occupancy*, where there is no other occupant; it being the clear and undoubted prerogative of the Crown that it has a special right to all that which is not in the occupation of anybody else—as wreck, waifes, estrays, &c.[2]

And perhaps here I may draw your Lordship's attention to that part of the proposition in the information which Mr. Bethell adverted

Bracton.

---

[1] See Jerwood, p. 89.

Appendix.

to, namely the additional allegation that the King has the right of "government and dominion" over the sea-shore. I may certainly clear my argument from all consideration of that kind; I of course am not denying that the Crown has *dominion and government* over the soil of the sea-shore—there is no doubt of that—neither am I in any degree denying that the Crown has *jurisdiction* over the sea-shore; by the Court of Admiralty, when it is covered by water, and by the common law when it assumes again the state of dry land. But none of these go in the slightest degree to show—on the other hand there is rather a contrary inference—that the Crown has any private property in the shore: a *jus privatum* in the shore is that which is set up by the Crown, and that is the only doctrine which I am combating: therefore, admitting the government—admitting the jurisdiction—admitting the right where there is no special occupant—I am contending that in all other cases the occupation and possession of the shore is so necessary to, and is so generally used and enjoyed by the owners of the adjoining land, that there is no pretence to any right in the Crown *preventing* that occupation. The occupation[1] of the sea-shore may be slight in point of evidence, I admit; perhaps it may be only the straying of cattle—perhaps it may be only for the purpose of taking advantage of the sea adjoining—embarking and disembarking: and therefore, the acts of occupation shown, may perhaps be few; but it will be familiar to your Lordship's mind that there is a case much stronger than that in which the Crown has not the possession nor the right to the soil; although the soil is called the King's soil, and although the owner of the adjoining land would seem, by the acts which he has done, to have excluded himself from possession of it. I am alluding to *Highways*. It has been said, indeed, that the sea-shore is the King's highway; it may be so called, and highways are so called;—but though the highway is generally separated from the lands of the owner by a hedge and ditch set up by his own act, and therefore he would seem to be limiting his property by making that boundary, yet your Lordship is well aware that it is the familiar law of the land that the soil of the highway is the property of the owners of the adjoining lands on each side; and therefore though as in a case of that kind, where there seems to be a strong inference to the contrary, yet the occupation of the owner of the adjoining land is still held sufficient, by presumption of law, to entitle him to the land of half the highway; so I say in the case of the sea-shore, where the occupation is more frequent, but perhaps difficult of direct proof, the legal inference is the same.

I was drawing your Lordship's attention to the case of *alluvion* which is referred to in Bracton, and Fleta who follows Bracton. *Britton*, an authority of a different description, and more conversant with the principles of the English law than either of the other writers, who chiefly founded themselves upon the Civil Law— Britton lays down the thing most strongly; even in some degree contrary to the doctrine of non-occupancy, which I was referring to before; for having first of all stated the case of alluvion, he says, "that if any isle rises in the sea, it becomes the property of " the lord of the adjoining manor." That seems to be an accidental property, attracted as it were to the adjoining manor in consequence of its adjacency to it, and where of course it would be under such circumstances much more difficult for the owner of that manor to show any right to it;—but that doctrine is there so laid down, showing at least that this author had no idea of such a prerogative right.

Britton.

Then, analogous to the Domesday Book, to which I before drew your Lordship's attention, there is a statute of the realm which gives an account of rights belonging to manors and others—the statute of *Extenta Manerii*, the 4 Edw. I.,[1] with the detail of the enumeration of which I will not trouble your Lordship; it is sufficient to say, that almost every species of right, connected with manors, that has any separate character, is enumerated. It is " a survey of the buildings, lands, commons, parks, woods, tenants, " &c. of the manor," &c. They are required to make " certain " returns of the buildings, demesnes, parks, woods, pawnage, herbage, " mills, and fishings, and of freeholders and their lands and tenements, " and customary tenants and the lands they hold—of forests and " their profits—and of fairs, markets, and the liberties, customs, " and services "—in short, every separate thing which could possibly belong to a manor. But there is no mention there whatever of the sea-shore as having any peculiar quality, or anything which would lead to its being held separately in any degree either by the Crown or the lord of the manor; or anything in point of fact which could induce any person to suppose that there was in that period

4 Edw. I. *Extenta Manerii.*

Toppesham.

of our law, any peculiar or mystical right connected with the shore of the sea, otherwise than as a part of the adjoining land.

In the treatise to which I have before adverted, there is the *Toppesham* case,[1] to which, with many others, I would draw your Lordship's attention, for the purpose of showing how the sea-shore, and the ports, and the navigable rivers, were treated as belonging to private individuals. In that case, "The Earls of Devon," in the 12 Edw. I., "had not only the " port of Toppesham, but the Record tells us, that *portus et piscaria* " *et mariscus de Topsham spectat Amiciæ Comitissæ Devon.*" And the same treatise quotes it again at a subsequent period:—" The " port and the fishing and the marsh of Toppesham belonged to " the Countess of Devon." It appears that there was a contest between the Countess of Devon and the mayor and burgesses of Exeter, who had the *port* of Exeter in fee farm, and eventually the Countess succeeds and the corporation are defeated. That, your Lordship observes, was a litigation between the Countess of Devon on the one part and the corporation of Exeter on the other; there was no interposition of the Crown.

Lord Chancellor.—Both might have claimed under the Crown.

Mr. Serjeant Merewether.—Yes, my Lord, I will not at all deny that they might have claimed under the Crown; they might have been grantees of the Crown both of the borough and town of Toppesham, and of the river, to hold under the Crown, (of which there are many other instances, but as grantees of the private property of the Crown) not of any distinct prerogative right, —but as part of the land—part and parcel of the borough or town.

Lord Chancellor.—" Fee farm :" still somebody else was the original proprietor.

Mr. Serjeant Merewether.—Certainly, my Lord, it might have been held under the Crown; but whether *jure privato* or *jure prærogativo* is the point; there seems no pretence for the latter.

Lord Chancellor.—The fact of there being a contest between the Corporation and an individual, does not show that the Crown had not the original title.

Mr. Serjeant Merewether.—No, my Lord; but I think your Lordship will see that if the Crown had had any title, it would have interposed, as was the practice in those days.

In the twentieth page of the same treatise, my Lord, there is

[1] " De Jure Maris," ante, xviii. and Jerwood, p. 49.

Speech of Mr. Serjeant Merewether. lxxxi

another authority quoted—the case of the Abbot of Tichfend [1]—who "impleaded the burgesses of Southampton that they had taken up "their weir at Cadeland. The burgesses replied that the weir was "placed there to the injury of our Lord the King and the town of "Southampton, and the ships and boats were impeded by which "they could the less come to the port. The Jurors say that from "time whereof the memory of man runneth not to the contrary "there was not any weir there, so that it was to the injury of those "passing by."

Tichfend.

Now upon this the author of this treatise observes, " That a sub-"ject *may* by prescription have a weir in the sea ; and consequently "have an interest below the low-water mark, for probably weirs be "such." I draw your Lordship's attention to that point, because it establishes that the right of the owners of the adjoining land is not limited, as is ordinarily conceived, to the low-water mark. I should contend that it goes further ; [2] *that in point of fact the owner of the adjoining land is entitled to go to the sea, wherever it may be ; to follow it as it recedes; and that his enjoyment is as far as he can make the sea capable of his occupation, and that as well by weirs, as by projections, which have from time immemorial been made all round this kingdom by the owners of the adjoining lands, who use the sea to the utmost point that they can make it available for their purposes.*

In the same reign there was a case of considerable importance against the Prior of Tinmouth.[3]—there the Attorney of His Majesty claimed for the King that river, *eò quod fluxu maris comprehenditur*. The judgment was signed against the Prior; and the treatise assumes that it was impliedly with respect to the soil. But if the case is looked at, my Lord, there is no pretence for that supposition —it was founded solely upon the ground of nuisance. The complaint was that the ships were impeded in their navigation ; and another complaint was that the Prior had set up a market contrary to the interests of the town of Newcastle :—it being clear by law, that no nuisance can be permitted to exist ; and no market can by law be set up within seven miles of any existing market. It is therefore obvious that there was abundant ground for that judgment without its being taken for granted that it impliedly affected the right to the soil.

Tinmouth case.

At the end of the reign of Edward I. and at the commencement

Year Books.

Statham, Fitzherbert.

Rolls of Parliament.

Hacchesham.

of the reign of Edward II. began that compilation of decided cases which will be familiar to your Lordship—I mean the Year Books. Those books date from that period up to the reign of Henry VIII. In them are recorded almost every question which by possibility could arise in the administration of the law:—and yet after the best search which I have been able to make in them, I cannot find one case which would give the slightest colour for this right which is now assumed to be in the Crown; and I am confirmed in that conclusion, because in all the *abridgements* which your Lordship is aware collect the cases out of the Year Books—in the early abridgements of *Statham* or *Fitzherbert*[1]—or any of those collections of cases—I cannot find the slightest trace of such a right as this. I am therefore confident that there is not at that period any appearance whatever of such a right in the Crown; and how, my Lord, it could possibly have been omitted to be mentioned, or to be called in question, if put in force, appears to me incredible; because this claim, if it applies to anything, applies to a considerable portion of the area of this sea-girt kingdom.

I have taken some pains in having the extent of the property claimed measured, as far as it is practicable from maps;[2] and I find it would apply, at the lowest possible calculation, to no less an amount than upwards of 700,000 acres of land. Now that such a claim as this should exist all around the kingdom, and that we should have in succeeding reigns minute records of the points decided in courts of law, but no trace whatever of such a proposition as this, is to me, I must confess, all but conclusive, that at that time of day such a right could not have existed. My Lord, the Year Books certainly lay a strong foundation for the inference I have drawn, and I think I shall satisfy your Lordship that there are other authorities leading to precisely the same conclusion.

In the *Rolls of Parliament* it will be found in the 8th of Edward II. that there was, with respect to the manor of *Hacchesham*,[3] a petition presented to the king claiming land which had been overflowed by the sea, and taken by the bishop of Bath and Wells:—to which the answer was, in the language of that day, " *Sequatur versùs Epis-* " *copum ad communem legem.*" The king directed that it should be decided according to the common law:—and it is justly enough observed in this book, " this would not have been the case, if the " king had been entitled." That is the language which I find in

Speech of Mr. Serjeant Merewether. lxxxiii

this treatise, upon which so much reliance is placed in support of this prerogative.

Lord Chancellor.—The only fair inference from that is this, " you cannot have it by favour ; " it entitles you by right and not by favour; it only refuses the favour.

Mr. Serjeant Merewether.—My Lord, if it were in the power of the Crown—if the Crown were seised, as it is alleged now to be, by right of prerogative——

Lord Chancellor.—Suppose the Crown does not choose to act; it says, Let the law take its course.

Mr. Serjeant Merewether.—Which it would have been quite unnecessary for the Crown to have said, if the Crown were in point of fact entitled.

Now here is another case which I will mention to your Lordship. As I am endeavouring to support a negative proposition of this kind, I do not mean to pass by any authority that may appear to impugn the argument I am enforcing. There is undoubtedly an extraordinary case to be met with in this book, and a still more extraordinary conclusion drawn from it—it is the case of the Abbot of St. Benedict Hulme in the 10th of Edward II. : [1]—" He impleads divers " for fishing *in ripariâ suâ* which extends itself from the Bridge of " Wroxham to a certain Lake called Blackdam. Pending the suit " the king's attorney came in, and alleged for the king that the said " *riparia* is an arm of the sea, which extends itself into the salt sea " and is the *riparia* of our lord the king, where the salt water flows " and reflows, and where ships and boats come and apply themselves " from the great sea to load and unload without paying toll to any " one, and it is a common fishery to every one ; and he says that it " was presented in the last *Iter*, before *Solomon de Roffa* and his " companions Justices Itinerant in that county, that the predecessor " of the abbot made a *purpresture* upon the king in the said *riparia*, " by placing *weirs* in the same, and by appropriating to him the " same fishing, holding it as if it were several. Upon which it was " considered that the weirs should be amoved, and that the water " should remain a common fishery. And the Attorney-General " sought a stay of proceedings, that they should not take any inqui- " sition thereon, until the justices were certified upon the record " and the process. Thereupon search is granted, and the record " certified. And afterwards a *procedendo* was obtained, and issue

Abbot of Hulme.

" being joined, it was found for the abbot, and judgment and execu-
" cution given against the defendant for the damages, namely
" £200." "Upon which record," says the author of this treatise
(it can hardly be possible that it should be Lord Hale), "these things
" are observable—First, that *de commune jure*, the right of such
" arms of the sea belongs to the king." That was the point asserted
by the attorney-general; the attorney-general said that he had a
record which would support it—and prayed a stay of proceedings
till it was examined. It was examined, and the decision was against
the effect of the record—they go to issue—and the issue is found
for the abbot. How, from such a case as that, a conclusion can be
drawn that by common right such an arm of the sea belongs to the
king, I must confess I cannot comprehend. And it is upon that
passage, my Lord, that this doctrine now rests, as being well-
founded: though I believe, when examined, it will turn out to be
totally unsustainable. I ought also to observe, upon that case, that
the Abbot of Hulme's title was founded upon a grant made to him
of the land *cum pertinentibus;* following out the same course to
which I before alluded with respect to the Saxon Charters.

14 Edw. II.   In Easter Term in the 14th of Edward II., there is a case with
respect to some boats which had been seized on the river Thames,
as being on the shore damage feasant; and it was there stated
that "there was no right to land without leave of the lord within
the flux and reflux of the tide." And therefore, that is at least
another case in which the soil of the river, within the flux and
reflux of the tide, was held to be in the lord, and that those who
entered upon it were trespassers.

17 Edw. II.   Now, my Lord, in the 17th of Edward II., there is the statute
which is ordinarily called the Statute "*De Prærogativâ Regis ;*"[1]
and in that statute there is a full mention of the prerogatives which
belong to the king. My Lord, the first chapter of that statute
relates to the custody of lands held in capite; the second, to the
marriage of wards; the third, to prime seizin; the fourth, to
widows dower; the fifth, to coparceners; the sixth, to women
marrying within age; and the seventh, to serjeanties. These seven
have all been put an end to by the statute of Charles II. The
remaining nine (sixteen altogether) relate to different subjects:—the
eighth to advowsons; the ninth, to the custody of idiots; the tenth,
to the custody of the lands of lunatics; the eleventh, to *wreck of*

Speech of Mr. Serjeant Merewether. lxxxv

the sea, whales and sturgeons; the twelfth, to the lands of Normans; the thirteenth, to the king's tenants in capite; the fourteenth, to the *escheats* of bishops' freeholders attainted for felony; the fifteenth, to lands, &c. *not to pass from the king but by express words;* and the sixteenth, to the goods and lands of felons. Now, my Lord, this is a very considerable enumeration of prerogatives of the Crown. Prerogatives connected with *wrecks* and *royal fish;* but no mention whatever of this alleged prerogative right of the crown. I shall not at all disguise from your Lordship that it is argued by some, that this statute does not contain all the prerogatives of the Crown. I must confess I am not aware of any that are not contained in it: but it is so said. Nevertheless, however strongly that may be asserted, and were it even found that there were two or three insignificant prerogatives of the Crown omitted in that statute, I should submit with confidence to your Lordship that such a right as the one claimed by the crown—so extensive as I have described it to be—could not by possibility have been omitted in the enumeration of so particularizing a statute, in which the subject-matter of the sea is brought under consideration, by reference to the prerogative of *wreck and royal fish.*

I will only observe with respect to "Horne's Myrrour of Justices,"[1] a book of great authority, which has a chapter on the rights of the Crown, that there is there again no trace whatever of this prerogative. And in the next reign (that book being published in the reign of Edward II.), in the reign of Edward III., I find a case which has always been referred to upon this subject—*Sir Henry Nevil's* case.[2] That is in the Year Book 5 Edw. III. Hil. fol. 11. As to the Year Books, I should however further state, that though they contain cases relative to *wreck* and to other subjects likely to have brought the sea prerogatives of the Crown into discussion, there are none that I can find relating to the seashore, further than those to which I shall draw your Lordship's attention. In page 27 of the treatise "De Jure Maris" it is said:[3]—" Consonant to this is the pleading of Sir Henry Nevil's case." He prescribed for *wreck* belonging to his manor, and succeeded in establishing that claim; the wreck being (as of course is usually the case) "*projectum super littus maris apud S. infrà*[4] *præcinctum manerii sive dominii illius.*" And there, without any express grant of the seashore, or anything

Horne's Myrrour.

Sir Hen. Nevil's case.

[1] Jerwood, p. 90. [2] *Ibid.* p. 54. [3] *Ante*, p. xxv.
[4] "Infrà" in the Law Latin of this date means "within." See Jerwood,

belonging to it, but under a grant of *wreck within the manor*, it was taken as being within the manor, being found upon the sea-shore. Therefore in that case, as well as two subsequent,—one of Sir *John*, and another of Sir *Henry* Constable,—which I shall refer to hereafter, your Lordship will see that the sea-shore was assumed to be part and parcel of the manor, and the property of the owner of the adjoining manor, who had a grant of the wreck *within* his manor.[1]

Abbot of St. Austin's case.

There is a case, in the same reign, of the Abbot of St. Austin of Canterbury, where there was an inquisition which found "*Quod non est solum nostrum, sed solum abbatis :*"—and that was a portion of what had been encroached upon in the creek, in the neighbourhood of Canterbury.

22 Edw. III. Lib. Assis.

In the 22 Edw. III., in the *Liber Assisarum*, there is a case which is often quoted—in the Banne Case—and over and over again in subsequent cases—but as far as I can see, it has no bearing whatever on this subject. It was founded upon the doctrine of Britton, with respect to the lands accruing to one manor, and taken off from the other by the violent course of a stream. It did not appear that it was a navigable river—nor was there any allusion to its being navigable—it was nothing more than an adjustment of the rights of ownership and occupation between two persons whose lands were opposite to each other by the side of the river, but whose relative boundaries were occasionally altered by the course of the stream. My only reason for mentioning this case is because it is quoted so unceasingly, as if it had something to do with the subject.

Abbot of Peterborough.

In the 23 Edw. III., the case occurred of Abbot of Peterborough:[2] "The Abbot of Peterborough was questioned at the king's suit for "acquiring thirty acres of marsh land in Gosberkile; the license of "the king not having been obtained. The abbot pleaded that by "the custom of the country from time whereof the memory of man "was not to the contrary, all and singular the lords of the lands of "the manors, and the lands upon the coasts of the sea particularly, "had all the marshes and salt marshes by the flux and reflux of the "sea; and he says that he has a certain manor in that vill, from "whence much land is adjacent to the coasts of the sea, and he "has by the flux and reflux of the sea about 300 acres of marsh "land adjacent; without this that he himself has acquired," &c. "Upon issue joined, it depended many years before it was tried. But

Speech of Mr. Serjeant Merewether. lxxxvii

"afterwards in Easter, 41 Edw. III., judgment was given, that
"according to the custom of the country, the lords of the manor
"near adjacent had the marshes and salt marshes increasing by the
"flux and reflux of the tide, and projected towards their land—*Ideò*
"*Abbas sine die*." The consequence was that he retained his possession over lands which certainly came within the description in the allegation of the Attorney-General's information.

That case, and others which I shall have occasion to quote to your Lordship, all show that in these instances the lords of the manors have enjoyed the sea-shore and possessed it without any regard at all to any prerogative right of the Crown.

In the Year Book also, there was another case in which a considerable quantity of land and *weirs* were recovered as parcel of the manor of Burnham in Essex.   Year Book, 34 Edw. III. pl. 11.

There are also during the reigns which I have been passing over, many *statutes* with regard to *weirs* in different parts of the country. Mr. Bethell referred to one of them, quoted in the Commission of Conservancy. All of those are still free from any mention whatever of any peculiar right of the Crown to the shore, upon which these *weirs* would have been an interference and an intrusion—if the prerogative right now claimed had existed.   Statutes.

In the 43 Edw. III. occurred the Abbot of Ramsey's case;—it is stated in this treatise. I do not read the treatise itself as an authority, but I refer to this case which is quoted there; it is also given by Sir Edward Coke in the Fourth Institutes in the chapter on the Court of Admiralty. He says :—" The case was that the "Abbot of Ramsey was seised of the manor of Brancaster in "Norfolk bordering upon the sea, upon sixty acres of marsh of "which manor the sea did flow and reflow; and yet it was adjudged "*parcel* of the abbot's manor, and by consequence within the body "of the county unto the low-water mark." I will read also another passage from Sir Edward Coke, which relates to a subsequent period. " It was adjudged in the 17 Eliz., in the Exchequer, "Diggs informing for the Queen, that the land between the flowing "and reflowing of the sea belonged to the lord of the manor "adjoining, as the Lord Dier doth there report." Judgment against the Crown.   Abbot of Ramsey.

Diggs v. Hammond.

In the sixth year of Richard II. there is a case which is frequently quoted; and a dictum which is supposed to bear upon the subject; but of which I must say that I cannot see the pertinency. It is with   6 Richard II.

lxxxviii   *Appendix.*

discussion, Belknap refused the grant of the protection, because he said, " The sea is of the ligeance of the king, as of his crown of " England." That has been quoted for the purpose of showing that the king is entitled to the sea; and by an odd mode of reasoning, because the king is entitled to the sea, he is argued to be entitled also to all the land over which the sea flows. But in truth this was nothing more than an application for a protection, to which the answer was, What is the protection wanted for? You are not out of the protection of the king on the sea. You do not want any protection for that purpose, because you are still in the ligeance of the king as of his crown of England. My Lord, this case is actually brought in for the purpose of supporting the alleged doctrine; and is quoted by some of the authors as the foundation of the King's prerogative.

2 Hen. VI. cap. 9.
In a statute in the 2nd of Henry VI. certain *weirs* on the river Thames are mentioned, and commissioners are appointed for the parts which were beyond the liberties of London. The Lord Mayor of London having the undoubted conservancy *jurisdiction* as to all *weirs* within the liberties of London, an Act of Parliament was passed to give the same power to other commissioners beyond them. In that Act the right of the owners (as in the instance of *Magna Charta* before mentioned) is expressly reserved; but there is no reservation of any right whatever in the Crown.

8 Edw. IV. fol. 18.
In the eighth year of Edward IV. in the Year Book will be found a case in which fishermen were proceeded against as trespassers on the shore for digging holes to put stakes in for drying their nets. They pleaded a custom that they had used to go there to dry their nets. It was held that was bad, because " there could be no custom " to dig *my* land although the sea flow over it," and " that it was a " destruction of the inheritance." That is a declaration of Chief-Justice Choke. But in that case again there is no reference whatever to any right of the Crown. An action was brought by the lord of the manor against those fishermen for trespassing upon his ground, and the words of the judgment are, " There could be no " custom to dig *my* land,"—evidently treating it as the land of the plaintiff, who succeeded in the action.

Year Book, 8 Edw. IV.
In the same Year Book, in the same reign, there is also another action of trespass for digging on the coast of the sea. The plea justified for erections as defences against the King's enemies; but it was held bad. There again there was no right of the Crown

was entitled to the shore, and those defences were put there. The lord of the manor however prohibits it, and brings an action. It is pleaded that they are defences for the protection of the country against the enemy, which would have prevailed if it had been set up under the authority of the *King* upon the *King's* own land.

My Lord, I have already adverted to the fact, (and therefore will not trouble your Lordship with it any further) that at this period of our legal history the *Abridgements* begin. *Statham's* Abridgement is in the reign of Edward IV.: and *Fitzherbert's* in the reign of Henry VIII.[1] Now during that time, as I have observed before, there is no trace of this doctrine. My Lord, the learned author of the Abridgment which I have last named was also the author of the well-known *Natura Brevium*, to which I am obliged to refer.

Abridgements.

Lord Chancellor.—It does not appear to me how this, being a general question, can be in issue now. The information says that the Crown is seised of the bed of the river, and upon that they rest part of their case. I do not see that that depends at all upon the general right of the Crown—it leaves it entirely open. They say, as to the particular bed of the river, the Crown is seised. *It may ultimately become a very material question*, when you come to try the right; and I may direct an issue to try the point as to the allegation of the information, that the Crown is seised of the bed of the river, met by a denial of that right, and an assertion of the right of the Defendants. As matter of pleading, *not saying what the ultimate right may be*, how am I to determine upon the general right of the Crown?

Mr. Serjeant Merewether.—My Lord, as far as the pleading goes, it is quite clear that there is an assertion of seisin on the one hand, and a denial of it on the other. You are not seised, we are:—that is the matter certainly to be tried in the cause, a matter of fact to be enquired into:—but I am now speaking of the proposition of *law*, my Lord, which precedes that allegation; and upon which the whole is founded—namely the prerogative right of the Crown.

Lord Chancellor.—That does not enter into it at all. Whatever the prerogative of the Crown may be with respect to other places, they do not give any opinion; but they say, As to the particular soil of the Thames we deny the right of the Crown, and assert the right of the Corporation; therefore the general prerogative in support of the Crown's right is not in issue. The question is, whether this matter now in discussion is raised by the answer, so as to make it necessary to decide it, in deciding whether the Defendants are to answer the question. Take the pleadings as they stand—take the answer as it stands—I want to be informed how it is that this general question is raised between the parties, the answer not denying, nor asserting, nor admitting, the *general* right, but saying as to the *particular* right in question, I deny that that is in the Crown. The general question is not raised in these pleadings at all—I wish to draw your attention to this fact.

Mr. Serjeant Merewether.—The Crown, your Lordship sees, asserts this prerogative, and it is the point upon which the exceptions rest.

Lord Chancellor.—The Defendant does not take issue upon that.

Mr. Serjeant Merewether.—There could be no issue taken upon that, my Lord—it is a proposition of law.

Lord Chancellor.—Then if there is not, it is no question upon the discovery.

Mr. Serjeant Merewether.—It is submitted to the Court, my Lord, by the answer, as a proposition of law should be.

Lord Chancellor.—The *Crown may not have that general right;* but there may be something peculiar in this case to show that it has a right in the bed of the Thames.

Mr. Randell.—The Attorney-General by this information, my Lord, does not allege that the Crown has any peculiar title, but he puts it upon the general prerogative title.

Lord Chancellor.—Then why does not the answer? It is clear enough upon the information that the discovery must be made; the question is raised upon the answer. The Defendants have set up an adverse title—the discovery sought relates to that adverse title, and not to the title of the Crown. That is the ground of the discovery. If that is so, that is as to the particular subject-matter. The answer does not deny the prerogative, and therefore deny the title; it denies the title altogether.

Mr. Serjeant Merewether.—*If your Lordship can be satisfied that the Crown has no such prerogative right as is asserted, how can this suit be maintained at all?*

Lord Chancellor.—That is not the question for discovery.

Mr. Serjeant Merewether.—If the suit could not be maintained, how could the Crown, as altogether a stranger, be entitled to call upon us to disclose our title, we being in possession?

Lord Chancellor.—It has a right to discovery from you in aid of

Speech of Mr. Serjeant Merewether.

Mr. Serjeant Merewether.—The proceedings in this case, my Lord, are so extremely expensive both to the Crown and the Corporation, and give so much trouble to all parties concerned, that I imagine it would be as much to the interest of the Crown as of the Corporation of London, that this, which is *the material point in the case*, should be settled.

Lord Chancellor.—I am no party to that agreement; *you may raise the question if you like:* after all it will be a decision not binding upon anybody, as it is not necessary for the purpose; if the decision as to the answer does not depend upon the question of the general prerogative, then whatever opinion might be afterwards expressed, would not be a decision upon the point at all. I am only throwing this out—it may be very material to the Crown no doubt —*it may be the foundation of their case;* but the Defendant does not put it upon that: on the contrary, he says, I have nothing to do with the general right—that is a matter of law; but I say, with regard to this particular question, I deny your right; the seisin in the Crown is denied, and an adverse seisin alleged in the Defendant.

Mr. Serjeant Merewether.—This first proposition is an earlier point in the case than that.

Lord Chancellor.—That is not the proposition which the Defendant meets; he meets it by a mere general denial of the Crown's right, whether supported by the prerogative or not; he denies the right, and asserts an adverse right of seisin in himself; that is the question between the parties. You are actually, under a question of this sort, trying a particular right, upon which the Crown may or may not rely *(in all probability it will of course)* in support of its claim.

Mr. Serjeant Merewether.—Surely, looking at the pleadings, the *information having alleged this so distinctly at the commencement, as the ground upon which the Attorney-General puts it;* and the Answer having denied it, and left it as a proposition of law for the judgment of the Court, it must be decided ——

Lord Chancellor.—Not as to this land—the general prerogative no doubt.

Mr. Serjeant Merewether.—The Master of the Rolls having given his judgment upon this very point; and the principal point in the exceptions which bring us here, being that we do not show the charter on which we claim this property from the Crown, to prove how it is out of the Crown—it does seem to me that the

it is in the Crown: then the right which is alleged is, that *by royal prerogative the Crown is entitled to the sea-shore all round the kingdom.* How that matter can be passed by, I do not very well see.

Lord Chancellor.—As I collect the answer, the proposition is not raised in that way. It is not that you rely upon a charter giving you the right, and that on that they ask for a discovery; but they say, that you have shown such a right as in point of fact shows the plaintiff's right.

Mr. Serjeant Merewether.—If this were a case between private individuals, and the party complaining alleged his title on the face of the bill, and it was afterwards, upon putting in an answer, said, But you do not show by what deed you have derived the title from us: is it not open to the defendant on that state of things to say, You have *no title* at all—you are *a stranger?* My argument [1] is with a view of showing, that *the Crown is altogether a* STRANGER *to this possession—that it has no right at all; that the right which is set out in the beginning of the information has no foundation in law;* therefore our not showing that we have any title derived from the Crown, is not any ground for calling for a discovery from us. If your Lordship has a decided opinion upon that point, so that I might not with propriety press the matter further before your Lordship ——

Lord Chancellor.—I throw it out for your consideration: you must exercise your own discretion about it; it is a difficulty which, no doubt, you have in the case.

Mr. Serjeant Merewether.—My Lord, I certainly should not have brought myself before your Lordship at all on this occasion, if it had not been from *a thorough conviction of the extreme importance of this matter to this suit;* and thinking also that the pleadings were such that *this must be decided in some way or other* before the disposal of the exceptions, and the judgment of the Master of the Rolls upon them. Being entrusted with the records of the Corporation, I am bound to resist the production of anything which would tend in any degree whatever to discover the title of the Corporation.

Lord Chancellor.—I cannot go any further than to suggest what exists in my mind as a difficulty.

Mr. Serjeant Merewether.—The further observations which I

Speech of Mr. Serjeant Merewether.

have to make to your Lordship will be for the purpose of showing *the period when this doctrine arose ; and that it has no foundation in law.* I am now, rather tediously I fear, going through the negative part of the case; but when I come to the other part, to show who were the authors of this doctrine—how it was attempted to be introduced—and how, when introduced, it was abandoned—how the charters granted in consequence of its assumption have been unavailing, and have been held by the Courts to be void—I think I shall make such an impression on your Lordship's mind as will lead you to the conclusion that *there is no such prerogative as that which is now claimed.*

Lord Chancellor.—What I have said, I have merely thrown out for your guidance.

Mr. Serjeant Merewether.—I am extremely obliged to your Lordship. I will avail myself of your Lordship's permission, by going through the remaining portions of my statement as speedily as possible.

The case to which I am now about to call your Lordship's attention is *Sir John Constable's.*[1] He was possessed of the lordship of Holderness, with the *wreck* from the sea *within* the manor; he brought an action for this wreck :—the grant under which he took is given at great length—and there are no special words giving him the *shore*, but simply the *wreck*. Now, my Lord, it is truly said that the sea-shore, being a prerogative right, could not pass out of the Crown without express words; therefore the word "wreck" only being used, and there being no express mention of the sea-shore, the decision that Sir John was entitled to that wreck, as being within his manor, is a decisive proof to show that the shore is a part of the manor, because the grant is " Wrecca infrà Manerium."—That occurred in Sir John Constable's case ; there is no judgment of the Court printed. But at a subsequent time, 43 Eliz., his son *Sir Henry Constable*, in a case reported at great length in the 5th Rep. 106, brought an action of trespass for the same cause, and after much discussion and full consideration, it was decided that he was entitled to the wreck, because it was assumed that the wreck must be on the sea-shore, and therefore he was entitled to it as infrà Manerium—showing the sea-shore to be *parcel* of the manor. Those cases have ever since been treated as authority. When the Attorney-General, on a recent occasion, set

Sir John Constable's case. 19 Eliz.

Sir Henry Constable's case. 43 Eliz.

up this prerogative, he was reminded of Constable's case;—and the Court said to him expressly, "If you are right, Mr. Attorney- "General, Sir Henry Constable's case is wrong." The Attorney- General set up the prerogative right of the Crown; and contended that no evidence could be received to explain a grant in general words; but that there must be a grant in special words of this pre- rogative right. Those cases therefore have been thought to be binding authorities, and have been much relied upon in reference to this subject. I will therefore, my Lord, not trouble you any farther with respect to the many cases which will be found where the right to the sea-shore was enjoyed by the lords of the manor and the owners of lands adjoining the sea-shore; about sixteen or seventeen of those actions were maintained for such a right without any interposition of the Crown.

My Lord, I have now arrived at that period of our legal history when undoubtedly this doctrine seems to have been introduced—

Jac. I. it was in the reign of James I.; and there are then some traces from which inferences have been drawn that the Crown has such a title.

8 Jac. I. Banne case.
In *Davies's Reports* [1] there is the well-known case of the *Banne* fishery, which has been supposed to support such a doctrine; but when it is looked into, my Lord, in point of fact it affords no inference of the kind; there is an observation in the course of it which looks that way, but the case was simply this:—The Crown by right of conquest being in possession of the land and territory immediately on the river *Banne*, had made a grant of some of that land to a person who claimed in consequence of it the fishery in the river; and the whole point decided in that case was, that under the general words granting the land, the fishery did not pass: however it was stated that there was some right in the Crown, and there are authorities quoted in the margin for it. These authorities I have already gone through—Britton and others—which, upon looking carefully into them, do not really bear out the proposition.

Noy. Shortly after that time, there is a case in *Noy*, in which the Court says, upon a diversion in the river Thames, that there should be a writ of *ad quod damnum*, or *a patent*. That is the first loose hint which I find of any right being supposed to be vested in the Crown —it was in fact a case of *purpresture;* and consequently does not support the private right in the Crown which is now set up.

Speech of Mr. Serjeant Merewether.

Then, my Lord, succeeds *Callis*,[1] a book supposed to be of authority. He was the Reader of Gray's Inn, and has certainly taken upon himself in his book to allege this prerogative right; but upon looking to the authorities which he quotes, it will be found that none support him in his position. He quotes the same authorities as are in the margin of the Banne case; but not one upon which any reliance can be placed. I am sure I shall not have occasion to urge to your Lordship that the mere authority of a text writer of that description, unless founded upon some decided case, cannot prevail.

Very soon after this time, charters began to be granted conveying the shore of the sea; and in the fourth year of Charles I. there was a charter granted to the *De Wandesfordes*, of the whole of the seashore; giving in the most extensive words all fisheries, marshes, lakes, mud-lands, oozes, and all wrecks, and all belonging to the sea as far as the tide flowed and reflowed. That charter was brought in question in the case of the *Attorney-General* v. *Parmeter*,[2] with respect to the harbour of Portsmouth; but upon its being produced and relied upon, it was stated that there had been no act done upon it whatever, and it never had been put in use; nor was that to be wondered at, because there were at that time parties entitled to that coast, and the sea-shore adjoining it: and in actual possession of it at the time of the grant, and have so continued ever since. The Duke of Norfolk, and many others all round Hayling Island and Langston Harbour (where there are large districts of mud-land and ooze and sea-shore), were in possession of them when this charter was granted. The moment that charter saw light in a court of justice, it was held to be void, and so treated.

As might be expected, this prerogative right being thus suggested, a case followed with respect to the river Thames, against *Philpot* and others; in which the Crown laid its claim to a considerable quantity of the shore as a purpresture, at the outside of Wapping Wall, on the north of the river Thames; and it procured a judgment.

Mr. Solicitor-General.—Where is that case?

Mr. Serjeant Merewether.—It is not reported; and I believe has never been acted upon. It is mentioned in the treatise *De Jure Maris*[3] thus:—"Consonant to this there was a decree Paschæ Car. I. " in the Exchequer entered in the Book of Orders of that term, folio " sixty-six, whereby it was decreed that the soil and ground lying be- " tween Wapping Wall and the river of Thames is *parcel of the Port*

Callis.

1629.
4 Car. I.

1633.
8 Car. I.

"*of London;* and therefore, and for that the same lies between the "high-water and low-water marks of the river of Thames, all the "houses built between the Hermitage Wharf and Dickshore east-"ward, and between the old wall of Wapping Wall on the north and "the river of Thames on the south, are decreed for the king, and "the same were accordingly seized into the king's hands." Now, my Lord, it is right that I should mention that case: but whenever it may be attempted to be cited as an authority, and the circumstances connected with it are looked into, I am sure it will not at this day be acted upon; as I believe it never has been; at least, if acted upon, it was disputed and called in question, and the proceedings under it were inch by inch fought by the Corporation of London. At that time, it is well known as a matter of history, the coffers of the Crown were not full; and it was desirable that proceedings of this kind should take place *for the improvement of the king's revenue;*[1] and accordingly it will be found, when that case is looked into, that the Lord High Treasurer and the Chancellor of the Exchequer sat with the learned Judges upon the Bench, and were present at the decision of that case. I think I may say with confidence, that case will not be relied upon.

Mr. Solicitor-General.—It is very possible.

Mr. Serjeant Merewether.—I shall be very glad if that case is relied upon, that the circumstances of it should be gone into; there are facts connected with it, which I think will be amusing and instructive to my learned friend, whenever he thinks fit to enter upon them. I do not find that case anywhere mentioned, excepting upon one occasion, in Whitaker *v.* Wise, Keble's Reports, 759; where it is said by the reporter at the end of his report, "That case was "decided against Sir Henry Constable's." I think therefore neither in law, nor in fact, will my learned friend be able to make anything of that case, so soon afterwards repudiated, when brought under consideration.

1647.
22 Car. I.

Johnson *v.* Barrett.

There is in the 22 Charles I. a case which I think is almost decisive, that this doctrine was not adopted as a known point of law at that time. It is a short note—and mentions only a part of the proceedings; but there is sufficient to show that it occurred at a *Trial at Bar.* It is the case of *Johnson* v. *Barrett,* Aleyn's Reports, page 10.[2] It related to a wharf at Yarmouth; the owner of which brought an action against the corporation for removing his wharf,

Speech of Mr. Serjeant Merewether. xcvii

it being supposed to be a nuisance to the harbour. In the course of the trial, as Aleyn reports, on its being asked to whom the land would belong if the wharf was removed, Rolle, counsel on one side, stated that " if it were above low-water it belonged to the owner of " adjoining land." But Hale, who was counsel on the other side, strenuously denied this, and said it was in the king. "But it was " agreed that if it were *below* low-water mark, it was in the Crown." Now I think it is hardly possible for any one to say that at that time it could be considered the law of this land, that " by the Royal pre-
" rogative, the ground and soil of the coasts and shores of the sea
" round this kingdom, and the ground and soil of every port and
" haven, and every navigable river into which the sea ebbs and flows,
" belonged to His Majesty." If so, the answer at the trial at bar would have been at once clear and plain, and it must have been instantly stated and assented to. Philpot's case would have been cited, if indeed anybody had had hardihood enough to do it—and you would probably have had this case of Johnson *v.* Barrett quoted by Hale, if Lord Hale was really the author of the treatise as asserted; Lord Hale himself being the counsel who stated that point in Court. But neither is Johnson *v.* Barrett quoted, nor any reference to it made in this treatise :—so that if it is Lord Hale's compilation, it must be inferred that Johnson *v.* Barrett was decided against his doctrine.

My Lord, this treatise, as far as it goes, is directly against the last proposition, that " if it were below low-water mark it was in the " Crown,"—because the book shows that weirs, which are generally below low-water mark, may belong to the owners of the adjoining land, which gives them a right beyond the mere line of low-water mark ; as Magna Charta also seems to assume.

Perhaps my learned friend will expect that in candour I should also refer to the case of *Bulstrode* v. *Hall*, Siderfin's Reports, 148, respecting some property at Blackwall; and where this note is inserted by the reporter: " In this case it was oftentimes affirmed " and not denied, that the soil of all rivers, so far as the flux and " reflux of the sea, is in the king and not in the lords of the manors, " except by prescription." Now I imagine, my Lord, that is the first distinct assertion of this doctrine now so much relied upon : it is a note of the reporter—not at all in the manner, as if it were the acknowledged law of the land ; but rather as one of the new notabilia, which he thought it was right to put down in his note-book.

1663.
15 Car. II.
Bulstrode
v. Hall.

side and not denied on the other, because it might have been admitted by both; as was the fact in a subsequent case, with respect to the Portsmouth Harbour, to which I drew your Lordship's attention before; where exactly the same took place. There it was admitted by the counsel on both sides, that the right did exist in the Crown:—but for the most obvious reason—that both parties *claimed under the Crown*. One party claimed under the Crown by that charter, which I have mentioned before to the De Wandesfords,—and the other claimed under the Crown by the general title—of course therefore the Crown's right was not disputed in that case. Such might have been the fact in Bulstrode *v.* Hall. But at all events it can never be said that this was stated in such a manner by this reporter, whatever his credit might have been, as to induce any one to believe that this prerogative right (which if it existed at all, must have existed from the earliest time) was then acknowledged law.

1664.
16 Car. II.
Trematon case.

In the same reign there was the important case of *Trematon ;*[1] and there have been more modern cases to the same point. That case related to the port and water of *Sutton Pool* at Plymouth, which was held, after (as is stated) seven years' evidence, to have passed as parcel of the manor of Trematon. There was no special mention of the water in the grant; and it is said in this treatise that the water passed " not by any prerogative right, but it passed by " strength of its being parcel of and appendant to the manor." Now this, my lord, is a matter of great importance:—because the Duchy of Cornwall would afford a full opportunity of sifting and testing this prerogative right. In a subsequent case, an information was filed against Sir John St. Aubyn by the Attorney-General of the Duchy of Cornwall,[2] for an encroachment upon the sea-shore at Devonport:—after a long trial and much discussion, it was at length found in favour of the lessee of the Duchy of Cornwall and against Sir John St. Aubyn; *not upon any prerogative right belonging to the duke or to the Crown*, but because the sea-shore belonged to the Duke of Cornwall as "*part and parcel of the manor of Trematon.*" The same was held in the case, to which I was just before drawing your lordship's attention; and also in a subsequent case with respect to Plymouth Harbour; and it is clear law that the sea-shore of those places belongs to the Duke of Cornwall, as *parcel of his manor* there, and *not by any prerogative right.* If the Attorney-General therefore sets up a prerogative right, a question must immediately occur between the Crown and the Duke of Cornwall: for it is clear law that such a right in the Crown cannot pass but by express words;— and there are no such express words in the charter which gives the Duchy of Cornwall to the Prince of Wales.—The charter is given at length in 3 Manning and Ryland's Reports, in the Appendix to Rowe *v*. Brenton.

<small>Rowe *v*. Brenton.</small>

I have already referred your Lordship to the treatise *De Jure Maris*.[1] I have made some observations upon it, and I am anxious not to trespass unnecessarily upon your time, therefore I will not repeat them; but I think I am justified in saying that if that treatise is examined carefully, it will be found, both from intrinsic as well as extrinsic circumstances, not to be entitled to the name which it has so long borne. I believe it is not Lord Hale's work: which may be justly tested by its intrinsic merits. There are some cases in it which seem accurately and well stated; but there are others which are contradictory to each other, and are perverted:—nevertheless this treatise has always been the authority referred to for the support of the doctrine I am now disputing.

<small>*De Jure Maris*.</small>

I will not trouble your lordship with any observations upon the subsequent *Abridgements*, which have added to the former works of that class: the former Abridgements, of Statham and Fitzherbert and Rolle, are all of them free from any assertion of this prerogative right, as I have already stated; but Comyn's Abridgement, Bacon's Abridgement, and Viner's Abridgement, all of them state it. However, I have gone through the authorities which they quote for it, and none of them support it; it is merely a statement made in those works without authority.

<small>Abridgements.</small>

I must make one observation upon Blackstone's Commentaries[2]— a book very likely to have promoted that general impression in the law, which has been entertained in modern times; for as we all read that book early in life, and imbibe its contents greedily and implicitly, so also we retain them long. This book therefore, from its style and composition and general use, is likely to have produced an effect upon the minds of most lawyers. Blackstone lays it down clearly and distinctly, that the shores belong to the king. But when you look at the authority he quotes for it, it is in fact a reference to the Commission of Sewers—he cites Fitzherbert's *Natura Brevium*, 149; which is nothing more than a transcript of the recital of the Commission of Sewers, in which it is alleged that inasmuch as His

<small>Blackstone.</small>

Majesty is bound to protect the country from foreign enemies, so is he also bound to protect the shores from the aggression of the sea. How so learned an author could have imagined that he was justified, from such an authority, in making such an assertion, I must confess I cannot explain.

I will not trouble your Lordship with a reference to a case, in which Mr. Justice Buller[1] quoted *obitèr* a passage on this subject; it is clear that he merely quoted from the treatise. But I hold in my hand the notes on the First Institutes, by Mr. Butler, who was the colleague (if I may use the expression) of Mr. Hargrave, and the note, a portion of which I am about to read, is the writing of Mr. Butler.[2] Probably it is not to be wondered at that Mr. Butler, who was so connected with Mr. Hargrave, should adopt the doctrine of the manuscript published by that gentleman. He says (quoting in fact the treatise):—" This being premised with respect to the " propriety or ownership of the sea and its soil, it may be considered " under these three distinct divisions, the high seas, the shore, or " the land between high-water mark and low-water mark, and the " soil and franchise of ports.

[margin: Butler's Notes. Co. Litt.]

" As to the high seas and their soil, the right of fishing in the sea " and its creeks and arms is originally lodged in the Crown, as the " right of depasturing is originally lodged in the owner of the waste " whereof he is lord ; the king has therefore of common right the " primary right of fishing."—(I think it would be difficult to support that by authority.)—" Yet the people of England have also, by " common right, a liberty of fishing in the sea and its creeks or " arms, as a public common of piscary ; yet in some cases the king " may enjoy a propriety exclusive of their common of piscary. He " also may grant it to a subject, and consequently a subject may be " entitled to it by prescription.

" As to the soil between high-water mark and low-water mark at " ordinary tides, this of common right belongs to the king. It *may* " however belong to a subject by grant or prescription." Then he refers to Sir Henry Constable's case,[3] which is contrary to the position he lays down:—and he states further also that " Wreck " may be *parcel* of a manor ! " Now there certainly can be no ground for such a proposition. Though I should speak with great respect of Mr. Butler's opinion, I cannot but think that on this occasion he

Speech of Mr. Serjeant Merewether.

was misled. A person of such authority as Mr. Hargrave having published a manuscript, as if written by Lord Hale, too many, like Mr. Butler, would be willing to take the doctrine on the authority of Lord Hale, without considering the foundation on which it really rests.

My lord, there is an Act of Parliament which seems to bear upon this subject—the 54 Geo. III. c. 159[1]—which authorizes the Admiralty to do certain acts upon the sea-shore, with the view of prohibiting sand and other things being improperly taken away from it; but there is a proviso, " That nothing in this Act shall abridge, " diminish, or take away, any *rights of property or ownership* which " any lord of a manor, or *other person*, may have on any port, or the " banks, shores, and sides thereof:"—and there being no reservation of the right of the Crown in that Act, it seems to go far as a legislative admission upon the point, that the subject is entitled to it as belonging to the land; and that the Crown is not.

54 Geo. III. c. 159.

For the reason which I have stated before, I will not weary your Lordship by a minute reference to those cases in which the rights of the lord of the manor have been established; but I would state shortly that in the case of *Brooke* v. *Spering*,[2] the right of the lord of the manor to the shores of Sheppy Island was upheld. In *Lord Grosvenor's* case, which occurred as to the river Thames, Lord Tenterden refers to the right of the soil in the City of London. Then in *Blundell* v. *Catterall*,[3] which was a question with respect to the right of bathing on the sea-shore; the inhabitants set up such a right, but the lord of the manor resisted it; the right of the lord of the manor was maintained:—and there was no reference to any right in the Crown. *Chad* v. *Tilsed*[4] is a case, my Lord, of considerable importance, because it is entirely consistent with the late case of the Duke of Beaufort, to which I before alluded, and which I think your Lordship will find to bear strongly on this point. Chad *v*. Tilsed was an action of trespass, brought by the owner of Brownsea Island in the Harbour of Poole, and a verdict was given for him :—the trespass being committed upon the sea-shore. The right of the plaintiff to recover was made out under a charter, which was produced, and also by acts of ownership by the lord; and those acts of ownership were held to be conclusive evidence of the right of the lord, without producing any grant by express words

Chad *v*. Tilsed.

from the Crown; which is most material with reference to the doctrine I have before mentioned, that a prerogative right (if it really exists in the Crown) cannot pass from it but by express words—Mr. Justice Richardson saying, "It was quite clear that an indi-"vidual might maintain a *right to such soil*, by *usage*, independently "of a grant." Now this case, my Lord, was cited in the very recent case of the *Duke of Beaufort*.—I pass over with a mere mention a case of the same description—*Gray* v. *Bond*,[1] giving the right to the lord of the manor—and come to *Dickens* v. *Shaw*,[2] at Brighton, with respect to taking sand from the shore:—there the case was also between the lord of the manor and the inhabitants of the town, but there was no interposition whatever by the Crown: and in the course of that case Mr. Justice Bayley (probably as much acquainted with this subject as any person could be) stated that " as far as the " Crown was concerned, the Crown had no beneficial right in the " soil; it had only a right for the protection of the public:"—which if your Lordship will allow me to call your recollection to what I stated at the commencement of my argument, is just the point upon which I rest. I say the Crown has certain rights on the sea-shore,[3]—the rights of dominion as alleged in the Information—the rights of jurisdiction by the Admiralty courts and by the common law courts,—and the duty to take care of the sea-shore for the purpose of navigation, and for the public use, as far as the public are entitled. To this extent the Crown has rights and duties: —but no beneficial interest—no right of private property—no right to take the fruits of the sea-shore:—which as my learned friend Mr. Bethell most properly put it, would be the case in effect, directly or indirectly, notwithstanding the arrangement which has been made that the Crown shall have its revenue out of the Consolidated Fund, and the hereditary revenues shall be in the administration of the Woods and Forests:—still, directly, or indirectly, this is a claim of private right in the Crown, and to the Crown would go the profits which would be derived by the establishment of this proposition.

In *Scratton* v. *Brown*,[4] the lord of the manor established his right expressly to the shore on the coast of Essex.

[1] Brod. and Bing. 667. And Oxenden *v.* Palmer, M.S., Kent, Herne Bay. The lord of the manor recovered against a surveyor of the roads for taking stones from the shore to mend the roads. And see Jerwood, p. 71.

Speech of Mr. Serjeant Merewether.

My Lord, there is a case of *Benest v. Pipon*, which was tried in Jersey, and eventually brought before the Privy Council, where Lord Wynford gave the judgment. He said " that occupation was " the foundation of most of the rights of property in land," and spoke of " that portion of the shore which was capable of being " usefully occupied;" and he laid down, that " What never has had " an individual owner, belongs to the sovereign in whose kingdom " it is; whatever any sovereign has allowed an individual to possess " or improve, he cannot take away, because he would be taking " from the occupant the value of the labour expended on it." Considering that this claim extends over the whole shore of the kingdom;—and that immense sums have been laid out by parties in improving their property by erections upon the sea-shore, to make it convenient for the purposes of commerce and trade—to require that all those improvements should be put at the mercy of this prerogative of the Crown, is a most formidable doctrine!— particularly when we must remember that much of this property has been made the subject of grants, of marriage settlements, mortgages, and other securities of that kind:—that those arrangements should be interfered with by a principle of this sort, when there are none but modern instances to support such a doctrine, or to show that such a right has ever been exercised, is, I repeat,.an alarming proposition.

These are the observations I have to press upon your Lordship; for with the exception of the case of the river Mersey, and a few cases, comparatively speaking, in the river Humber, where parties, tired of proceedings with the Crown, which never pays costs, consented to take leases at small rents under the Crown—with the exception of those cases, and two within this last year, I believe there is no proof whatever of this prerogative right, extensive as it is alleged to be, ever having been put in force:—and I believe I am fully within compass when I say that these cases are within the last twenty years.

A late friend of mine, Mr. Ward of *West Cowes* in the Isle of Wight, was indicted[1] for a nuisance in the river Medina, on the shore; injuring, as it was said, the navigation: but nobody ever dreamt of claiming the soil from him; no right whatever was set up in the Crown; though at that time (as in the Humber) much attention was given to the asserted regalia of the Crown. One can

Benest v. Pipon.

Modern instances.

West Cowes.

hardly suppose a stronger case than this, in which the Crown did not interfere, if indeed it had really such a title as is alleged.

American case.
There is an American case[1] which would bear upon the subject: but perhaps your Lordship would not think it very material: though the American law is now certainly considered as of some authority in this country.

Portland.
To the island of *Portland* I may also refer, as rather curiously illustrative of the rights of the Crown. I believe it will be found that in that island Her Majesty is the lady of the manor, and in that character she has used the shore, and has made grants of it, and deals with it as belonging to Her Majesty; but in right of the manor, and not of any prerogative.[2]

Duke of Beaufort's Case.
With regard to the case of the *Duke of Beaufort*,[3] to which I was drawing your Lordship's attention, that was an action brought by the Duke of Beaufort against the mayor and corporation of *Swansea*, for a trespass upon what had been theretofore a part of the sea-shore. Ships had from time to time lodged their ballast there; by which means the shore had been so much raised and made fit for occupation, that I believe the corporation had formed public walks or something of that description upon it: but the Duke brought an action against them for trespass, in order to try the right to the soil. The Duke it seemed claimed under some deed from the Earl of Warwick, and produced the grant in Court—the grant was read—it contained only general words—it conveyed the *land*—the *terra* and the lordship of the manor of Gower—and nothing further: and it was contended that this sea-shore was parcel of that manor. Acts of ownership, by his Grace and his predecessors, upon the sea-shore, were shown; and were left to the jury for them to say whether they proved or not that the sea-shore passed under the words "Terra de Gower." A verdict was given for the Duke of Beaufort. The corporation were dissatisfied with that verdict, and they moved in the Court of Exchequer for a new trial. When the rule *Nisi* came on for discussion, the Attorney-General appeared to support the motion for a new trial; and he put the case distinctly upon the ground, that the right to the shore was the prerogative right of the Crown, and that such a prerogative right could not pass out of it but by

---

[1] Martin *v.* Waddell, 16 Peters' U. S. Rep. 369.
[2] See the "Case of Swans" at Abbotsbury, in the same neighbourhood, 7 Rep. 86; also the "History of Weymouth and its Neighbourhood."

express words, which were not to be found in this grant. The learned Judge had directed the jury that in his judgment the grant was not sufficient of itself without explanation to carry the sea-shore; but he said to the jury, " You are to take into your " consideration all the acts of ownership done by the Duke of " Beaufort and his predecessors, and say upon the whole, whether " you are satisfied or not, that the sea-shore did pass under the " grant and was part and parcel of the manor." The jury gave deliberate answers to all the questions put to them, affirming that it did pass under the grant and that it was part of the manor. But the Attorney-General, when he supported the rule, contending that sea-shore was the prerogative right of the Crown, said that the grant could not convey any right to the shore to the Duke of Beaufort, unless it was by express words; so of course the evidence of acts of ownership could not give that effect to the grant; and it was put to him distinctly by Mr. Baron Rolfe, " Then, Mr. Attorney, " why do you refer to the evidence at all? because you say, that " no possible evidence could have such an effect: for your proposi- " tion is, that the prerogative right existing in the Crown cannot " pass out of it without express words." Here the Court, consisting of some of the first lawyers in this country, the Lord Chief Baron, Mr. Baron Parke, Mr. Baron Alderson, and Mr. Baron Rolfe, concurred unanimously in opinion that the direction of the learned Judge was right, and consequently overruled the position of the Attorney-General, that there was any such prerogative right in the Crown.

My Lord, there are other cases which would bear upon the subject, but I will not trouble you with them.

Lord Chancellor.—The Duke of Beaufort's title was not derived directly from the Crown.

Mr. Serjeant Merewether.—No, my Lord.

Mr. Solicitor-General.—Yes, my Lord; the only question in that case was (I do not think it will be very material upon this argument,) but the question in that case really was, whether in the grant which came from the Crown, from the Duchy of Lancaster, the extent of the manor did include this part of the shore which was in the harbour of Swansea.

Mr. Serjeant Merewether.—I think my learned friend is mistaken, in saying that the Duke claimed from the Duchy of Lancaster.

Mr. Solicitor-General.—That was the express question, whether the Crown directly or indirectly, to the Duke of Beaufort, it came from the Crown possessed in its *private right*, and not *jure coronæ*. It was originally in a subject, and being seized by the Crown was afterwards granted to Robert de Brios, from whom the present plaintiff derived his title.

Mr. Solicitor-General.—It is stated in a report by a gentleman at the bar, "This was an action of trespass, tried before Mr. Justice "Vaughan Williams, for certain erections made between high and "low-water mark, alleged to belong to the plaintiff, as passing to "him under the general words in a grant from the Crown of the "Seignory of Gower." The question I believe was, simply, whether the words *cum pertinentibus* included this. It came from the Crown.

Mr. Serjeant Merewether.—Not from the Crown *jure coronæ*. The Crown may derive from me, or from the learned Solicitor-General, property, which it may hold in its *private right*, and then grant out in the same way as any other private individual; but I believe there is no foundation whatever for saying that in that case the ground which the Duke of Beaufort enjoyed was not the right originally of a private individual, and as such, granted from the Crown to the Duke of Beaufort's predecessors. As to the other statement which the learned Solicitor-General has made, as far as I could follow him, it is exactly what I stated, which is, that the question was, whether the shore did pass under the general words or not; and the Attorney-General, pressing his argument, was reminded of *Sir Henry Constable's* case,[1] as being directly contrary to what he urged; which was simply that the prerogative right could not pass without express words. But, said Mr. Baron Parke, "If you are right, Mr. Attorney, Sir Henry Constable's case is "wrong;"—and that case has always been assumed to be an authority.

I therefore submit to your Lordship that this case of the Duke of Beaufort has incidentally decided this point. And if your Lordship will excuse me for one moment, I will just remind you that the nature of my argument has been this:—That up to the period when the Stuarts succeeded to the throne, there is not the slightest pretence or shadow of a case—or document—or record—to show that any such prerogative existed:—that from that period, precedents ought to be taken with the utmost caution :—and I am justified in saying so, by the words of Mr. Baron Wood's judgment[2] in one of those cases to which I referred your Lordship—I say therefore that from that period precedents must be looked at with suspicion;—not but that there might be in those days decisions sound in law—quoted from time to time—acted upon—and dealt with as law:—and which, whatever the times were, would be regarded as authority. —But if you find at such a period only a text author suggesting this doctrine—without any authority quoted for it—the matter loosely mooted—a sort of *obitèr* argument by the counsel on the one side and the other,—followed up by such a case as the one I have referred to [1]—not finding that case afterwards quoted except to be repudiated, by the statement that it was contrary to Constable's case—charters granted by the Crown at that same time, pretending to deal with the shore (there was that of the De Wandesfords, to which I have alluded, and one also relating to part of the shore of Dorset, both however held to be void)—how this doctrine, now revived, can be supported merely upon the authority of text authors, and the *obitèr dicta* of learned Judges, misled by the treatise published under the name of Lord Hale, but not I think rightly so, I must confess I am at a great loss to understand. I believe my learned friends will in vain look through all our books upon the law for a single case which will support this doctrine. I challenge my learned friends to that point:—and when it is remembered that it was the Attorney-General himself who argued the case of the Duke of Beaufort,—and we know all his assiduity, his intelligence and his zeal,—we may be quite sure that he would not have passed by the opportunity of quoting any authority upon the point, if he could with his numerous assistants have found one. The only authority referred to was the case of Sir Henry Constable, which, he was reminded, was directly against him.

With the thorough conviction therefore that *there is no ground in Law for this prerogative right*, I close the argument which I have addressed to your Lordship, to prove that *this right cannot be maintained;* and consequently that we ought not to be required further to answer the Crown on this point :—for *the Crown having no title in itself*, cannot as a *stranger* to this matter *call upon the Defendants to discover the evidence of theirs.*

dents revived in this reign; or if they do take a temporary root, they will soon be eradicated.—Per Wood, B. in the case of the Attorney-General of the Prince of Wales *v.* Sir St. Aubyn."—Wightwick's Rep. 187.

[1] Philpot's Case, 8 Car. I. See before, p. xcv.

COPIES OF FORMS IN COMMON USE AT THE BOARD OF TRADE

RELATIVE TO THE RIGHTS AND INTERESTS OF THE CROWN IN THE SHORES AND BED OF THE SEA.

HE following is the form upon which any works or encroachments, or other interferences with the foreshore or bed of the sea or tidal rivers, are reported to the Board of Trade, by officers of Coast Guard and of Customs.

Division,
187 .

Sir,
WITH reference to instructions received by me from the Commodore Controller General of the Coast Guard, by circular dated   , I beg to forward upon the other side the particulars of a
at   within this Division.

I am,

Sir,

Your obedient Servant,

Inspecting Commander,

To the Secretary,   Division.

Appendix.

COAST GUARD   DIVISION

RETURN AS TO WORKS OR ENCROACHMENTS ON, OR OTHER INTERFERENCES WITH, FORESHORE OR BED OF THE SEA.

Nature and Description of Ownership or Encroachment.	Position of Foreshore, as near as it can be described.	Name and Address of Person or Persons exercising or claiming or making the Act of Ownership, or making the Encroachment (as the Case may be).	Is the Act done by virtue of a Claim of a Proprietary Title, or not? If not, by what Authority?	† Does the Act or Encroachment interfere with any Rights hitherto enjoyed by the Public? If so, describe them.	If it does not so interfere at present, is it likely hereafter to interfere with any such Rights? If so, state Particulars.	Will the Work be likely to prove injurious to Navigation, &c.

† Whether docks, walls, piers, drains, embankments, reclamation of land, or other description of works, laying telegraphic cables, shingle, ballast, seaweed, or other material from the foreshore, such as bathing or walking on the beach or foreshore, boating, landing, fishing, &c., or the like.

Any additional remarks or information within the knowledge of the person making this Return.

Signature ———————

Note.—If the person making this return has the means, a plan or tracing of the ground, showing as distinctly as possible the portion of foreshore affected, should be forwarded at the same time to the Board of Trade, or if this cannot easily be done, the Board of Trade should be asked whether they desire a plan, and if so, how it should be made.

Forms in use at the Board of Trade.

The following are the forms in common use by the Board of Trade in dealing with ordinary applications for the rights and interests of the Crown in the foreshore or bed of the sea or tidal rivers. The varying circumstances of different cases, however, render alterations and omissions frequently necessary.

(1.) Upon an application being received, the following communications are addressed:
    (*a.*) To the applicant.
    (*b.*) The officer commanding the nearest Coast Guard Division, or, if there is no Coast Guard, to an officer of Customs.

(*a.*) *To the Applicant.*

Board of Trade (Harbour Department),
Whitehall Gardens, S.W., 187 .

I AM directed by the Board of Trade to acknowledge your letter of the   proposing
a certain portion of the foreshore
and in reply, I am directed to acquaint you, that before entering upon the consideration of your proposal, this Board desire to be informed,

1. What is the use contemplated to be made of the soil of the shore proposed to be   by

2. What use is at present, or has been hitherto, made of the shore in question, either by fishermen, boatmen, or the public generally? Whether the shore is now, or has been hitherto, used by the public for walking, bathing, boating, landing, fishing, gathering seaweed, &c., or for any other purpose?

3. If any of the public have used or enjoyed, or do use or enjoy, the shore in question for any of the above-named purposes, whether the use of the shore contemplated by
                    will interfere with or abridge any, and which, of such uses or enjoyments?

4. What are the names and addresses of both the owners and occupiers of the land adjacent to the shore in question?

I am to add, that it is not the desire of the Board of Trade to

cxii   *Appendix.*

prevent any useful work, but simply to see that the public rights are not interfered with.

I am, &c.

Assistant Secretary.

To

(*b.*) *To the Officer commanding the nearest Coast Guard Division.*

Board of Trade (Harbour Department),
Sir,   Whitehall, S.W.,   187 .

I AM directed by the Board of Trade to acquaint you that, by "The Crown Lands Act, 1866," the management of the Crown's rights and interests in the foreshore has been transferred from the Office of Woods to the Board of Trade.

An application has been made to the Board by   for the   of a portion of the foreshore   as shown on the accompanying plan.

I am to request that you will ascertain and report, for the information of this Board :—

1. What use is at present, or has hitherto been, made of the shore in question, either by fishermen, boatmen, or the public generally, and whether the shore is now, or has been hitherto, used by the public for walking, bathing, boating, landing, fishing, gathering seaweed, &c., or for any other purpose?

2. Whether the   of the foreshore in question will, in your opinion, interfere with or abridge the exercise of any rights or privileges now or hitherto enjoyed by the public thereon, or with any use thereof which is now or has hitherto been made by anyone for any of the purposes before mentioned?

3. The names and addresses of both the owners and the occupiers of the land adjacent to the shore in question.

The Board desire also to be informed, in the event of their proceeding with this application, what are the most advantageous places at which, and what are the best means by which, public notice of their intention should be given, in order that the popula-

Forms in use at the Board of Trade.

hitherto been accustomed to make any use of the shore, may not, without their knowledge, be deprived of any rights to which they are properly entitled.

Any additional information with regard to the application may be added to your report.

I am, &c.
(signed)
To the Inspecting Commander   Assistant Secretary.
of the Coast Guard.

(2.) When the names of the owners and occupiers of the land adjacent to the shore in respect of which the application is made are known, the following communication is addressed to each of them. If the shore is in a harbour, a similar communication is forwarded to the Harbour authority.

Board of Trade (Harbour Department),
Whitehall Gardens, S.W.,   187 .

I AM directed by the Board of Trade to acquaint you that an application has been made to them by
for a   of the rights and interests of the Crown in a certain portion of the foreshore of
and, as the Board are informed that some of the adjacent land is   by
, I am to request that you will have the goodness to favour them with any observations which
may have to offer on the application.

I am, &c.

Assistant Secretary.
To

(3.) If the case is proceeded with and is considered to be one in which a survey may be dispensed with, the following communication is addressed to the applicant. This form applies to a lease; if a grant is proposed to be made, the requisite alteration is made in the letter.

Board of Trade (Harbour Department),
Whitehall Gardens,   187 .

Appendix.

the approval of the Board of Trade to the plans for proposed   at

I am directed by the Board to acquaint you that there is no objection to the plans, but that the Board are unable to give their formal assent thereto, without further communication with

By the Crown Lands Act, 1866 (29 & 30 Vict. cap. 62), the management of the rights and interests of the Crown in the foreshore and bed of the sea has been transferred from the Office of Woods to the Board of Trade, and consequently any application or negotiation for the purchase or lease of such rights and interests in the land which may be affected by the construction of the   in question, must now be made to or with this Board.

It appears to the Board of Trade that the construction of the   in question is a case in which the necessity and expense of a survey may, in pursuance of the 62nd section of the 10 Geo. 4, cap. 50, be dispensed with, and I am therefore directed to inform you that this Board, on the part of the Crown, are prepared to grant   a lease of the foreshore and bed of the sea, upon which the proposed   is to be erected, upon the terms specified below. The lease will contain clauses or covenants on the part of the lessee similar to such of the sections of "The Railways Clauses Act, 1863," sects 13-19, as are applicable to the case of the   now proposed to be constructed, and will also contain such other clauses or covenants as the Board may consider necessary for the purpose of reserving for the public rights of walking, bathing, boating, landing, fishing, &c.

All the expenses of and incidental to this arrangement will have to be paid by

Upon receiving from you an acceptance of these proposals, the plans will be forwarded to you inscribed with the assent of the Board of Trade, without waiting for the formal completion and execution of the lease.

I am, &c.

Assistant Secretary.

PROPOSED TERMS OF LEASE.

Term   .   .   .   .   years.
Annual Rent   .   .   £

Forms in use at the Board of Trade.

(4.) If the case is proceeded with, and is considered to be one in which a survey should be made, the applicant is addressed as follows:—

Board of Trade (Harbour Department),
Whitehall Gardens, S.W., 187

WITH reference to your letter of the ,
applying for the approval of the Board of Trade to the plans for proposed   at
 I am directed by the Board to acquaint you that there is no objection to the plans, but that they are unable to give their formal assent thereto, without further communication with

By the Crown Lands Act, 1866 (29 & 30 Vict. c. 62), the management of the rights and interests of the Crown in the foreshore and bed of the sea has been transferred from the Office of Woods to the Board of Trade, and consequently any application or negotiation for the purchase or lease of such rights and interests in the land which may be affected by the construction of the
            in question, must now be made to or with this Board.

Conveyances and leases of foreshore, made by this Board, will contain covenants or clauses, similar to such of the sections of " The Railways Clauses Act, 1863," sects. 13-19, as are applicable to the case of the   now proposed to be constructed, and also such other covenants and clauses as this Board may consider necessary for the purpose of reserving for the public rights of walking, bathing, boating, landing, fishing, &c., and other similar rights.

On hearing from you that
  are prepared to make compensation to this Board on the part of the Crown, by taking either a conveyance or a lease of the interest of the Crown in the land in question, upon the conditions above mentioned, the Board of Trade will direct a valuation to be made for the purpose of adjusting the purchase money or rent, as the case may be, and the plans will be forwarded to you, inscribed with the assent of this Board, without waiting for the formal completion of the

All the expenses of and incidental to this arrangement will have to be paid by

I am, &c.
Assistant Secretary.

Appendix.

(5.) The following are the forms in which grants and leases of the rights and interests of the Crown in foreshore, &c. are usually made by the Board of Trade. They have been prepared with a view of embracing all points which may arise; it consequently is seldom that every clause is applicable to the case under consideration, and omissions or additions (as the case may be), are then made.

(a.) *Common Form of Grant.*

This Indenture, made the   day of
18   between the Queen's Most Excellent Majesty of the first part, the Board of Trade acting in exercise of such of the powers conferred by the Acts 10 Geo 4, c. 50, and 15 & 16 of Her Majesty, c. 62, or any other Act, as were transferred to the Board of Trade by "The Crown Lands Act, 1866," of the second part, and

                                      hereinafter called the grantee   , of the third part, witnesseth, that in consideration of the sum of
                               by the grantee   paid to the Accountant of the Board of Trade, the receipt whereof is hereby acknowledged, the Board of Trade, on behalf of Her Majesty, and with the consent of the Commissioners of Her Majesty's Treasury, signified by their warrant, dated the   day of   18 , do by these presents grant unto the grantee   and [his or her] heirs all that piece of land being part of the fore-shore and bed of the   below high-water mark situate opposite to   in the parish of   in the county of
            and extending   which said premises hereby granted are intended to be delineated in the plan annexed to these presents, and to be therein coloured

Except, nevertheless, and always reserving to the Queen's Majesty, Her heirs and successors, out of this present grant, full and free right for Her and them, and for all persons by Her or their permission (which permission shall be assumed to have been granted unless the contrary be shown), to ride, drive, walk, or otherwise pass to and fro over, and to fish and bathe upon, and to gather seaweed and ware from the premises hereby granted, and to land thereon goods and passengers from vessels and boats, and to embark therefrom goods and passengers in vessels and boats, but so that erections or works constructed or placed on the said premises,

Forms in use at the Board of Trade. cxvii

vided, shall not be prejudiced or interfered with by reason of the aforesaid exception and reservation.

And also except and always reserving as aforesaid all rights of way and access to and over the premises now existing by means of any public road, footpath, bridge, or other means, or by means of any road, footpath, or bridge shown on the said plan hereto annexed, as made or intended to be made.

And also except and reserving to the Queen's Majesty, Her heirs and successors, and to the Board of Trade, and any other body or person duly authorised in right of the Queen's Majesty, Her heirs and successors, full right to enter on the premises hereby granted, and remove therefrom all buildings, works, or erections which may have become dilapidated or abandoned, or which may have been constructed without the consent or approval hereby required thereto, or which may, in the opinion of the Board of Trade, be injurious to navigation or the public interest, and to restore the site to the former or proper condition thereof, and to erect or construct any buildings or works which may, in the opinion of the Board of Trade, be required for the purpose of navigation or the public interest.

To have and to hold the premises hereby granted unto and to the use of the grantee , [his or her] assigns for ever.

Yielding and paying unto the Queen's Majesty, Her heirs and successors, the yearly rent of one shilling on the first day of January in every year, if demanded.

And the grantee doth hereby for himself or herself [his or her] heirs and assigns, covenant with the Queen's Majesty, Her heirs and successors, in manner following; that is to say, that the grantee , [his or her] heirs and assigns, will not, without the consent in writing of the Board of Trade first obtained, erect or place on the premises hereby granted any building or work. And also will, in case the Board of Trade shall consent to any building or work being erected or placed on the premises hereby granted, erect, place, or construct the same according to such plan and under such restrictions and regulations as may be approved of in writing by the Board of Trade, and not otherwise.

And also will not, in case any such building or work shall have been so erected or placed on the premises hereby granted, at any time alter or extend the same without the like consent and approval of the Board of Trade having been first obtained.

And also will not, without the consent in writing of the Board of

premises hereby granted, which may, in the opinion of the Board of Trade, prejudice or obstruct navigation, or be or become injurious to the public interest.

And also will at all times keep the premises in a good and proper state of repair, and in proper condition, free from all defects injurious to navigation or the adjacent lands or the public interest.

And also will, during the whole time of constructing, altering, or extending any work upon the premises hereby granted, exhibit and keep burning every night from sunset to sunrise such lights (if any) as the Board of Trade shall from time to time require.

And also that it shall be lawful for the Queen's Majesty, Her heirs and successors, and the Board of Trade, and any persons duly authorised by Her or them, from time to time and at all reasonable times to enter into and upon and inspect the premises hereby granted, and the state and condition thereof, and of any want of repair or of any defect to give notice, and to place such notice in some conspicuous position upon the said premises, and that the grantee , [his or her] heirs or assigns, will, on receipt of any such notice, or upon any such notice being placed in some conspicuous position on the premises hereby granted, forthwith, and within three calendar months from the giving or placing of such notice, restore the premises hereby granted to a proper state and condition, and substantially and properly execute the repairs and amendments, and remove the defects specified in such notice.

And also that it shall be lawful for the Queen's Majesty, Her heirs or successors, and the Board of Trade, and any persons duly authorised as aforesaid, at any time to enter upon the premises hereby granted, and to remove therefrom and abate all buildings, works, or materials, which may have become dilapidated or abandoned, or which may have been constructed without the consent or approval hereby required thereto, or which may, in the opinion of the Board of Trade, be injurious to navigation or the public interest, and to restore the site to the former or proper condition thereof, and to erect or construct any buildings or works which, in the opinion of the Board of Trade, may be required for the purpose of navigation or the public interest.

And also will pay to the Queen's Majesty, Her heirs or successors, all expenses incurred by the Queen's Majesty, Her heirs or successors, or the Board of Trade, or any persons duly authorised as aforesaid, of and incidental to a survey of the premises hereby granted,

Forms in use at the Board of Trade. cxix

or of or incidental to any consent or approval hereby required to be given thereto, or which may be incurred in removing buildings, works, or materials which may have become dilapidated or been abandoned, or which may have been constructed without the consent or approval hereby required, or which may, in the opinion of the Board of Trade, be injurious to navigation or the public interest, and all other expenses incurred in restoring the premises hereby granted to the former or proper condition thereof.

And also will not in any way hinder or obstruct the due exercise and enjoyment of any other right or privilege excepted and reserved out of the grant hereby made.

And also will duly observe and perform all the stipulations and provisions contained in the Schedule hereto.

Provided always, that if the rent hereby reserved shall be unpaid for the space of 21 days after the same shall have become due and been legally demanded, or in case default shall be made in observance or performance of any covenant or provision herein contained, and on the part of the grantee ,[his or her] heirs or assigns, to be observed and performed, then and in either of such cases, or in case the works authorised by the   Act are not completed within the time fixed by the said Act, it shall be lawful for the Queen's Majesty, Her heirs or successors, into and upon the premises hereby granted, or any part thereof in the name of the whole, to re-enter, and to put an end to the grant hereby made, and thereupon the grant hereby made shall become void accordingly, without prejudice to any remedy of the Queen's Majesty, Her heirs and successors, under any covenant by the said grantee herein contained.

Provided also, and it is hereby agreed and declared, that if the Queen's Majesty, Her heirs or successors, or the Board of Trade, shall at any time be desirous of purchasing the premises hereby granted, then the grantee ,[his or her] heirs or assigns, shall sell the same to the Queen's Majesty, Her heirs or successors, at such price as shall be agreed upon, or if not agreed upon, as shall be ascertained by arbitration under the provisions of "The Lands Clauses Consolidation Act, 1845," with respect to the purchase of lands otherwise than by agreement, and on payment of the purchase money so ascertained the premises shall be reconveyed to the Queen's Majesty, Her heirs or successors.

Provided also, that this deed shall be deemed sufficiently enrolled

Records and Enrolments, and the filing or making an entry of such deposit by the Keeper of the said Records and Enrolments.

In witness whereof one of the secretaries or assistant secretaries of the Board of Trade and the grantee   have hereunto set their respective hands and seals, the day and year first above written.

   Signed, sealed, and delivered by   in the presence of

   Signed, sealed, and delivered by the above-named grantee in the presence of

    Received from the above-named grantee   the amount
    of the consideration money above mentioned . .   } £

    The SCHEDULE above referred to.

(*b.*) *Common Form of Lease.*

THIS Indenture, made the day of 18   between the Queen's Most Excellent Majesty of the first part, the Board of Trade acting in exercise of such of the powers conferred by the Acts 10 Geo. 4, c. 50, and 15th & 16th of Her Majesty, c. 62, or any other Act, as were transferred to the Board of Trade by "The Crown Lands Act, 1866," of the second part, and
           hereinafter called the lessee , of the third part, witnesseth that the Board of Trade on behalf of Her Majesty, and with the consent of the Commissioners of Her Majesty's Treasury, signified by their warrant, dated the
day of   18 , do by these presents grant and demise unto the lessee   all that piece of land being part of the foreshore and bed of the below high-water mark situate opposite to
   in the parish of   in the county of
and extending   which said premises hereby demised are intended to be delineated in the plan annexed to these presents and to be therein coloured .

Except, nevertheless, and always reserving to the Queen's Majesty, Her heirs and successors, out of this present grant and demise, full and free right for her and them, and for all persons by Her or their permission (which permission shall be assumed to have been granted unless the contrary be shown) to ride, drive, walk, or otherwise pass to and fro over, and to fish and bathe upon, and to gather seaweed

Forms in use at the Board of Trade. cxxi

or ware from the demised premises, and to land thereon goods and passengers from vessels and boats, and to embark therefrom goods and passengers in vessels and boats, but so that erections or works constructed or placed on the demised premises, with the consent and approval of the Board of Trade, as hereby provided, shall not be prejudiced or interfered with by reason of the aforesaid exception and reservation.

And also except and always reserving as aforesaid all rights of way and access to or over the demised premises now existing by means of any public road, footpath, bridge, or other means, or by means of any road, footpath, or bridge shown on the said plan hereto annexed, as made or intended to be made.

And also except and always reserving to the Queen's Majesty, Her heirs and successors, and to the Board of Trade, and any other body or person duly authorised in right of the Queen's Majesty, Her heirs or successors, full right to enter on the said demised premises, and remove therefrom all buildings, works, or erections which may have become dilapidated or abandoned, or which may have been constructed without the consent or approval hereby required thereto, or which may, in the opinion of the Board of Trade, be injurious to navigation or the public interest, and to restore the site to the former or proper condition thereof, and to erect or construct any buildings or works which may, in the opinion of the Board of Trade, be required for the purpose of navigation or the public interest.

To have and to hold the said hereby demised premises unto the lessee , [his or her] executors, administrators, and assigns, for the term of   years from the   day of   18 , yielding and paying therefor, during the said term unto the Queen's Majesty, Her heirs and successors, the yearly rent of   pounds, to be paid to the accountant for the time being of the Board of Trade at the office of the Board of Trade in London by equal half-yearly payments on the   day of   and the   day of   in every year, free from all deductions on account of present or future landlords' or tenants' taxes, rates, charges, or impositions, except landlords' property tax, the first half-yearly payment to be made on the   day of   18 , and the payment of the rent for the last half-year of the said term to be made on the   day of   next preceding the expiration of the said term.

And the lessee doth hereby, for [his or her] heirs, executors, and administrators, covenant with the Queen's Majesty, Her heirs and

[his or her] executors, administrators, and assigns, will duly pay the yearly rent hereby reserved, at the times and in manner hereby provided.

And also will pay the land tax, and all other present and future landlords' and tenants' taxes, rates, charges, and impositions, except landlords' property tax, payable in respect of the demised premises, or by the landlord or tenant on account thereof.

And also will not, without the consent in writing of the Board of Trade first obtained, erect or place on the demised premises any building or work.

And also will in case the Board of Trade shall consent to any building or work being erected or placed on the demised premises, erect, place, and construct the same according to such plan and under such restrictions and regulations as may be approved of in writing by the Board of Trade, and not otherwise.

And also will not, in case any such building or work shall have been so erected or placed on the demised premises, at any time alter or extend the same without the like consent and approval of the Board of Trade having been first obtained.

And also will not, without the consent in writing of the Board of Trade first obtained, place any materials, or do any other act on the demised premises which may, in the opinion of the Board of Trade, prejudice or obstruct or tend to prejudice or obstruct navigation, or be or become injurious to the public interest.

And also will not commit or suffer any waste, spoil, or destruction on the demised premises.

And also will, at all times during the term hereby granted, keep the demised premises in a good and proper state of repair, and in proper condition, free from all defects injurious to navigation or the adjacent lands or the public interest.

And also will, during the whole time of constructing, altering, or extending any work upon the demised premises, exhibit and keep burning every night from sunset to sunrise such lights (if any) as the Board of Trade shall from time to time require.

And also that it shall be lawful for the Queen's Majesty, Her heirs and successors, and the Board of Trade, and any persons duly authorised by Her or them, from time to time and at all reasonable times, to enter into and upon and inspect the demised premises and the state and condition thereof, and of any want of repair or of any defect to give notice and to place such notice in some conspicuous

Forms in use at the Board of Trade. cxxiii

executors, administrators, or assigns, will, on receipt of any such notice, or upon any such notice being placed in some conspicuous position upon the demised premises forthwith and within three calendar months from the giving or placing of such notice restore the demised premises to a proper state and condition, and substantially and properly and to the satisfaction of the Board of Trade, execute the repairs and amendments, and remove the defects specified in such notice.

And also that it shall be lawful for the Queen's Majesty, Her heirs or successors, and the Board of Trade, and any persons duly authorised as aforesaid, at any time to enter upon the demised premises and to remove therefrom and abate all buildings, works, or materials which may have become dilapidated or abandoned, or which may have been constructed without the consent or approval hereby required thereto or which may, in the opinion of the Board of Trade, be injurious to navigation or the public interest, and to restore the site to the former or proper condition thereof, and to erect or construct any buildings or works which, in the opinion of the Board of Trade, may be required for the purpose of navigation or the public interest.

And also will pay to the Queen's Majesty, Her heirs or successors, all expenses incurred by the Queen's Majesty, Her heirs or successors, or the Board of Trade, or any persons duly authorised as aforesaid, of and incidental to a survey of the demised premises preparatory to the erection or construction of buildings or works, or of or incidental to any consent or approval hereby required to be given thereto or which may be incurred in removing buildings, works, or materials which may have become dilapidated or been abandoned, or which may have been constructed without the consent or approval hereby required, or which may, in the opinion of the Board of Trade, be injurious to navigation or the public interest, and all other expenses incurred in restoring the demised premises to the former or proper condition thereof.

And also will not in any way hinder or obstruct the due exercise and enjoyment of any other right or privilege excepted and reserved out of the demise hereby made.

And also will not assign or underlet the demised premises or any part thereof, without the consent in writing of the Board of Trade first obtained.

And also will cause all assignments of the demised premises or bates and letters of administration affecting the same premises, to be, within six calendar months after the date thereof, entered and enrolled in the Office of Land Revenue Records and Enrolments.

And also will duly observe and perform all the stipulations and provisions contained in the Schedule hereto.

And also will, at the expiration or other sooner determination of the term hereby granted, deliver up the demised premises to the Queen's Majesty, Her heirs or successors, in good and substantial repair and proper condition, having regard to the erections and works to be authorised pursuant to the provisions of these presents.

Provided always, that if the rent hereby reserved shall be unpaid for 21 days after any day hereby appointed for payment thereof, whether legally demanded or not, or in case default shall be made in observance or performance of any covenant or provision herein contained, and on the part of the lessee , [his or her] executors, administrators, or assigns, to be observed and performed, or if any act shall be done or suffered, whereby the demised premises or any part thereof shall, without the assent of the Board of Trade first obtained, become vested in any person other than the lessee , or other than any of the following persons, namely, an assignee becoming such with such assent as aforesaid, or an executor, or administrator, or legatee of the lessee , or of any such assignee, then the term hereby granted shall cease without prejudice to any remedy of the Queen's Majesty, Her heirs or successors, under any covenant by the said lessee herein contained.

Provided also, and it is hereby agreed and declared, that if the Queen's Majesty, Her heirs or successors, or the Board of Trade, shall at any time be desirous of purchasing the demised premises for all the residue of the term hereby granted, then the lessee , [his or her] executors, administrators, or assigns, shall sell the same to the Queen's Majesty, Her heirs or successors, at such price as shall be agreed upon, or if not agreed upon as shall be ascertained by arbitration under the provisions of "The Lands Clauses Consolidation Act, 1845," with respect to the purchase of lands otherwise than by agreement, and on payment of the purchase money so ascertained, the demised premises shall be surrendered to the Queen's Majesty, Her heirs or successors, to the intent that the term hereby granted may merge and be extinguished.

Provided always, that this deed shall be deemed sufficiently enrolled by the deposit of a duplicate thereof in the Office of Land

Forms in use at the Board of Trade.

entry of such deposit by the Keeper of the said Records and Enrolments.

In witness whereof, one of the secretaries or assistant secretaries of the Board of Trade and the lessee have hereunto set their respective hands and seals the day and year first above written.

Signed, sealed, and delivered by

Signed, sealed, and delivered by the above-named lessee in the presence of

The SCHEDULE above referred to.

INDEX.

₊ *The references in Roman numerals are to pages in the Appendix.*

	Page
ABBOT of Benedict Hulm, Case of	57, xvii, lxxxiii
of Ramsey, Case of	118, xxvi, lxxxvii
of Peterborough, Case of	119, xxvi, lxxxvi
of St. Austin's, Case of	xi, lxxxvi
of Tichfend, Case of	xviii, lxxxi

ABRIDGMENTS, &c., on Crown's Right to the Shore, cited by Mr. Serjeant Merewether:—
Bacon xcix
Comyns xcix
Fitzherbert . . . . lxxxii, lxxxix
Rolle xcix
Statham . . . . lxxxii, lxxxix
Viner xcix
ACTS OF OWNERSHIP, continuous, may show the shore to be
 parcel of a manor. [See "Ownership."] 15
 may raise presumption of lost grant 15
 in one part of a bank no evidence of ownership of a particular
 spot 101
ADVERSE POSSESSION, title by 22, 23, 24
 may be confirmed by statute law but not by prescriptive rights
 to wreck, &c. 39
AGRICULTURE, advantages to, from a right to dig for manures on
 the shore 211, 216
ALIENATION OF CROWN LANDS, prohibited 106
ALLUVION, defined . . . . . 108, 109, xi, xxv
 belongs to the owner of the adjacent *terra firma* . . 111, xxvi
 as to the ownership when it is produced by artificial causes 111
 what ownership of adjacent soil entitles to it . . . 112
 as copyhold 113
 as freehold 113

	Page
ALLUVION (*continued*)—	
the lord's right	113, 114
as to the lord's claim when the alluvion is waste	114
same as imperceptible derelictions	114, 126
title to, whether it lie in custom or prescription	118, 120, xii, xxvii
distinguished from " derelict land "	125
meaning of imperceptible	126, 127
Crown hath title to sudden increase	126, 129, xi, xxvi
is not by sudden accession	130, xxvii
AMERICA, when rivers navigable in	4
to whom the shore belongs	13
grants from the State construed strictly	21
as to obstructions in rivers	44
several fishery	48
navigation	48
law of, as to alluvion	111
law of, as to islands	141
law of, as to banks	163
public right to take shell fish on the shore	186
public right to dig for shell fish on the shore	186
profits à prendre	197, 202, 203
ANALOGY, in the evidences of title to the sea-shore, and to inland estate	32
between profits à prendre in inland wastes and in the sea shore	195
ANCHORAGE, in a grant may pass the shore	18
right to anchor a necessary part of right to navigate	43
evidence of mere immemorial usage will not support a claim of dues for	43
ANCIENT GRANTS, from the king	6, 14
when they may be presumed	15
APPENDANT AND APPURTENANT, prescription concerns things	34
land cannot be to land	34
an exclusive right of fishing for oysters may	35
" several " fishery to manors	49
" several " fishery cannot be to a "several" pasture	50
fishing in the sea being a matter of common right, a prescription for it as appurtenant to a particular township is void	174
AQUA, what passes by the word	147
ARMS OF THE SEA, their limits. (See also " Sea" and " Shore.")	3, vii, ix
king's title therein	3, vii, ix, xiv, lxiv
extent and nature	3, 4, 5, vii

ARMS OF THE SEA (*continued*)—
public right of fishing in 3, 41, 42, 46
public right of navigation in 42, 43
when owned by a subject does not change its ownership if
 left derelict or dry . . . 129, 134, 142, xii, xxix, xxxi
ATTORNEY-GENERAL *v.* LONDON, Mayor and Corporation of,
 case of lxix
AUTHENTICITY OF "DE JURE MARIS" . . . 5, lxxv, xcix

BANK, shore may pass under the term of 18
distinguished from shore 162
definition of, in America 163
definition of, in England 9, 163
text of Bracton on the subject 163
right of way over 173
right to land upon 174
right of way along, above high-water mark 175
towage of boats along 176, 215
on the right of fishermen to drag their boats upon . . 176
the practice of drying nets upon 176
BANNE RIVER, case of . . . . . 20, 41, 65, v, xciv
BARON OF BARCLAY'S CASE . . . . . . 84, xiii, xxxii
BATHING, as to the public right of, on the shore 156
decision that the public have no common law right . . 157
silence in the books as to the right of 158
antiquity and universality of custom of . . . 159, 169
distinction between the custom as claimed in respect of the
 sea and inland waters 160
Bracton's text favouring the right 161
custom of bathing preceded law both of England and Rome 165
opinion of the Court in Blundell *v.* Caterall as to bathing in
 machines 170, 183
as to its inconsistency with private rights 171
a several fishery may exclude the right to bathe where the
 bathing would injure the several fishery 172
right to bathe is a mere right of way into the sea . . 181
right to bathe will not occasion other more beneficial uses to
 be put down as nuisances 181
national advantage of 182
as to its being a local, and not general custom . . . 183
distinction between, from the shore and in machines . . 183
as to the profits derived from 184
the supposed advantage of subjecting bathing to the regula-

Index.

	Page
BEACH, when materials must not be taken from to repair highways	198
equity will restrain removal of materials from	198
BLACKSTONE, opinion of, on Crown's right to the shore	xcix
opinion of, on royal fish	80
opinion of, on alluvion	109, 111
BOARD OF TRADE, the management of Crown's rights by	4, 5
power of, to sell, lease, or otherwise deal with Crown property	5
power of, to protect the shore	46
forms used by	cix—cxxv
BOATS, the right to land on shore from	174
to drag vessels above the reach of the tides	174, 176
BOUNDARIES OF THE SEA-SHORE	9, 10, 13, l, lxiv
Callis's opinion on	9
evidence of, in titles	38, 89, 99
BRACTON, doctrine of, on Crown's right to the sea-shore	lxxvii
doctrine of, on ownership of shore	105
doctrine of, on alluvion	110
doctrine of, on derelictions	110
doctrine of, on islands arising in the sea	141, xxxv
text of, favouring the right of bathing	161
text of, bearing on distinction between the bank and the shore	163
doctrine of, on *communis usus littorum*	161 *et seq.*
BRITISH SEAS AND ARMS OF THE SEA, the limits of	1, vii, ix
of the king's title therein	2, vii, ix
include the sea and the land covered by it	2
extent and nature	2, 3, vii
of the title which subjects may have therein	3, 6, 14, xiv
king's title to land under the sea	6
if a portion be granted by the Crown to a subject, it does not change its ownership if left dry	7, 142, xii, xv, xxix, xxxi
BUTLER'S DOCTRINE, as to prescription giving a title to the sea-shore	26
notes to Co. Lit. cited by Mr. Serjeant Merewether	c
as to the proofs of title to the ownership of the sea-shore considered	31
CALLIS, on grants by the king of land, sea-covered	7
on custom and prescription	7
on tides	11
on the shore	13
Mr. Serjeant Merewether on	xcv
CHARTERS, Saxon, quoted by Mr. Serjeant Merewether	lxxi, lxxiii

Index. cxxxi

	Page
CIVIL LAW, doctrine of, as to the ownership of the sea and sea-shore	104

coincidence of, with the Common law, in some rights in the
shore 164, 165
Bracton's text compared with 164, 165
CONSERVATORS, concerning, and waterbailiffs . . . xx, xxi
CONSTABLE, Sir Henry, case of . . . . 15, xxiv, xli, xciii
CONSTABLE, Sir John, case of xciii
COPYHOLDER, his title to the alluvion of the shore when next his
tenement 113
his title to the alluvion of the shore as part of the wastes . 113
his right in respect of his tenement 113
as to the lord's right as opposed to that of the . . . 113
CORNWALL, right of inhabitants to dig sand on the shore 94 *et seq.*
207, xxiv
CREEKS, title to. (See also "Arms of the sea," "British seas")'. 3
CROWN, title of, to the sea and sea-shore . 1-6, vii, ix, x, xv, lxiv
to navigable rivers 3-4
rights of, managed by Board of Trade 4, 5, 46
rights of, forms used by Board of Trade in dealing with cix-cxxv
grants by, of portions of land, sea-covered . . 6, xii, xv, xxxi
grants by, of sea-shore . . . . . 14, 15, 17, xiv, xv
grants construed strictly 20, 21, 65, 103, 106
title of, to shore is by the Common law 39
whether right of fishing is originally lodged in . . 42, vii
title of, to wreck . . . . . . 44, 80, xxxvi, lxiv
grant of shore by, and no more words will not pass wreck, &c. 82
title of, to shore ought to be preserved on grounds of public
policy 104
alienation of lands by, prohibited 106, 220
title of, to derelict land . . . . . 115, 129, xxvii
title of, to lakes and marshes 115
title of, to islands arising *de novo* . . . . . 140, xxxv
Bracton's doctrine . . . . 141, xxxv
CUSTOM, of one manor not evidence of custom of another . . 89
to dig sand, &c. See "Prescription" . . 93, 94, 207, xxiv
is a good one 93
whether evidence of title to shore 93
whether title to alluvion lies in . . . 118, 120, xii, xxvi
whether title to derelict land lies in . . 131, 142, xi, xxviii
whether if a man has a port by, that will carry the soil . . 137
cannot entitle to derelict lands . . . 104, 132, 142, xxix
of bathing, its antiquity and universality 159
of bathing in the sea and inland rivers 160
of bathing preceded the law both of England and Rome . 165

cxxxii   *Index.*

	Page
CUSTOM (*continued*)—	
of bathing immemorial	169
of bathing too general to be construed a local	182
manorial, local not general	195
for all the inhabitants to fish is bad	196
for all the inhabitants to take shingle	197, 198
to dig shells, how it must be prescribed for as a local	203
whether as a local, the digging of shells, &c. can be prescribed for by inhabitants	204
whether it is of common right	206
is general throughout maritime countries	207
importance of to agriculture, and the general interests of the realm	211
coeval with the culture of land	212
and as general	212
support of, desirable on grounds of public utility	216
DE JURE MARIS. Appendix I., authenticity of, questioned by Mr. Serjeant Merewether	5, lxxv, xcix
by Mr. Phear	5
by Mr. Houck	5
"DE PRÆROGATIVO REGIS," 17 Ed. II., quoted by Mr. Serjeant Merewether	lxxxiv
DERELICT LAND, defined. See "Alluvion"	108, 115, xi, xxvii
"imperceptible," same as alluvion, goes to the owner of the adjacent soil	110, 111, 115, 127
title to	111, 115, 117, 126, xi
whether imperceptible or not a question for a jury	115
distinguished from alluvion	125
meaning of the word "imperceptible"	127
sudden and perceptible goes to the Crown	129, xii
if marks can be ascertained, it remains to the original owner, or returns when the water is gone	129, xi
title to does not lie in custom or prescription	131, 142, xi, xxviii
arm of the sea owned by a subject does not change its ownership if left derelict and dry	134, 142, xii, xxix, xxxi
DIGGING FOR SAND, the custom of	93, 94, 207, xxiv
whether evidence of title to shore	93, li
custom is a good one	93, li
a local or general custom	94
stat. of 1 Jac. I. ch. 18, as to digging it in Devon and Cornwall	94, 204, 207, xxiv
effect of express manor grants of right	97
as to the public right to dig for it on the shore	186, 191, 194

Index. cxxxiii

DIGGING FOR SAND (*continued*)—
 is a profit à prendre 194
 analogy between the right on the shore and in inland wastes 195
 as to right to dig for it as a local custom on the shore . . 196
 a general practice of the shore 206
 importance of general right of, on the shore 211
 the custom of, coeval with the culture of the land . . . 212
 support of custom of, desirable on grounds of public utility . 216
" DOOMSDAY BOOK," silence in, as to Crown's rights . . . lxxiv

EASEMENTS, distinction between, and profits à prendre . . 194
 prescription for . . . . 198 *et seq.*
22 ED. III., *Liber Assisarum* case in, quoted by Mr. Serjeant
 Merewether lxxxvi
34 ED. III. pl. 11, quoted by Mr. Serjeant Merewether . lxxxvii
EGRESS AND REGRESS, grant of wreck implies, over the shore . 83
 public right of fishery implies, over the shore . . 48, 173
 right to land from boats on the shore 174
 right of way for fishing and navigation over the shore . . 176
EMBANKING, distinction between, and wears 75
 its evidence of title to the shore 98, 99
 difference between, against the sea and against a river 167, 168, 169
ENCROACHMENT cannot be made on the property of the Crown
 or its grantee 99
EVIDENCE of shore being parcel of a manor . . . 15, xxiv
 of shore being parcel of a vill or parish . . . . 15, xxiv
 of Crown's propriety in the sea and arms thereof . . . ix
 what, to entitle juries to presume an ancient lost grant from
  the Crown 15
 that the shore passed under a grant 18
 of title to the shore. . . . . . 30, 31, 32, xxiv, l
 of title to the shore and to inland estate, analogy between . 32
 of boundaries in titles 38, 88
 of immemorial usage alone will not support a claim of dues
  for anchorage 43
 of a several fishery 50
 what amount of, sufficient for a jury to presume a legal grant
  of a several fishery 50
 that the shore may belong to a subject in gross . 77, 78, xxiv, lxi
 or as parcel of a manor . . . . . . 77, 78, xxiv, lxi
 of custom in one manor is not evidence of the custom of another 89
 as to digging for sand being evidence of title to the shore 92 *et seq.*
 as to embanking being evidence of title to the shore . 98 *et seq.*

Index.

	Page
EVIDENCE, whether proof of jurisdiction to present and punish purprestures on the shore evidence of ownership	100
of exercise of acts of ownership in other parts no evidence of right to do acts on a particular spot	101
EXTENTA MANERII 4 Ed. I., quoted by Mr. Serjeant Merewether	lxxix

FISH, royal, what are	40, 44, 80, xli
not necessarily included in a grant of a sea-coast manor	19
not always appurtenant to a manor	19
may be parcel of or belonging to an hundred	xli
a royal franchise	40, 44, 80, xli, xlii
a subject may have, by grant or prescription	40, 81, xlii
whether it gives a title to the shore	81, 82
doctrine of Hale, C.J., on this point	78, xxv
his doctrine considered	79, 80
public right to fish on shore	174, 175
public not compellable to land fish caught at sea at the port	175
as to public right to catch on the shore shell-fish	186, 191
a custom for all the inhabitants of a parish to catch fish is bad	196
FISHERY, the right of, originally lodged in the Crown	42, vii
yet there is a public common of	viii, xvii
a subject may have the interest of, in an arm of the sea, &c., not only " free " but " several "	xv
public cannot acquire right of, by immemorial usage in a non-tidal river	37
in the sea, &c., public right of	3, 41, 46, viii, xvii
includes egress and regress over the shore	41, 48, 49, 173, xlvii
may be of two kinds	50, xv
with the net, as a liberty without the soil	51, xvi
or in concomitance with the soil	51, xvi
or a local fishing that ariseth from the propriety of the soil	51, xvi
such may be held by usage either in gross	49, xvi
or as parcel of, or appendant to the manor	49, xvi
public and private incompatible	52
the public have a right to fish on the shore as well as on the sea	175
fishing is subject to the laws for the conservation of fish and fry	192, xx
"several," what it is	47, 49, 50, xv, xvii
may be in gross	49, xvi
or appendant and appurtenant to manors	49, xvi
whether there may be a prescriptive right to	50
under what words it passes	50
"sole and exclusive," after verdict equivalent to	50

FISHERY (*continued*)—

"several," cannot be appendant to a several pasture . 50
legally granted before Magna Charta does not merge
  by forfeiture to the Crown 51
created before Magna Charta can be granted afterwards 51
trespass lies for breaking into. 51
where it is claimed in the arms of the sea, the exclusive
  claim must be set up in the pleadings . . . 51
will not shift with the altered course of the river . . 51
considered as giving title to the shore . 52, 55, xvii, xviii
ownership of soil does not entitle such owner to establish
  an exclusive fishery . . . . . . 53 *et seq.*
doctrine of Hale, C. J., on these points . . 56, xviii *et seq.*
Mr. Hargrave's opinion 60
distinction between, in places not within the tides, and
  in the sea and tide rivers 56, 62, 72
exclusive and fixed discountenanced by law . . 69, xix
no inference from the statutes against wears, &c., that
  such exclusive fisheries carry the soil 71
wears and fixed fisheries to be construed strictly . . 72
an express grant of, and no more words will not include
  the soil 74
may exclude the right to bathe where the bathing would
  injure the fishery 172
free, definition of 50, 66, 68
  as distinguished from "several" 66
  difference between "libera," "separalis," and "com-
    munis" piscaria 68
FITZWALTER'S (Lord) case 53, 56, 85
FLOTSAM, definition of . . . . . . 40, 41, 80, xl
  Crown's title to . . . . 40, 41, 80, xl
  confers no title to the shore 81
  doctrine of Hale, C. J. xxv
  may belong to a subject. . . . . . 81, xxv
  may belong to a subject by charter or prescription . . xli
  does not pass by grant of "Wreccum Maris" . . . xl
  if taken up in wide ocean belongs to the finder if the owner
    cannot be found xl
  if in the narrow seas *primâ facie* belongs to the Crown . . xl
  if the owner can be found belongs to him . . . xl
  may be parcel of, or belonging to an hundred . . . xli
FORMS, report of works, encroachments, &c. . . . cix
  official return of the above cx
  letter from Board of Trade to a person proposing to take a

	Page

FORMS (*continued*)—
   to the officer of Coast Guard relating to the shore . . . cxii
   to occupiers of adjacent land cxiii
   to the applicant dispensing with a survey . . . cxiii
   to the applicant where a survey is to be made. . . . cxv
   grant by Board of Trade cxvi
   form of lease cxx

GATEWARD'S CASE 199
GLANVILLE, quoted by Mr. Serjeant Mereweather, as having no
   reference to the Crown's prerogative to the sea-shore . lxxv
GOODS, when said to be landed 10
GRANTS by the king of portions of land sea-covered . 6, xii, xv, xxxi
   opinion of Callis 7
   of the sea-shore . . . . . . 14, 15, 17, xiv, xv
   the shore may be the subject of express 15, 17
   under what words the above may pass . . . 14, 18, xiv, xv
   juries may sometimes presume an ancient lost grant from the
     Crown 15
   of the Crown construed strictly . . . 20, 21, 65, 103, 106
   from one subject to another, in favour of the grantee . . 20
   of a separate fishery, and no more words will not include the soil 74
   of wreck, &c. *per se* do not carry the soil. . . . 76 *et seq.*
   of shore do not *per se* give wreck or other regalia . . . 82
   flotsam, &c. do not pass under grant of "Wreccum Maris" . xl
GROYNES, as to the right in a subject to make them on the shore . 167

HACCHESHAM MANOR, case of . . . . . . xii, lxxxii
HALE, C. J., "De jure Maris" i
   authenticity of, questioned 5
HERON, Sir Edward, case of . . . . 12, xxiii
HIGH spring tides. See "Tides" and "Spring tides."
   definition of . . . . 10, ix, xxiii
   the soil subject to, is no part of the shore . . . 12, ix
HORNE'S "Myrrour of Justices," silence in, as to Crown's right to
   the sea-shore lxxxv

IMMEMORIAL USAGE. See "Usage."
   in prescription for a customary privilege it is allowed to raise
     the presumption of an ancient grant 23
   whether it can alone raise a title to land considered . 25 *et seq.*
   the essence of prescription 36, 37
   the public cannot acquire by, a right of fishing in a non-tidal
     river 37
   by the public of an open waste, what inference . . 37

Index.

	Page
IMMEMORIAL USAGE will not support a claim to dues for anchorage	43
towing paths may be acquired by, as a local custom	48
INCREMENTA MARITIMA defined. (See "Alluvion," "Derelict," and "Islands")	xi, xxxv
what may pass under	xiv, xv
INFRA, meaning of	79, lxxxv
INTAKINGS, their evidence of title to the shore	100
INUNDATIONS, as distinct from tides	8
as to title to land subject to	xii
ISLANDS, arising in the sea, &c.	140, 141, xiv, xxxiv, xxxv
Crown has a *primâ facie* title to	140, 141, xxxiv, xxxv
when a subject may have	140, 141, xxxiv, xxxv
Bracton's texts	141
as to the law in America	141
JETSAM, definition of	40, 41, 80, xl
Crown's title to	40, 41, 80, xl
confers no title to the shore	81
Hale, C. J., opinion of	xxv
may belong to a subject	81
by charter or prescription	xli
does not pass under grant of "Wreccum Maris"	xl
if taken up in wide ocean belongs to the finder, if owner cannot be found	xl
if in the narrow seas *primâ facie* belongs to the Crown	xl
if the owner can be found, to him	xl
may be parcel of or belonging to an hundred	xli
KING, title of, to the sea and sea-shore	1-6, vii, ix, x, xv, lxiv
title of, to navigable rivers	3, 4
rights of, managed by Board of Trade	4, 5, 46
rights of, forms used by the Board of Trade in dealing with	cix-cxxv
grants by, of portions of land sea-covered	6, xii, xv, xxxi
grants by, of sea-shore	14, 15, 17, xiv, xv
grants by, construed strictly	20, 21, 65, 103, 106
title of, to shore is by the Common law	39
whether right of fishing is originally lodged in	42, vii
title of, to wreck	44, 80, xxxvi, lxiv
grant of shore by, and no more words will not pass wreck, &c.	82
title of, to shore ought to be preserved on grounds of public policy	104
alienation of lands by, prohibited	106, 220
title of, to derelict land	115, 129, xxvii
title of, to lakes and marshes	115
title of, to islands arising *de novo*	140, xxxv

	Page
LAKE, title to soil of	4
when gained from the sea	115
title of king	115
title of owner of adjoining lands	116
LAND, prescription gives no title to	22
title to, by grants	22
title to, by adverse possession aided by the Statute law	22
shore is technically	32
cannot be appendant or appurtenant to land	34, 35
cannot be prescribed for	38
alienation of, by Crown, prohibited by Statute	106, 220
LAWS of William I. and Henry I., no reference therein to Crown's rights to the sea-shore (quoted by Mr. Serjeant Merewether)	lxxv
LAWS, Saxon, quoted by Mr. Serjeant Merewether	lxxiv
LIGAN, definition of	40, 41, 80, xl
Crown's title to	40, 41, 80, xl
confers no title to the shore	81
doctrine of Hale, C. J.	xxv
may belong to a subject	81, xxv
by charter or prescription	xli
does not pass by grant of "Wreccum Maris"	xl
if taken in wide ocean belongs to the finder, if the owner cannot be found	xl
if in the narrow seas *primâ facie* belongs to the Crown	xl
if the owner can be found, belongs to him	xl
may be parcel of or belonging to an hundred	xli
LITTUS, or the shore, is *primâ facie* the king's. (See "Sea-shore")	13
technically land	32
distinction between, and "ripam"	162
LORDS OF THE MANOR, their claims to the shore	17
grants by the Crown to	17, 18
ownership of, in the sea-shore by prescription considered	21
may have a separate fishery	52
mere ownership of the shore by, will not include a separate fishery	53
title of, to alluvion	113
their rights as opposed to copyholders	113
title of, to land imperceptibly derelict	114
MACHINES, bathing in, as to the rights of	170, 183
MAGNA CHARTA, quoted by Mr. Serjeant Merewether	lxxv
MANOR, shore may be parcel of	15, ix, xxiv
what proof necessary	15, xxiv

MANOR (*continued*)—
 claim of lord of, to the shore 17
 under what words the shore will pass in a grant of . 14, 18, xiv
 grants by the Crown to lords of 18
 on the coast does not necessarily include the shore . . 18
 on the coast does not necessarily include the regalia of wreck 19
 or royal fish 19
 ownership of lord of, in the sea-shore by prescription considered 21
 lord of, may have a separate fishery 52
 mere ownership of the shore by a lord of manor will not include a separate fishery 53
 title to alluvion by lord of 113
 his rights as opposed to copyholder's 113
 title to land " imperceptibly " derelict by lord of . . . 114
 lands acquired " *per relictionem maris* " are not prescribable as part of a 131
MANURES, as to public right to dig for on the shore . 92, 206, xlvi
 antiquity and utility of using marine, in agriculture . 213, 214
MARITIMA INCREMENTA, Crown has a title to. (See "Alluvion," " Derelict," and " Islands.") . . . . . xi, xxv
 what may pass under . . . . xiv, xv
MARSHES, gained from the sea 10, 115
 king's ownership in 10, 115
 title of adjoining owner to 116
MINES, under the sea in Cornwall are vested in the Duke of Cornwall 18

NAVIGABLE RIVER, what is a . . . . 4, 13, vii, xiv
 to whom the soil belongs 3, 4
 rights of crown to soil of 3, 4
 management of Crown's rights in, by Board of Trade . . 4, 46
 public rights of fishing and navigation in . . . 3, 42, 46, vii *et seq.*, xvii
 bed of, *primâ facie* extra-parochial 15
 may be parcel of a vill or parish . . . . . 15, xxiv
 is within the adjoining county . . . . . 16, vii
 nuisance must not be created in . . . . 43, v, xxxiv
 as to vessels sunk in 45
 of conservators of . . . . xx, xxi
NAVIGATION, public right of, in the seas, &c. . . . 42, 43
 obstruction to, must not be created in a tidal river 43, v, xxxiv
 liability to remove such obstruction 45
 in America, what it includes 48
 towing is not, properly so called 48

	Page
NEAP TIDES. (See "Tides.")	
are ordinary tides	10, xxiv
boundary of the shore is by the medium tide between the springs and the	9, 10
shore covered by, may belong to a subject	xxiv
NETS, fishing with	51
public fishery is a floating right with	52
right of drying, on the bank	176
NEVILLE, Sir Henry, case of	79, 83, xxv, lxxxv
NOY, case in, quoted by Mr. Serjeant Merewether	xciv
NUISANCE, must not be created in a river	43, v, xxxiv
when indictable	44, v, vi
what amounts to a	45
is a question for a jury	45
used sometimes to be reformed in the King's Bench	vi
sometimes by Special Commission	vi
OBSTRUCTION, to navigation must not be created	43, 44, v, xxxiv
what liability to remove	45
OWNERSHIP of the soil of the sea and navigable rivers	3, 108
value of proof of, acts of	15
as to whether, in the sea-shore can be claimed by prescription	21
Mr. Butler's opinion as to the proofs of the title to the ownership of sea-shore	26, 31
what acts can oust the king's, in the shore	33
of several fishery	47
of the soil of the shore does not entitle such owner to establish an exclusive fishery	53
mere ownership of the soil will not exclude the public	54 et seq.
of exclusive fishery does not give a title to the shore	55 et seq.
of royal franchises does not necessarily include, of the shore itself	81
of shore does not necessarily include royal franchises	82 et seq.
as to digging for sand being evidence of, to the shore	92 et seq.
as to embanking being evidence of, to the shore	98
acts of, in one part no evidence of right to do acts on another part of the shore	101
franchises, &c. which will not give, to the soil	103
of the shore, doctrine of the Civil Law writers on	104, 105
of alluvion and derelictions imperceptible	110 et seq.
what, of adjacent land entitles to the alluvion, &c.	112
of lords of the manor	113, 114

Index. cxli

	Page
OWNERSHIP, of soil in ports	135 *et seq.*
of islands	140, 141
OYSTER FISHERIES, acts relating to	192

PARCEL OF A MANOR, shore may be	15, xxiv
what proof necessary	15, xxiv
PARISH, shore may be part of adjoining	15
but *primâ facie* it is extra-parochial	15
PLYMOUTH AND SUTTON POOLE, case of	138, 146, xxxii, xcviii
PORT OF TOPPESHAM, case of	57, 137, 145, xviii, xxxii, lxxx
PORTS, title to the soil of	135, xxx
belongs like the shore to the king *primâ facie*	135, xxx
but may belong to a subject	137, xxxi
creation of new ports	135
franchise of, distinct from the soil	137, xxxi
the franchise may belong to a subject either with or without the soil	137, xxxi
whether the word " port " will *per se* carry the soil in an express grant	137, 144, xxxi
ancient survey of	139
whether prescription for a " port " includes the soil	137, 143, xxxi
doctrine of Hale, C. J., on this point	137, 145, xxxi
distinction between possession of it by a subject and by the king	153
whether fish or goods not customable must be landed in	175, 177
PRESCRIPTION, title by, to the shore considered	16, 21, l
gives no title to lands	22
positive and negative	22
Prescription Act, what is within	23
Mr. Phear on the Act	23
by statutes of limitation	24
as to the old law of	25
modern law of	26
doctrine of Hale, C. J., and Mr. Butler as to its giving title to the shore	26, 27
concerns things appendant and appurtenant	34
what things may or may not be prescribed for	35
plea of, by what evidence supported	36, 37
usage, the essence of	36
a subject may have the interest of fishing in arm of the sea by	xv
seizin and, distinguished	37, 38
prescriptive rights no proof of title	39
ceases with its subject matter	75

PRESCRIPTION (*continued*)—
   a right lying in, ought not to include more than it would if
      expressly granted 97
   for a port, whether it will include the soil . . . 137 *et seq.*
   whether land covered by the sea can be prescribed . . 142
   derelict soil does not lie in 131
   for profits à prendre 194, 196, 200
   distinction between, *in que* estate and as an inhabitant . 197
   for a profit à prendre by inhabitants not good . . . 199
   for easements 200
   mere habitancy not sufficient to support a plea for profit
      à prendre 202
   for a local custom to dig sand, &c. 203
   whether any distinction in prescribing for inland profit and
      profit on the shore 204
PRIOR DE CONINGSHED, case of xvi
   of Christ Church, Canterbury . . . . 138, xxxii
   of Stoke xvi
   of Tinmouth . . . . x, lxxxi
PROFITS À PRENDRE, in gross, do not come within the Prescription
   Act 23-24
   distinction between easements and 194
   what 194, 195
   analogy between, in inland wastes and in sea-shore . . 195
   prescription for 196, 197
   must be prescribed for in the "*que estate*" . . 197-199
   but not as inhabitants 198, 199, 201
PUBLIC RIGHTS of fishing in the sea, &c. . 41, 42, 46, 49, viii, xvii
   of navigation . . . . 42, xxxiv
   of egress and regress over the shore from boats . . 48, 175
   are to be construed strictly 107
   on the shore 156, 186, 191
   of bathing 156
   of way over the shore on foot and in carriages . . 171, 184
   of disembarking on the "ripam" 173, 174
   of laying up boats on the shore 174, 176
   of way for, and public right of fishing on the shore 173, 174, 175
   of way along the "ripam" above high-water mark . . 175
   of towing paths 176, 215
   of drying nets on the shore 176
   of taking shell fish on the shore 186
   is part of the public fishery 191
   of digging sand, &c. on the shore 191, 194
   of digging for manures on the shore 206, 218

Index. cxliii

	Page
PURPRESTURES, meaning of	100, l
whether jurisdiction to prevent and punish evidence of ownership of the shore	100, l
QUAYS, WHARFS, &c., on the shore	179
QUE ESTATE, prescription in	197 *et seq.*
RAMSEY, Abbot of, case of	118, xxvi, lxxxvii
RIPA, shore may pass under the term of	18
distinguished from shore	162
definition of, in America	163
definition of, in England	9, 163
text of Bracton on the subject	163
right of way over	173
right to land fish upon	174
right of way along, above high-water mark	175
towage of boats along	176, 215
on the rights of fishermen to drag their boats upon	176
the practice of drying nets upon	176
RIVERS, fresh, belong to the owners of the soil adjacent, "*usque filum aquæ*"	i
special usage may alter common presumption	ii
as to sudden and insensible gains on one or other side	ii
special custom may alter the case in great rivers	ii
of the right of prerogative in fresh rivers	iii, iv
public, what are	4-13
title to the soil of	3-4
rights of Crown to soil of	3-4
management of Crown's rights in, by Board of Trade	4, 46
public rights of fishing and navigation in	3, 42, 46, vii, xvii
bed of, *primâ facie* extra-parochial	15
may be parcel of a vill or parish	15, xxiv
is within the adjoining county	16, vii
nuisance must not be created in	43, v, xxxiv
as to vessels sunk in	45
of conservators of	xx, xxi
as to property in islands arising in	140, xiv, xxxv
ROYAL FISH, what are	40, 44, 80, xli
not necessarily included in a grant of a sea-coast manor	19
not always appurtenant to a manor	19
may be parcel of or belonging to a hundred	xli
a royal franchise	40, 41, 80, xli, xlii
a subject may have by grant or prescription	40, 81, xlii
whether it gives a title to the shore	81, 82

cxliv   *Index.*

	Page
ROYAL FISH, doctrine of Hale, C. J., on this point	78, xxv
his doctrine considered	79, 80

SALMON, as to the Crown's right in Scotland 192
SAND, as to digging and taking, being evidence of title to shore 92, 103, xlv
    stat. of 1 Jac. I. ch. 18, as to digging it in Devon and Cornwall . . . . 94, 204, 207, xxiv
    effect of express manor grants of right to dig . . . 97
    as to the public right to dig for it on the shore . 186, 191, 194
    is a profit à prendre 194
    analogy between the right on the shore and in inland wastes 195
    as to right to dig for it, as a local custom, on the shore . 196
    a general practice on the shore 206
    importance of general right to dig, on the shore . . 211
SAXON charters quoted by Mr. Serjeant Merewether . . lxxi, lxxiii
    laws, quoted by Mr. Serjeant Merewether . . . lxxiv
SEAS, British, and the arms thereof, &c., the limits of . . 1, vii, ix
    of the king's title therein . . . . . 2, vii, ix
    includes the sea and the land covered by it 2
    extent and nature . . . . 2, 3, 4, vii
    of the title which subjects may have therein . . 3, 6, 14, xiv
    king's title to the land under the sea 6
    if a portion be granted by the Crown to a subject, it does not change its ownership if left dry . 7, 142, xii, xv, xxix, xxxi
SEA-BOTTOM, definition of 8
    belongs to the king 6, 13
SEA-COAST, manor on, does not necessarily include the shore . 18, l
    nor wreck nor royal fish 19
SEA-SHORE, definition of . . . . . . 8, 9, 13, ix
    boundaries . . . . . 8, 9, 13, ix, xiv, xxiv, lxiv
    belongs *primâ facie* to the king . . 9-13, ix, xiv, xxiii, lxiv
    but subject to the right of passage over 3
    the title which subjects may have therein . 14, ix, xxxiii, lxiv
    title proofs of, same as in inland estate . . 14, ix, xxxiii, lxiv
    under what words in a grant it may pass . 14, 15, 18, xiv, xv
    grants of, by Crown . . . . . . 14, 15, xiv
    may be made the subject of express grant . . . 15
    may be parcel of a manor, vill, or parish . . 15, ix, xxiv
    but *primâ facie* extra-parochial . . . . 15, ix, xxiv
    title to, by prescription . . . . . 16, 21, xv, xxxi
    Mr. Butler's doctrine considered 26, 31
    is part of adjoining county . . . . . 16, vii
    title of lords of the manor 17, 18, 19

Index. cxlv

SEA-SHORE (*continued*)—
   grants to lords of manor 17
   not necessarily included in a grant of a sea-coast manor . 18, 1
   technically land 32
   is capable of seizin in law 33
   king's title to, is positive and by common law . . . 39, ix
   title to, by adverse possession confirmed by Statute law . 39
   ownership of, does not necessarily include a several fishery 52, 53
   of manor often of great extent 73
   not included in an express grant of a several fishery . . 74
   grant of, *per se*, does not give wreck or other regalia . . 82
   Bracton's doctrine as to ownership of 105
   right of way over, for fishing, &c. 171
   public right to fish on 174, 175, 186, 191
   right to land from boats on 174
   whether right to dry nets on 176
   digging sand, shells, &c. on . . . . . . 194 *et seq.*
   right of way over, on foot and in carriage . . . 184, 193
SEA-WEED, title to. 92
   of the right to take it 92
SEIZIN, shore capable of 33
   difference between, and prescription 37
   proofs of . . . . 100 *et seq.*
SELDEN'S doctrine of Crown's title to the sea and land covered
   by it . . . . 2, vii
SEVERAL FISHERY, definition of . . . . 47, 49, 50, xv, xvii
   may be in gross . . . . 49, xvi
   or appendant and appurtenant to manors . . . 49, xvi
   whether there may be a prescriptive right to 50
   under what words it passes 50
   "sole and exclusive" after verdict equivalent to . . . 50
   what evidence is sufficient for a jury to presume a legal
      grant of 50
   cannot be appendant to a several pasture 50
   legally granted before Magna Charta does not merge by for-
      feiture to the Crown 51
   created before Magna Charta can be granted afterwards . 51
   trespass lies for breaking into 51
   where it is claimed in the arms of the sea, the exclusive
      claim must be set up in the pleadings 51
   will not shift with the altered course of the river . . . 51
   considered as giving title to the shore . . 52, 55, xvii, xviii
   ownership of soil does not entitle such owner to establish an
      exclusive fishery . . . . 53 *et seq.*

Index.

SEVERAL FISHERY (*continued*)—
    doctrine of Hale, C. J., on these points . . . 56, xviii *et seq.*
    Mr. Hargrave's opinion 60
    distinction between, in places not within the tides and in the
        sea and tide rivers 56, 62, 72
    exclusive and fixed, discountenanced by law . . . 69, xix
    no reference from the statutes against wears, &c., that such
        exclusive fisheries carry the soil 71
    wears and fixed fisheries to be construed strictly . . . 72
    an express grant of, and no more words, will not include the
        soil 74
    may exclude the right to bathe where the bathing would
        injure the fishery 172
SEVERN, River, case of . . . . . 84 *et seq.* ii, xiii, xxxii, lxxvi
SHELLS, concerning the right to dig and take, on shore . 187, 194
    decision in Bagott *v.* Orr 191
    of the right to take, on the shore by local custom . . 196
SHELL-FISH, as to the public right to catch and take, on the shore 186
        et seq.
    is of common right 191
    is part of the public fishery 192
SIR HENRY CONSTABLE, case of . . . . 15, xxiv, xli, xciii
SIR JOHN CONSTABLE, case of xciii
SIR HENRY NEVILLE, case of . . . . . 79, xxv, lxxxv
SPRING TIDES explained . . . . 10, xxiii
    not ordinary tides 11, 12
    soil subject to no part of the shore . . . . . 12, ix
SOIL OF THE SEA, to whom it belongs . . . . 3, ix, xxiii
    of a navigable river . . . . 3, ix, xxiii
    of a fresh river . . . . i, ii, iii
    of a lake 4, 115, 116
    subject to high spring tides, &c., is "terra firma" . . 12, 13
STATUTES, 21 Hen. I. c. 18 . . . . 70, xix
    9 Hen. III. c. 23 lxxv
    20 Hen. III. 25
    3 Ed. I. 1 "Westminster," c. 4 xxxvi
    4 Ed. I. "Extenta Manerii" lxxix
    13 Ed. I. c. 47 xxi
    17 Ed. II. "De prærogativa Regis" . . . xxxix, lxxxiv
    25 Ed. III. c. 4 . . . . 69, xix
    27 Ed. III. c. 13 . . . . . . xxxvi, xxxviii, xl
    45 Ed. III. c. 2 . . . . 69, xix
    13 Rich. II. c. 19 xxi
    15 Rich. II. c. 3 xxxvi

Index. cxlvii

STATUTES (*continued*)—
	Page
17 Rich. II. c. 9	xx, xx
1 Hen. IV. c. 12	69, xix, xxi
4 Hen. IV. c. 11	69, xix
2 Hen. VI. c. 9	lxxxviii
12 Ed. IV. c. 7	69, 70, 72, xix
4 Hen. VII. c. 15	70, xix, xxi
11 Hen. VII. c. 5	70, xix
14 Hen. VIII. c. 13	70, xix
23 Hen. VIII. c. 5	168, iv
23 Hen. VIII. c. 18	70, xix
27 Hen. VIII. c. 18	70, xix, xxi
31 Hen. VIII. c. 4	70, xix
1 Eliz. c. 17	xx, xxi
3 Jac. I. c. 12	70, xix
3 Jac. I. c. 20	70, xix
7 Jac. I. c. 18	94, 205, 207, xxiv, l, lxxiv
21 Jac. I. c. 2	26
1 Anne, c. 7, s. 5	106
9 Geo. III. c. 16	26
50 Geo. III. c. 38	xlix
54 Geo. III. c. 159, s. 19	ci
54 Geo. III. c. 170, s. 9	197
2 & 3 Will. IV. c. 1	5
2 & 3 Will. IV. c. 71	23, 24, 32, 36, 50
2 & 3 Will. IV. c. 112	5
3 & 4 Will. IV. c. 52, s. 50	81
3 & 4 Will. IV. c. 69	5
5 & 6 Will. IV. c. 50, s. 52	198
5 Vict. c. 1	5
8 & 9 Vict. c. 20, s. 17	46
8 & 9 Vict. c. 99	5
10 Vict. c. 27, s. 12	46
10 Vict. c. 89, s. 69	186
13 & 14 Vict. c. 88, s. 1	50
14 & 15 Vict. c. 42	5
15 & 16 Vict. c. 62	5
16 & 17 Vict. c. 56	5
16 & 17 Vict. c. 107, s. 9	134
17 & 18 Vict. c. 104, ss. 458, 472	81
21 & 22 Vict. c. 98, s. 44	186
21 & 22 Vict. c. 109	18
24 & 25 Vict. c. 109	70, 192
25 & 26 Vict. c. 69	46

Index.

	Page
STATUTES (*continued*)—	
26 & 27 Vict. c. 92, ss. 13-19	46
28 & 29 Vict. c. 121	70
29 & 30 Vict. c. 62	4, 5
29 & 30 Vict. c. 85	192
30 Vict. c. 18	192
31 & 32 Vict. c. 45	42, 192
31 & 32 Vict. c. 122, s. 27	16
32 & 33 Vict. c. 31	192
36 Vict. c. 13	70
37 & 38 Vict. c. 40	5
SUTTON MARSH, case of	131, xi, xxiv, xxviii
SUTTON POOL, case of	138, 146, xxxii, xcviii
comments on	150
SWANS, case of	civ
TERRA FIRMA, definition of	8
includes land subject to spring and high spring tides	13
divided into manors and freeholds	17
by new formation	108 *et seq.*
distinguished from shore	162
THAMES, River, case of	13, x, lxxxiv, xcv, cvii
TICHFEND, Abbot of, case of	xviii, lxxxi
TIDES, definition of	10, xxiii
three kinds of	10, xxiii
spring, whether ordinary	11, xxiii
high spring, the soil subject to is no part of the shore	12, ix, xxiii
spring, soil subject to is no part of the shore	11, xxiii
neap, are "ordinary"	10, xxiv
shore covered by, may belong to a subject	14, 15, ix, xxiv, l
what, are the boundaries of the shore	9, 13, ix, l
TINMOUTH, Prior of	x, lxxxi
TOLL for anchorage	43
for using banks	208
as a capstan rent	xlv
TOPPESHAM CASE	57, 137, 145, xviii, xxxii, lxxx
TOWING PATHS, not a general right along the banks	48, 176, 215
nor along navigable rivers	215
but may be acquired by usage or prescription as a local custom	48
TRADE, Board of, as to the management of Crown property by	4, 5, 46
forms used by	cix, cxxv

Index. cxlix

	Page

USAGE, to prove the shore parcel of a manor 15
   in prescription for a customary privilege immemorial, is
   allowed to raise the presumption of ancient grant . 23, 24
   whether immemorial, can raise a title to land considered 25 *et seq.*
   the essence of prescription 36, 37
   the public cannot acquire by, a right of fishing in a non-tidal
   river 37
   by the public of an open waste, what inference . . . 37
   a subject may by, have a several fishing in an arm of the sea xvii
   will not *per se* support a claim to dues for anchorage . . 43
   towing paths may be acquired by, as a local custom . . 48

VANHAESDANKE'S CASE . . . . 12, ix, xxiii

WAY, right of, over the shore 171, 184
   for fishing 173
   along the bank 175
   general, on the shore 184
WEARS, a mode of private fisheries . . 51, *et seq.* 68 xviii, xix
   discountenanced by law . . . . 69, xix
   when legal 70
   do not carry the soil 71
   are opposed to the *jus publicum* 71
   and must be construed strictly 72
   distinguished from embanking and intaking 75
WHARVES, on the shore 179
   whether an obstruction to navigation 44, 45
WORDS, meaning of "alluvion" . . . . . . 108 *et seq.*
   "anchorage" 18
   "aqua" 147
   "derelict land" . . . . 108 *et seq.*
   fishery "libera" 66, 67, 68
   fishery "separalis" . . . . 47 *et seq.*
   fishery "communis" 46
   "flotsam" . . . . 40, 41, 80, xl
   "high spring tides" 10
   "imperceptible" 127
   "jetsam" . . . . 40, 41, 80, xl
   "land" 8, 32
   "landed" 10
   "littus" . . . . 8, 13, ix
   "ligan" . . . . 40, 41, 80, xl
   "marettum" 149
   "neap tides" . . . . 10, xxiv

Index.

WORDS (*continued*)—
 "profits à prendre" 194
 "que estate" 197
 "ripa" 9, 162, 163
 "royal fish" . . . . 40, 44, 80, xli
 "sea bottom" 8
 "sea grounds" 149
 "shore" . . . . 8 *et seq.* 13, ix
 "spring tides" . . . . 10 *et seq.*
 "terra firma" 8, 162
 "wreck" . . . . . . 40, 44, 80, xxxvi *et seq.*
WRECK, definition of . . . . 40, 44, 80, xxxvi *et seq.*
 is a royal franchise . . . . 40, 44, 80, xxxix, lxiv
 may belong to a subject by grant or prescription . 40, 81, xxxix
 will not *per se* confer a title to the shore . 20, 76 *et seq.* lvi
 doctrine of Hale, C.J., that it will raise a presumption of
  ownership in the shore . . . . . 78, xxiv, xxv
 his doctrine considered 79
 grant of so much shore by the king and no more words will
  not pass 82
 grant of shore does not *per se* include wreck . . . 82, lvi
 implies the right of egress and regress to take it . . 82
              xxv, lxvi
 grant of a sea-coast manor does not necessarily include the
  regalia of wreck, &c. 19
YARBOROUGH, Lord, case of 120-128
YEAR BOOKS, on Crown's right to the sea-shore quoted by Mr.
 Serjeant Merewether lxxxii
 22 Ed. III. Liber Assisarum case in, also quoted by him lxxxvi
 34 Ed. III. pl. 11, case in, also quoted by him . . lxxxvii
 6 Rich. II. case in, also quoted by him . . . lxxxvii
 8 Ed. IV. fol. 18, case in, also quoted by him . . lxxxviii

THE END.

www.ingramcontent.com/pod-product-compliance
Lightning Source LLC
Chambersburg PA
CBHW032022220426
43664CB00006B/329